Resistance

Resistance

Val McDermid

with art by

Kathryn Briggs

BLACK CAT
NEW YORK

ADAPTED BY KATHRYN BRIGGS AND VAL MCDERMID
ART BY KATHRYN BRIGGS

FIRST PUBLISHED IN GREAT BRITAIN IN 2021 BY PROFILE BOOKS LTD
IN ASSOCIATION WITH WELLCOME COLLECTION

PUBLISHED SIMULTANEOUSLY IN CANADA
PRINTED IN CANADA

FIRST GROVE ATLANTIC PAPERBACK EDITON: JUNE 2021

ISBN 978-0-8021-5872-7
EISBN 978-0-8021-5873-4

LIBRARY OF CONGRESS CATALOGING-IN-PUBLICATION DATA
IS AVAILABLE FOR THIS TITLE.

BLACK CAT
AN IMPRINT OF GROVE ATLANTIC
154 WEST 14TH STREET
NEW YORK, NY 10011

DISTRIBUTED BY PUBLISHERS GROUP WEST

GROVEATLANTIC.COM

21 22 23 24 10 9 8 7 6 5 4 3 2 1

To all the scientists who lent me their expertise
in the realisation of this project, and whose
efforts to save lives continue daily.

– Val

To the healthcare workers.

– Kathryn

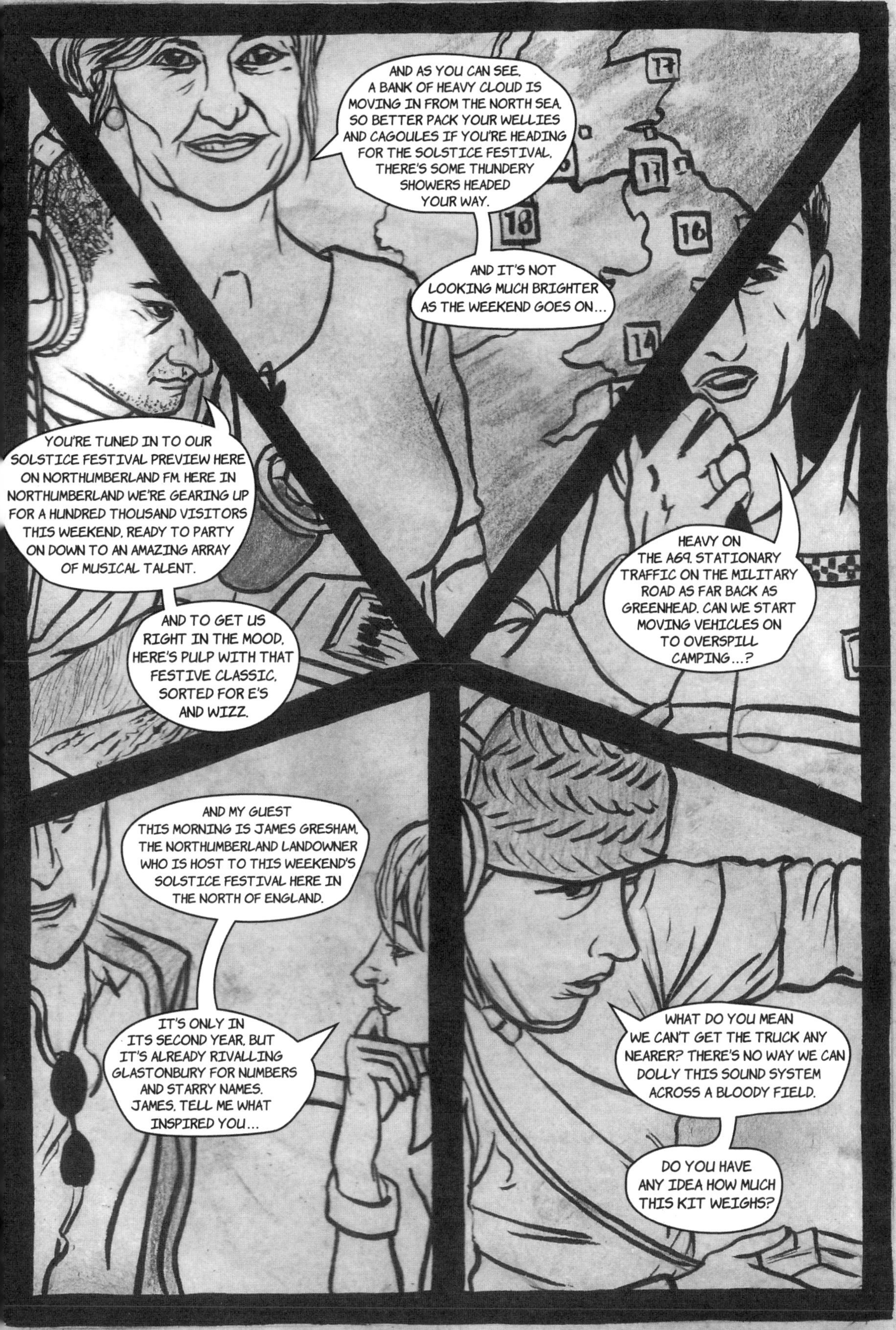
AND AS YOU CAN SEE, A BANK OF HEAVY CLOUD IS MOVING IN FROM THE NORTH SEA. SO BETTER PACK YOUR WELLIES AND CAGOULES IF YOU'RE HEADING FOR THE SOLSTICE FESTIVAL. THERE'S SOME THUNDERY SHOWERS HEADED YOUR WAY.
AND IT'S NOT LOOKING MUCH BRIGHTER AS THE WEEKEND GOES ON…
17
17
18
16
14
YOU'RE TUNED IN TO OUR SOLSTICE FESTIVAL PREVIEW HERE ON NORTHUMBERLAND FM. HERE IN NORTHUMBERLAND WE'RE GEARING UP FOR A HUNDRED THOUSAND VISITORS THIS WEEKEND, READY TO PARTY ON DOWN TO AN AMAZING ARRAY OF MUSICAL TALENT.
AND TO GET US RIGHT IN THE MOOD, HERE'S PULP WITH THAT FESTIVE CLASSIC, SORTED FOR E'S AND WIZZ.
HEAVY ON THE A69. STATIONARY TRAFFIC ON THE MILITARY ROAD AS FAR BACK AS GREENHEAD. CAN WE START MOVING VEHICLES ON TO OVERSPILL CAMPING…?
AND MY GUEST THIS MORNING IS JAMES GRESHAM, THE NORTHUMBERLAND LANDOWNER WHO IS HOST TO THIS WEEKEND'S SOLSTICE FESTIVAL HERE IN THE NORTH OF ENGLAND.
IT'S ONLY IN ITS SECOND YEAR, BUT IT'S ALREADY RIVALLING GLASTONBURY FOR NUMBERS AND STARRY NAMES. JAMES, TELL ME WHAT INSPIRED YOU…
WHAT DO YOU MEAN WE CAN'T GET THE TRUCK ANY NEARER? THERE'S NO WAY WE CAN DOLLY THIS SOUND SYSTEM ACROSS A BLOODY FIELD.
DO YOU HAVE ANY IDEA HOW MUCH THIS KIT WEIGHS?

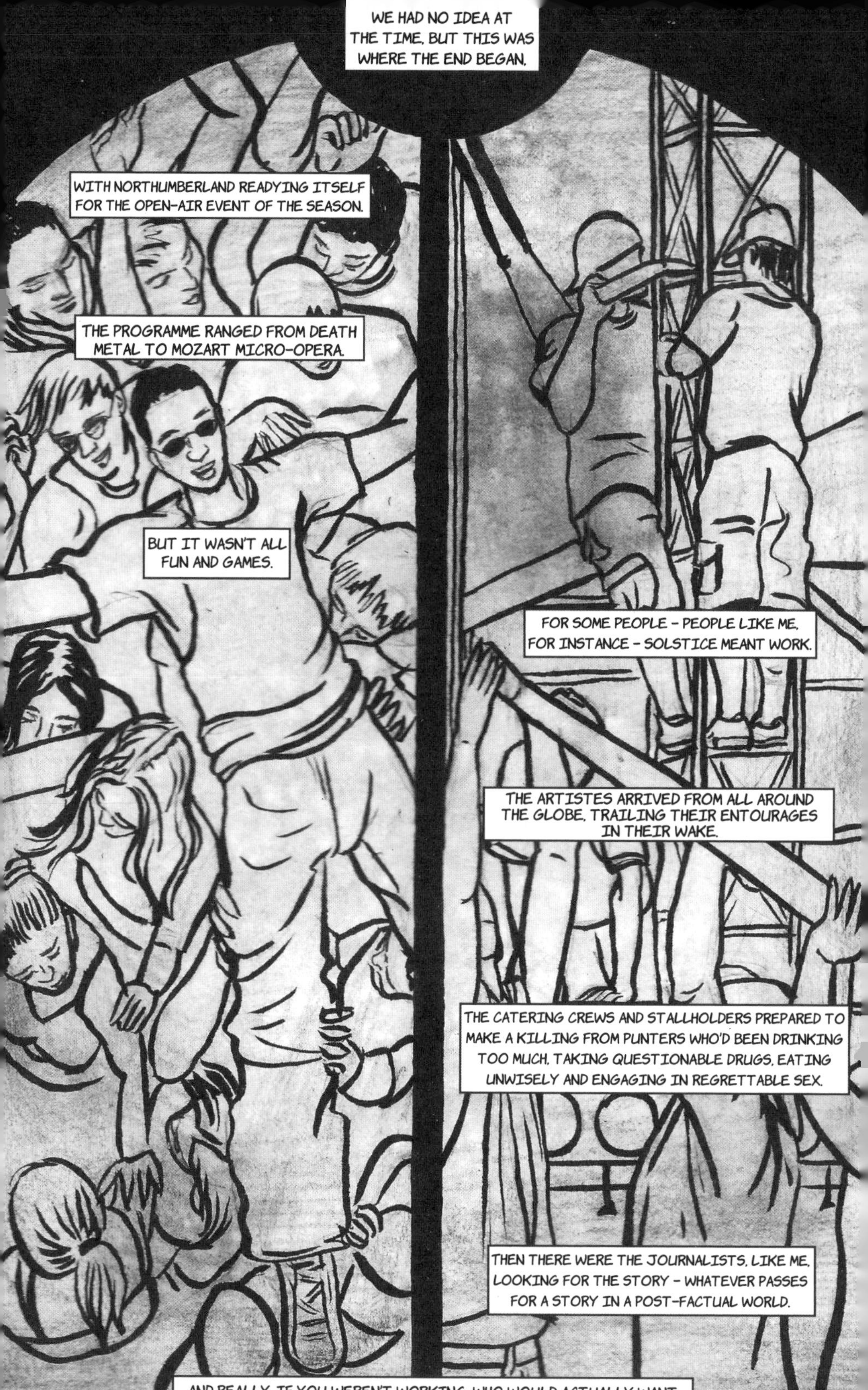
WE HAD NO IDEA AT THE TIME, BUT THIS WAS WHERE THE END BEGAN.
WITH NORTHUMBERLAND READYING ITSELF FOR THE OPEN-AIR EVENT OF THE SEASON.
THE PROGRAMME RANGED FROM DEATH METAL TO MOZART MICRO-OPERA.
BUT IT WASN'T ALL FUN AND GAMES.
FOR SOME PEOPLE - PEOPLE LIKE ME, FOR INSTANCE - SOLSTICE MEANT WORK.
THE ARTISTES ARRIVED FROM ALL AROUND THE GLOBE, TRAILING THEIR ENTOURAGES IN THEIR WAKE.
THE CATERING CREWS AND STALLHOLDERS PREPARED TO MAKE A KILLING FROM PUNTERS WHO'D BEEN DRINKING TOO MUCH, TAKING QUESTIONABLE DRUGS, EATING UNWISELY AND ENGAGING IN REGRETTABLE SEX.
THEN THERE WERE THE JOURNALISTS, LIKE ME, LOOKING FOR THE STORY - WHATEVER PASSES FOR A STORY IN A POST-FACTUAL WORLD.
AND REALLY, IF YOU WEREN'T WORKING, WHO WOULD ACTUALLY WANT TO BE THERE, SPENDING A WEEKEND IN THE RAIN WITHOUT ADEQUATE SANITATION IN A FARMER'S FIELD MILES FROM THE NEAREST HOT BATH?

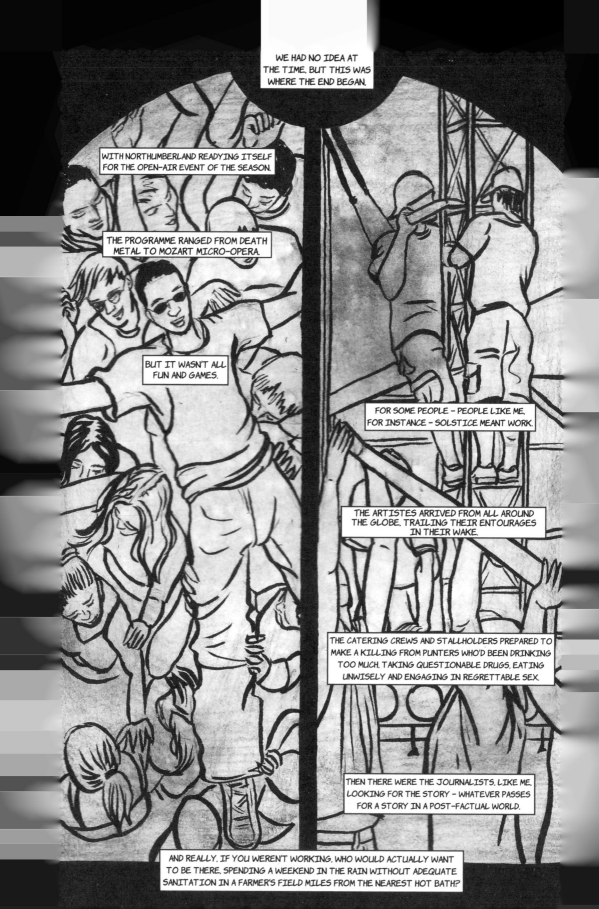

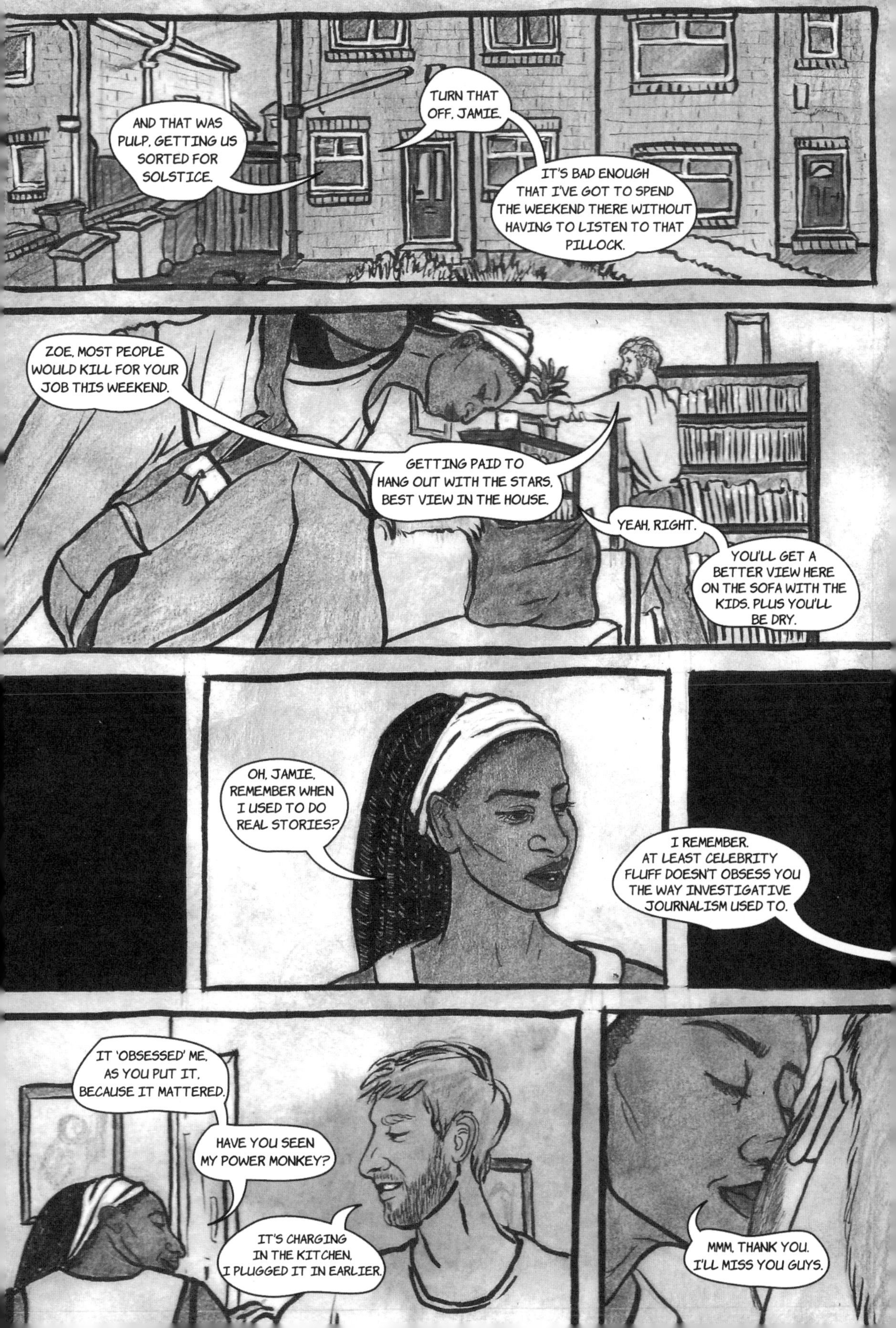
AND THAT WAS PULP, GETTING US SORTED FOR SOLSTICE.
TURN THAT OFF, JAMIE.
IT'S BAD ENOUGH THAT I'VE GOT TO SPEND THE WEEKEND THERE WITHOUT HAVING TO LISTEN TO THAT PILLOCK.
ZOE, MOST PEOPLE WOULD KILL FOR YOUR JOB THIS WEEKEND.
GETTING PAID TO HANG OUT WITH THE STARS. BEST VIEW IN THE HOUSE.
YEAH, RIGHT.
YOU'LL GET A BETTER VIEW HERE ON THE SOFA WITH THE KIDS. PLUS YOU'LL BE DRY.
OH, JAMIE, REMEMBER WHEN I USED TO DO REAL STORIES?
I REMEMBER. AT LEAST CELEBRITY FLUFF DOESN'T OBSESS YOU THE WAY INVESTIGATIVE JOURNALISM USED TO.
IT 'OBSESSED' ME, AS YOU PUT IT, BECAUSE IT MATTERED.
HAVE YOU SEEN MY POWER MONKEY?
IT'S CHARGING IN THE KITCHEN. I PLUGGED IT IN EARLIER.
MMM, THANK YOU. I'LL MISS YOU GUYS.

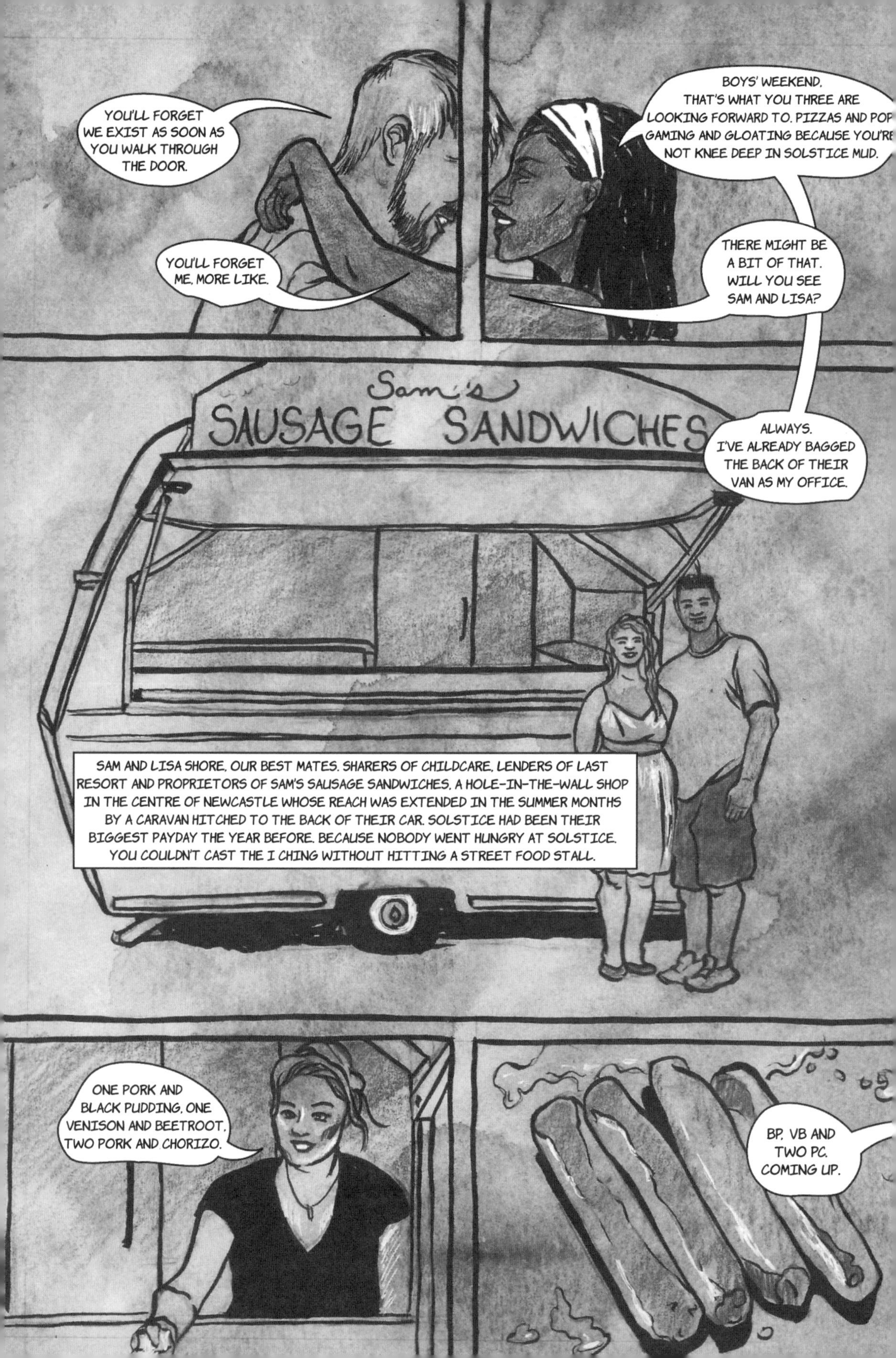
YOU'LL FORGET WE EXIST AS SOON AS YOU WALK THROUGH THE DOOR.
YOU'LL FORGET ME, MORE LIKE.
BOYS' WEEKEND. THAT'S WHAT YOU THREE ARE LOOKING FORWARD TO. PIZZAS AND POP GAMING AND GLOATING BECAUSE YOU'RE NOT KNEE DEEP IN SOLSTICE MUD.
THERE MIGHT BE A BIT OF THAT. WILL YOU SEE SAM AND LISA?
ALWAYS. I'VE ALREADY BAGGED THE BACK OF THEIR VAN AS MY OFFICE.
Sam's SAUSAGE SANDWICHES
SAM AND LISA SHORE, OUR BEST MATES. SHARERS OF CHILDCARE, LENDERS OF LAST RESORT AND PROPRIETORS OF SAM'S SAUSAGE SANDWICHES, A HOLE-IN-THE-WALL SHOP IN THE CENTRE OF NEWCASTLE WHOSE REACH WAS EXTENDED IN THE SUMMER MONTHS BY A CARAVAN HITCHED TO THE BACK OF THEIR CAR. SOLSTICE HAD BEEN THEIR BIGGEST PAYDAY THE YEAR BEFORE. BECAUSE NOBODY WENT HUNGRY AT SOLSTICE. YOU COULDN'T CAST THE I CHING WITHOUT HITTING A STREET FOOD STALL.
ONE PORK AND BLACK PUDDING, ONE VENISON AND BEETROOT, TWO PORK AND CHORIZO.
BP, VB AND TWO PC. COMING UP.

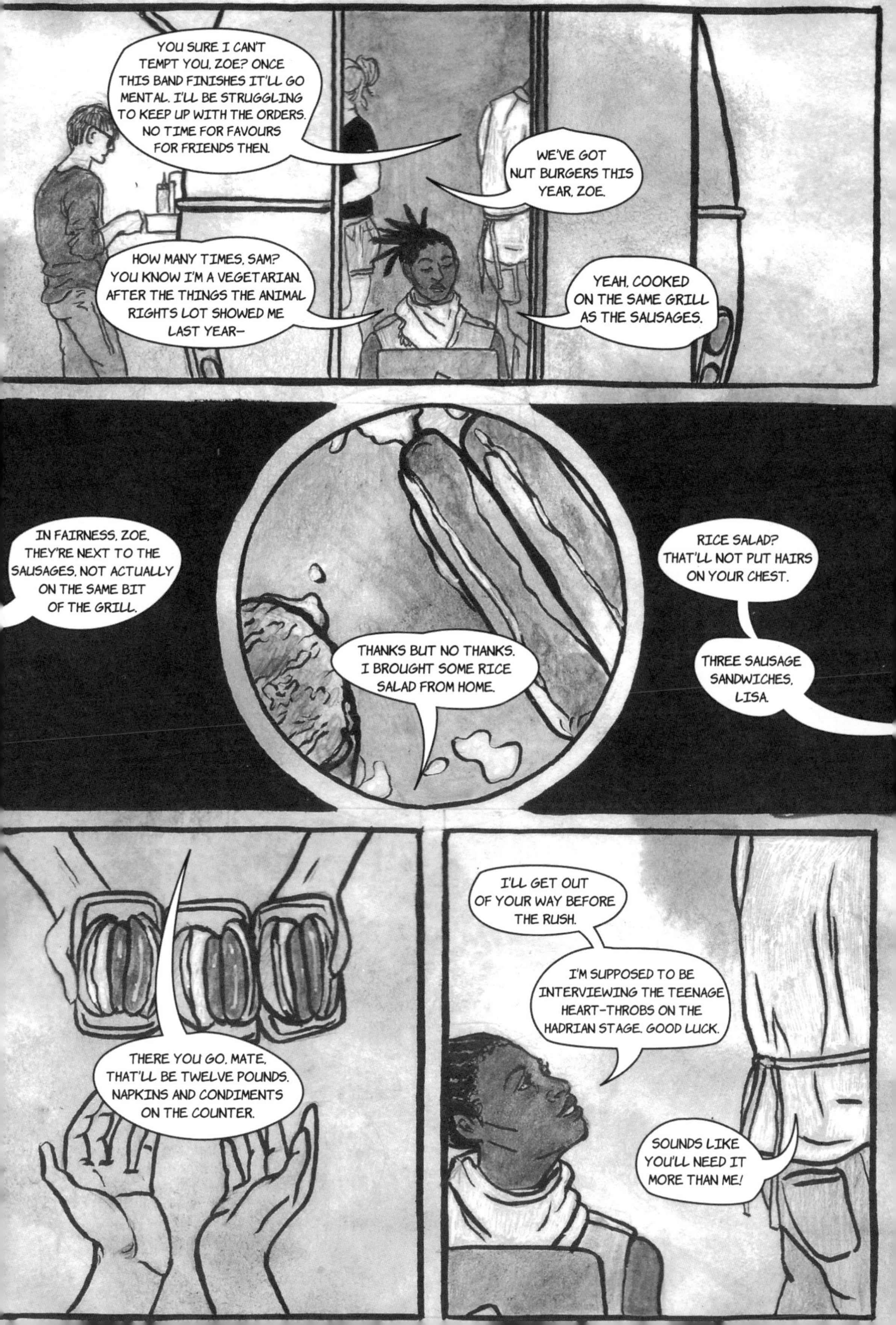
YOU SURE I CAN'T TEMPT YOU, ZOE? ONCE THIS BAND FINISHES IT'LL GO MENTAL. I'LL BE STRUGGLING TO KEEP UP WITH THE ORDERS. NO TIME FOR FAVOURS FOR FRIENDS THEN.
WE'VE GOT NUT BURGERS THIS YEAR, ZOE.
HOW MANY TIMES, SAM? YOU KNOW I'M A VEGETARIAN. AFTER THE THINGS THE ANIMAL RIGHTS LOT SHOWED ME LAST YEAR—
YEAH, COOKED ON THE SAME GRILL AS THE SAUSAGES.
IN FAIRNESS, ZOE, THEY'RE NEXT TO THE SAUSAGES, NOT ACTUALLY ON THE SAME BIT OF THE GRILL.
THANKS BUT NO THANKS. I BROUGHT SOME RICE SALAD FROM HOME.
RICE SALAD? THAT'LL NOT PUT HAIRS ON YOUR CHEST.
THREE SAUSAGE SANDWICHES, LISA.
THERE YOU GO, MATE. THAT'LL BE TWELVE POUNDS. NAPKINS AND CONDIMENTS ON THE COUNTER.
I'LL GET OUT OF YOUR WAY BEFORE THE RUSH.
I'M SUPPOSED TO BE INTERVIEWING THE TEENAGE HEART-THROBS ON THE HADRIAN STAGE. GOOD LUCK.
SOUNDS LIKE YOU'LL NEED IT MORE THAN ME!

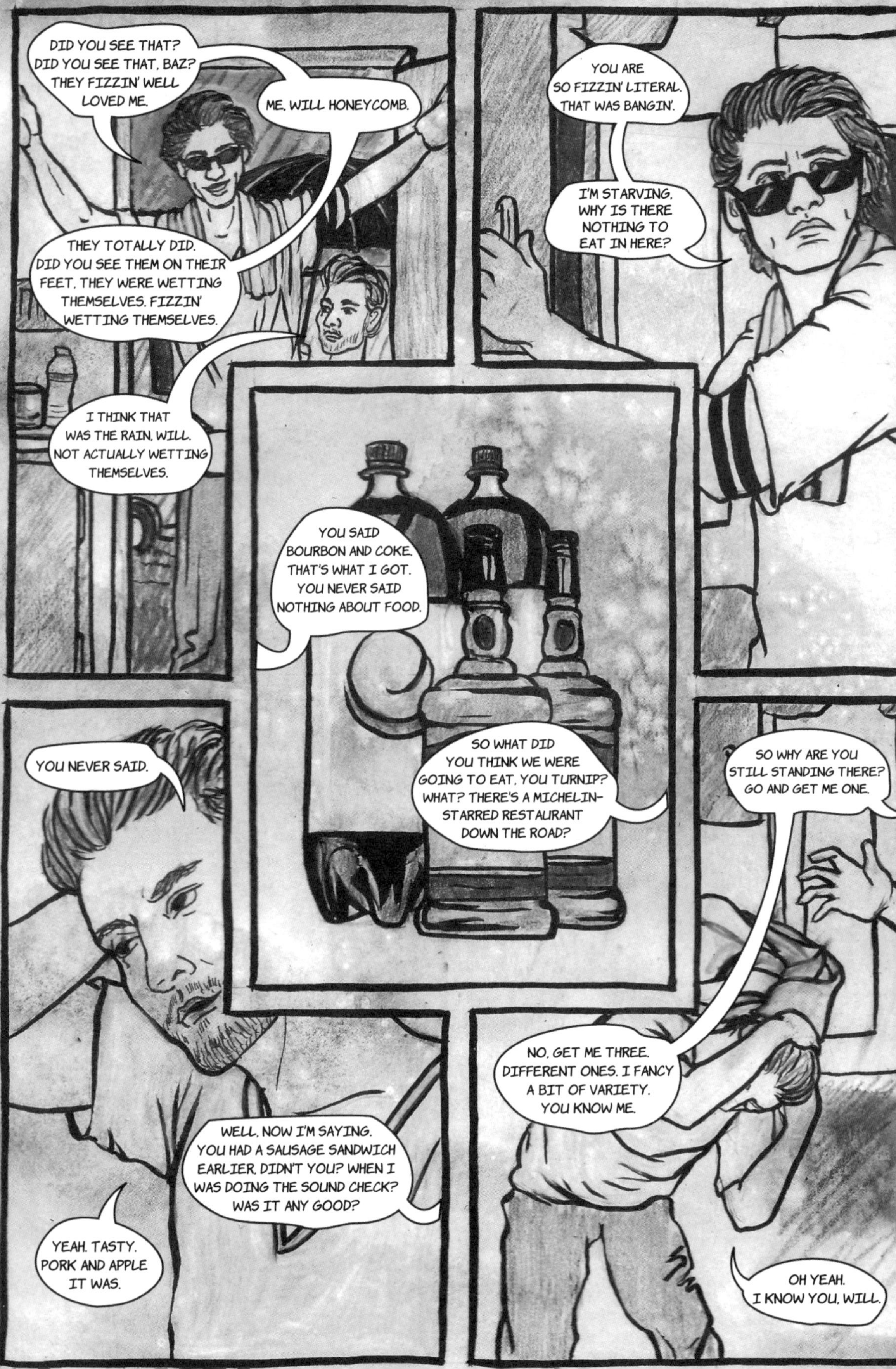
DID YOU SEE THAT? DID YOU SEE THAT, BAZ? THEY FIZZIN' WELL LOVED ME.
ME, WILL HONEYCOMB.
THEY TOTALLY DID. DID YOU SEE THEM ON THEIR FEET, THEY WERE WETTING THEMSELVES. FIZZIN' WETTING THEMSELVES.
I THINK THAT WAS THE RAIN, WILL. NOT ACTUALLY WETTING THEMSELVES.
YOU ARE SO FIZZIN' LITERAL. THAT WAS BANGIN'.
I'M STARVING. WHY IS THERE NOTHING TO EAT IN HERE?
YOU SAID BOURBON AND COKE. THAT'S WHAT I GOT. YOU NEVER SAID NOTHING ABOUT FOOD.
SO WHAT DID YOU THINK WE WERE GOING TO EAT, YOU TURNIP? WHAT? THERE'S A MICHELIN-STARRED RESTAURANT DOWN THE ROAD?
YOU NEVER SAID.
WELL, NOW I'M SAYING. YOU HAD A SAUSAGE SANDWICH EARLIER, DIDN'T YOU? WHEN I WAS DOING THE SOUND CHECK? WAS IT ANY GOOD?
YEAH. TASTY. PORK AND APPLE IT WAS.
SO WHY ARE YOU STILL STANDING THERE? GO AND GET ME ONE.
NO, GET ME THREE. DIFFERENT ONES. I FANCY A BIT OF VARIETY. YOU KNOW ME.
OH YEAH. I KNOW YOU, WILL.

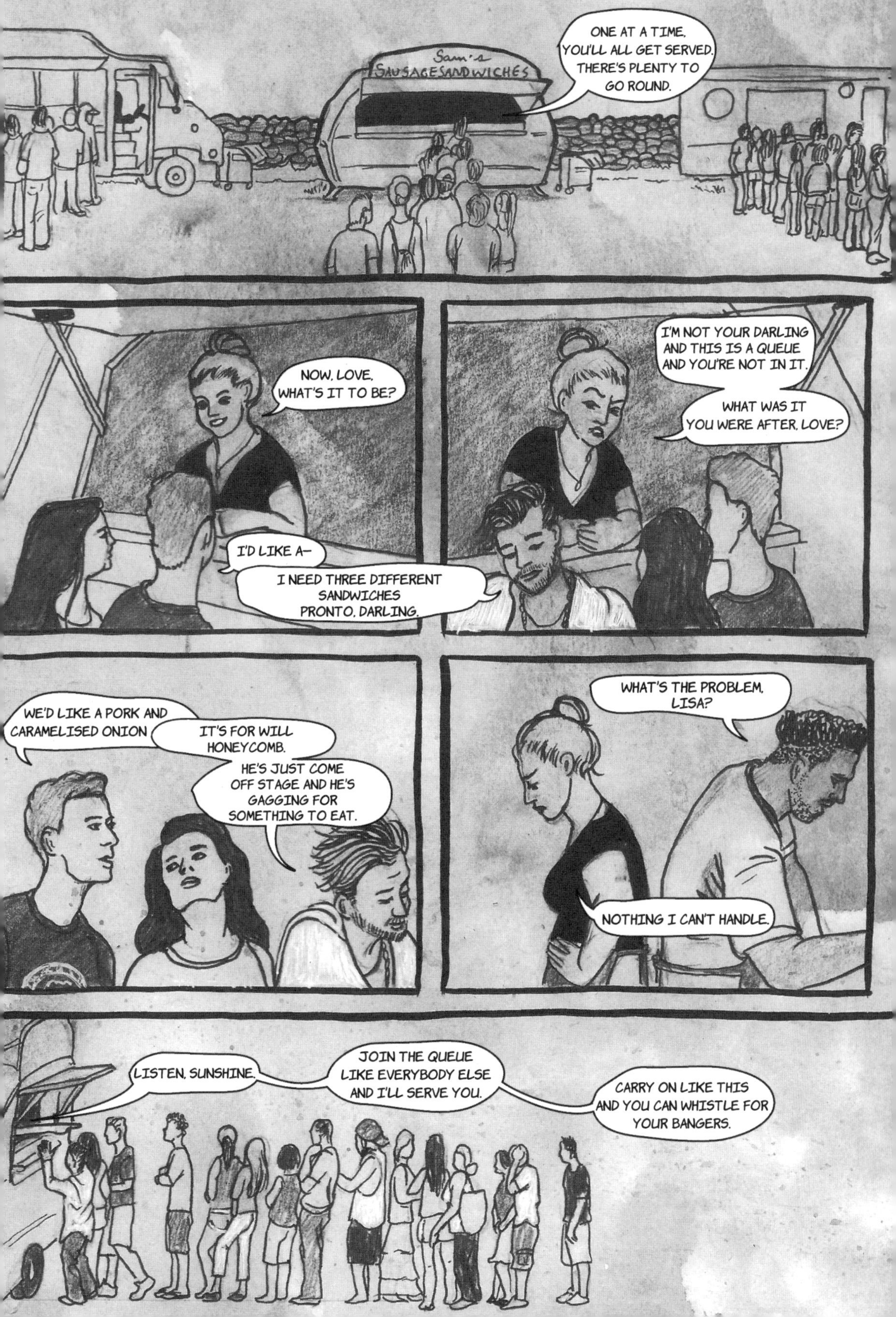
Sam's
SAUSAGE SANDWICHES
ONE AT A TIME. YOU'LL ALL GET SERVED. THERE'S PLENTY TO GO ROUND.
NOW, LOVE, WHAT'S IT TO BE?
I'D LIKE A—
I NEED THREE DIFFERENT SANDWICHES PRONTO, DARLING.
I'M NOT YOUR DARLING AND THIS IS A QUEUE AND YOU'RE NOT IN IT.
WHAT WAS IT YOU WERE AFTER, LOVE?
WE'D LIKE A PORK AND CARAMELISED ONION
IT'S FOR WILL HONEYCOMB.
HE'S JUST COME OFF STAGE AND HE'S GAGGING FOR SOMETHING TO EAT.
WHAT'S THE PROBLEM, LISA?
NOTHING I CAN'T HANDLE.
LISTEN, SUNSHINE.
JOIN THE QUEUE LIKE EVERYBODY ELSE AND I'LL SERVE YOU.
CARRY ON LIKE THIS AND YOU CAN WHISTLE FOR YOUR BANGERS.

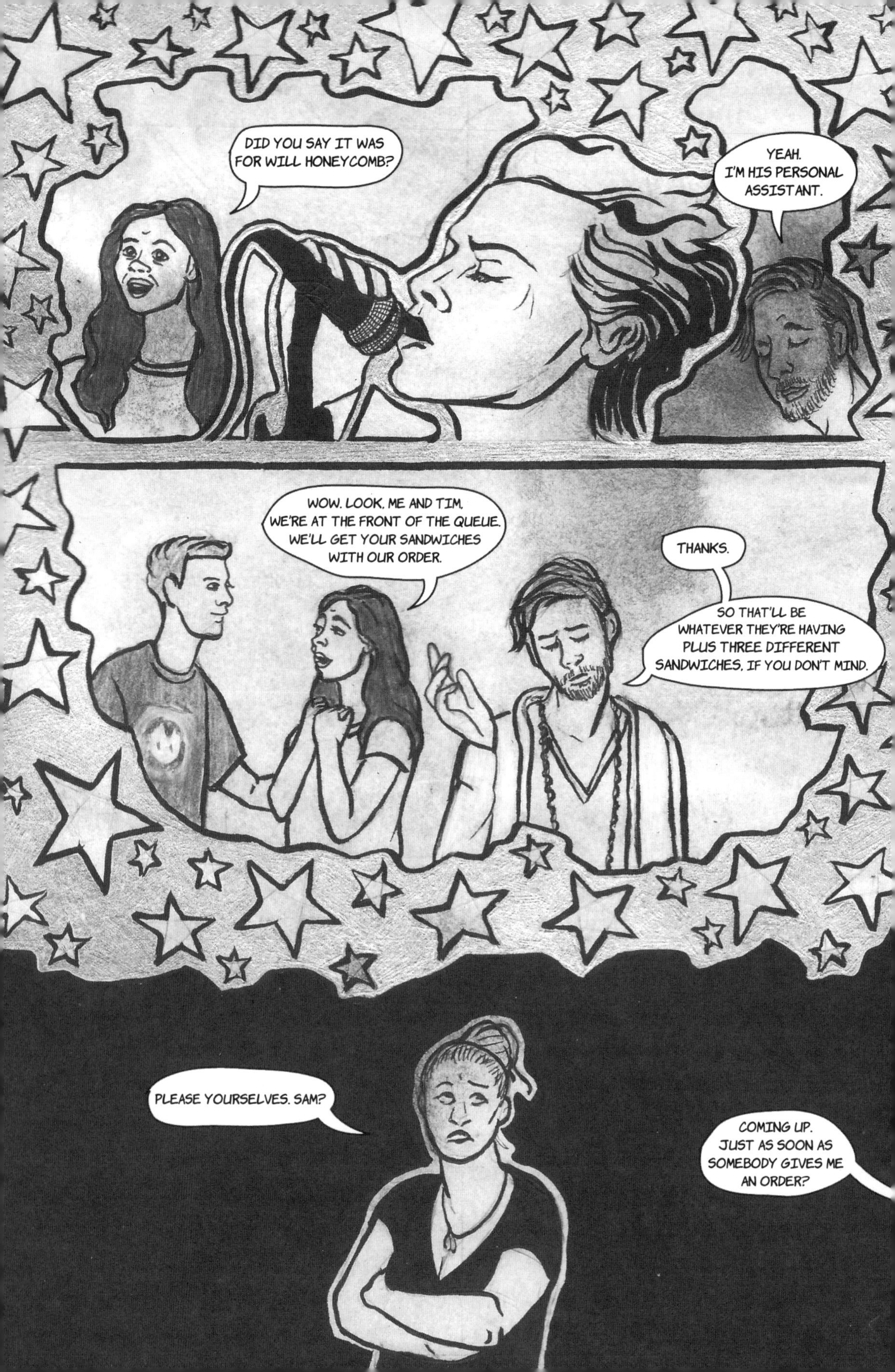
DID YOU SAY IT WAS FOR WILL HONEYCOMB?
YEAH. I'M HIS PERSONAL ASSISTANT.
WOW. LOOK, ME AND TIM, WE'RE AT THE FRONT OF THE QUEUE. WE'LL GET YOUR SANDWICHES WITH OUR ORDER.
THANKS.
SO THAT'LL BE WHATEVER THEY'RE HAVING PLUS THREE DIFFERENT SANDWICHES, IF YOU DON'T MIND.
PLEASE YOURSELVES. SAM?
COMING UP. JUST AS SOON AS SOMEBODY GIVES ME AN ORDER?

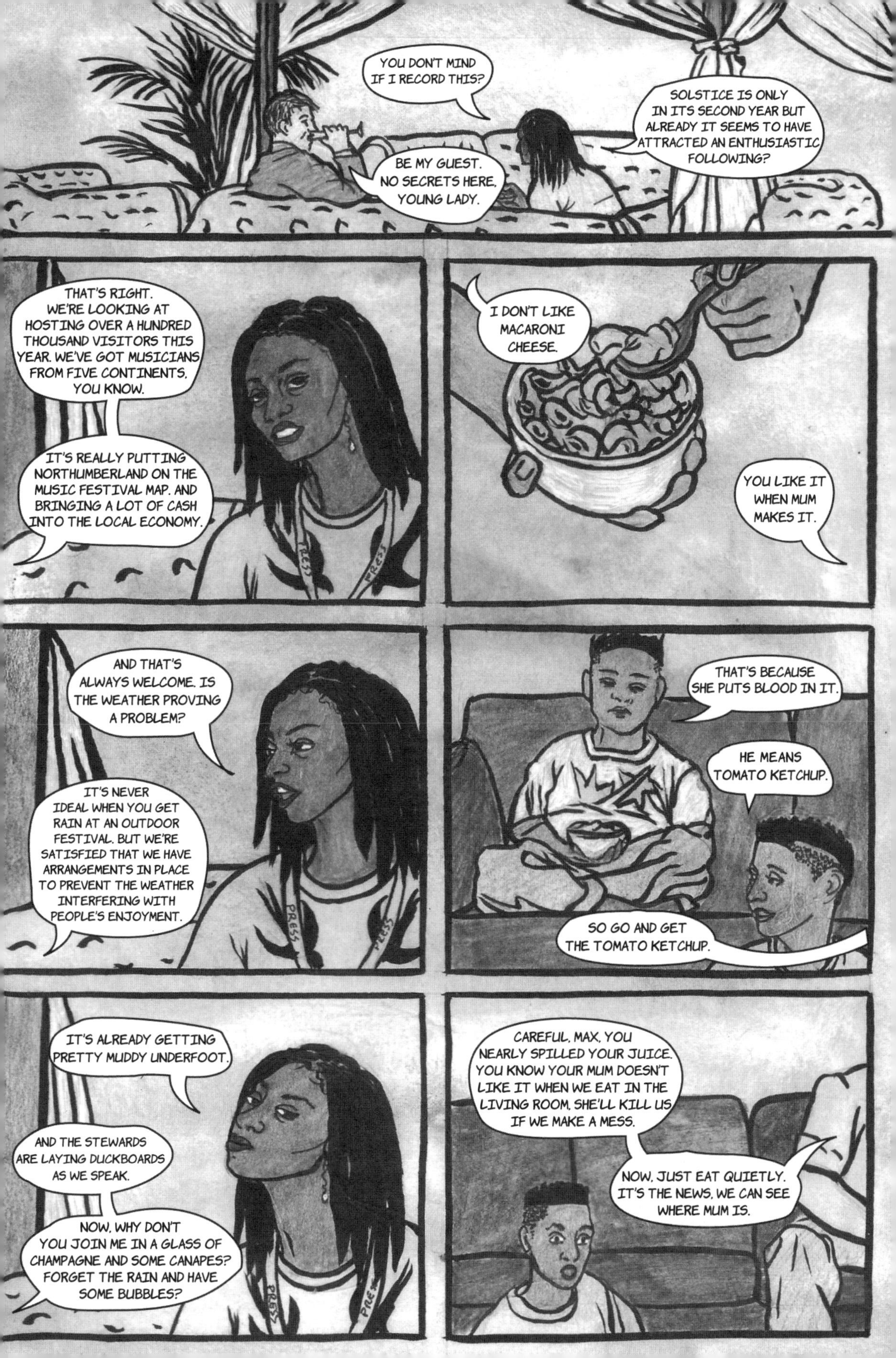

YOU DON'T MIND IF I RECORD THIS?
BE MY GUEST. NO SECRETS HERE, YOUNG LADY.
SOLSTICE IS ONLY IN ITS SECOND YEAR BUT ALREADY IT SEEMS TO HAVE ATTRACTED AN ENTHUSIASTIC FOLLOWING?
THAT'S RIGHT. WE'RE LOOKING AT HOSTING OVER A HUNDRED THOUSAND VISITORS THIS YEAR. WE'VE GOT MUSICIANS FROM FIVE CONTINENTS, YOU KNOW.
IT'S REALLY PUTTING NORTHUMBERLAND ON THE MUSIC FESTIVAL MAP. AND BRINGING A LOT OF CASH INTO THE LOCAL ECONOMY.
PRESS
I DON'T LIKE MACARONI CHEESE.
YOU LIKE IT WHEN MUM MAKES IT.
AND THAT'S ALWAYS WELCOME. IS THE WEATHER PROVING A PROBLEM?
IT'S NEVER IDEAL WHEN YOU GET RAIN AT AN OUTDOOR FESTIVAL. BUT WE'RE SATISFIED THAT WE HAVE ARRANGEMENTS IN PLACE TO PREVENT THE WEATHER INTERFERING WITH PEOPLE'S ENJOYMENT.
PRESS
THAT'S BECAUSE SHE PUTS BLOOD IN IT.
HE MEANS TOMATO KETCHUP.
SO GO AND GET THE TOMATO KETCHUP.
IT'S ALREADY GETTING PRETTY MUDDY UNDERFOOT.
AND THE STEWARDS ARE LAYING DUCKBOARDS AS WE SPEAK.
NOW, WHY DON'T YOU JOIN ME IN A GLASS OF CHAMPAGNE AND SOME CANAPES? FORGET THE RAIN AND HAVE SOME BUBBLES?
PRESS
CAREFUL, MAX, YOU NEARLY SPILLED YOUR JUICE. YOU KNOW YOUR MUM DOESN'T LIKE IT WHEN WE EAT IN THE LIVING ROOM. SHE'LL KILL US IF WE MAKE A MESS.
NOW, JUST EAT QUIETLY. IT'S THE NEWS, WE CAN SEE WHERE MUM IS.

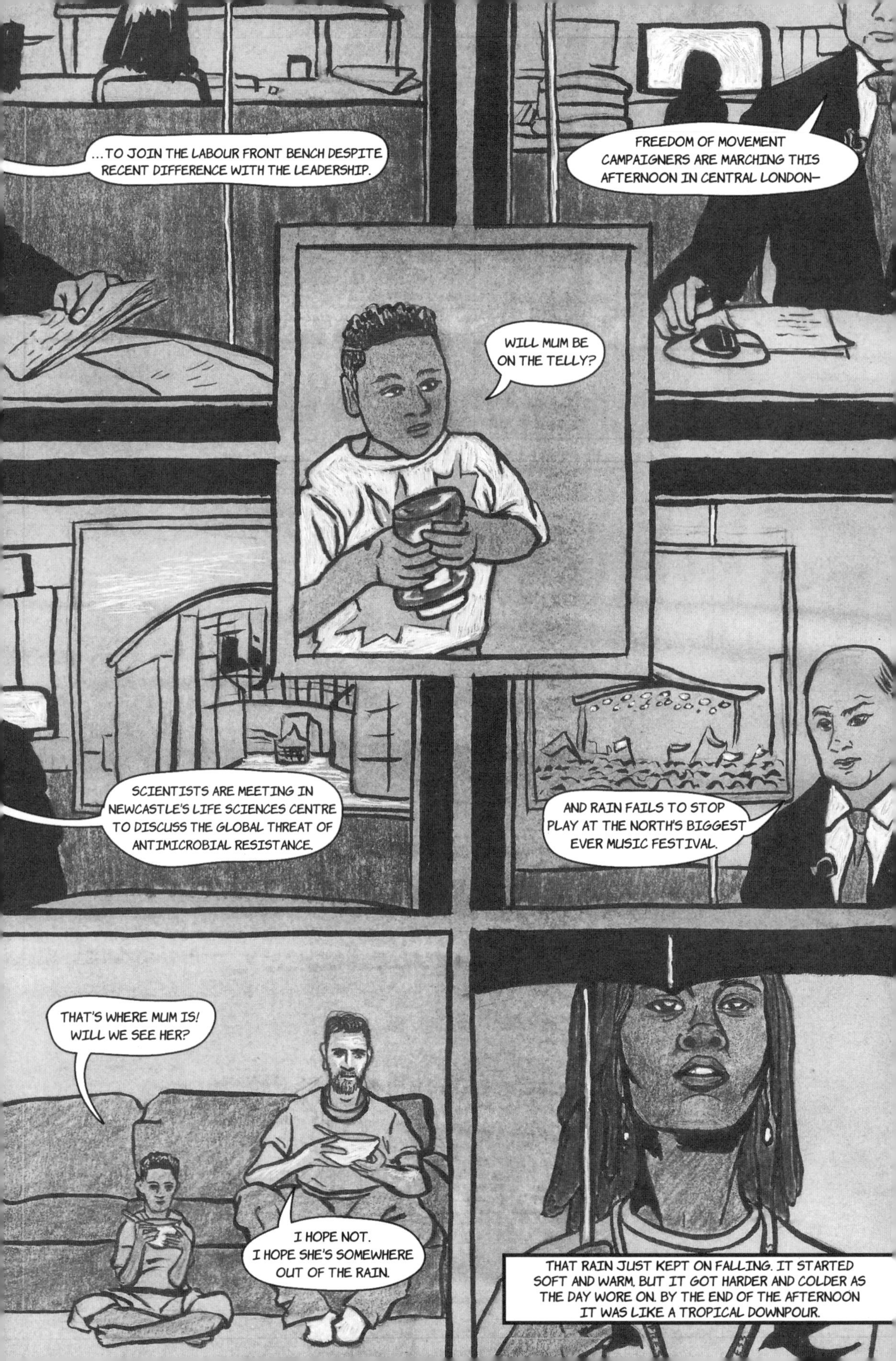
…TO JOIN THE LABOUR FRONT BENCH DESPITE RECENT DIFFERENCE WITH THE LEADERSHIP.
FREEDOM OF MOVEMENT CAMPAIGNERS ARE MARCHING THIS AFTERNOON IN CENTRAL LONDON—
WILL MUM BE ON THE TELLY?
SCIENTISTS ARE MEETING IN NEWCASTLE'S LIFE SCIENCES CENTRE TO DISCUSS THE GLOBAL THREAT OF ANTIMICROBIAL RESISTANCE.
AND RAIN FAILS TO STOP PLAY AT THE NORTH'S BIGGEST EVER MUSIC FESTIVAL.
THAT'S WHERE MUM IS! WILL WE SEE HER?
I HOPE NOT. I HOPE SHE'S SOMEWHERE OUT OF THE RAIN.
THAT RAIN JUST KEPT ON FALLING. IT STARTED SOFT AND WARM, BUT IT GOT HARDER AND COLDER AS THE DAY WORE ON. BY THE END OF THE AFTERNOON IT WAS LIKE A TROPICAL DOWNPOUR.

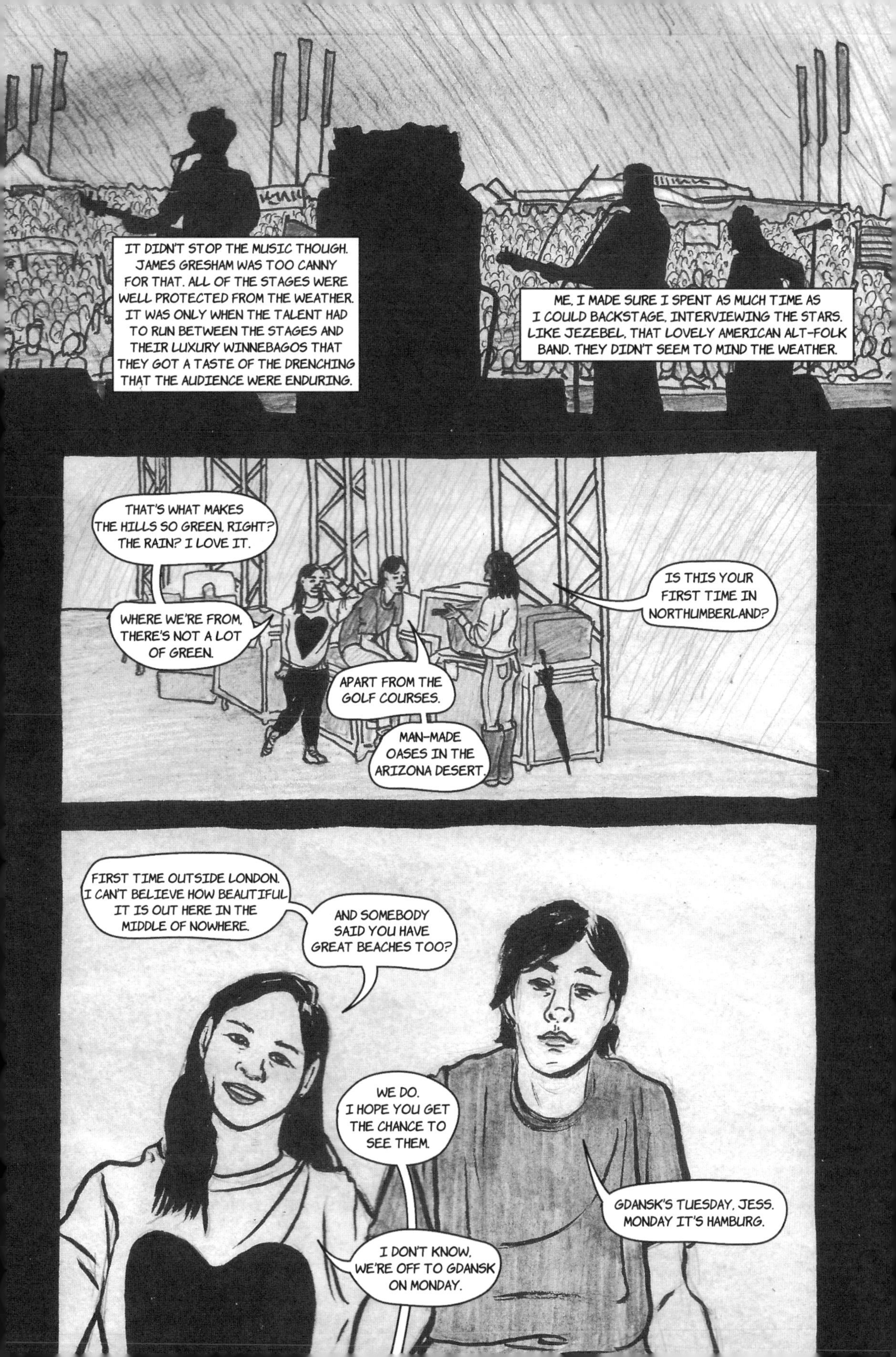
IT DIDN'T STOP THE MUSIC THOUGH. JAMES GRESHAM WAS TOO CANNY FOR THAT. ALL OF THE STAGES WERE WELL PROTECTED FROM THE WEATHER. IT WAS ONLY WHEN THE TALENT HAD TO RUN BETWEEN THE STAGES AND THEIR LUXURY WINNEBAGOS THAT THEY GOT A TASTE OF THE DRENCHING THAT THE AUDIENCE WERE ENDURING.
ME, I MADE SURE I SPENT AS MUCH TIME AS I COULD BACKSTAGE, INTERVIEWING THE STARS. LIKE JEZEBEL, THAT LOVELY AMERICAN ALT-FOLK BAND. THEY DIDN'T SEEM TO MIND THE WEATHER.
THAT'S WHAT MAKES THE HILLS SO GREEN, RIGHT? THE RAIN? I LOVE IT.
WHERE WE'RE FROM, THERE'S NOT A LOT OF GREEN.
IS THIS YOUR FIRST TIME IN NORTHUMBERLAND?
APART FROM THE GOLF COURSES.
MAN-MADE OASES IN THE ARIZONA DESERT.
FIRST TIME OUTSIDE LONDON. I CAN'T BELIEVE HOW BEAUTIFUL IT IS OUT HERE IN THE MIDDLE OF NOWHERE.
AND SOMEBODY SAID YOU HAVE GREAT BEACHES TOO?
WE DO. I HOPE YOU GET THE CHANCE TO SEE THEM.
I DON'T KNOW, WE'RE OFF TO GDANSK ON MONDAY.
GDANSK'S TUESDAY, JESS. MONDAY IT'S HAMBURG.

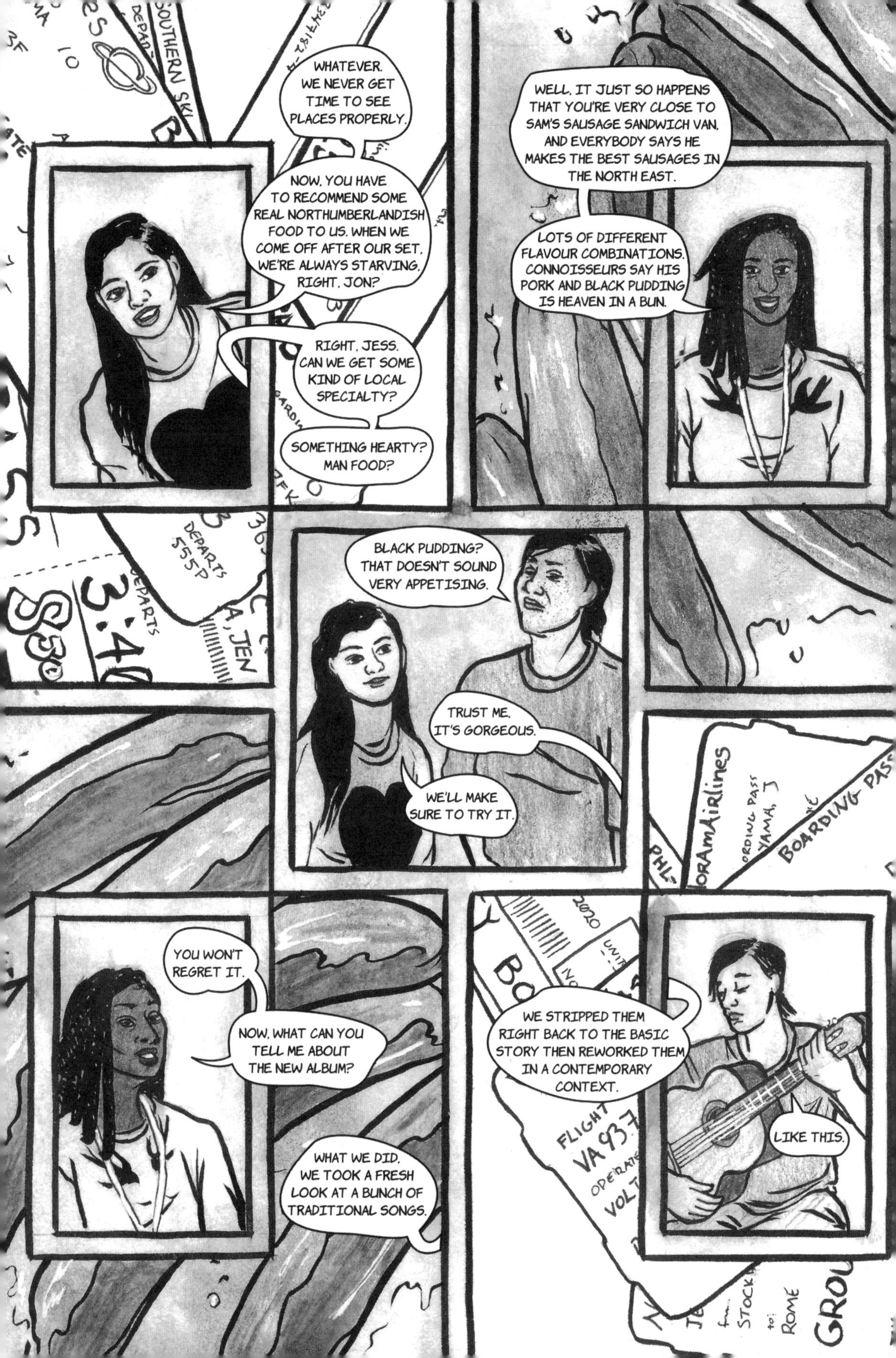
WHATEVER. WE NEVER GET TIME TO SEE PLACES PROPERLY.
NOW, YOU HAVE TO RECOMMEND SOME REAL NORTHUMBERLANDISH FOOD TO US. WHEN WE COME OFF AFTER OUR SET, WE'RE ALWAYS STARVING. RIGHT, JON?
RIGHT, JESS. CAN WE GET SOME KIND OF LOCAL SPECIALTY?
SOMETHING HEARTY? MAN FOOD?
WELL, IT JUST SO HAPPENS THAT YOU'RE VERY CLOSE TO SAM'S SAUSAGE SANDWICH VAN, AND EVERYBODY SAYS HE MAKES THE BEST SAUSAGES IN THE NORTH EAST.
LOTS OF DIFFERENT FLAVOUR COMBINATIONS. CONNOISSEURS SAY HIS PORK AND BLACK PUDDING IS HEAVEN IN A BUN.
BLACK PUDDING? THAT DOESN'T SOUND VERY APPETISING.
TRUST ME, IT'S GORGEOUS.
WE'LL MAKE SURE TO TRY IT.
YOU WON'T REGRET IT.
NOW, WHAT CAN YOU TELL ME ABOUT THE NEW ALBUM?
WHAT WE DID, WE TOOK A FRESH LOOK AT A BUNCH OF TRADITIONAL SONGS.
WE STRIPPED THEM RIGHT BACK TO THE BASIC STORY THEN REWORKED THEM IN A CONTEMPORARY CONTEXT.
LIKE THIS.

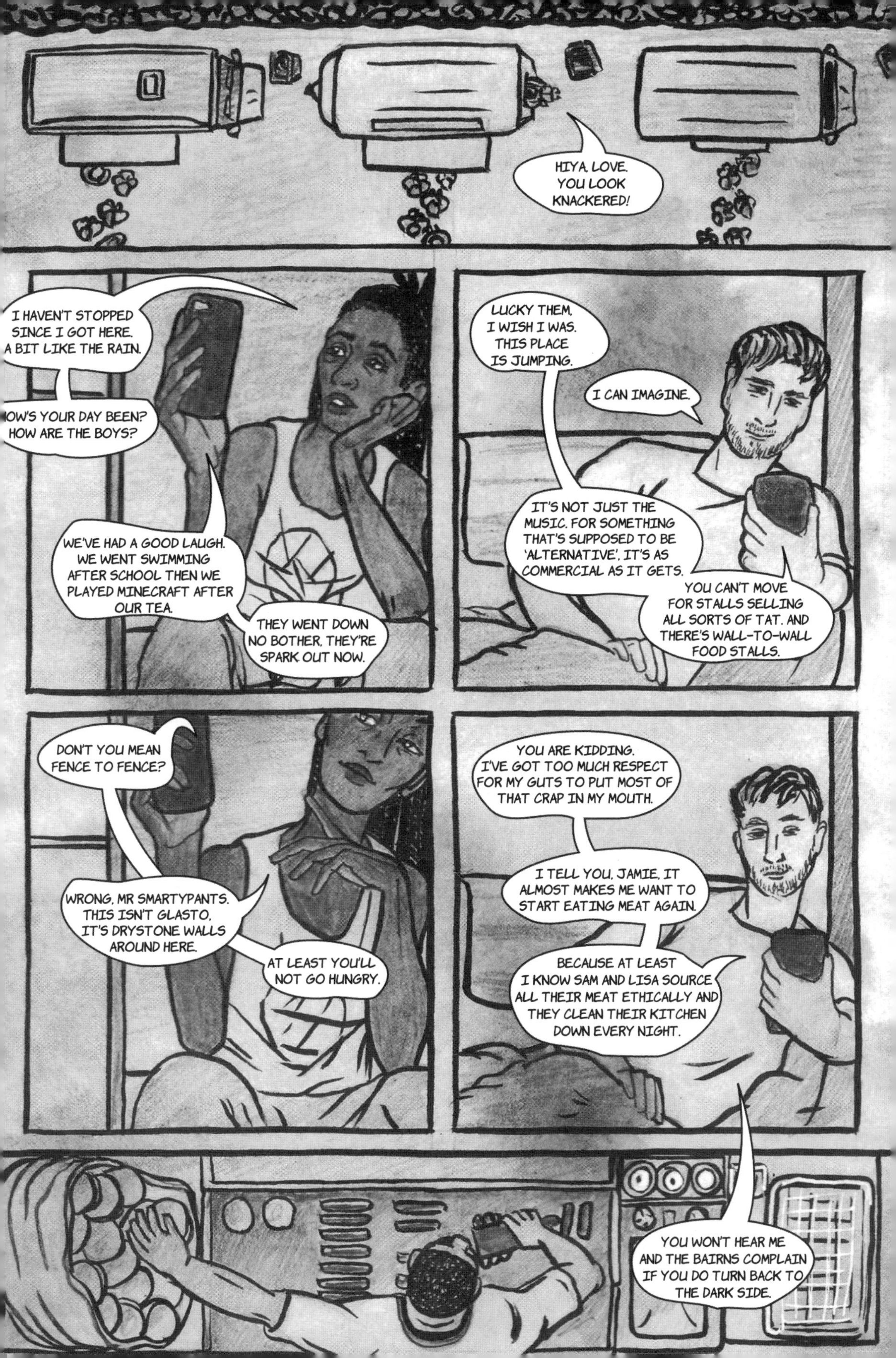
HIYA, LOVE. YOU LOOK KNACKERED!
I HAVEN'T STOPPED SINCE I GOT HERE. A BIT LIKE THE RAIN.
HOW'S YOUR DAY BEEN? HOW ARE THE BOYS?
WE'VE HAD A GOOD LAUGH. WE WENT SWIMMING AFTER SCHOOL THEN WE PLAYED MINECRAFT AFTER OUR TEA.
THEY WENT DOWN NO BOTHER. THEY'RE SPARK OUT NOW.
LUCKY THEM. I WISH I WAS. THIS PLACE IS JUMPING.
I CAN IMAGINE.
IT'S NOT JUST THE MUSIC. FOR SOMETHING THAT'S SUPPOSED TO BE 'ALTERNATIVE', IT'S AS COMMERCIAL AS IT GETS.
YOU CAN'T MOVE FOR STALLS SELLING ALL SORTS OF TAT. AND THERE'S WALL-TO-WALL FOOD STALLS.
DON'T YOU MEAN FENCE TO FENCE?
WRONG, MR SMARTYPANTS. THIS ISN'T GLASTO, IT'S DRYSTONE WALLS AROUND HERE.
AT LEAST YOU'LL NOT GO HUNGRY.
YOU ARE KIDDING. I'VE GOT TOO MUCH RESPECT FOR MY GUTS TO PUT MOST OF THAT CRAP IN MY MOUTH.
I TELL YOU, JAMIE, IT ALMOST MAKES ME WANT TO START EATING MEAT AGAIN.
BECAUSE AT LEAST I KNOW SAM AND LISA SOURCE ALL THEIR MEAT ETHICALLY AND THEY CLEAN THEIR KITCHEN DOWN EVERY NIGHT.
YOU WON'T HEAR ME AND THE BAIRNS COMPLAIN IF YOU DO TURN BACK TO THE DARK SIDE.

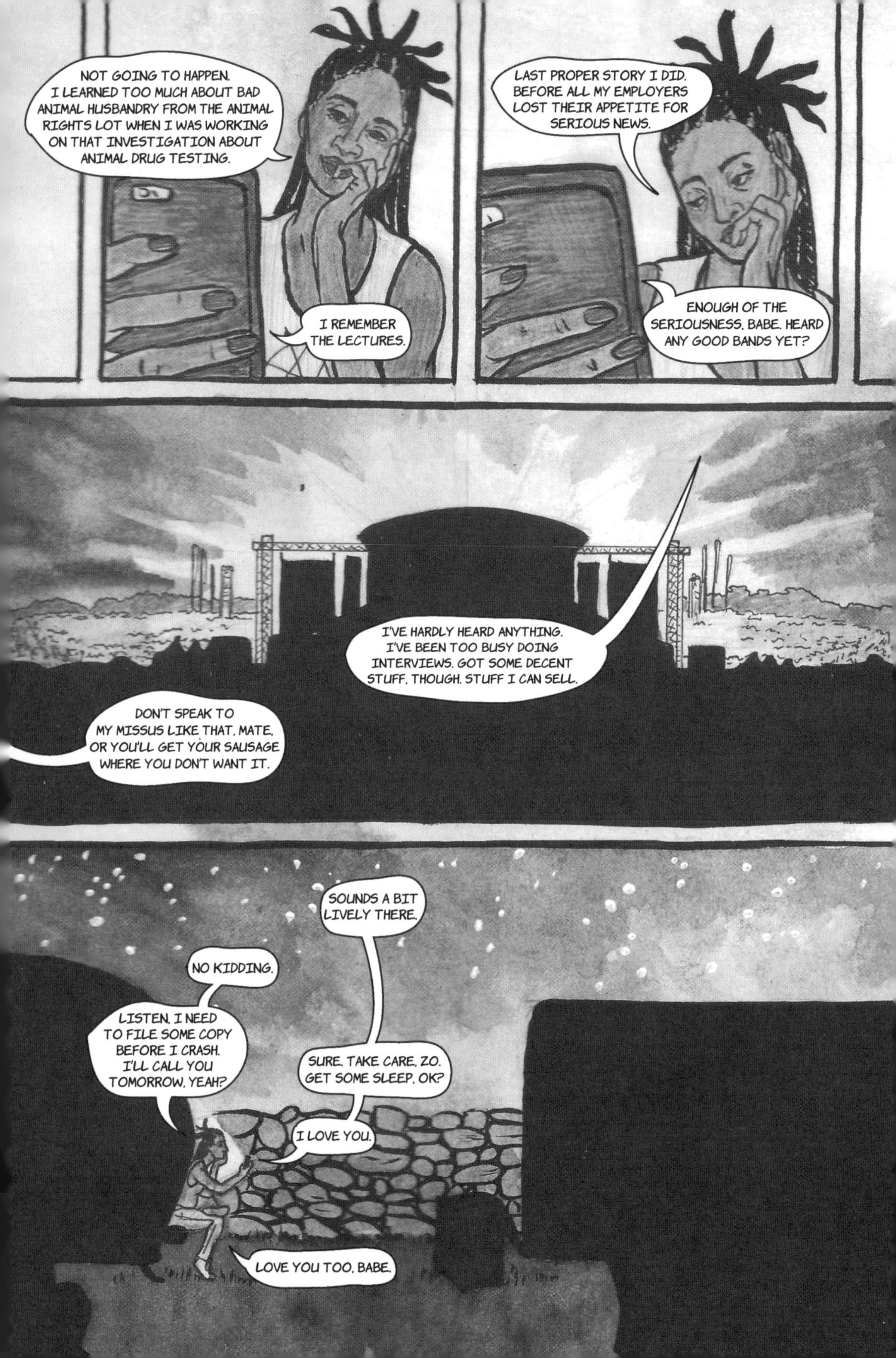
NOT GOING TO HAPPEN. I LEARNED TOO MUCH ABOUT BAD ANIMAL HUSBANDRY FROM THE ANIMAL RIGHTS LOT WHEN I WAS WORKING ON THAT INVESTIGATION ABOUT ANIMAL DRUG TESTING.
I REMEMBER THE LECTURES.
LAST PROPER STORY I DID. BEFORE ALL MY EMPLOYERS LOST THEIR APPETITE FOR SERIOUS NEWS.
ENOUGH OF THE SERIOUSNESS, BABE. HEARD ANY GOOD BANDS YET?
I'VE HARDLY HEARD ANYTHING. I'VE BEEN TOO BUSY DOING INTERVIEWS. GOT SOME DECENT STUFF, THOUGH. STUFF I CAN SELL.
DON'T SPEAK TO MY MISSUS LIKE THAT, MATE, OR YOU'LL GET YOUR SAUSAGE WHERE YOU DON'T WANT IT.
SOUNDS A BIT LIVELY THERE.
NO KIDDING.
LISTEN, I NEED TO FILE SOME COPY BEFORE I CRASH. I'LL CALL YOU TOMORROW, YEAH?
SURE. TAKE CARE, ZO. GET SOME SLEEP, OK?
I LOVE YOU.
LOVE YOU TOO, BABE.

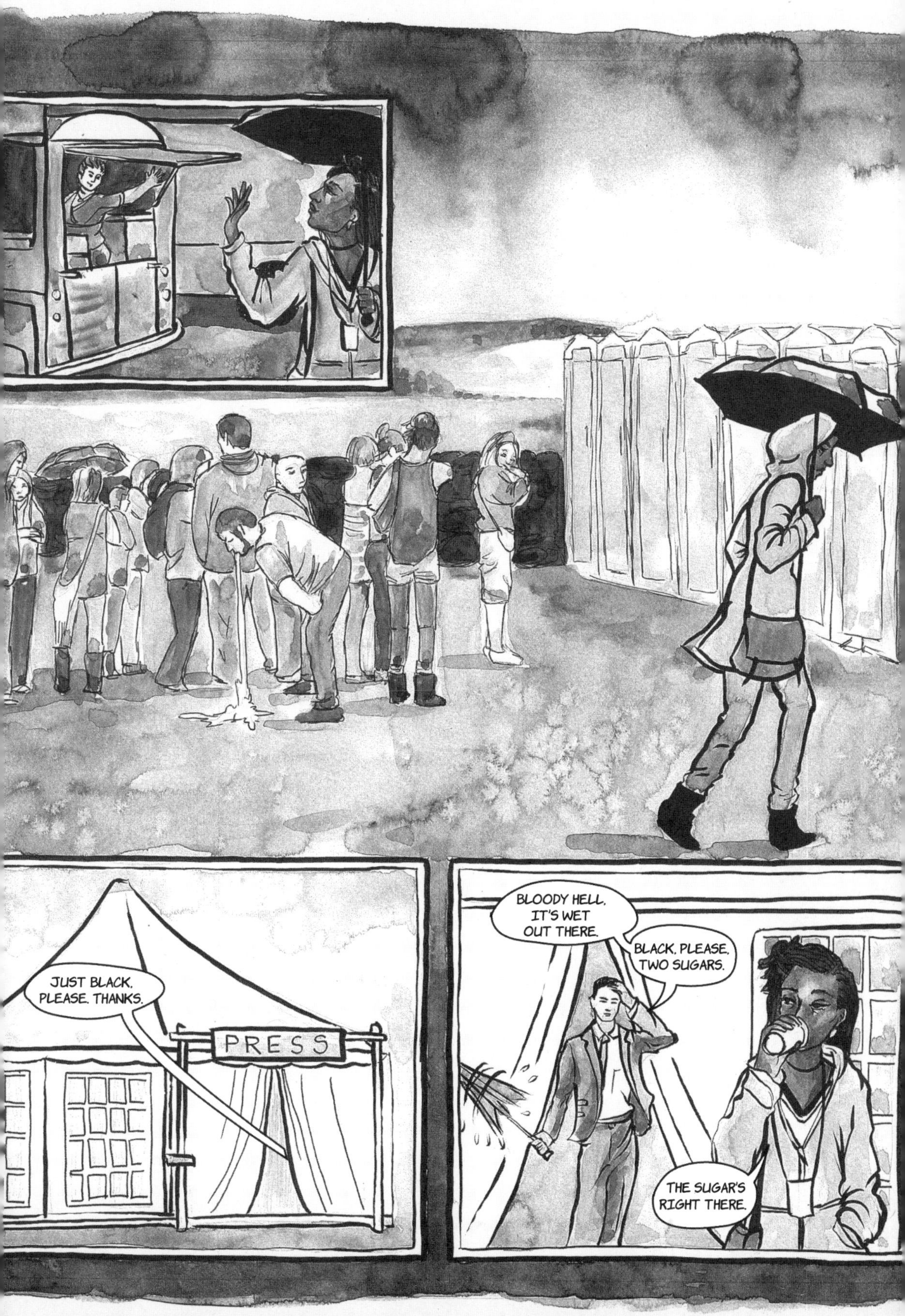
JUST BLACK. PLEASE. THANKS.
PRESS
BLOODY HELL. IT'S WET OUT THERE.
BLACK, PLEASE. TWO SUGARS.
THE SUGAR'S RIGHT THERE.

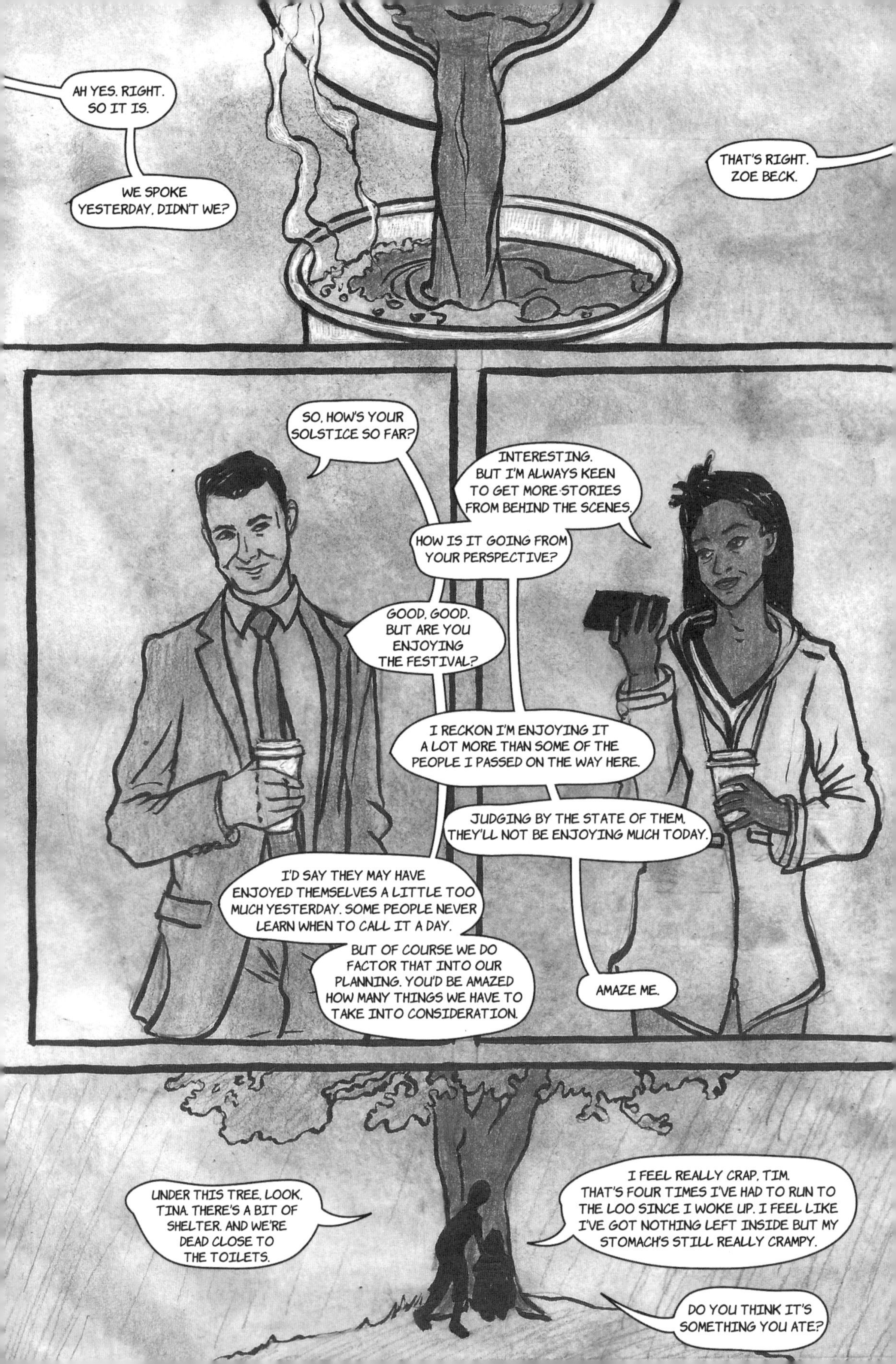
AH YES. RIGHT. SO IT IS.
WE SPOKE YESTERDAY, DIDN'T WE?
THAT'S RIGHT. ZOE BECK.
SO, HOW'S YOUR SOLSTICE SO FAR?
INTERESTING. BUT I'M ALWAYS KEEN TO GET MORE STORIES FROM BEHIND THE SCENES.
HOW IS IT GOING FROM YOUR PERSPECTIVE?
GOOD, GOOD. BUT ARE YOU ENJOYING THE FESTIVAL?
I RECKON I'M ENJOYING IT A LOT MORE THAN SOME OF THE PEOPLE I PASSED ON THE WAY HERE.
JUDGING BY THE STATE OF THEM, THEY'LL NOT BE ENJOYING MUCH TODAY.
I'D SAY THEY MAY HAVE ENJOYED THEMSELVES A LITTLE TOO MUCH YESTERDAY. SOME PEOPLE NEVER LEARN WHEN TO CALL IT A DAY.
BUT OF COURSE WE DO FACTOR THAT INTO OUR PLANNING. YOU'D BE AMAZED HOW MANY THINGS WE HAVE TO TAKE INTO CONSIDERATION.
AMAZE ME.
UNDER THIS TREE, LOOK, TINA. THERE'S A BIT OF SHELTER. AND WE'RE DEAD CLOSE TO THE TOILETS.
I FEEL REALLY CRAP, TIM. THAT'S FOUR TIMES I'VE HAD TO RUN TO THE LOO SINCE I WOKE UP. I FEEL LIKE I'VE GOT NOTHING LEFT INSIDE BUT MY STOMACH'S STILL REALLY CRAMPY.
DO YOU THINK IT'S SOMETHING YOU ATE?

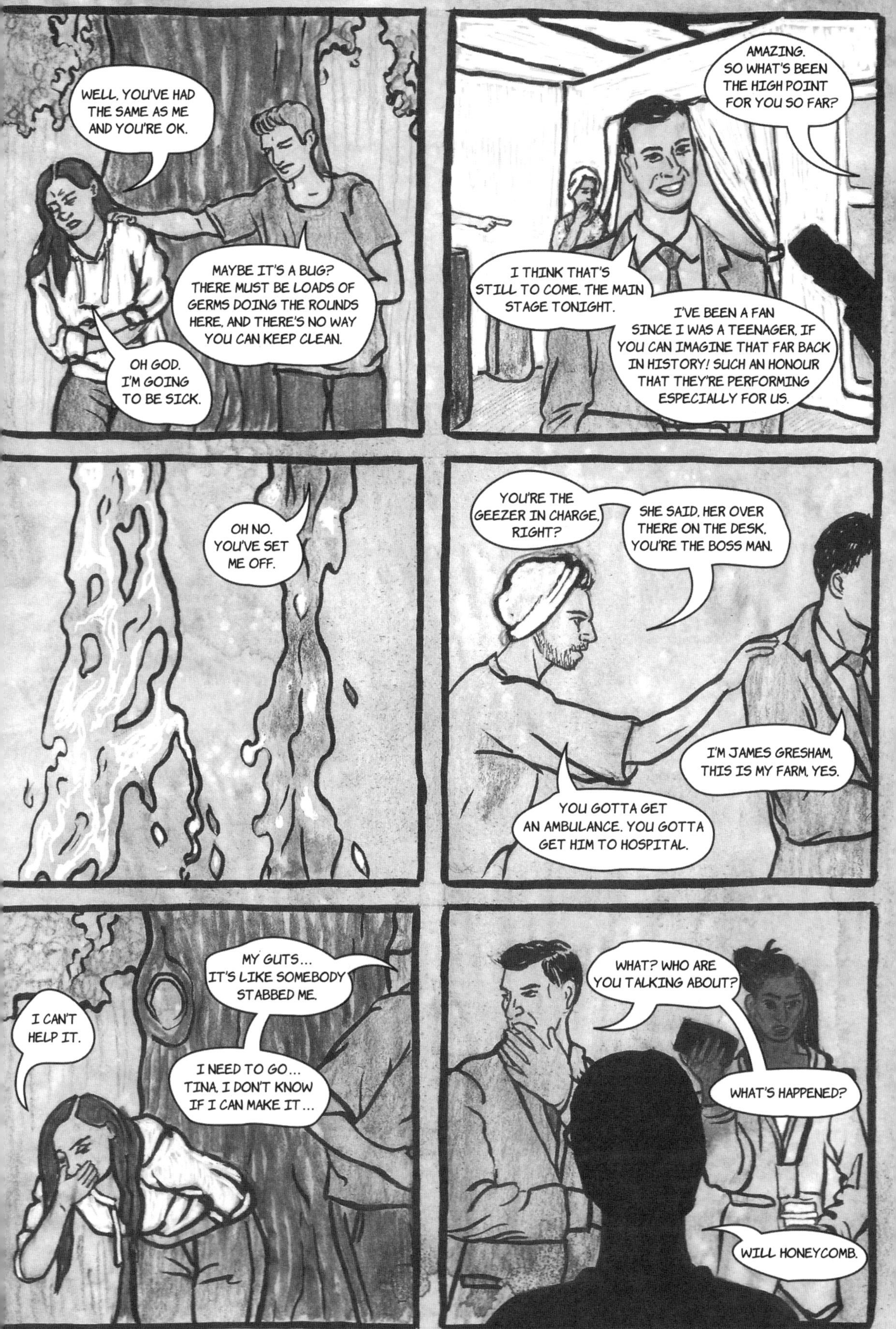
WELL, YOU'VE HAD THE SAME AS ME AND YOU'RE OK.
MAYBE IT'S A BUG? THERE MUST BE LOADS OF GERMS DOING THE ROUNDS HERE, AND THERE'S NO WAY YOU CAN KEEP CLEAN.
OH GOD. I'M GOING TO BE SICK.
AMAZING. SO WHAT'S BEEN THE HIGH POINT FOR YOU SO FAR?
I THINK THAT'S STILL TO COME. THE MAIN STAGE TONIGHT.
I'VE BEEN A FAN SINCE I WAS A TEENAGER, IF YOU CAN IMAGINE THAT FAR BACK IN HISTORY! SUCH AN HONOUR THAT THEY'RE PERFORMING ESPECIALLY FOR US.
OH NO. YOU'VE SET ME OFF.
YOU'RE THE GEEZER IN CHARGE, RIGHT?
SHE SAID, HER OVER THERE ON THE DESK, YOU'RE THE BOSS MAN.
I'M JAMES GRESHAM, THIS IS MY FARM, YES.
YOU GOTTA GET AN AMBULANCE. YOU GOTTA GET HIM TO HOSPITAL.
I CAN'T HELP IT.
MY GUTS… IT'S LIKE SOMEBODY STABBED ME.
I NEED TO GO… TINA, I DON'T KNOW IF I CAN MAKE IT…
WHAT? WHO ARE YOU TALKING ABOUT?
WHAT'S HAPPENED?
WILL HONEYCOMB.

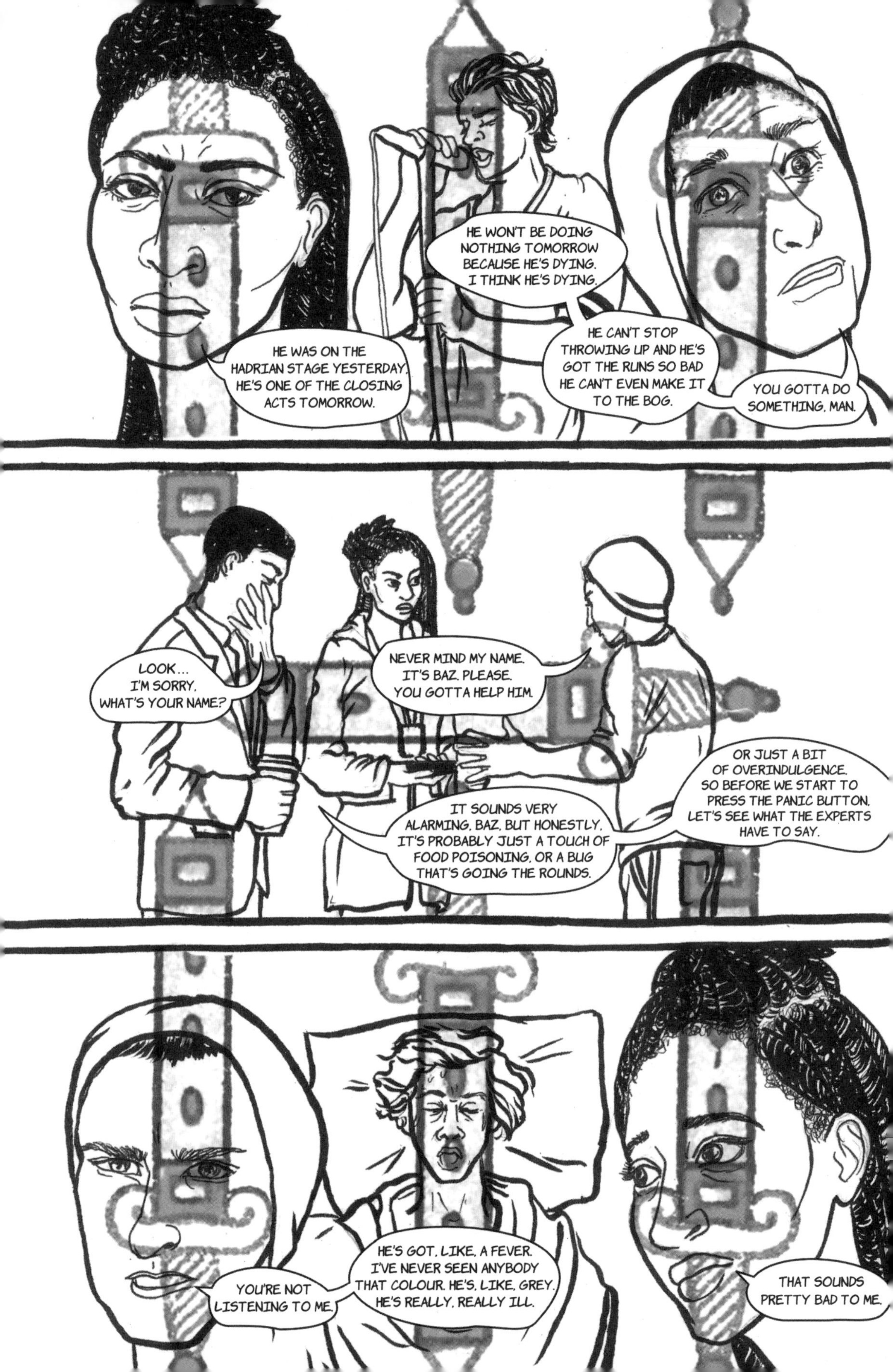
HE WAS ON THE HADRIAN STAGE YESTERDAY. HE'S ONE OF THE CLOSING ACTS TOMORROW.
HE WON'T BE DOING NOTHING TOMORROW BECAUSE HE'S DYING. I THINK HE'S DYING.
HE CAN'T STOP THROWING UP AND HE'S GOT THE RUNS SO BAD HE CAN'T EVEN MAKE IT TO THE BOG.
YOU GOTTA DO SOMETHING, MAN.
LOOK... I'M SORRY. WHAT'S YOUR NAME?
NEVER MIND MY NAME. IT'S BAZ. PLEASE. YOU GOTTA HELP HIM.
IT SOUNDS VERY ALARMING, BAZ, BUT HONESTLY, IT'S PROBABLY JUST A TOUCH OF FOOD POISONING, OR A BUG THAT'S GOING THE ROUNDS.
OR JUST A BIT OF OVERINDULGENCE. SO BEFORE WE START TO PRESS THE PANIC BUTTON, LET'S SEE WHAT THE EXPERTS HAVE TO SAY.
YOU'RE NOT LISTENING TO ME.
HE'S GOT, LIKE, A FEVER. I'VE NEVER SEEN ANYBODY THAT COLOUR. HE'S, LIKE, GREY. HE'S REALLY, REALLY ILL.
THAT SOUNDS PRETTY BAD TO ME.

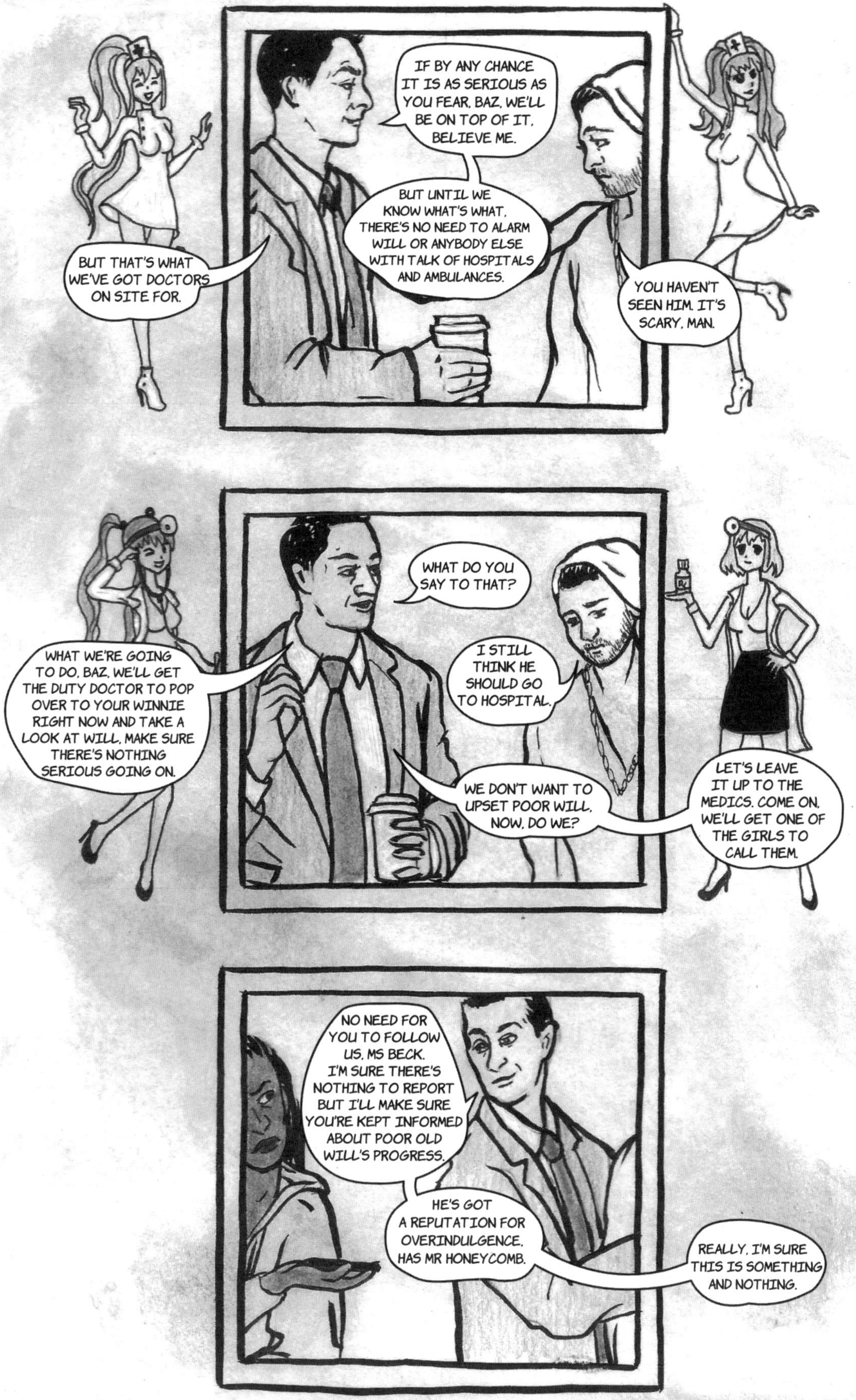
IF BY ANY CHANCE IT IS AS SERIOUS AS YOU FEAR, BAZ, WE'LL BE ON TOP OF IT, BELIEVE ME.
BUT UNTIL WE KNOW WHAT'S WHAT, THERE'S NO NEED TO ALARM WILL OR ANYBODY ELSE WITH TALK OF HOSPITALS AND AMBULANCES.
BUT THAT'S WHAT WE'VE GOT DOCTORS ON SITE FOR.
YOU HAVEN'T SEEN HIM. IT'S SCARY, MAN.
WHAT DO YOU SAY TO THAT?
I STILL THINK HE SHOULD GO TO HOSPITAL.
WHAT WE'RE GOING TO DO, BAZ, WE'LL GET THE DUTY DOCTOR TO POP OVER TO YOUR WINNIE RIGHT NOW AND TAKE A LOOK AT WILL, MAKE SURE THERE'S NOTHING SERIOUS GOING ON.
WE DON'T WANT TO UPSET POOR WILL, NOW, DO WE?
LET'S LEAVE IT UP TO THE MEDICS. COME ON, WE'LL GET ONE OF THE GIRLS TO CALL THEM.
NO NEED FOR YOU TO FOLLOW US, MS BECK. I'M SURE THERE'S NOTHING TO REPORT BUT I'LL MAKE SURE YOU'RE KEPT INFORMED ABOUT POOR OLD WILL'S PROGRESS.
HE'S GOT A REPUTATION FOR OVERINDULGENCE, HAS MR HONEYCOMB.
REALLY, I'M SURE THIS IS SOMETHING AND NOTHING.

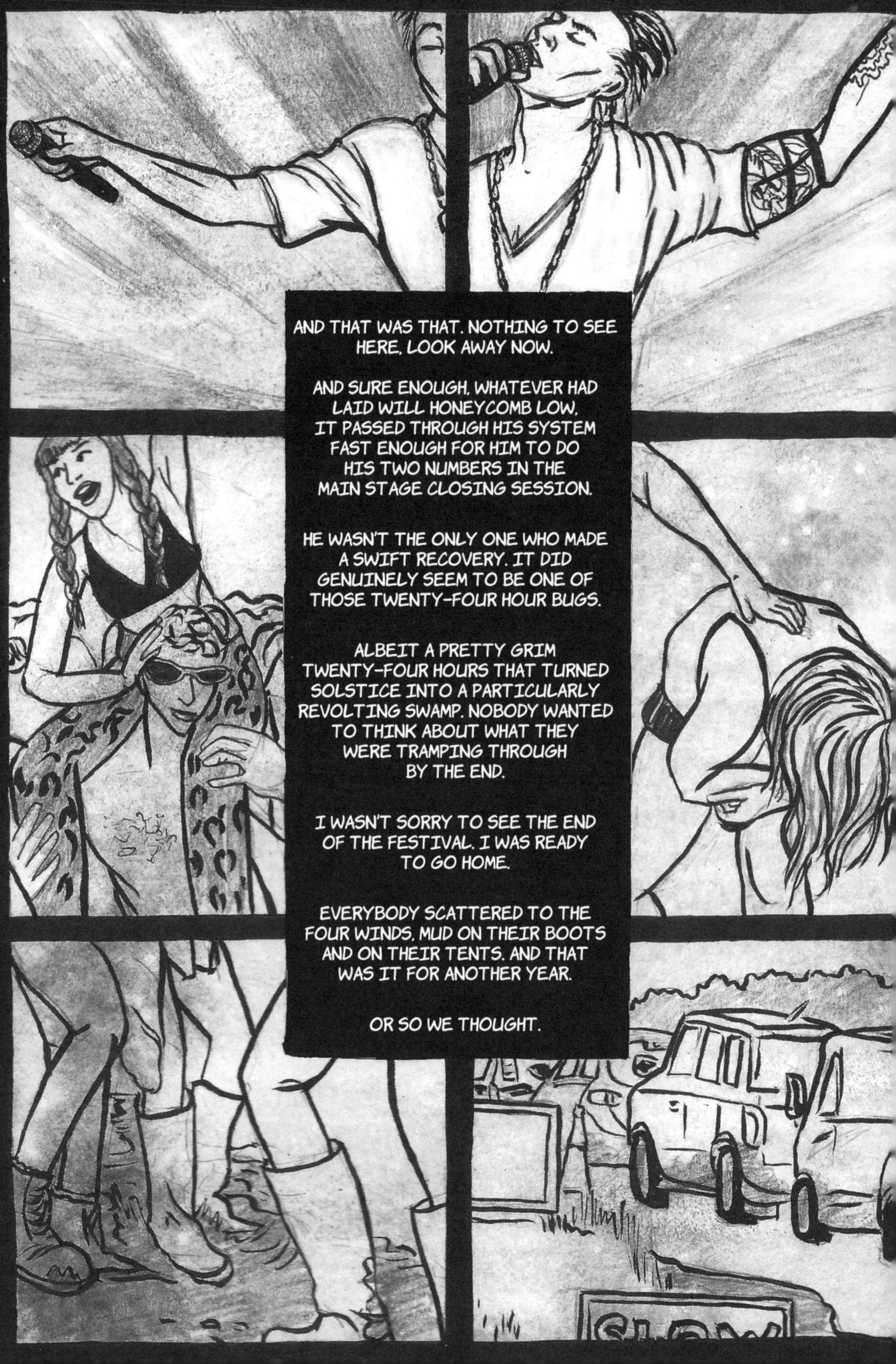
AND THAT WAS THAT. NOTHING TO SEE HERE, LOOK AWAY NOW.
AND SURE ENOUGH, WHATEVER HAD LAID WILL HONEYCOMB LOW, IT PASSED THROUGH HIS SYSTEM FAST ENOUGH FOR HIM TO DO HIS TWO NUMBERS IN THE MAIN STAGE CLOSING SESSION.
HE WASN'T THE ONLY ONE WHO MADE A SWIFT RECOVERY. IT DID GENUINELY SEEM TO BE ONE OF THOSE TWENTY-FOUR HOUR BUGS.
ALBEIT A PRETTY GRIM TWENTY-FOUR HOURS THAT TURNED SOLSTICE INTO A PARTICULARLY REVOLTING SWAMP. NOBODY WANTED TO THINK ABOUT WHAT THEY WERE TRAMPING THROUGH BY THE END.
I WASN'T SORRY TO SEE THE END OF THE FESTIVAL. I WAS READY TO GO HOME.
EVERYBODY SCATTERED TO THE FOUR WINDS, MUD ON THEIR BOOTS AND ON THEIR TENTS. AND THAT WAS IT FOR ANOTHER YEAR.
OR SO WE THOUGHT.

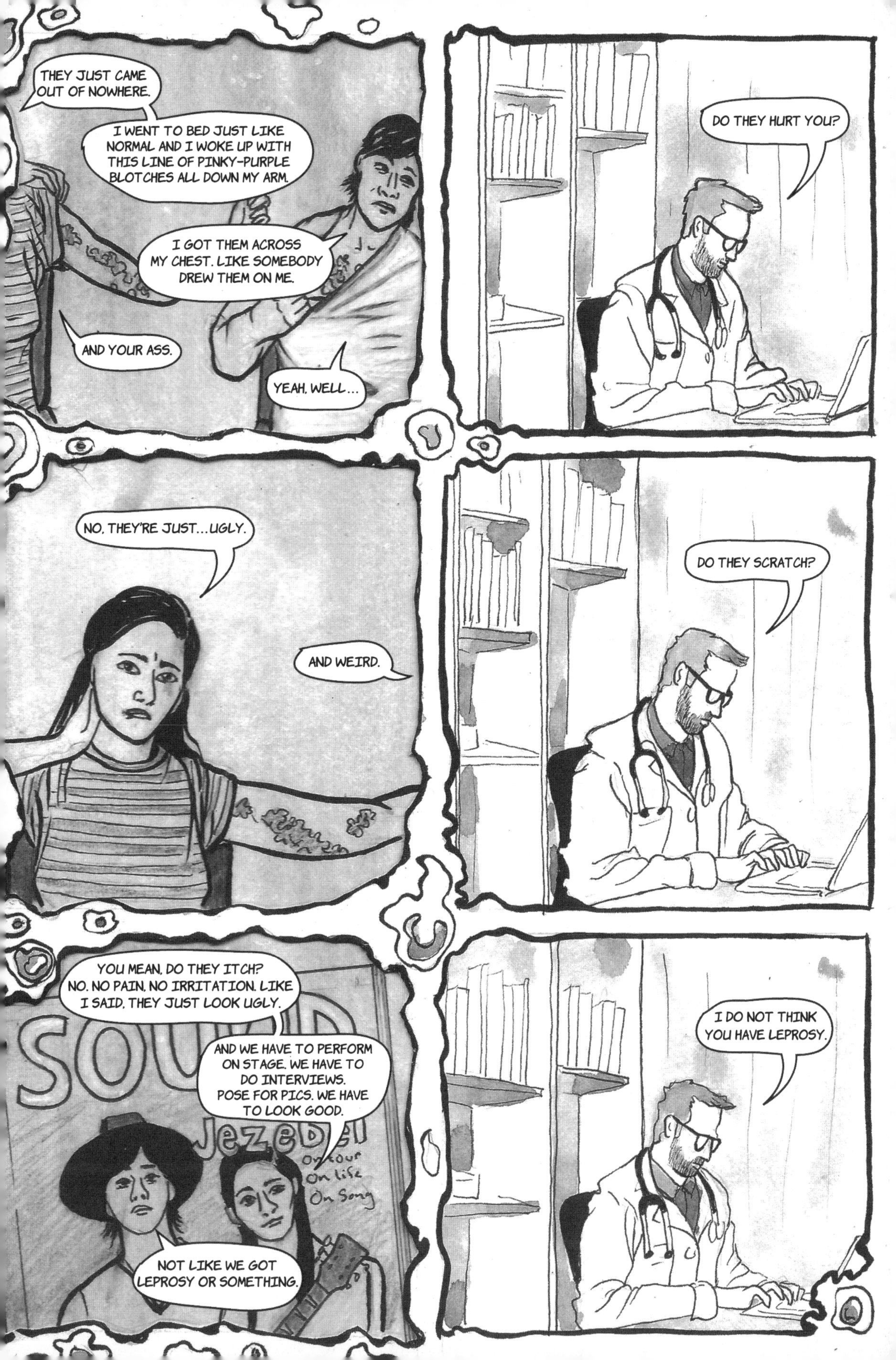
THEY JUST CAME OUT OF NOWHERE.
I WENT TO BED JUST LIKE NORMAL AND I WOKE UP WITH THIS LINE OF PINKY-PURPLE BLOTCHES ALL DOWN MY ARM.
I GOT THEM ACROSS MY CHEST. LIKE SOMEBODY DREW THEM ON ME.
AND YOUR ASS.
YEAH, WELL...
DO THEY HURT YOU?
NO, THEY'RE JUST...UGLY.
AND WEIRD.
DO THEY SCRATCH?
YOU MEAN, DO THEY ITCH? NO. NO PAIN, NO IRRITATION. LIKE I SAID, THEY JUST LOOK UGLY.
AND WE HAVE TO PERFORM ON STAGE. WE HAVE TO DO INTERVIEWS. POSE FOR PICS. WE HAVE TO LOOK GOOD.
On life
On Song
NOT LIKE WE GOT LEPROSY OR SOMETHING.
I DO NOT THINK YOU HAVE LEPROSY.

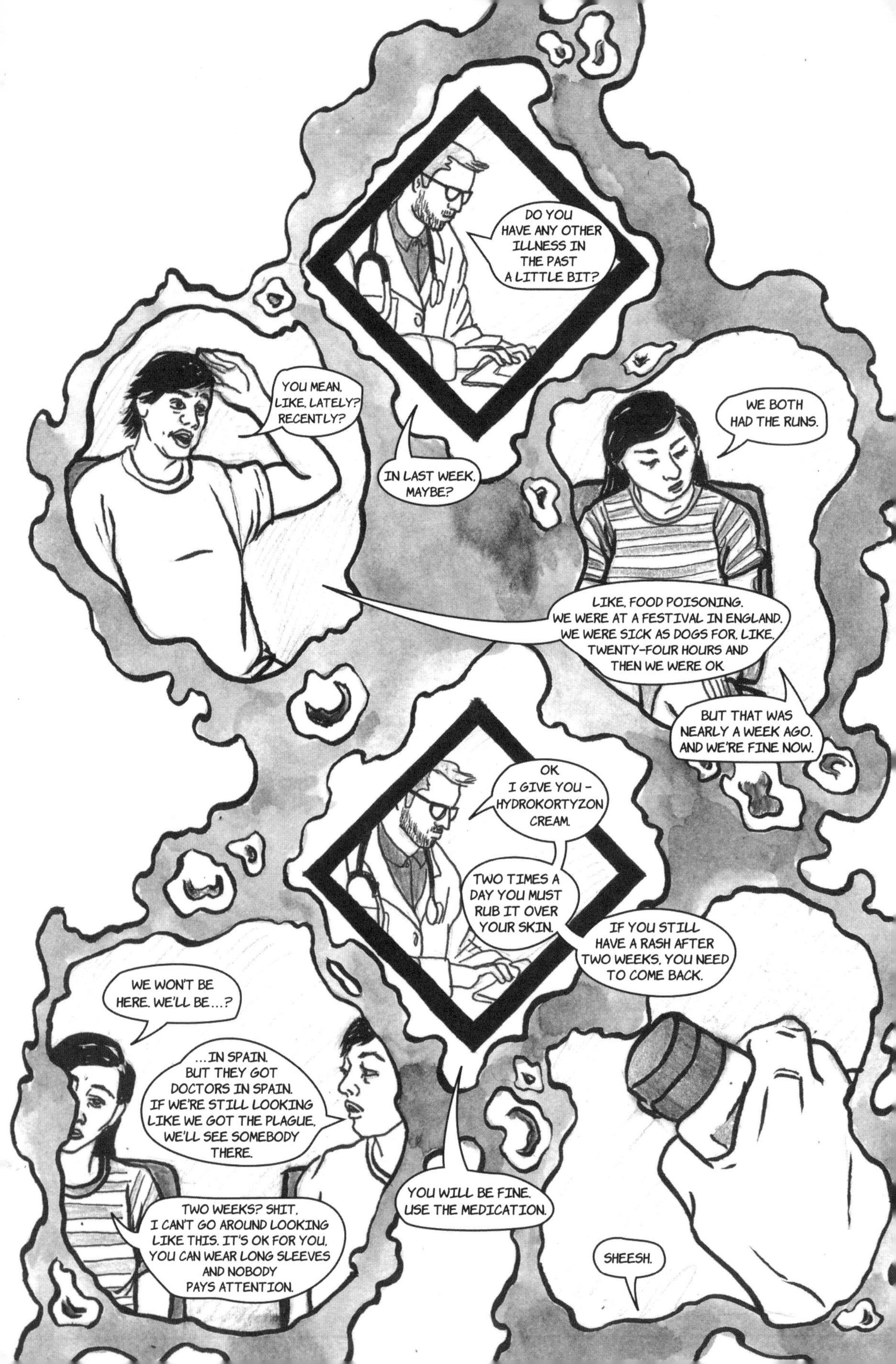
DO YOU HAVE ANY OTHER ILLNESS IN THE PAST A LITTLE BIT?
YOU MEAN. LIKE, LATELY? RECENTLY?
IN LAST WEEK. MAYBE?
WE BOTH HAD THE RUNS.
LIKE, FOOD POISONING. WE WERE AT A FESTIVAL IN ENGLAND. WE WERE SICK AS DOGS FOR, LIKE, TWENTY-FOUR HOURS AND THEN WE WERE OK.
BUT THAT WAS NEARLY A WEEK AGO. AND WE'RE FINE NOW.
OK I GIVE YOU - HYDROKORTYZON CREAM.
TWO TIMES A DAY YOU MUST RUB IT OVER YOUR SKIN.
IF YOU STILL HAVE A RASH AFTER TWO WEEKS, YOU NEED TO COME BACK.
WE WON'T BE HERE. WE'LL BE...?
...IN SPAIN. BUT THEY GOT DOCTORS IN SPAIN. IF WE'RE STILL LOOKING LIKE WE GOT THE PLAGUE, WE'LL SEE SOMEBODY THERE.
TWO WEEKS? SHIT. I CAN'T GO AROUND LOOKING LIKE THIS. IT'S OK FOR YOU. YOU CAN WEAR LONG SLEEVES AND NOBODY PAYS ATTENTION.
YOU WILL BE FINE. USE THE MEDICATION.
SHEESH.

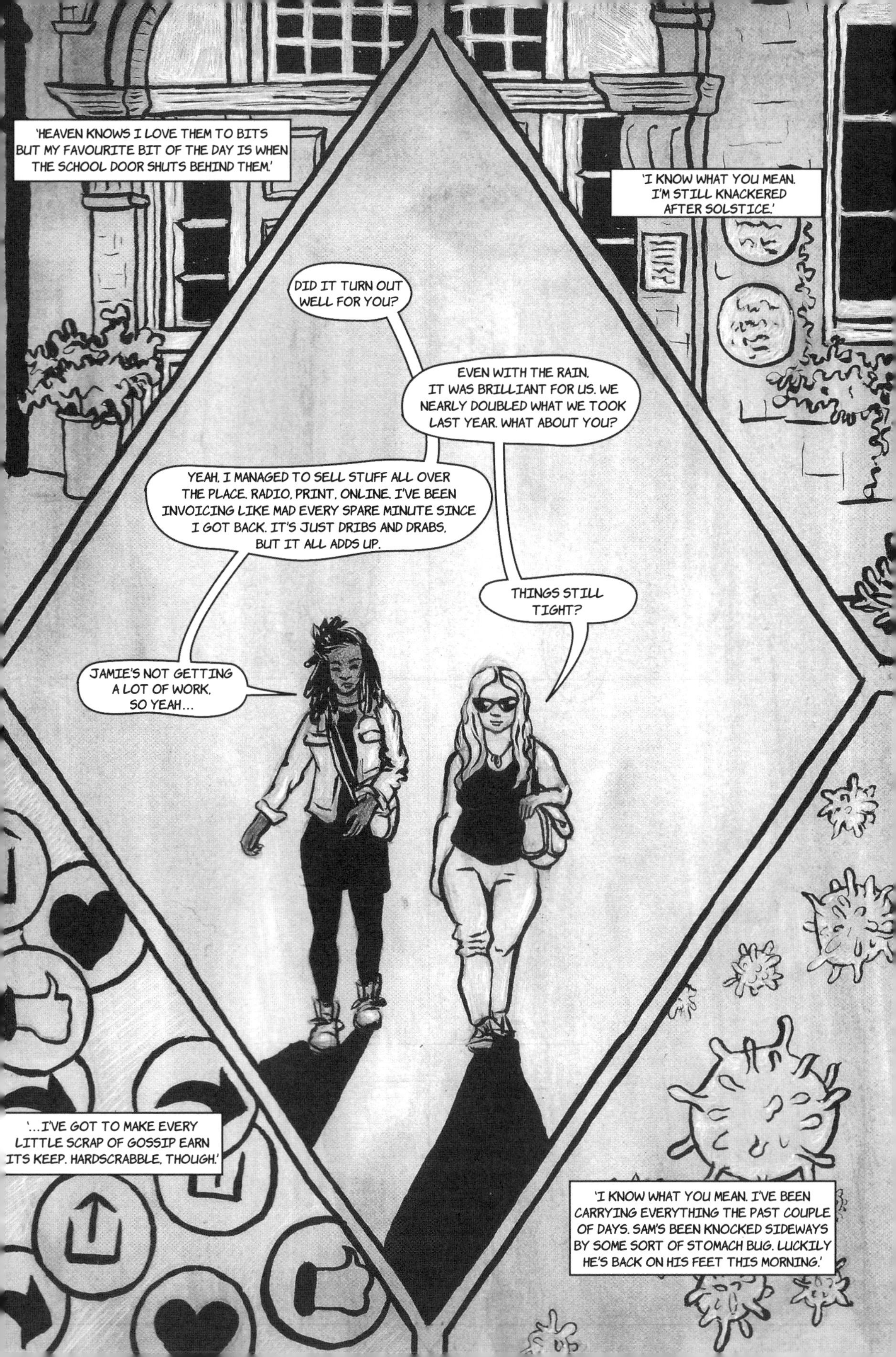
'HEAVEN KNOWS I LOVE THEM TO BITS BUT MY FAVOURITE BIT OF THE DAY IS WHEN THE SCHOOL DOOR SHUTS BEHIND THEM.'
'I KNOW WHAT YOU MEAN. I'M STILL KNACKERED AFTER SOLSTICE.'
DID IT TURN OUT WELL FOR YOU?
EVEN WITH THE RAIN, IT WAS BRILLIANT FOR US. WE NEARLY DOUBLED WHAT WE TOOK LAST YEAR. WHAT ABOUT YOU?
YEAH, I MANAGED TO SELL STUFF ALL OVER THE PLACE. RADIO, PRINT, ONLINE. I'VE BEEN INVOICING LIKE MAD EVERY SPARE MINUTE SINCE I GOT BACK. IT'S JUST DRIBS AND DRABS, BUT IT ALL ADDS UP.
THINGS STILL TIGHT?
JAMIE'S NOT GETTING A LOT OF WORK, SO YEAH…
'…I'VE GOT TO MAKE EVERY LITTLE SCRAP OF GOSSIP EARN ITS KEEP. HARDSCRABBLE, THOUGH.'
'I KNOW WHAT YOU MEAN. I'VE BEEN CARRYING EVERYTHING THE PAST COUPLE OF DAYS. SAM'S BEEN KNOCKED SIDEWAYS BY SOME SORT OF STOMACH BUG. LUCKILY HE'S BACK ON HIS FEET THIS MORNING.'

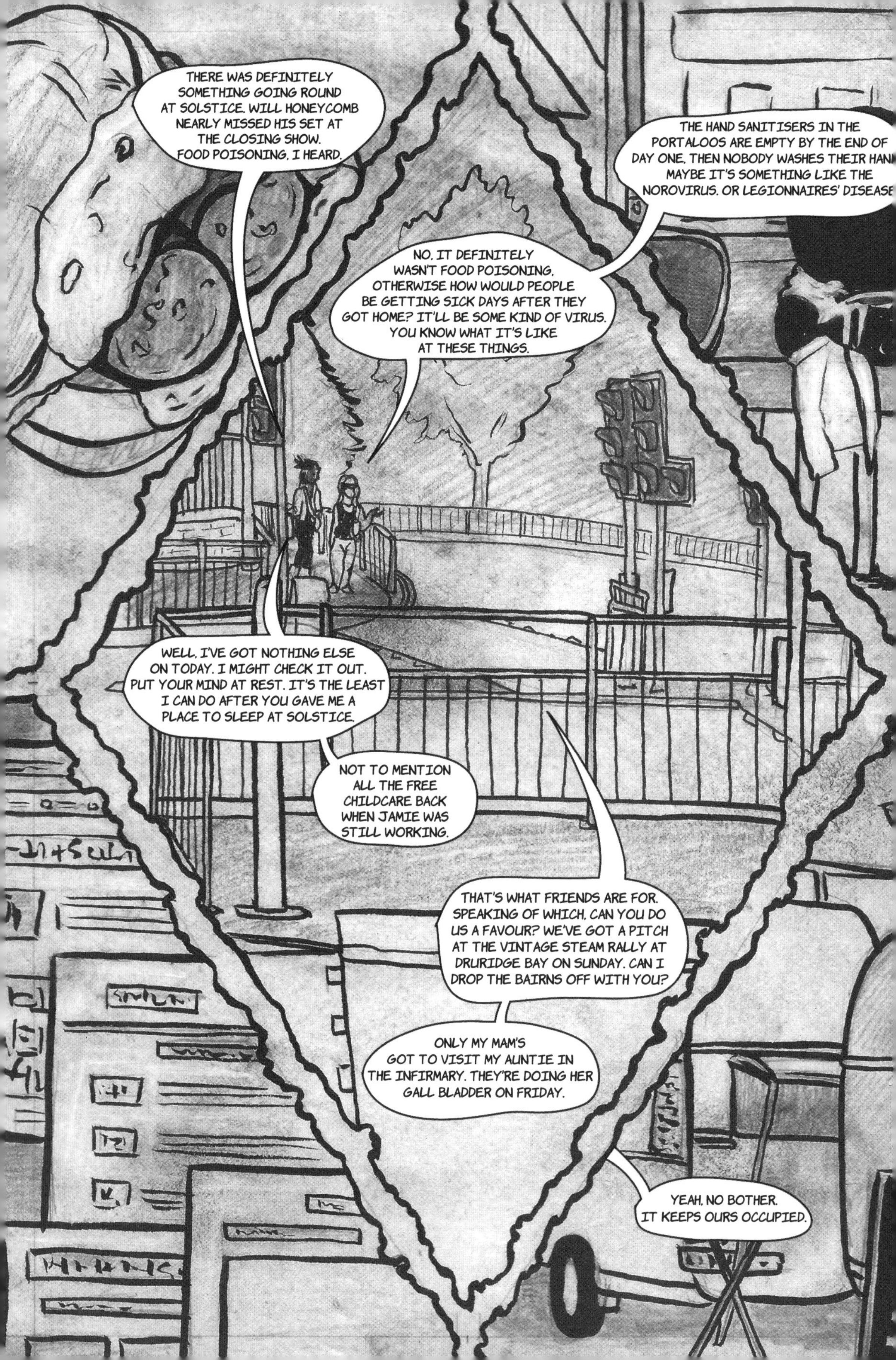
THERE WAS DEFINITELY SOMETHING GOING ROUND AT SOLSTICE. WILL HONEYCOMB NEARLY MISSED HIS SET AT THE CLOSING SHOW. FOOD POISONING, I HEARD.
NO, IT DEFINITELY WASN'T FOOD POISONING, OTHERWISE HOW WOULD PEOPLE BE GETTING SICK DAYS AFTER THEY GOT HOME? IT'LL BE SOME KIND OF VIRUS. YOU KNOW WHAT IT'S LIKE AT THESE THINGS.
THE HAND SANITISERS IN THE PORTALOOS ARE EMPTY BY THE END OF DAY ONE, THEN NOBODY WASHES THEIR HAN
MAYBE IT'S SOMETHING LIKE THE NOROVIRUS. OR LEGIONNAIRES' DISEASE
WELL, I'VE GOT NOTHING ELSE ON TODAY. I MIGHT CHECK IT OUT. PUT YOUR MIND AT REST. IT'S THE LEAST I CAN DO AFTER YOU GAVE ME A PLACE TO SLEEP AT SOLSTICE.
NOT TO MENTION ALL THE FREE CHILDCARE BACK WHEN JAMIE WAS STILL WORKING.
THAT'S WHAT FRIENDS ARE FOR. SPEAKING OF WHICH, CAN YOU DO US A FAVOUR? WE'VE GOT A PITCH AT THE VINTAGE STEAM RALLY AT DRURIDGE BAY ON SUNDAY. CAN I DROP THE BAIRNS OFF WITH YOU?
ONLY MY MAM'S GOT TO VISIT MY AUNTIE IN THE INFIRMARY. THEY'RE DOING HER GALL BLADDER ON FRIDAY.
YEAH, NO BOTHER. IT KEEPS OURS OCCUPIED.

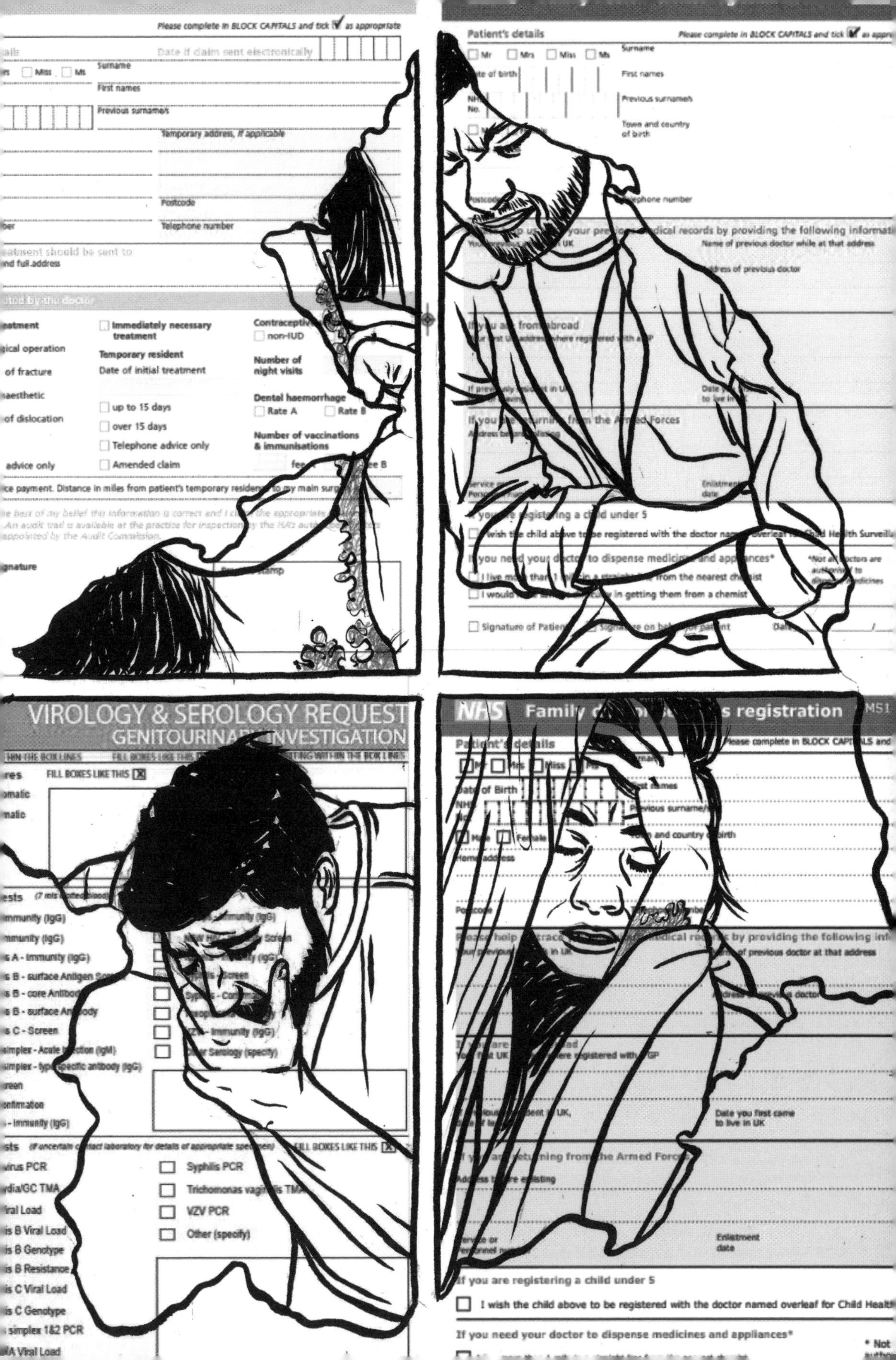

Please complete in BLOCK CAPITALS and tick as appropriate
Date if claim sent electronically
Surname
First names
Previous surname/s
Temporary address, if applicable
Postcode
Telephone number
Immediately necessary treatment
Temporary resident
Date of initial treatment
up to 15 days
over 15 days
Telephone advice only
Amended claim
Contraceptive
non-IUD
Number of night visits
Dental haemorrhage
Rate A
Rate B
Number of vaccinations & immunisations
Patient's details
Please complete in BLOCK CAPITALS and tick as appropriate
Mr
Mrs
Miss
Ms
Surname
First names
Previous surnames
Town and country of birth
Telephone number
Name of previous doctor while at that address
If you are registering a child under 5
I would have serious difficulty in getting them from a chemist
Signature of Patient
VIROLOGY & SEROLOGY REQUEST
GENITOURINARY INVESTIGATION
FILL BOXES LIKE THIS
Syphilis PCR
Trichomonas vaginalis TMA
VZV PCR
Other (specify)
NHS
Family doctor services registration
GMS1
Please complete in BLOCK CAPITALS and tick as appropriate
Date of Birth
Home address
Postcode
Date you first came to live in UK
Enlistment date
If you are registering a child under 5
I wish the child above to be registered with the doctor named overleaf for Child Health
If you need your doctor to dispense medicines and appliances*

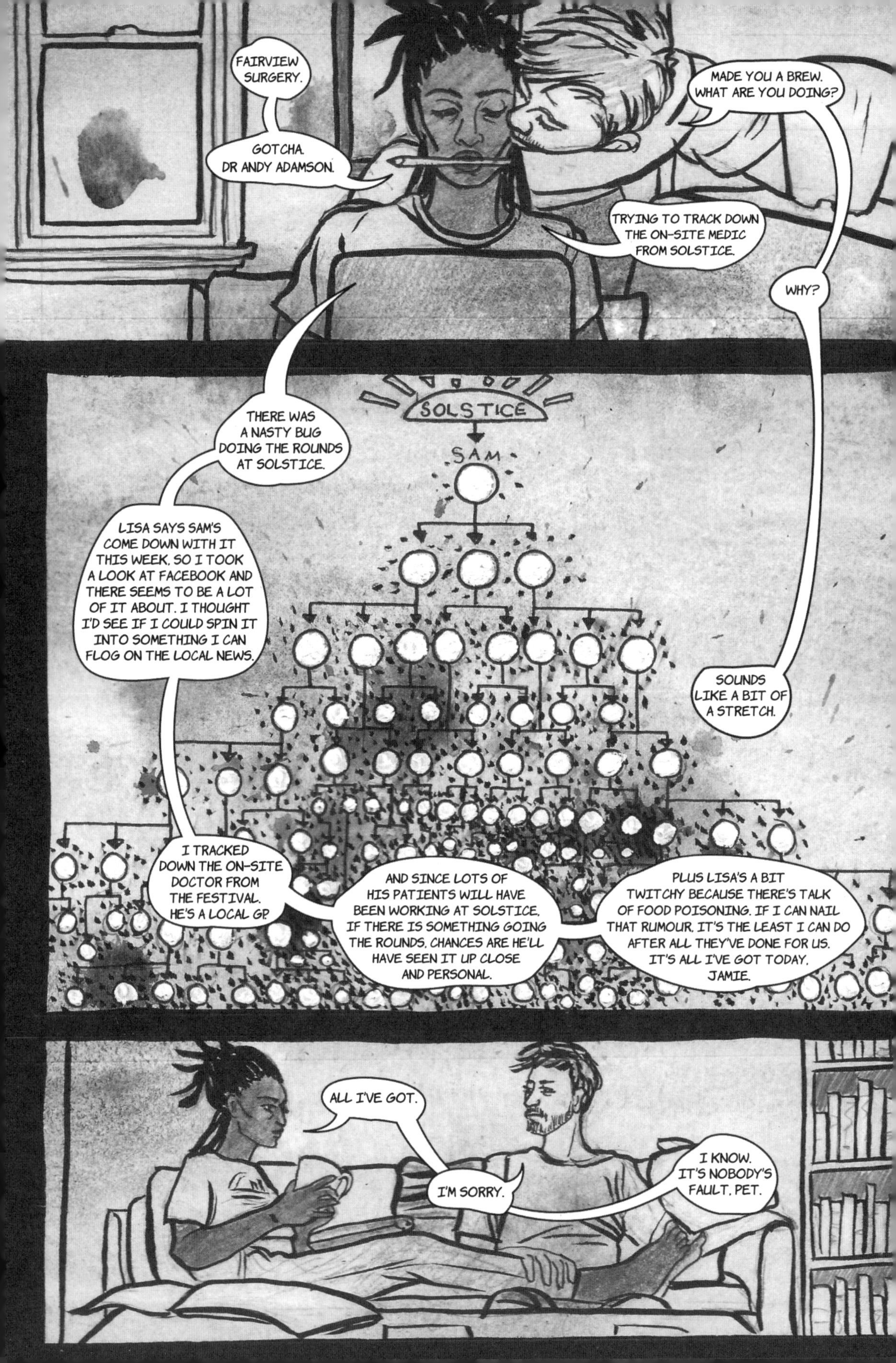
FAIRVIEW SURGERY.
GOTCHA. DR ANDY ADAMSON.
MADE YOU A BREW. WHAT ARE YOU DOING?
TRYING TO TRACK DOWN THE ON-SITE MEDIC FROM SOLSTICE.
WHY?
THERE WAS A NASTY BUG DOING THE ROUNDS AT SOLSTICE.
SOLSTICE
SAM
LISA SAYS SAM'S COME DOWN WITH IT THIS WEEK, SO I TOOK A LOOK AT FACEBOOK AND THERE SEEMS TO BE A LOT OF IT ABOUT. I THOUGHT I'D SEE IF I COULD SPIN IT INTO SOMETHING I CAN FLOG ON THE LOCAL NEWS.
SOUNDS LIKE A BIT OF A STRETCH.
I TRACKED DOWN THE ON-SITE DOCTOR FROM THE FESTIVAL. HE'S A LOCAL GP.
AND SINCE LOTS OF HIS PATIENTS WILL HAVE BEEN WORKING AT SOLSTICE, IF THERE IS SOMETHING GOING THE ROUNDS, CHANCES ARE HE'LL HAVE SEEN IT UP CLOSE AND PERSONAL.
PLUS LISA'S A BIT TWITCHY BECAUSE THERE'S TALK OF FOOD POISONING. IF I CAN NAIL THAT RUMOUR, IT'S THE LEAST I CAN DO AFTER ALL THEY'VE DONE FOR US. IT'S ALL I'VE GOT TODAY, JAMIE.
ALL I'VE GOT.
I'M SORRY.
I KNOW. IT'S NOBODY'S FAULT, PET.

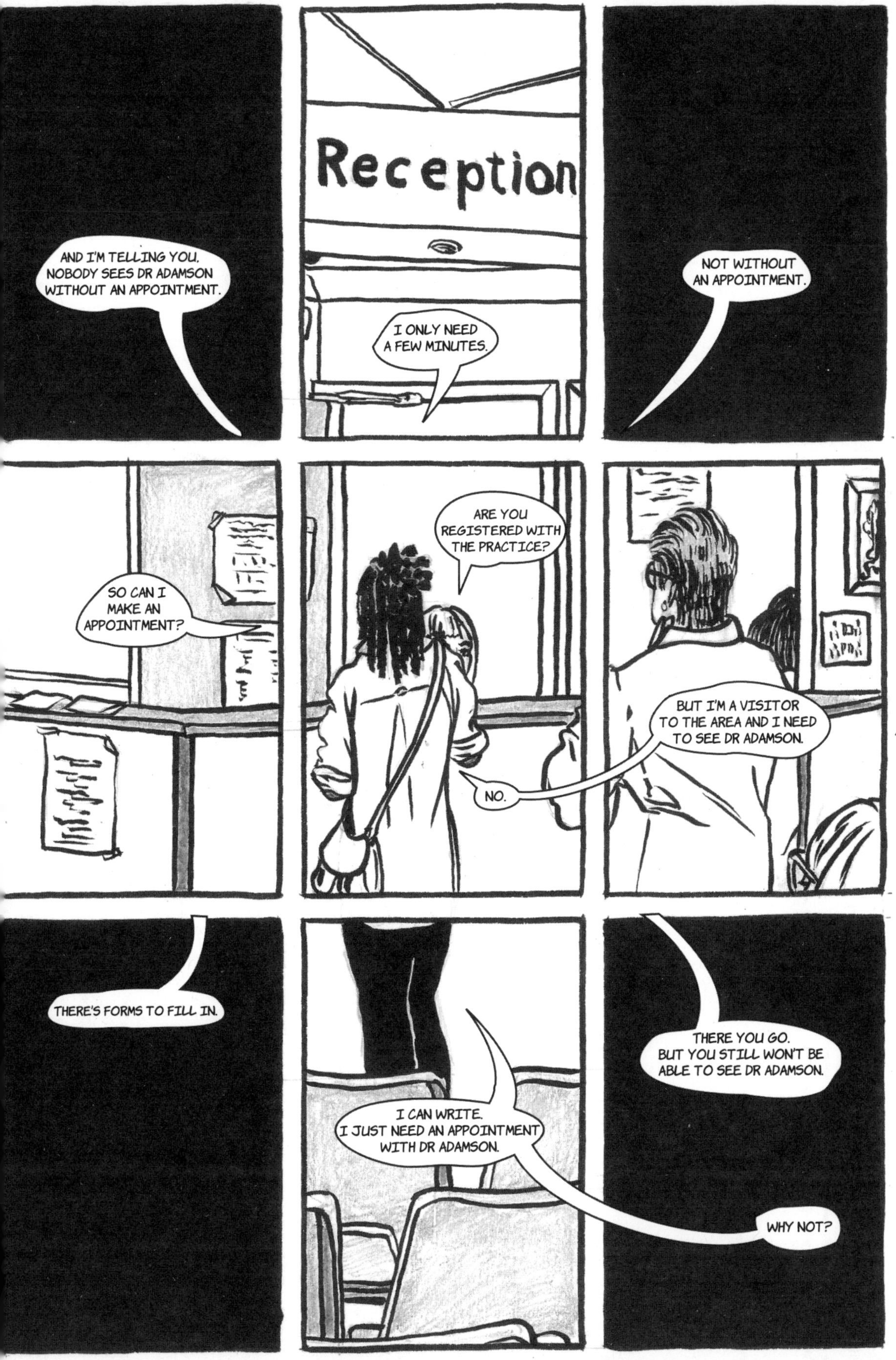
Reception
AND I'M TELLING YOU, NOBODY SEES DR ADAMSON WITHOUT AN APPOINTMENT.
I ONLY NEED A FEW MINUTES.
NOT WITHOUT AN APPOINTMENT.
SO CAN I MAKE AN APPOINTMENT?
ARE YOU REGISTERED WITH THE PRACTICE?
NO.
BUT I'M A VISITOR TO THE AREA AND I NEED TO SEE DR ADAMSON.
THERE'S FORMS TO FILL IN.
I CAN WRITE. I JUST NEED AN APPOINTMENT WITH DR ADAMSON.
THERE YOU GO. BUT YOU STILL WON'T BE ABLE TO SEE DR ADAMSON.
WHY NOT?

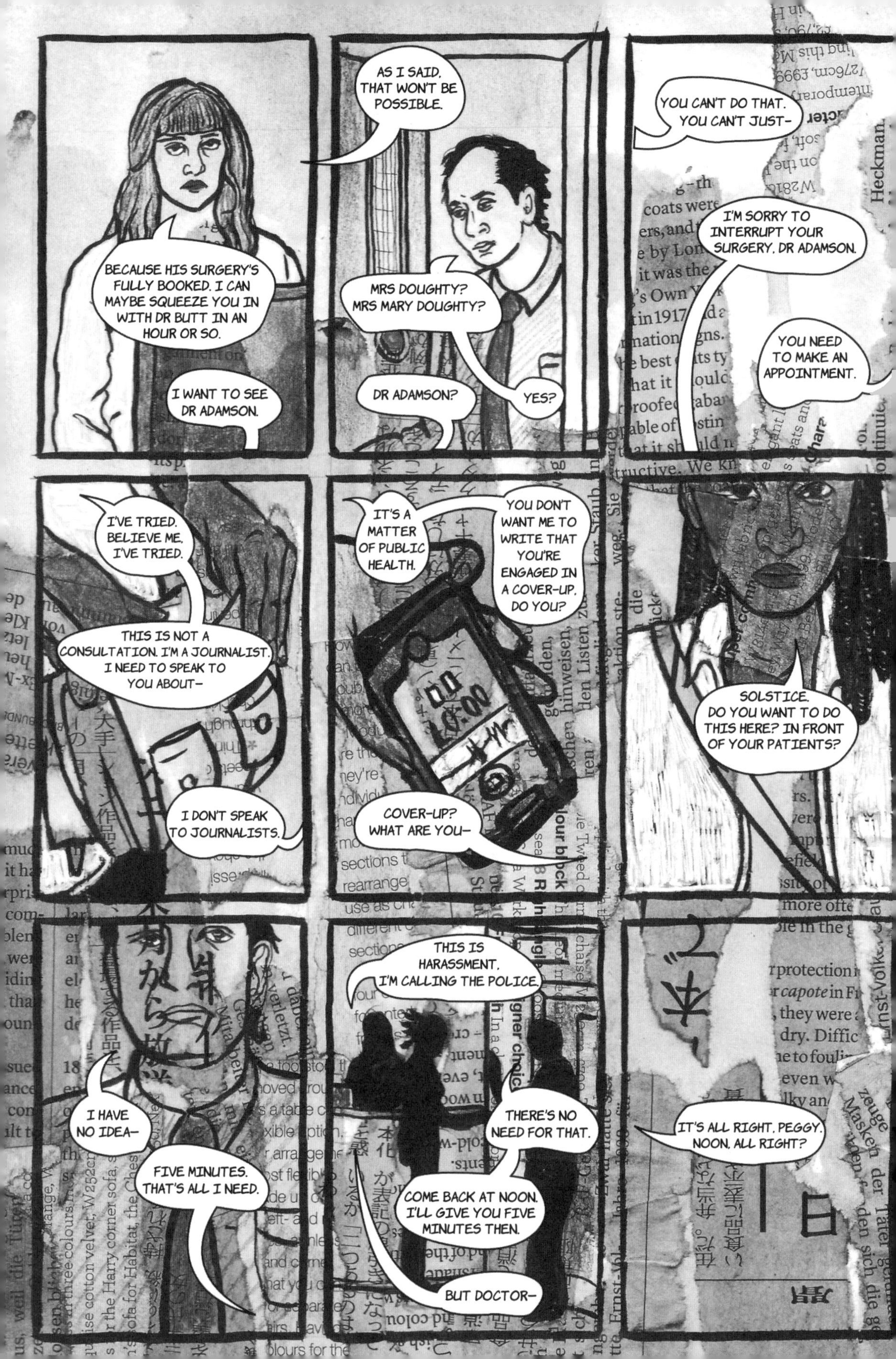
BECAUSE HIS SURGERY'S FULLY BOOKED. I CAN MAYBE SQUEEZE YOU IN WITH DR BUTT IN AN HOUR OR SO.
I WANT TO SEE DR ADAMSON.
AS I SAID, THAT WON'T BE POSSIBLE.
MRS DOUGHTY? MRS MARY DOUGHTY?
DR ADAMSON?
YES?
YOU CAN'T DO THAT. YOU CAN'T JUST-
I'M SORRY TO INTERRUPT YOUR SURGERY, DR ADAMSON.
YOU NEED TO MAKE AN APPOINTMENT.
I'VE TRIED. BELIEVE ME, I'VE TRIED.
THIS IS NOT A CONSULTATION. I'M A JOURNALIST. I NEED TO SPEAK TO YOU ABOUT-
I DON'T SPEAK TO JOURNALISTS.
IT'S A MATTER OF PUBLIC HEALTH.
YOU DON'T WANT ME TO WRITE THAT YOU'RE ENGAGED IN A COVER-UP, DO YOU?
COVER-UP? WHAT ARE YOU-
SOLSTICE. DO YOU WANT TO DO THIS HERE? IN FRONT OF YOUR PATIENTS?
I HAVE NO IDEA-
FIVE MINUTES. THAT'S ALL I NEED.
THIS IS HARASSMENT. I'M CALLING THE POLICE.
THERE'S NO NEED FOR THAT.
COME BACK AT NOON. I'LL GIVE YOU FIVE MINUTES THEN.
BUT DOCTOR-
IT'S ALL RIGHT, PEGGY. NOON, ALL RIGHT?

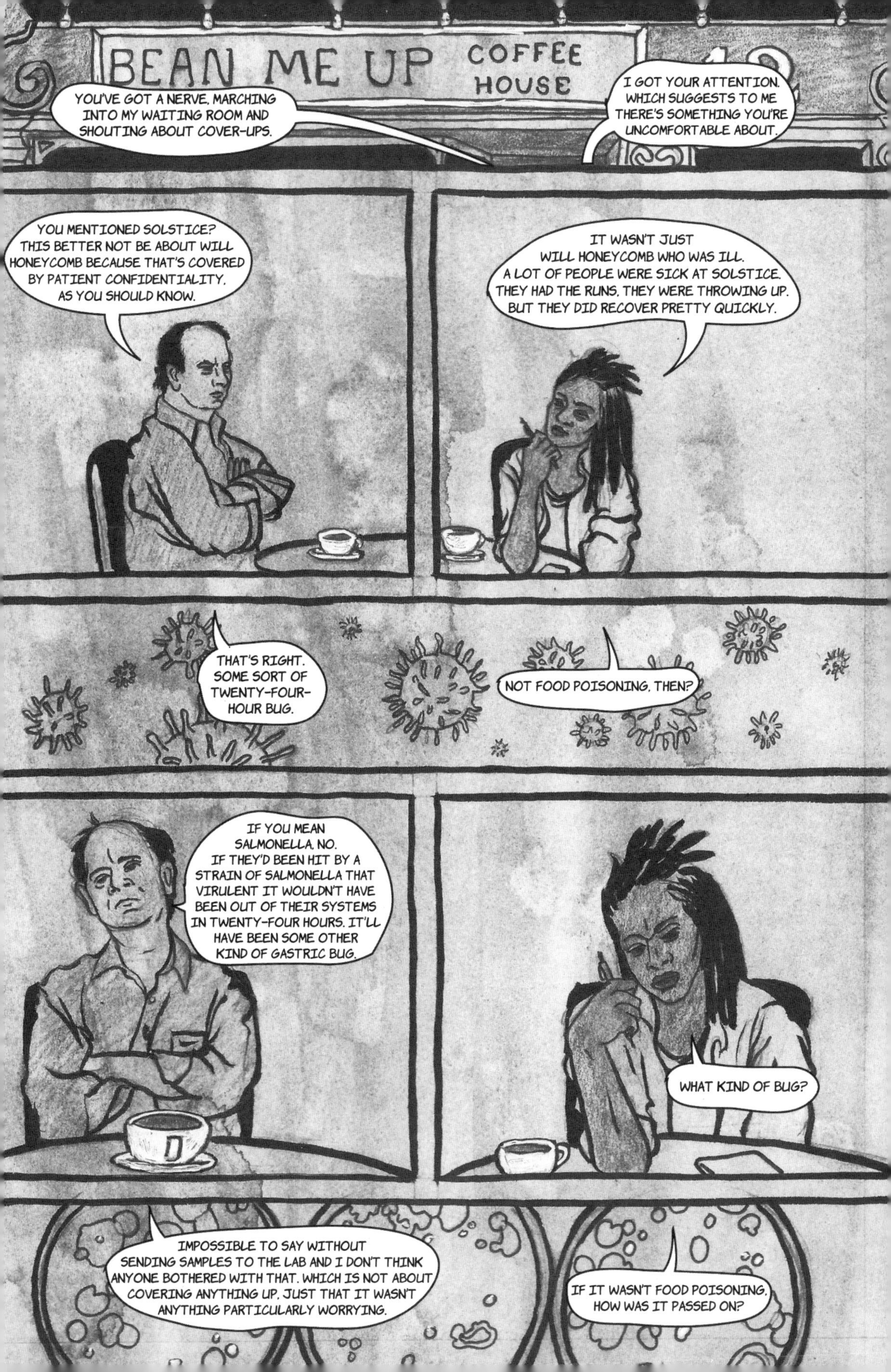
BEAN ME UP COFFEE HOUSE
YOU'VE GOT A NERVE, MARCHING INTO MY WAITING ROOM AND SHOUTING ABOUT COVER-UPS.
I GOT YOUR ATTENTION. WHICH SUGGESTS TO ME THERE'S SOMETHING YOU'RE UNCOMFORTABLE ABOUT.
YOU MENTIONED SOLSTICE? THIS BETTER NOT BE ABOUT WILL HONEYCOMB BECAUSE THAT'S COVERED BY PATIENT CONFIDENTIALITY, AS YOU SHOULD KNOW.
IT WASN'T JUST WILL HONEYCOMB WHO WAS ILL. A LOT OF PEOPLE WERE SICK AT SOLSTICE. THEY HAD THE RUNS, THEY WERE THROWING UP. BUT THEY DID RECOVER PRETTY QUICKLY.
THAT'S RIGHT. SOME SORT OF TWENTY-FOUR-HOUR BUG.
NOT FOOD POISONING, THEN?
IF YOU MEAN SALMONELLA, NO. IF THEY'D BEEN HIT BY A STRAIN OF SALMONELLA THAT VIRULENT IT WOULDN'T HAVE BEEN OUT OF THEIR SYSTEMS IN TWENTY-FOUR HOURS. IT'LL HAVE BEEN SOME OTHER KIND OF GASTRIC BUG.
WHAT KIND OF BUG?
IMPOSSIBLE TO SAY WITHOUT SENDING SAMPLES TO THE LAB AND I DON'T THINK ANYONE BOTHERED WITH THAT. WHICH IS NOT ABOUT COVERING ANYTHING UP, JUST THAT IT WASN'T ANYTHING PARTICULARLY WORRYING.
IF IT WASN'T FOOD POISONING, HOW WAS IT PASSED ON?

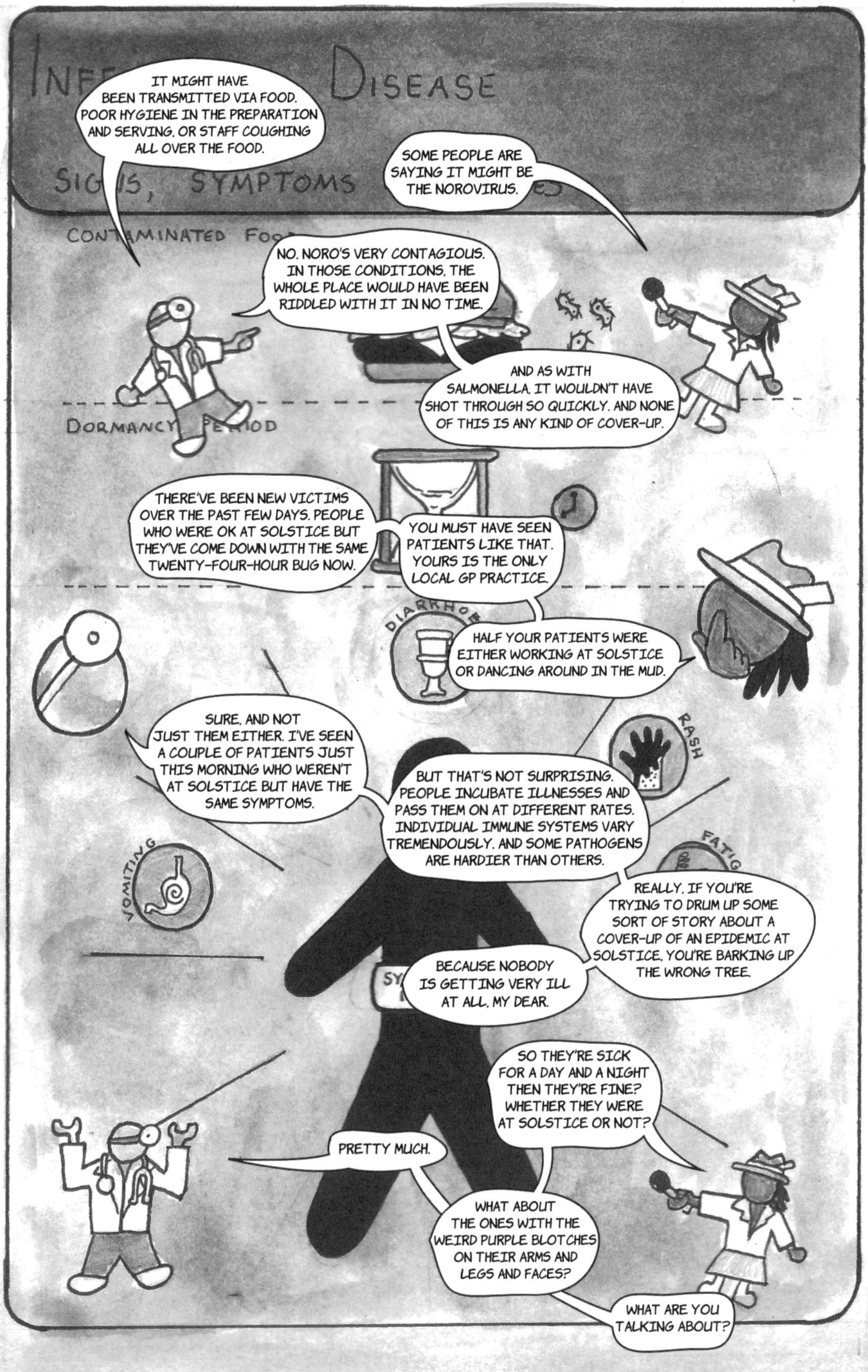
DISEASE
SYMPTOMS
IT MIGHT HAVE BEEN TRANSMITTED VIA FOOD. POOR HYGIENE IN THE PREPARATION AND SERVING, OR STAFF COUGHING ALL OVER THE FOOD.
SOME PEOPLE ARE SAYING IT MIGHT BE THE NOROVIRUS.
NO. NORO'S VERY CONTAGIOUS. IN THOSE CONDITIONS, THE WHOLE PLACE WOULD HAVE BEEN RIDDLED WITH IT IN NO TIME.
AND AS WITH SALMONELLA, IT WOULDN'T HAVE SHOT THROUGH SO QUICKLY. AND NONE OF THIS IS ANY KIND OF COVER-UP.
THERE'VE BEEN NEW VICTIMS OVER THE PAST FEW DAYS. PEOPLE WHO WERE OK AT SOLSTICE BUT THEY'VE COME DOWN WITH THE SAME TWENTY-FOUR-HOUR BUG NOW.
YOU MUST HAVE SEEN PATIENTS LIKE THAT. YOURS IS THE ONLY LOCAL GP PRACTICE.
HALF YOUR PATIENTS WERE EITHER WORKING AT SOLSTICE OR DANCING AROUND IN THE MUD.
SURE, AND NOT JUST THEM EITHER. I'VE SEEN A COUPLE OF PATIENTS JUST THIS MORNING WHO WEREN'T AT SOLSTICE BUT HAVE THE SAME SYMPTOMS.
BUT THAT'S NOT SURPRISING. PEOPLE INCUBATE ILLNESSES AND PASS THEM ON AT DIFFERENT RATES. INDIVIDUAL IMMUNE SYSTEMS VARY TREMENDOUSLY. AND SOME PATHOGENS ARE HARDIER THAN OTHERS.
RASH
VOMITING
REALLY, IF YOU'RE TRYING TO DRUM UP SOME SORT OF STORY ABOUT A COVER-UP OF AN EPIDEMIC AT SOLSTICE, YOU'RE BARKING UP THE WRONG TREE.
BECAUSE NOBODY IS GETTING VERY ILL AT ALL, MY DEAR.
SO THEY'RE SICK FOR A DAY AND A NIGHT THEN THEY'RE FINE? WHETHER THEY WERE AT SOLSTICE OR NOT?
PRETTY MUCH.
WHAT ABOUT THE ONES WITH THE WEIRD PURPLE BLOTCHES ON THEIR ARMS AND LEGS AND FACES?
WHAT ARE YOU TALKING ABOUT?

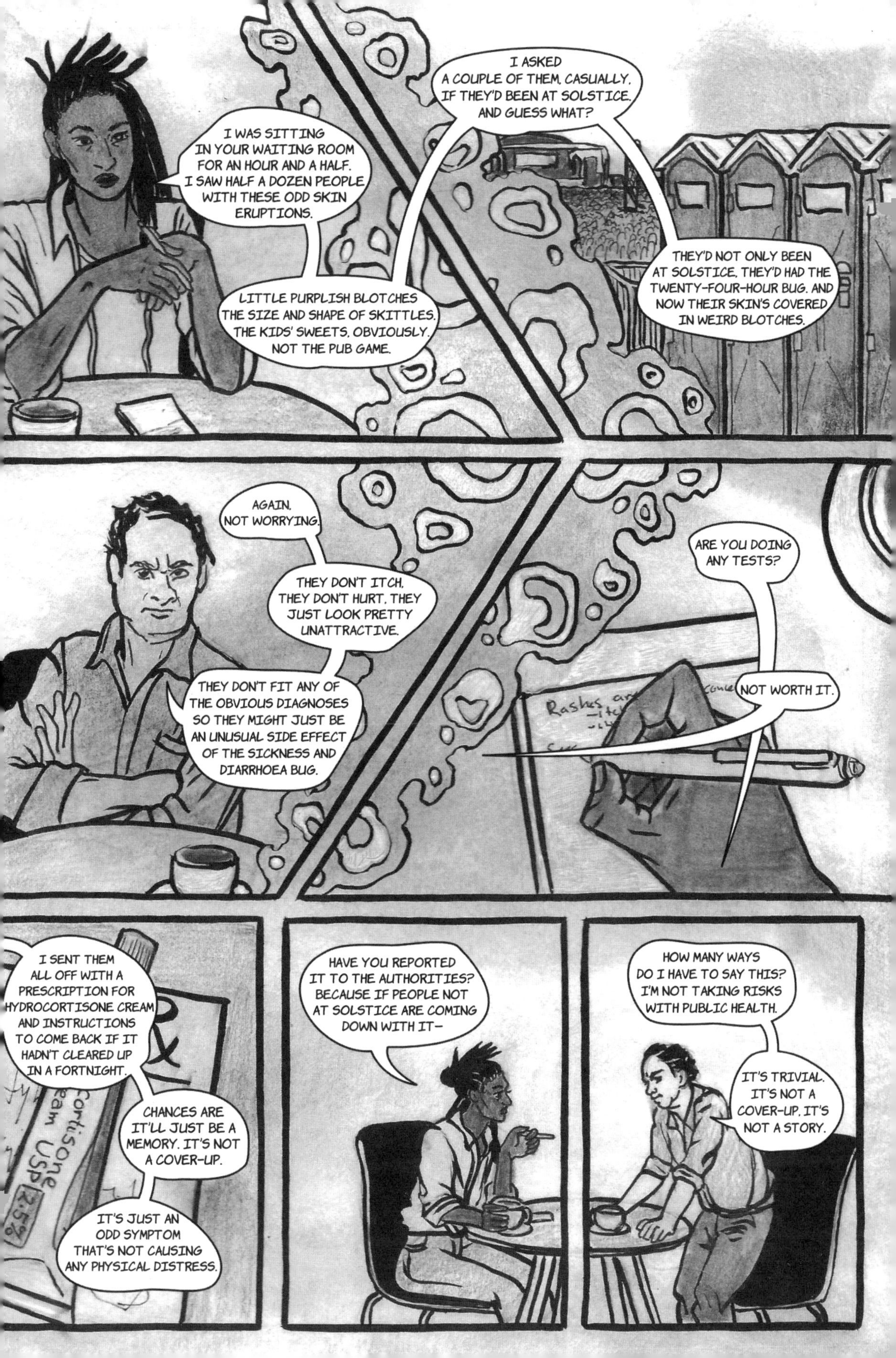
I WAS SITTING IN YOUR WAITING ROOM FOR AN HOUR AND A HALF. I SAW HALF A DOZEN PEOPLE WITH THESE ODD SKIN ERUPTIONS.
LITTLE PURPLISH BLOTCHES THE SIZE AND SHAPE OF SKITTLES. THE KIDS' SWEETS, OBVIOUSLY. NOT THE PUB GAME.
I ASKED A COUPLE OF THEM, CASUALLY, IF THEY'D BEEN AT SOLSTICE. AND GUESS WHAT?
THEY'D NOT ONLY BEEN AT SOLSTICE, THEY'D HAD THE TWENTY-FOUR-HOUR BUG. AND NOW THEIR SKIN'S COVERED IN WEIRD BLOTCHES.
AGAIN, NOT WORRYING.
THEY DON'T ITCH, THEY DON'T HURT, THEY JUST LOOK PRETTY UNATTRACTIVE.
THEY DON'T FIT ANY OF THE OBVIOUS DIAGNOSES SO THEY MIGHT JUST BE AN UNUSUAL SIDE EFFECT OF THE SICKNESS AND DIARRHOEA BUG.
ARE YOU DOING ANY TESTS?
NOT WORTH IT.
I SENT THEM ALL OFF WITH A PRESCRIPTION FOR HYDROCORTISONE CREAM AND INSTRUCTIONS TO COME BACK IF IT HADN'T CLEARED UP IN A FORTNIGHT.
CHANCES ARE IT'LL JUST BE A MEMORY. IT'S NOT A COVER-UP.
IT'S JUST AN ODD SYMPTOM THAT'S NOT CAUSING ANY PHYSICAL DISTRESS.
HAVE YOU REPORTED IT TO THE AUTHORITIES? BECAUSE IF PEOPLE NOT AT SOLSTICE ARE COMING DOWN WITH IT–
HOW MANY WAYS DO I HAVE TO SAY THIS? I'M NOT TAKING RISKS WITH PUBLIC HEALTH.
IT'S TRIVIAL. IT'S NOT A COVER-UP. IT'S NOT A STORY.

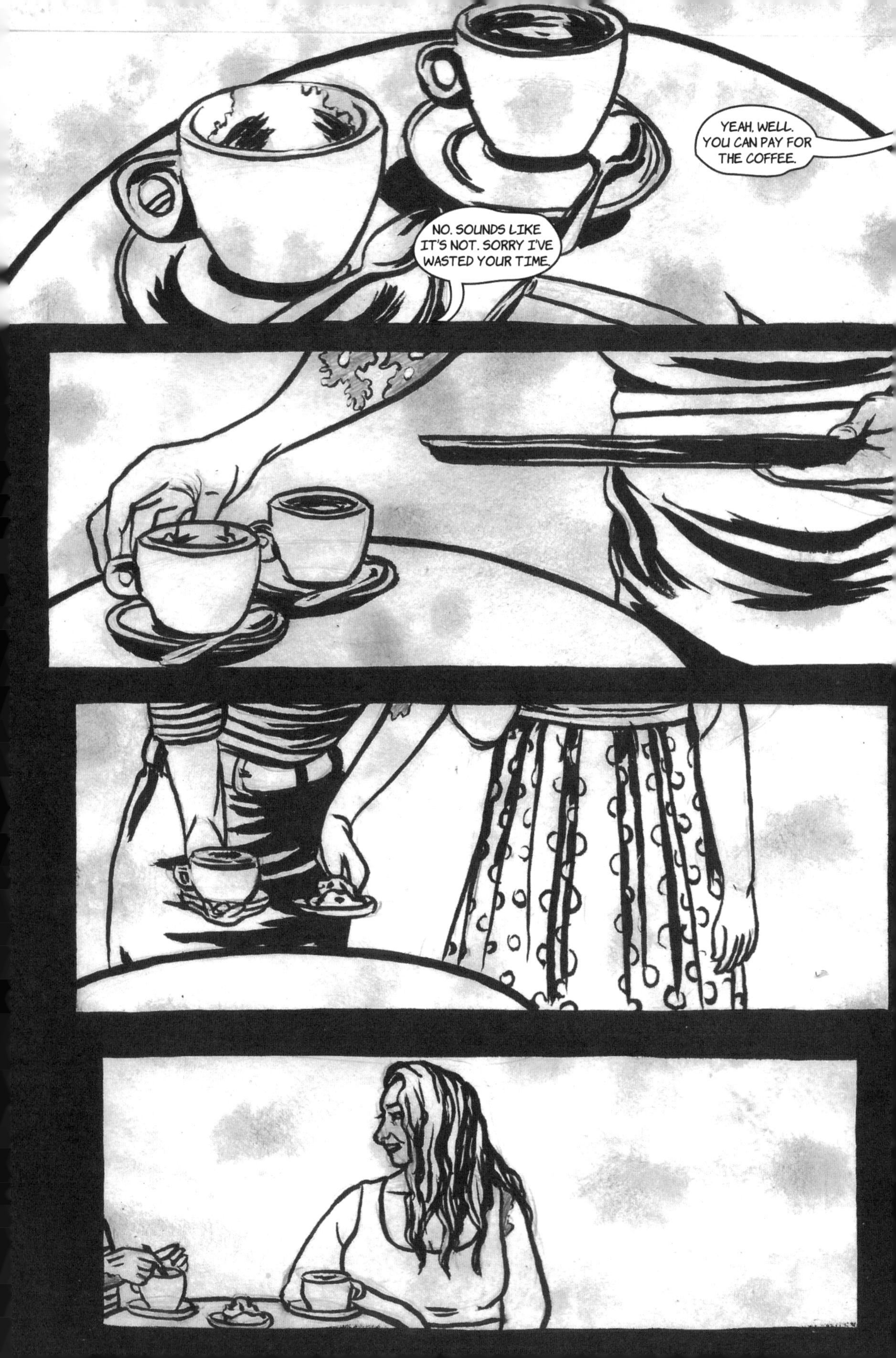
YEAH, WELL. YOU CAN PAY FOR THE COFFEE.
NO. SOUNDS LIKE IT'S NOT. SORRY I'VE WASTED YOUR TIME.

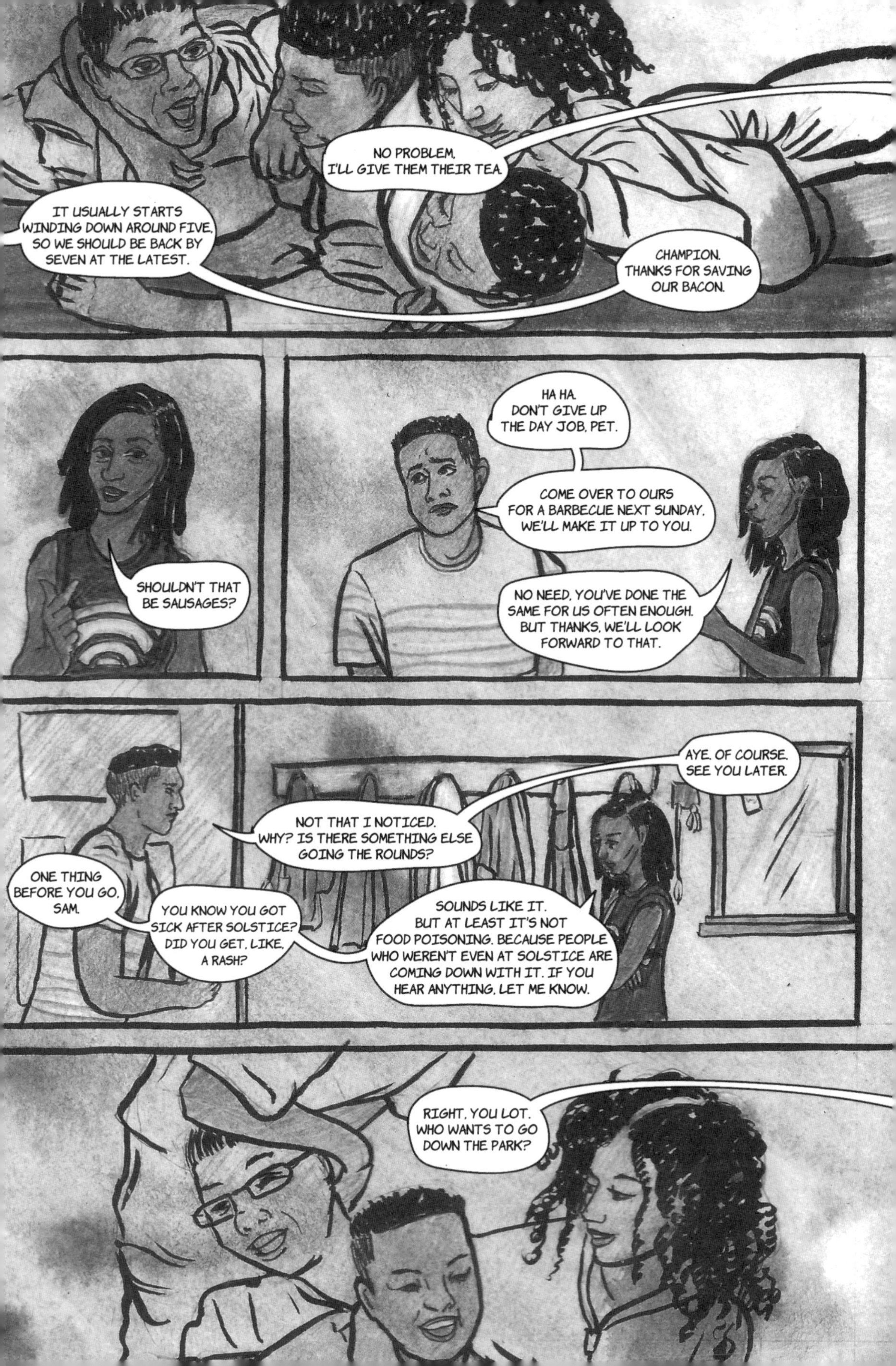
IT USUALLY STARTS WINDING DOWN AROUND FIVE, SO WE SHOULD BE BACK BY SEVEN AT THE LATEST.
NO PROBLEM. I'LL GIVE THEM THEIR TEA.
CHAMPION. THANKS FOR SAVING OUR BACON.
SHOULDN'T THAT BE SAUSAGES?
HA HA. DON'T GIVE UP THE DAY JOB, PET.
COME OVER TO OURS FOR A BARBECUE NEXT SUNDAY. WE'LL MAKE IT UP TO YOU.
NO NEED, YOU'VE DONE THE SAME FOR US OFTEN ENOUGH. BUT THANKS, WE'LL LOOK FORWARD TO THAT.
ONE THING BEFORE YOU GO, SAM.
YOU KNOW YOU GOT SICK AFTER SOLSTICE? DID YOU GET, LIKE, A RASH?
NOT THAT I NOTICED. WHY? IS THERE SOMETHING ELSE GOING THE ROUNDS?
SOUNDS LIKE IT. BUT AT LEAST IT'S NOT FOOD POISONING. BECAUSE PEOPLE WHO WEREN'T EVEN AT SOLSTICE ARE COMING DOWN WITH IT. IF YOU HEAR ANYTHING, LET ME KNOW.
AYE. OF COURSE. SEE YOU LATER.
RIGHT, YOU LOT. WHO WANTS TO GO DOWN THE PARK?

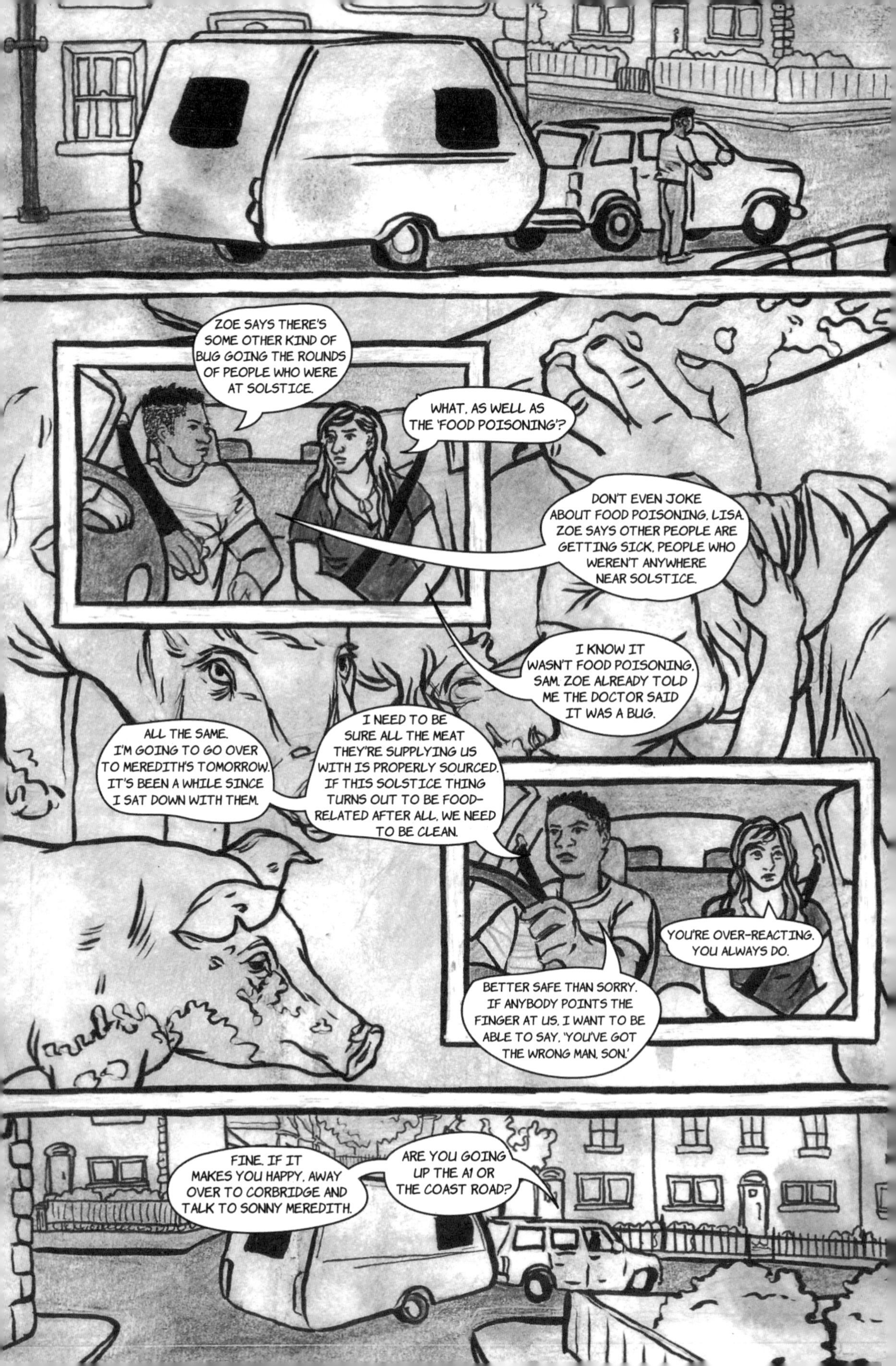
ZOE SAYS THERE'S SOME OTHER KIND OF BUG GOING THE ROUNDS OF PEOPLE WHO WERE AT SOLSTICE.
WHAT, AS WELL AS THE 'FOOD POISONING'?
DON'T EVEN JOKE ABOUT FOOD POISONING, LISA. ZOE SAYS OTHER PEOPLE ARE GETTING SICK, PEOPLE WHO WEREN'T ANYWHERE NEAR SOLSTICE.
I KNOW IT WASN'T FOOD POISONING, SAM. ZOE ALREADY TOLD ME THE DOCTOR SAID IT WAS A BUG.
ALL THE SAME. I'M GOING TO GO OVER TO MEREDITH'S TOMORROW. IT'S BEEN A WHILE SINCE I SAT DOWN WITH THEM.
I NEED TO BE SURE ALL THE MEAT THEY'RE SUPPLYING US WITH IS PROPERLY SOURCED. IF THIS SOLSTICE THING TURNS OUT TO BE FOOD-RELATED AFTER ALL, WE NEED TO BE CLEAN.
YOU'RE OVER-REACTING. YOU ALWAYS DO.
BETTER SAFE THAN SORRY. IF ANYBODY POINTS THE FINGER AT US, I WANT TO BE ABLE TO SAY, 'YOU'VE GOT THE WRONG MAN, SON.'
FINE. IF IT MAKES YOU HAPPY, AWAY OVER TO CORBRIDGE AND TALK TO SONNY MEREDITH.
ARE YOU GOING UP THE A1 OR THE COAST ROAD?

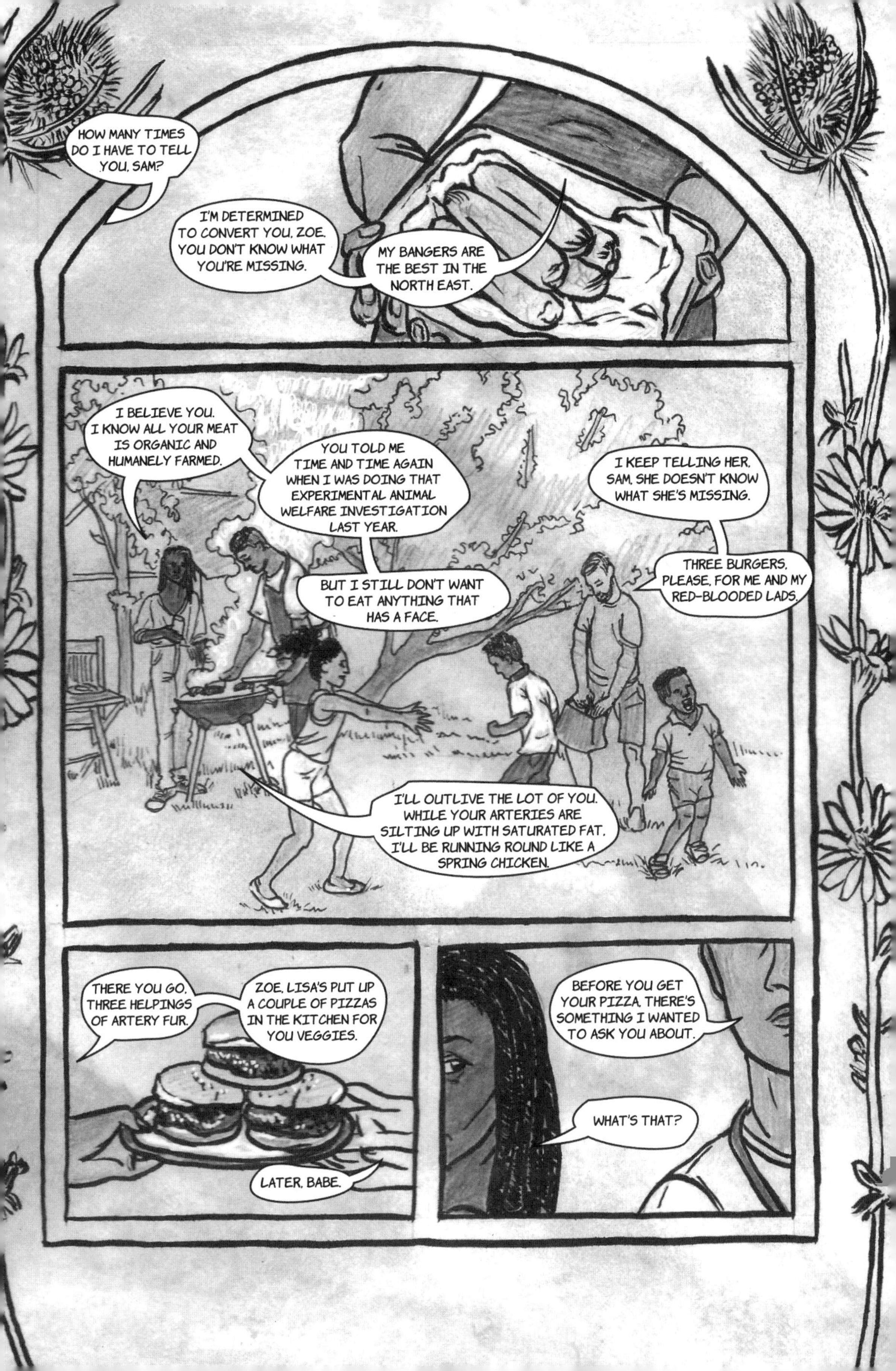
HOW MANY TIMES DO I HAVE TO TELL YOU, SAM?
I'M DETERMINED TO CONVERT YOU, ZOE. YOU DON'T KNOW WHAT YOU'RE MISSING.
MY BANGERS ARE THE BEST IN THE NORTH EAST.
I BELIEVE YOU. I KNOW ALL YOUR MEAT IS ORGANIC AND HUMANELY FARMED.
YOU TOLD ME TIME AND TIME AGAIN WHEN I WAS DOING THAT EXPERIMENTAL ANIMAL WELFARE INVESTIGATION LAST YEAR.
BUT I STILL DON'T WANT TO EAT ANYTHING THAT HAS A FACE.
I KEEP TELLING HER, SAM. SHE DOESN'T KNOW WHAT SHE'S MISSING.
THREE BURGERS, PLEASE, FOR ME AND MY RED-BLOODED LADS.
I'LL OUTLIVE THE LOT OF YOU. WHILE YOUR ARTERIES ARE SILTING UP WITH SATURATED FAT, I'LL BE RUNNING ROUND LIKE A SPRING CHICKEN.
THERE YOU GO, THREE HELPINGS OF ARTERY FUR.
ZOE, LISA'S PUT UP A COUPLE OF PIZZAS IN THE KITCHEN FOR YOU VEGGIES.
LATER, BABE.
BEFORE YOU GET YOUR PIZZA, THERE'S SOMETHING I WANTED TO ASK YOU ABOUT.
WHAT'S THAT?

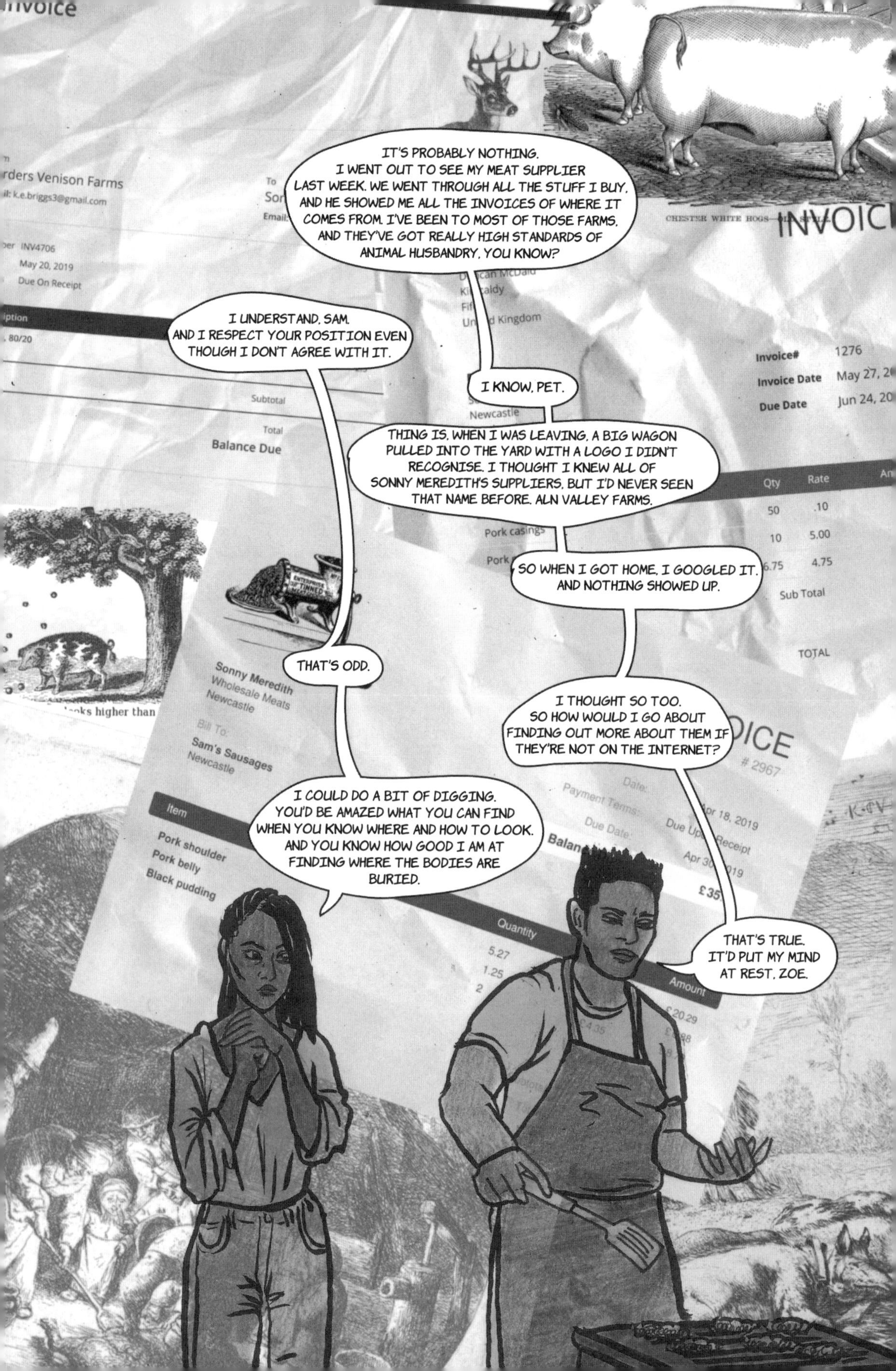
IT'S PROBABLY NOTHING. I WENT OUT TO SEE MY MEAT SUPPLIER LAST WEEK. WE WENT THROUGH ALL THE STUFF I BUY, AND HE SHOWED ME ALL THE INVOICES OF WHERE IT COMES FROM. I'VE BEEN TO MOST OF THOSE FARMS, AND THEY'VE GOT REALLY HIGH STANDARDS OF ANIMAL HUSBANDRY, YOU KNOW?
I UNDERSTAND, SAM. AND I RESPECT YOUR POSITION EVEN THOUGH I DON'T AGREE WITH IT.
I KNOW, PET.
THING IS, WHEN I WAS LEAVING, A BIG WAGON PULLED INTO THE YARD WITH A LOGO I DIDN'T RECOGNISE. I THOUGHT I KNEW ALL OF SONNY MEREDITH'S SUPPLIERS, BUT I'D NEVER SEEN THAT NAME BEFORE. ALN VALLEY FARMS.
SO WHEN I GOT HOME, I GOOGLED IT. AND NOTHING SHOWED UP.
THAT'S ODD.
I THOUGHT SO TOO. SO HOW WOULD I GO ABOUT FINDING OUT MORE ABOUT THEM IF THEY'RE NOT ON THE INTERNET?
I COULD DO A BIT OF DIGGING. YOU'D BE AMAZED WHAT YOU CAN FIND WHEN YOU KNOW WHERE AND HOW TO LOOK. AND YOU KNOW HOW GOOD I AM AT FINDING WHERE THE BODIES ARE BURIED.
THAT'S TRUE. IT'D PUT MY MIND AT REST, ZOE.

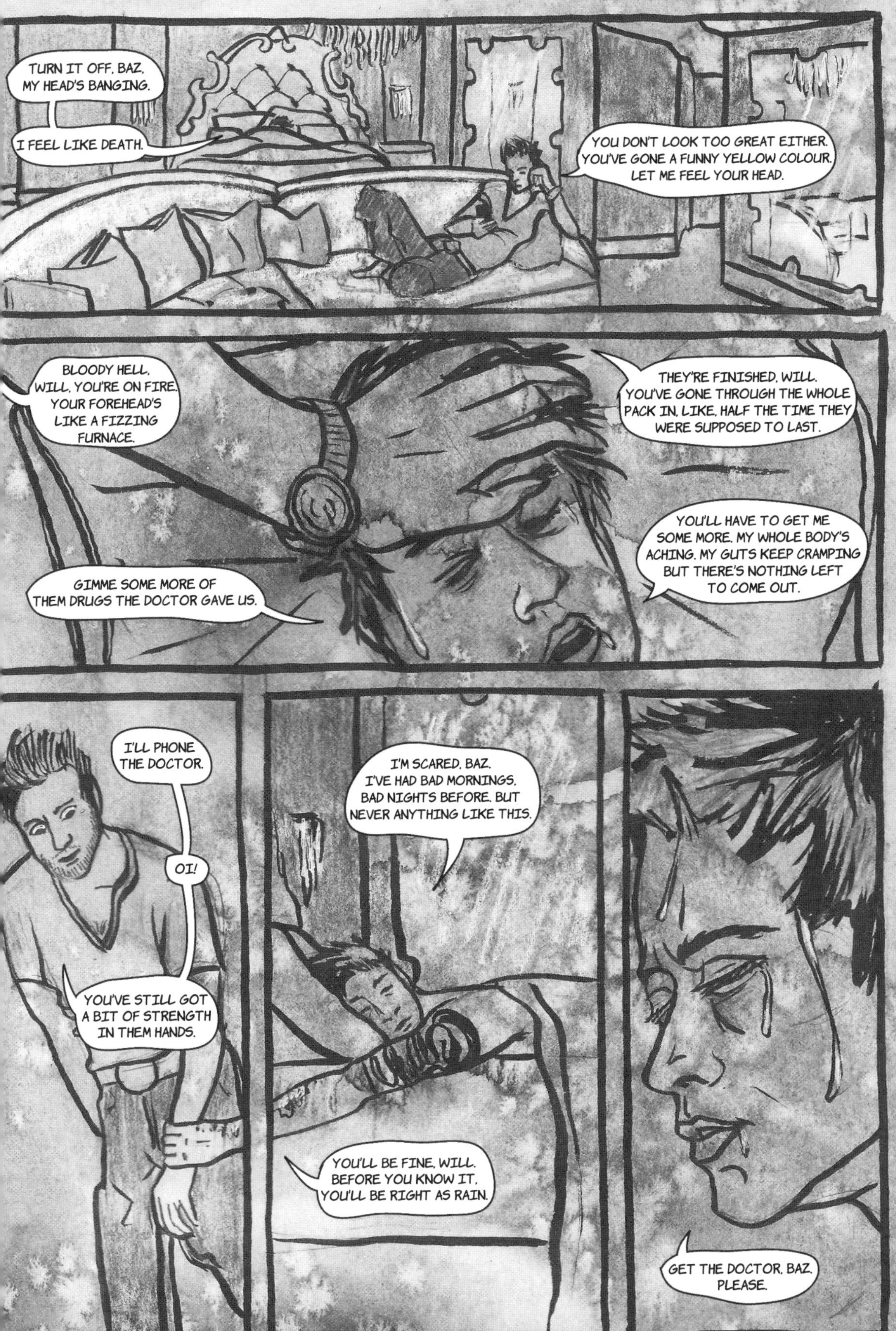
TURN IT OFF, BAZ, MY HEAD'S BANGING.
I FEEL LIKE DEATH.
YOU DON'T LOOK TOO GREAT EITHER. YOU'VE GONE A FUNNY YELLOW COLOUR. LET ME FEEL YOUR HEAD.
BLOODY HELL, WILL, YOU'RE ON FIRE. YOUR FOREHEAD'S LIKE A FIZZING FURNACE.
GIMME SOME MORE OF THEM DRUGS THE DOCTOR GAVE US.
THEY'RE FINISHED, WILL. YOU'VE GONE THROUGH THE WHOLE PACK IN, LIKE, HALF THE TIME THEY WERE SUPPOSED TO LAST.
YOU'LL HAVE TO GET ME SOME MORE. MY WHOLE BODY'S ACHING. MY GUTS KEEP CRAMPING BUT THERE'S NOTHING LEFT TO COME OUT.
I'LL PHONE THE DOCTOR.
OI!
YOU'VE STILL GOT A BIT OF STRENGTH IN THEM HANDS.
I'M SCARED, BAZ. I'VE HAD BAD MORNINGS, BAD NIGHTS BEFORE. BUT NEVER ANYTHING LIKE THIS.
YOU'LL BE FINE, WILL. BEFORE YOU KNOW IT, YOU'LL BE RIGHT AS RAIN.
GET THE DOCTOR, BAZ. PLEASE.

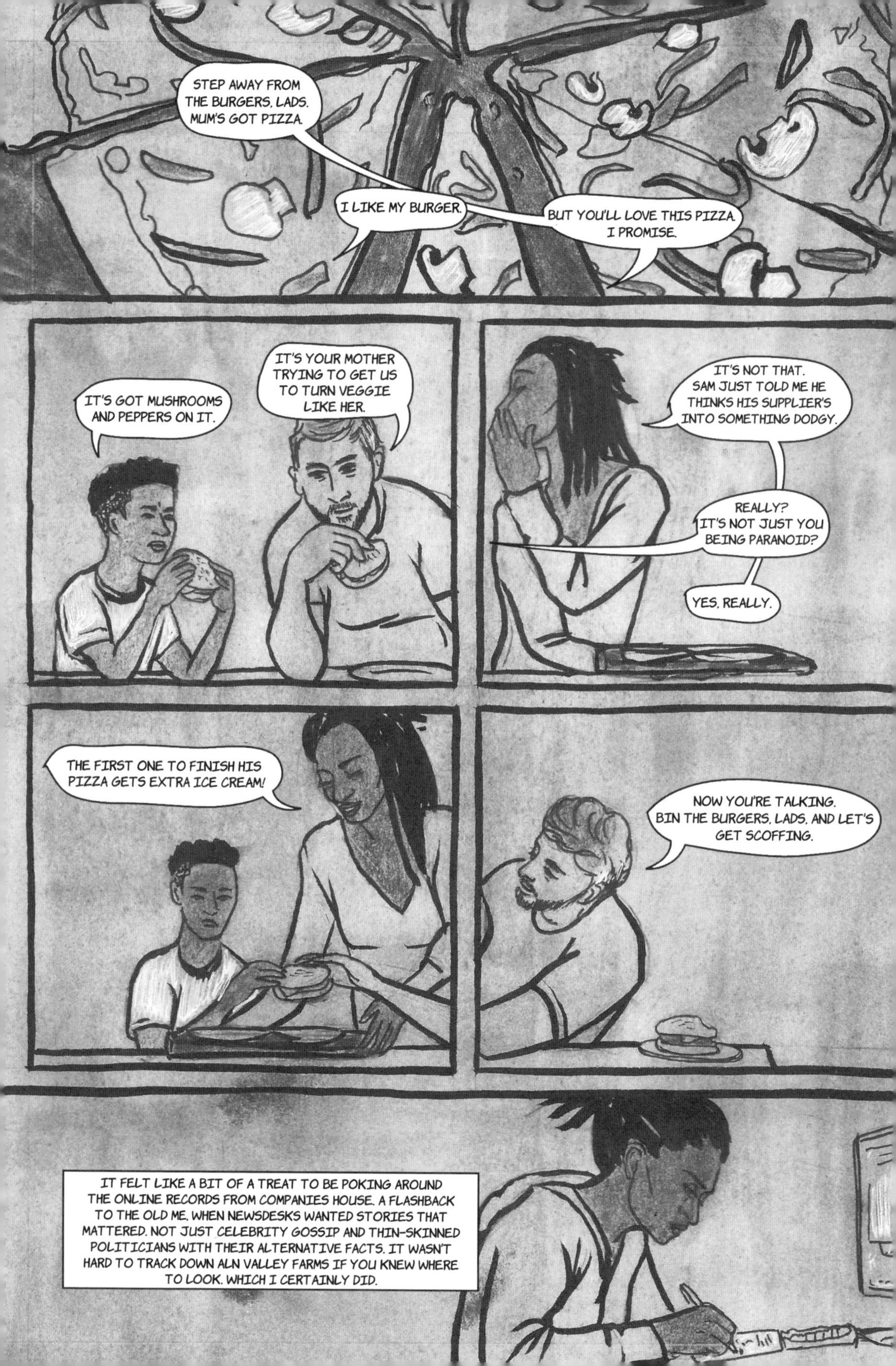
STEP AWAY FROM THE BURGERS, LADS. MUM'S GOT PIZZA.
I LIKE MY BURGER.
BUT YOU'LL LOVE THIS PIZZA. I PROMISE.
IT'S GOT MUSHROOMS AND PEPPERS ON IT.
IT'S YOUR MOTHER TRYING TO GET US TO TURN VEGGIE LIKE HER.
IT'S NOT THAT. SAM JUST TOLD ME HE THINKS HIS SUPPLIER'S INTO SOMETHING DODGY.
REALLY? IT'S NOT JUST YOU BEING PARANOID?
YES, REALLY.
THE FIRST ONE TO FINISH HIS PIZZA GETS EXTRA ICE CREAM!
NOW YOU'RE TALKING. BIN THE BURGERS, LADS, AND LET'S GET SCOFFING.
IT FELT LIKE A BIT OF A TREAT TO BE POKING AROUND THE ONLINE RECORDS FROM COMPANIES HOUSE. A FLASHBACK TO THE OLD ME, WHEN NEWSDESKS WANTED STORIES THAT MATTERED. NOT JUST CELEBRITY GOSSIP AND THIN-SKINNED POLITICIANS WITH THEIR ALTERNATIVE FACTS. IT WASN'T HARD TO TRACK DOWN ALN VALLEY FARMS IF YOU KNEW WHERE TO LOOK. WHICH I CERTAINLY DID.

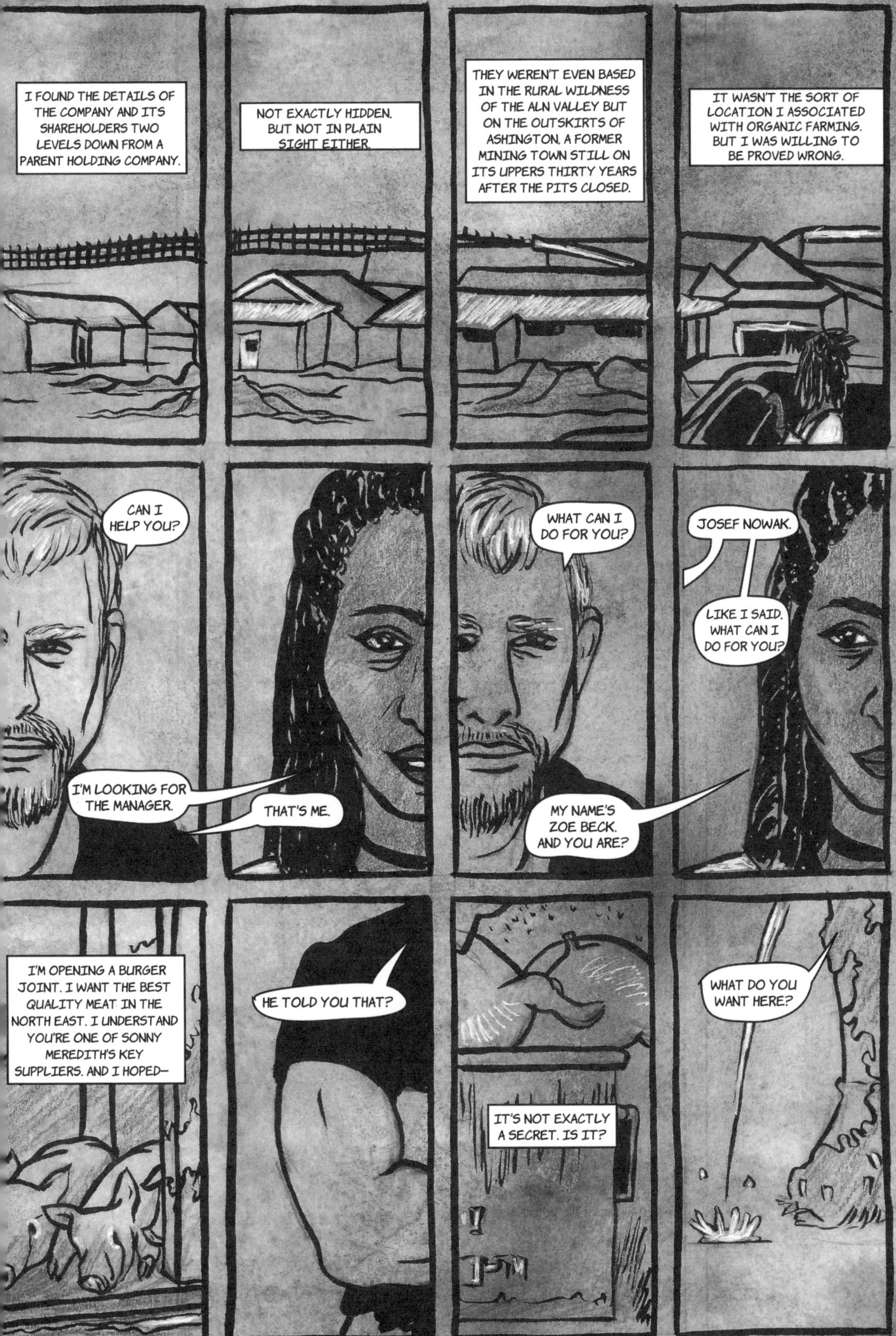
I FOUND THE DETAILS OF THE COMPANY AND ITS SHAREHOLDERS TWO LEVELS DOWN FROM A PARENT HOLDING COMPANY.
NOT EXACTLY HIDDEN. BUT NOT IN PLAIN SIGHT EITHER.
THEY WEREN'T EVEN BASED IN THE RURAL WILDNESS OF THE ALN VALLEY BUT ON THE OUTSKIRTS OF ASHINGTON, A FORMER MINING TOWN STILL ON ITS UPPERS THIRTY YEARS AFTER THE PITS CLOSED.
IT WASN'T THE SORT OF LOCATION I ASSOCIATED WITH ORGANIC FARMING. BUT I WAS WILLING TO BE PROVED WRONG.
CAN I HELP YOU?
I'M LOOKING FOR THE MANAGER.
THAT'S ME.
WHAT CAN I DO FOR YOU?
MY NAME'S ZOE BECK. AND YOU ARE?
JOSEF NOWAK.
LIKE I SAID. WHAT CAN I DO FOR YOU?
I'M OPENING A BURGER JOINT. I WANT THE BEST QUALITY MEAT IN THE NORTH EAST. I UNDERSTAND YOU'RE ONE OF SONNY MEREDITH'S KEY SUPPLIERS. AND I HOPED—
HE TOLD YOU THAT?
IT'S NOT EXACTLY A SECRET. IS IT?
WHAT DO YOU WANT HERE?

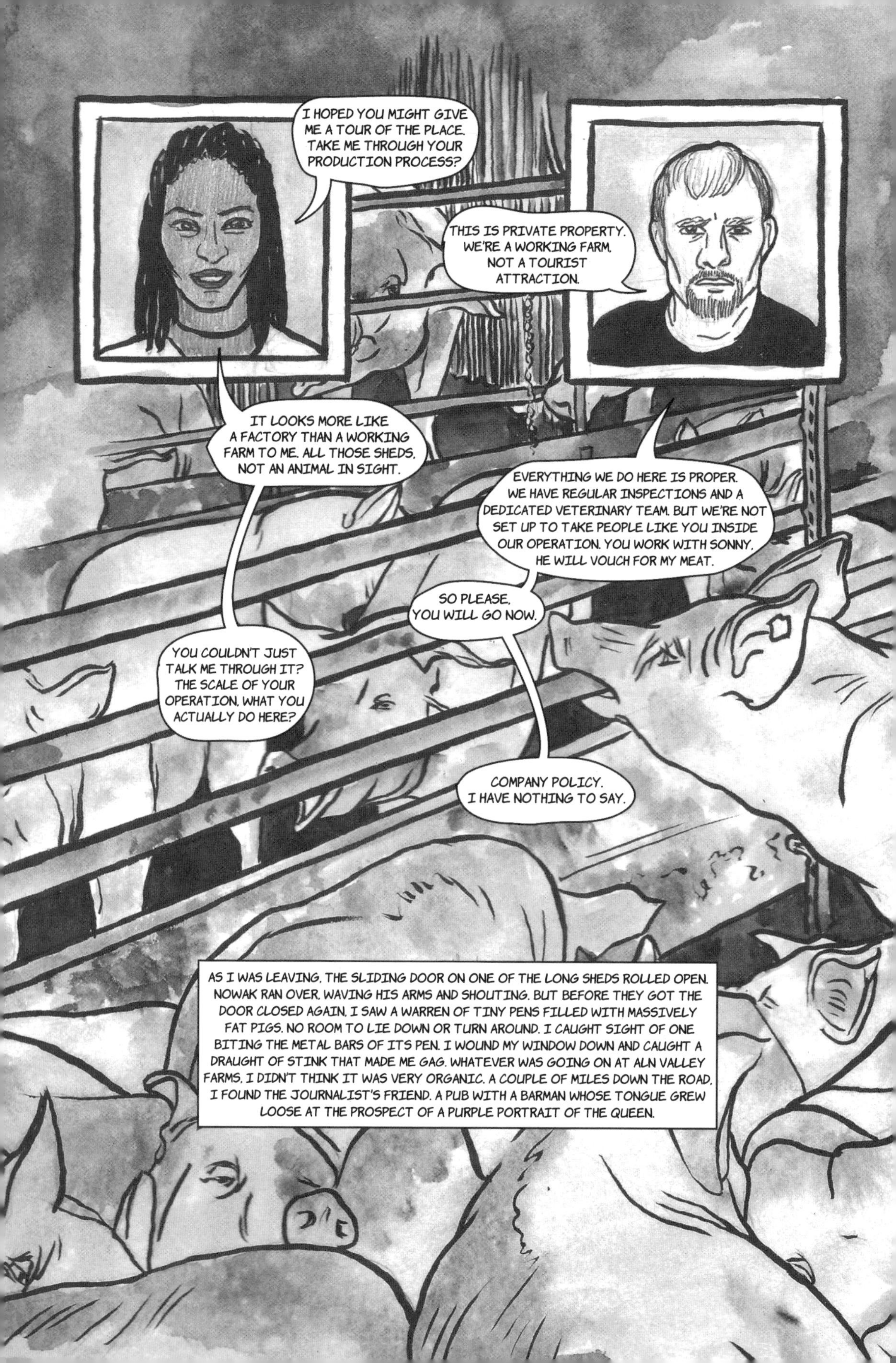
I HOPED YOU MIGHT GIVE ME A TOUR OF THE PLACE. TAKE ME THROUGH YOUR PRODUCTION PROCESS?
THIS IS PRIVATE PROPERTY. WE'RE A WORKING FARM, NOT A TOURIST ATTRACTION.
IT LOOKS MORE LIKE A FACTORY THAN A WORKING FARM TO ME. ALL THOSE SHEDS, NOT AN ANIMAL IN SIGHT.
EVERYTHING WE DO HERE IS PROPER. WE HAVE REGULAR INSPECTIONS AND A DEDICATED VETERINARY TEAM. BUT WE'RE NOT SET UP TO TAKE PEOPLE LIKE YOU INSIDE OUR OPERATION. YOU WORK WITH SONNY, HE WILL VOUCH FOR MY MEAT.
SO PLEASE, YOU WILL GO NOW.
YOU COULDN'T JUST TALK ME THROUGH IT? THE SCALE OF YOUR OPERATION, WHAT YOU ACTUALLY DO HERE?
COMPANY POLICY. I HAVE NOTHING TO SAY.
AS I WAS LEAVING, THE SLIDING DOOR ON ONE OF THE LONG SHEDS ROLLED OPEN. NOWAK RAN OVER, WAVING HIS ARMS AND SHOUTING. BUT BEFORE THEY GOT THE DOOR CLOSED AGAIN, I SAW A WARREN OF TINY PENS FILLED WITH MASSIVELY FAT PIGS. NO ROOM TO LIE DOWN OR TURN AROUND. I CAUGHT SIGHT OF ONE BITING THE METAL BARS OF ITS PEN. I WOUND MY WINDOW DOWN AND CAUGHT A DRAUGHT OF STINK THAT MADE ME GAG. WHATEVER WAS GOING ON AT ALN VALLEY FARMS, I DIDN'T THINK IT WAS VERY ORGANIC. A COUPLE OF MILES DOWN THE ROAD, I FOUND THE JOURNALIST'S FRIEND. A PUB WITH A BARMAN WHOSE TONGUE GREW LOOSE AT THE PROSPECT OF A PURPLE PORTRAIT OF THE QUEEN.

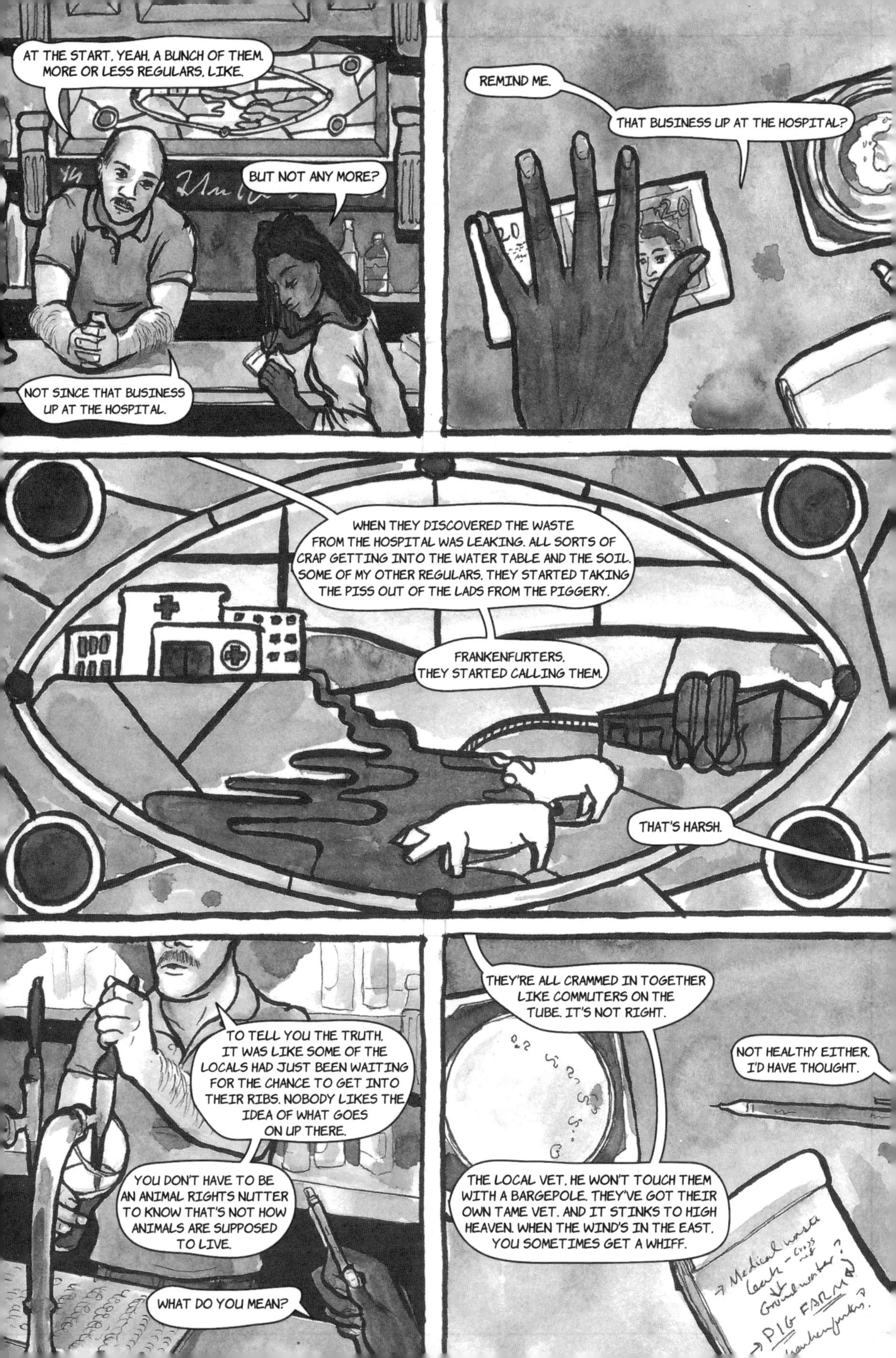
AT THE START, YEAH, A BUNCH OF THEM. MORE OR LESS REGULARS, LIKE.
BUT NOT ANY MORE?
NOT SINCE THAT BUSINESS UP AT THE HOSPITAL.
REMIND ME.
THAT BUSINESS UP AT THE HOSPITAL?
WHEN THEY DISCOVERED THE WASTE FROM THE HOSPITAL WAS LEAKING. ALL SORTS OF CRAP GETTING INTO THE WATER TABLE AND THE SOIL. SOME OF MY OTHER REGULARS, THEY STARTED TAKING THE PISS OUT OF THE LADS FROM THE PIGGERY.
FRANKENFURTERS, THEY STARTED CALLING THEM.
THAT'S HARSH.
TO TELL YOU THE TRUTH, IT WAS LIKE SOME OF THE LOCALS HAD JUST BEEN WAITING FOR THE CHANCE TO GET INTO THEIR RIBS. NOBODY LIKES THE IDEA OF WHAT GOES ON UP THERE.
YOU DON'T HAVE TO BE AN ANIMAL RIGHTS NUTTER TO KNOW THAT'S NOT HOW ANIMALS ARE SUPPOSED TO LIVE.
WHAT DO YOU MEAN?
THEY'RE ALL CRAMMED IN TOGETHER LIKE COMMUTERS ON THE TUBE. IT'S NOT RIGHT.
NOT HEALTHY EITHER, I'D HAVE THOUGHT.
THE LOCAL VET, HE WON'T TOUCH THEM WITH A BARGEPOLE. THEY'VE GOT THEIR OWN TAME VET. AND IT STINKS TO HIGH HEAVEN. WHEN THE WIND'S IN THE EAST, YOU SOMETIMES GET A WHIFF.
Medical waste
Groundwater?
PIG FARM

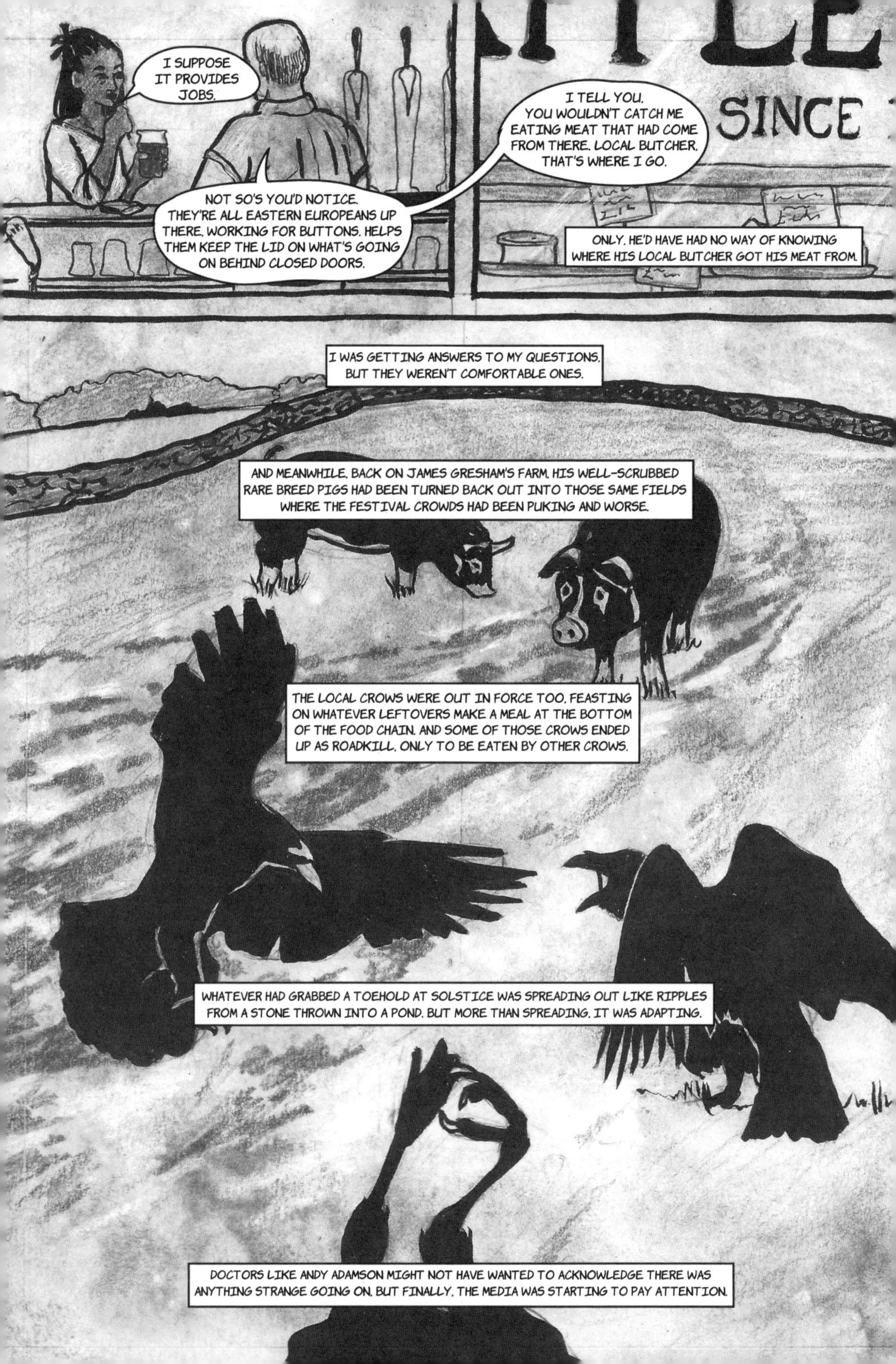
SINCE
I SUPPOSE IT PROVIDES JOBS.
NOT SO'S YOU'D NOTICE. THEY'RE ALL EASTERN EUROPEANS UP THERE, WORKING FOR BUTTONS. HELPS THEM KEEP THE LID ON WHAT'S GOING ON BEHIND CLOSED DOORS.
I TELL YOU, YOU WOULDN'T CATCH ME EATING MEAT THAT HAD COME FROM THERE. LOCAL BUTCHER, THAT'S WHERE I GO.
ONLY, HE'D HAVE HAD NO WAY OF KNOWING WHERE HIS LOCAL BUTCHER GOT HIS MEAT FROM.
I WAS GETTING ANSWERS TO MY QUESTIONS, BUT THEY WEREN'T COMFORTABLE ONES.
AND MEANWHILE, BACK ON JAMES GRESHAM'S FARM, HIS WELL-SCRUBBED RARE BREED PIGS HAD BEEN TURNED BACK OUT INTO THOSE SAME FIELDS WHERE THE FESTIVAL CROWDS HAD BEEN PUKING AND WORSE.
THE LOCAL CROWS WERE OUT IN FORCE TOO, FEASTING ON WHATEVER LEFTOVERS MAKE A MEAL AT THE BOTTOM OF THE FOOD CHAIN. AND SOME OF THOSE CROWS ENDED UP AS ROADKILL, ONLY TO BE EATEN BY OTHER CROWS.
WHATEVER HAD GRABBED A TOEHOLD AT SOLSTICE WAS SPREADING OUT LIKE RIPPLES FROM A STONE THROWN INTO A POND. BUT MORE THAN SPREADING, IT WAS ADAPTING.
DOCTORS LIKE ANDY ADAMSON MIGHT NOT HAVE WANTED TO ACKNOWLEDGE THERE WAS ANYTHING STRANGE GOING ON, BUT FINALLY, THE MEDIA WAS STARTING TO PAY ATTENTION.

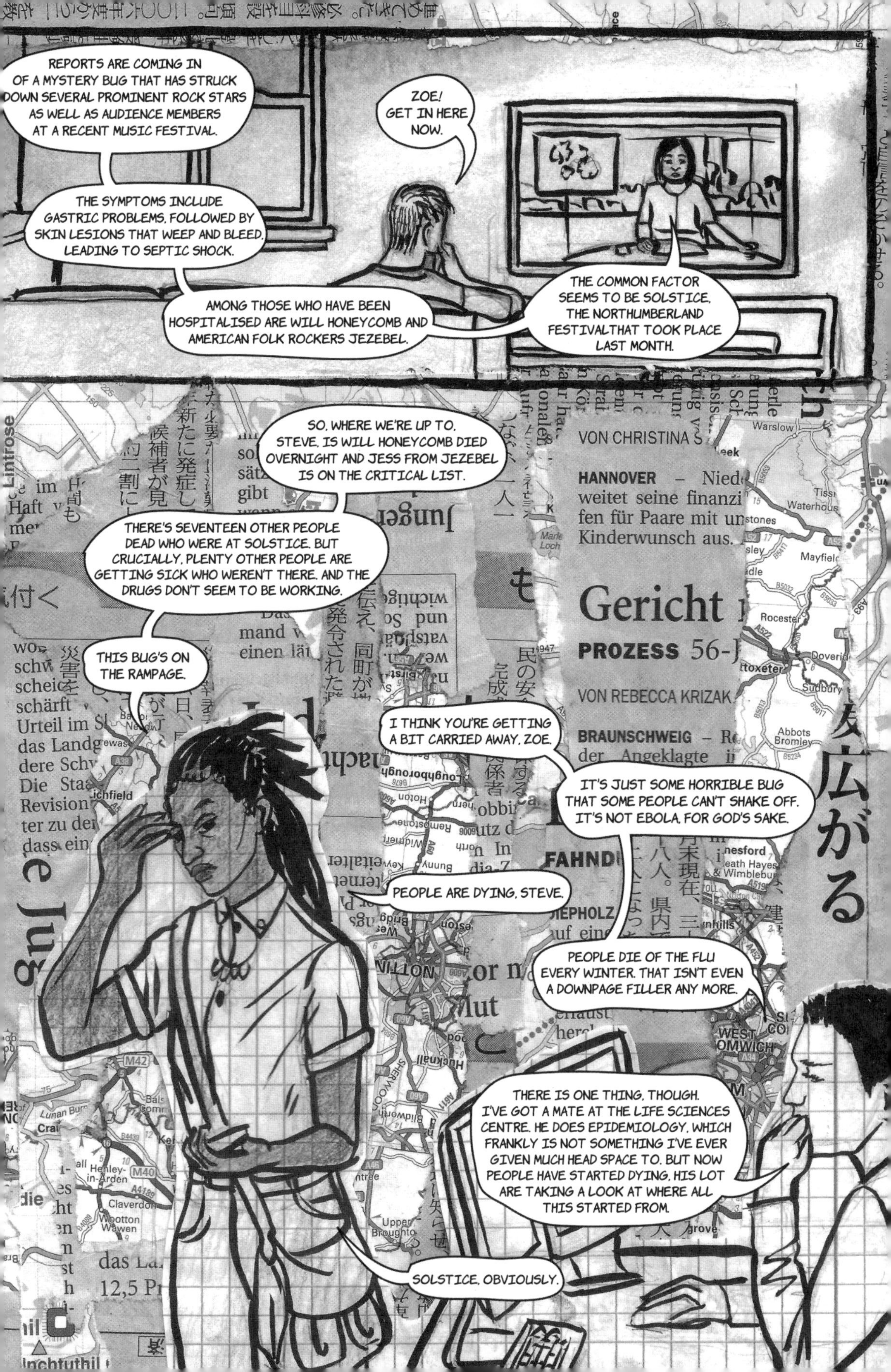
REPORTS ARE COMING IN OF A MYSTERY BUG THAT HAS STRUCK DOWN SEVERAL PROMINENT ROCK STARS AS WELL AS AUDIENCE MEMBERS AT A RECENT MUSIC FESTIVAL.
ZOE! GET IN HERE NOW.
THE SYMPTOMS INCLUDE GASTRIC PROBLEMS, FOLLOWED BY SKIN LESIONS THAT WEEP AND BLEED, LEADING TO SEPTIC SHOCK.
AMONG THOSE WHO HAVE BEEN HOSPITALISED ARE WILL HONEYCOMB AND AMERICAN FOLK ROCKERS JEZEBEL.
THE COMMON FACTOR SEEMS TO BE SOLSTICE, THE NORTHUMBERLAND FESTIVALTHAT TOOK PLACE LAST MONTH.
SO, WHERE WE'RE UP TO, STEVE, IS WILL HONEYCOMB DIED OVERNIGHT AND JESS FROM JEZEBEL IS ON THE CRITICAL LIST.
THERE'S SEVENTEEN OTHER PEOPLE DEAD WHO WERE AT SOLSTICE. BUT CRUCIALLY, PLENTY OTHER PEOPLE ARE GETTING SICK WHO WEREN'T THERE. AND THE DRUGS DON'T SEEM TO BE WORKING.
THIS BUG'S ON THE RAMPAGE.
I THINK YOU'RE GETTING A BIT CARRIED AWAY, ZOE.
IT'S JUST SOME HORRIBLE BUG THAT SOME PEOPLE CAN'T SHAKE OFF. IT'S NOT EBOLA, FOR GOD'S SAKE.
PEOPLE ARE DYING, STEVE.
PEOPLE DIE OF THE FLU EVERY WINTER. THAT ISN'T EVEN A DOWNPAGE FILLER ANY MORE.
THERE IS ONE THING, THOUGH. I'VE GOT A MATE AT THE LIFE SCIENCES CENTRE. HE DOES EPIDEMIOLOGY, WHICH FRANKLY IS NOT SOMETHING I'VE EVER GIVEN MUCH HEAD SPACE TO. BUT NOW PEOPLE HAVE STARTED DYING, HIS LOT ARE TAKING A LOOK AT WHERE ALL THIS STARTED FROM.
SOLSTICE, OBVIOUSLY.

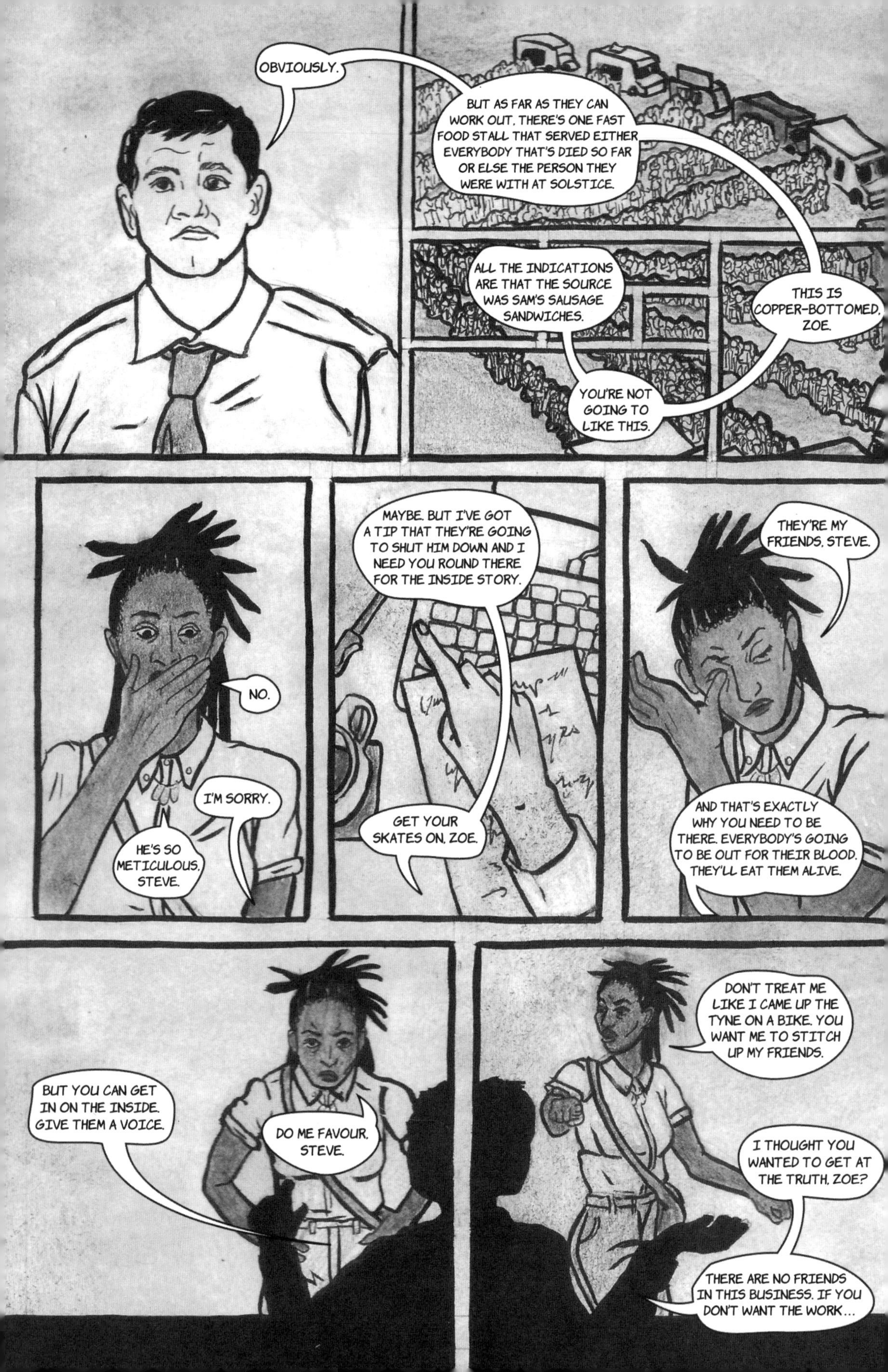
OBVIOUSLY.
BUT AS FAR AS THEY CAN WORK OUT, THERE'S ONE FAST FOOD STALL THAT SERVED EITHER EVERYBODY THAT'S DIED SO FAR OR ELSE THE PERSON THEY WERE WITH AT SOLSTICE.
THIS IS COPPER-BOTTOMED, ZOE.
ALL THE INDICATIONS ARE THAT THE SOURCE WAS SAM'S SAUSAGE SANDWICHES.
YOU'RE NOT GOING TO LIKE THIS.
NO.
I'M SORRY.
HE'S SO METICULOUS, STEVE.
MAYBE. BUT I'VE GOT A TIP THAT THEY'RE GOING TO SHUT HIM DOWN AND I NEED YOU ROUND THERE FOR THE INSIDE STORY.
GET YOUR SKATES ON, ZOE.
THEY'RE MY FRIENDS, STEVE.
AND THAT'S EXACTLY WHY YOU NEED TO BE THERE. EVERYBODY'S GOING TO BE OUT FOR THEIR BLOOD. THEY'LL EAT THEM ALIVE.
DO ME FAVOUR, STEVE.
BUT YOU CAN GET IN ON THE INSIDE. GIVE THEM A VOICE.
DON'T TREAT ME LIKE I CAME UP THE TYNE ON A BIKE. YOU WANT ME TO STITCH UP MY FRIENDS.
I THOUGHT YOU WANTED TO GET AT THE TRUTH, ZOE?
THERE ARE NO FRIENDS IN THIS BUSINESS. IF YOU DON'T WANT THE WORK...

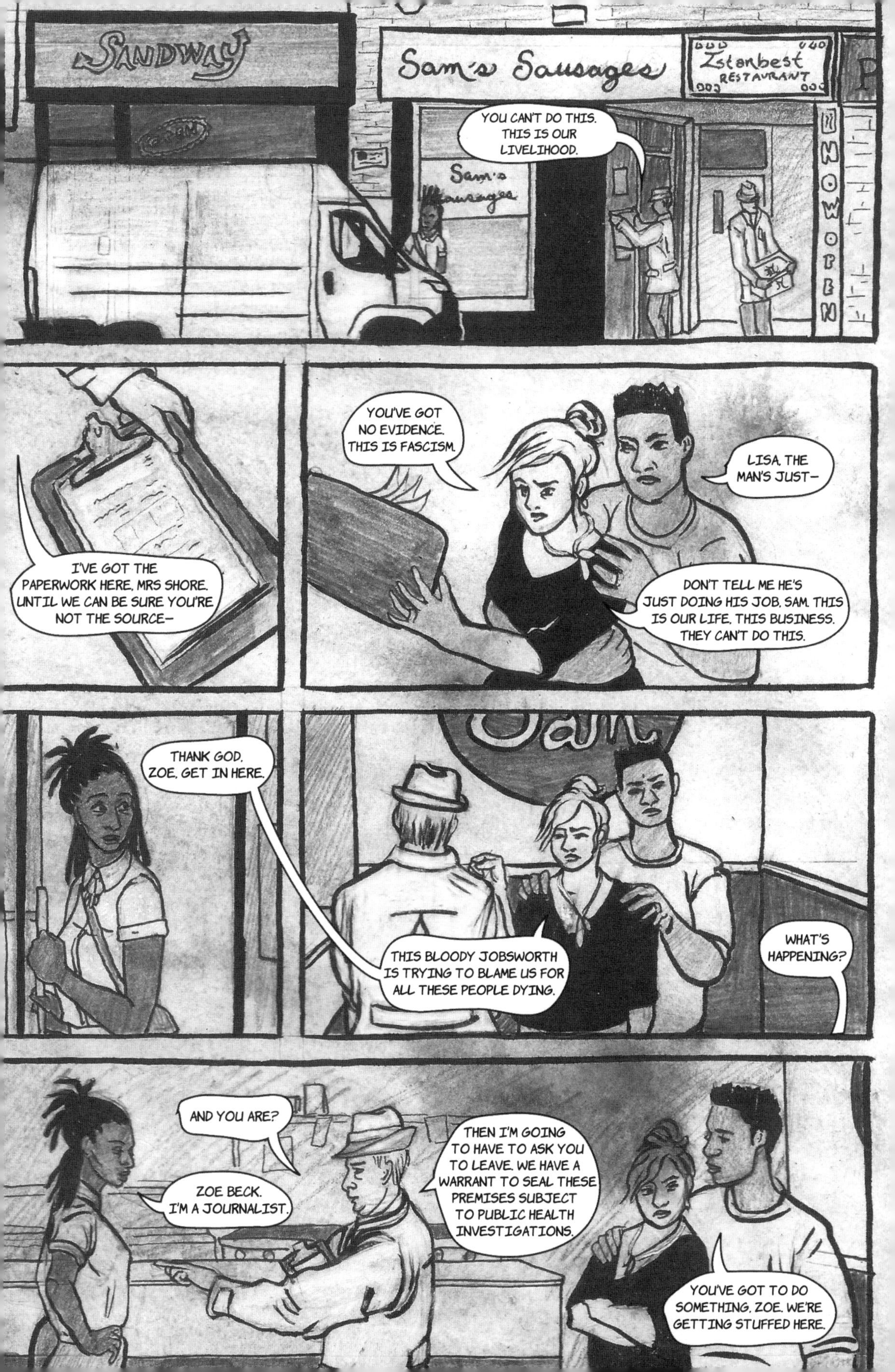
SANDWAY
Sam's Sausages
Zstanbest RESTAURANT
NOW OPEN
Sam's Sausages
YOU CAN'T DO THIS. THIS IS OUR LIVELIHOOD.
I'VE GOT THE PAPERWORK HERE, MRS SHORE. UNTIL WE CAN BE SURE YOU'RE NOT THE SOURCE–
YOU'VE GOT NO EVIDENCE. THIS IS FASCISM.
LISA, THE MAN'S JUST–
DON'T TELL ME HE'S JUST DOING HIS JOB, SAM. THIS IS OUR LIFE, THIS BUSINESS. THEY CAN'T DO THIS.
THANK GOD. ZOE, GET IN HERE.
THIS BLOODY JOBSWORTH IS TRYING TO BLAME US FOR ALL THESE PEOPLE DYING.
WHAT'S HAPPENING?
AND YOU ARE?
ZOE BECK. I'M A JOURNALIST.
THEN I'M GOING TO HAVE TO ASK YOU TO LEAVE. WE HAVE A WARRANT TO SEAL THESE PREMISES SUBJECT TO PUBLIC HEALTH INVESTIGATIONS.
YOU'VE GOT TO DO SOMETHING, ZOE. WE'RE GETTING STUFFED HERE.

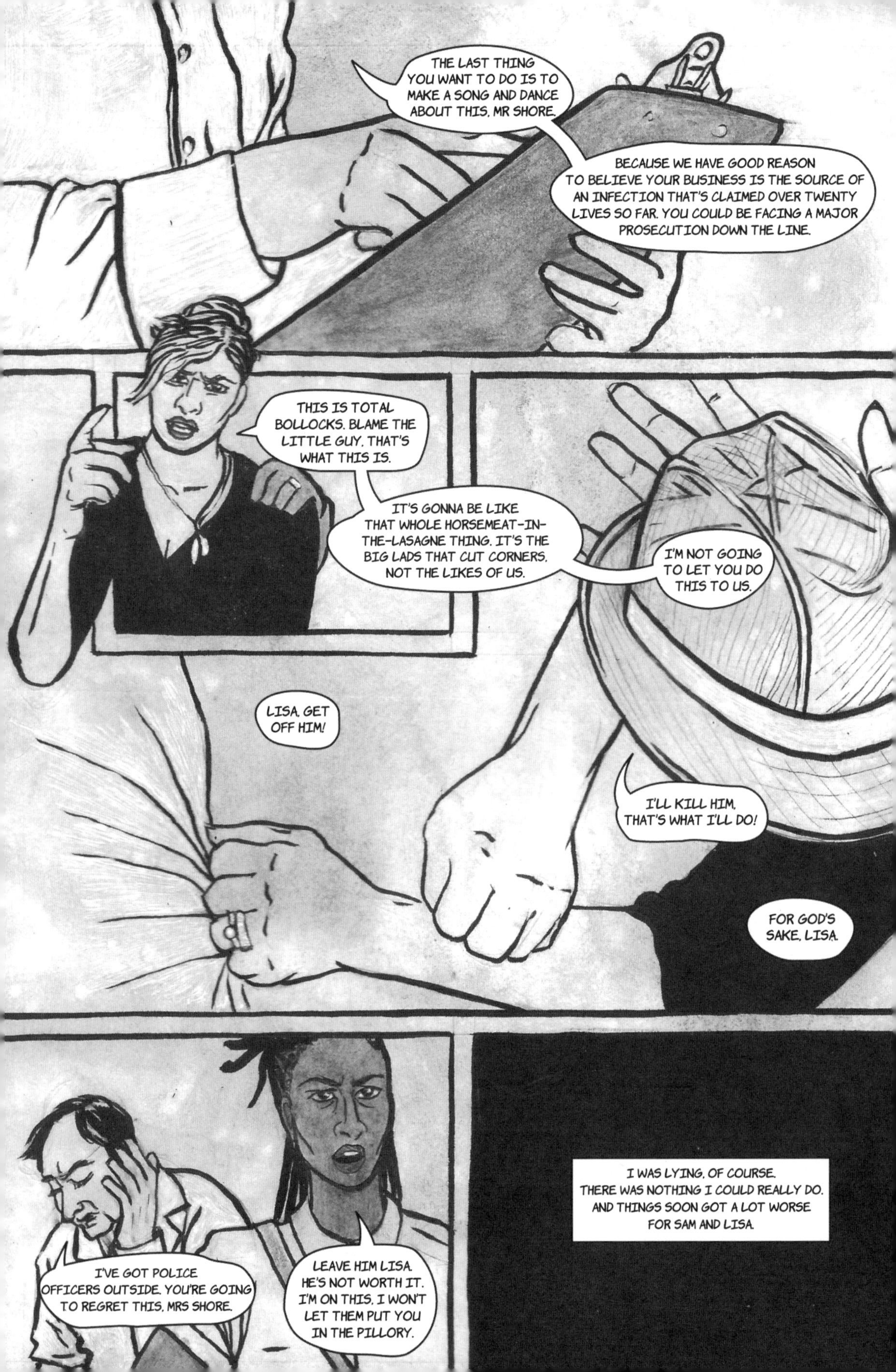
THE LAST THING YOU WANT TO DO IS TO MAKE A SONG AND DANCE ABOUT THIS, MR SHORE.
BECAUSE WE HAVE GOOD REASON TO BELIEVE YOUR BUSINESS IS THE SOURCE OF AN INFECTION THAT'S CLAIMED OVER TWENTY LIVES SO FAR. YOU COULD BE FACING A MAJOR PROSECUTION DOWN THE LINE.
THIS IS TOTAL BOLLOCKS. BLAME THE LITTLE GUY. THAT'S WHAT THIS IS.
IT'S GONNA BE LIKE THAT WHOLE HORSEMEAT-IN-THE-LASAGNE THING. IT'S THE BIG LADS THAT CUT CORNERS, NOT THE LIKES OF US.
I'M NOT GOING TO LET YOU DO THIS TO US.
LISA. GET OFF HIM!
I'LL KILL HIM, THAT'S WHAT I'LL DO!
FOR GOD'S SAKE, LISA.
I'VE GOT POLICE OFFICERS OUTSIDE. YOU'RE GOING TO REGRET THIS, MRS SHORE.
LEAVE HIM LISA. HE'S NOT WORTH IT. I'M ON THIS. I WON'T LET THEM PUT YOU IN THE PILLORY.
I WAS LYING, OF COURSE. THERE WAS NOTHING I COULD REALLY DO. AND THINGS SOON GOT A LOT WORSE FOR SAM AND LISA.

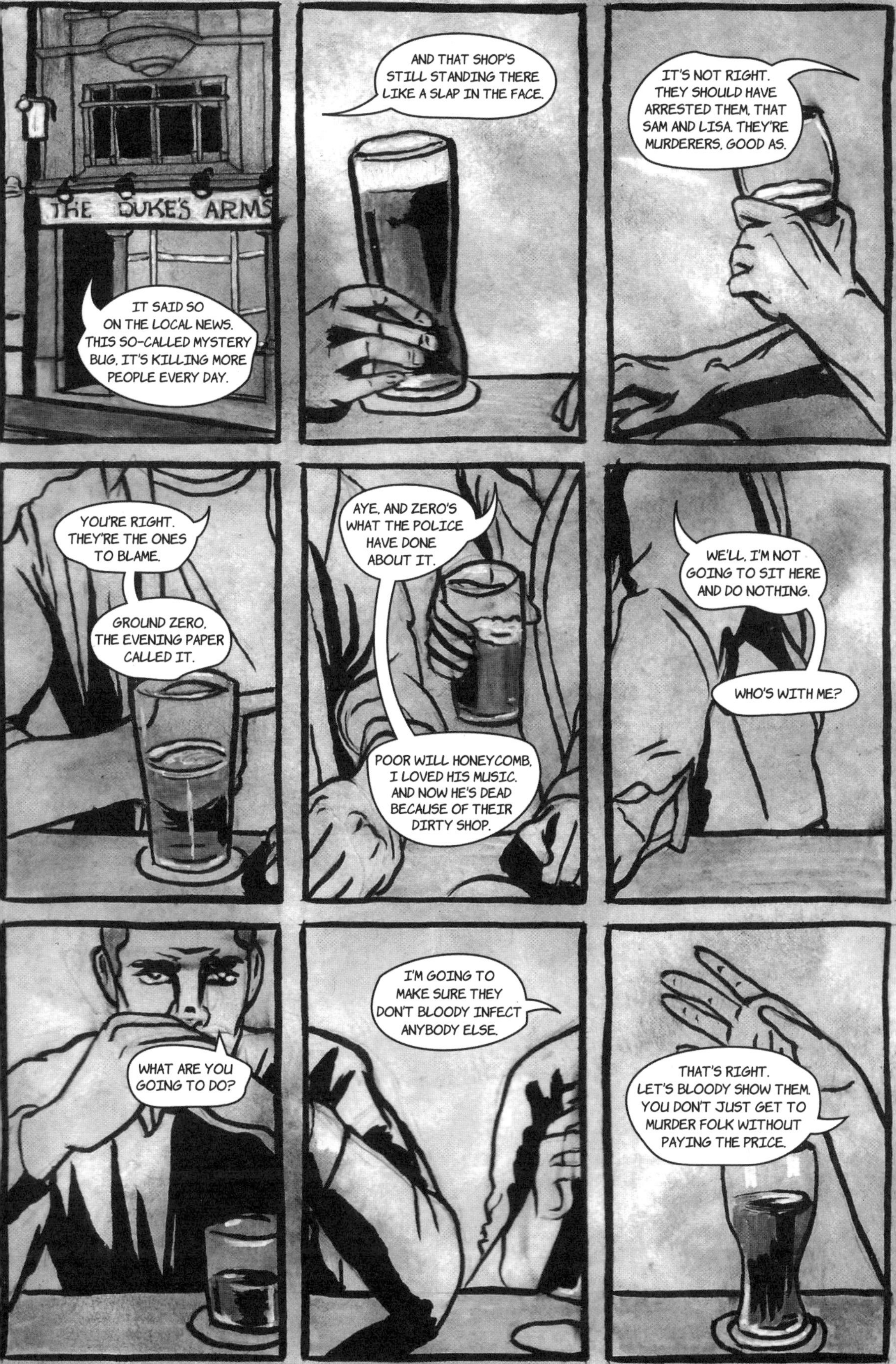
THE DUKE'S ARMS
IT SAID SO ON THE LOCAL NEWS. THIS SO-CALLED MYSTERY BUG, IT'S KILLING MORE PEOPLE EVERY DAY.
AND THAT SHOP'S STILL STANDING THERE LIKE A SLAP IN THE FACE.
IT'S NOT RIGHT. THEY SHOULD HAVE ARRESTED THEM, THAT SAM AND LISA. THEY'RE MURDERERS, GOOD AS.
YOU'RE RIGHT. THEY'RE THE ONES TO BLAME.
GROUND ZERO, THE EVENING PAPER CALLED IT.
AYE, AND ZERO'S WHAT THE POLICE HAVE DONE ABOUT IT.
POOR WILL HONEYCOMB, I LOVED HIS MUSIC. AND NOW HE'S DEAD BECAUSE OF THEIR DIRTY SHOP.
WE'LL, I'M NOT GOING TO SIT HERE AND DO NOTHING.
WHO'S WITH ME?
WHAT ARE YOU GOING TO DO?
I'M GOING TO MAKE SURE THEY DON'T BLOODY INFECT ANYBODY ELSE.
THAT'S RIGHT. LET'S BLOODY SHOW THEM. YOU DON'T JUST GET TO MURDER FOLK WITHOUT PAYING THE PRICE.

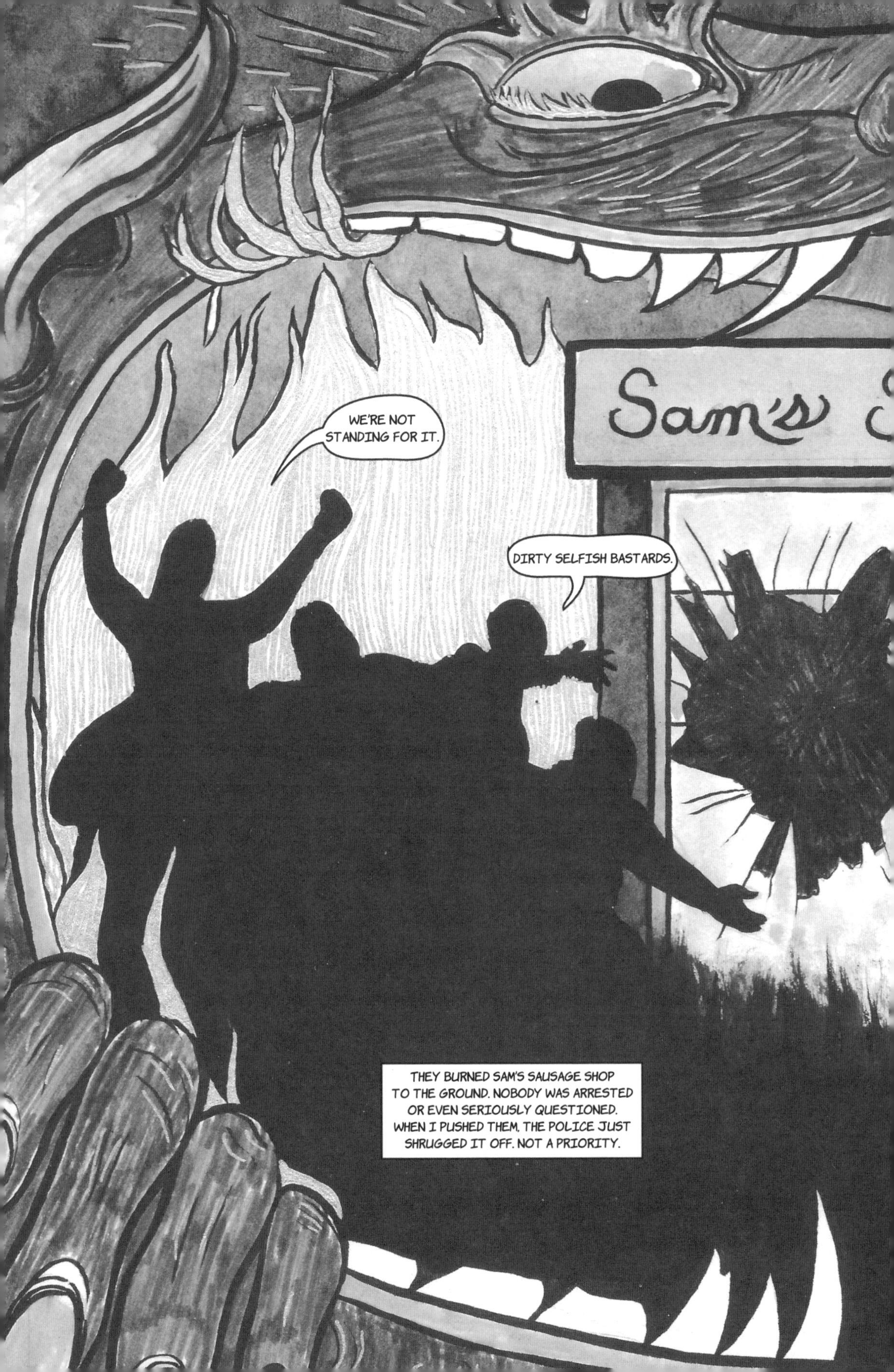
Sam's
WE'RE NOT STANDING FOR IT.
DIRTY SELFISH BASTARDS.
THEY BURNED SAM'S SAUSAGE SHOP TO THE GROUND. NOBODY WAS ARRESTED OR EVEN SERIOUSLY QUESTIONED. WHEN I PUSHED THEM, THE POLICE JUST SHRUGGED IT OFF. NOT A PRIORITY.

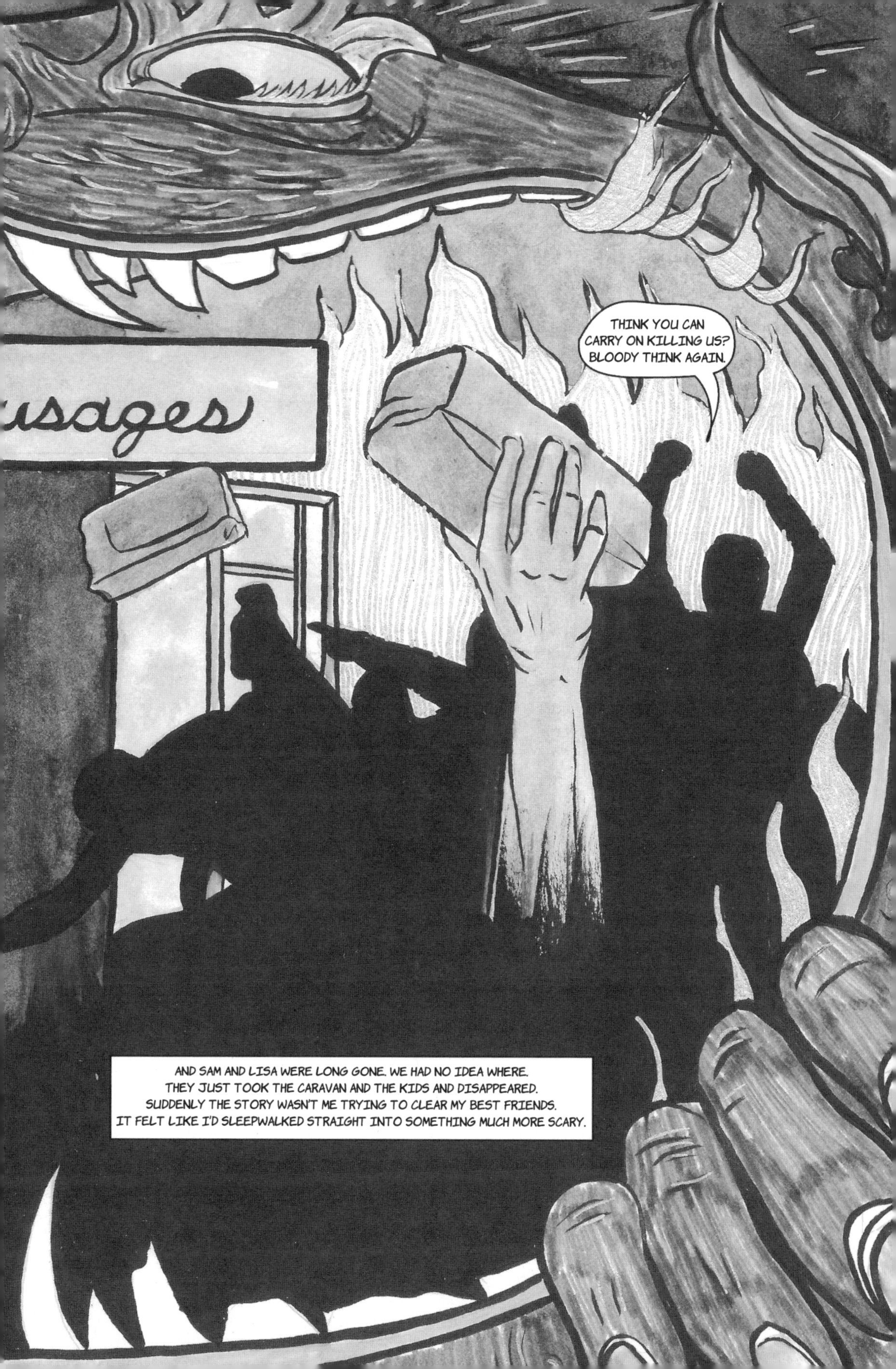

usages
THINK YOU CAN CARRY ON KILLING US? BLOODY THINK AGAIN.
AND SAM AND LISA WERE LONG GONE. WE HAD NO IDEA WHERE. THEY JUST TOOK THE CARAVAN AND THE KIDS AND DISAPPEARED. SUDDENLY THE STORY WASN'T ME TRYING TO CLEAR MY BEST FRIENDS. IT FELT LIKE I'D SLEEPWALKED STRAIGHT INTO SOMETHING MUCH MORE SCARY.

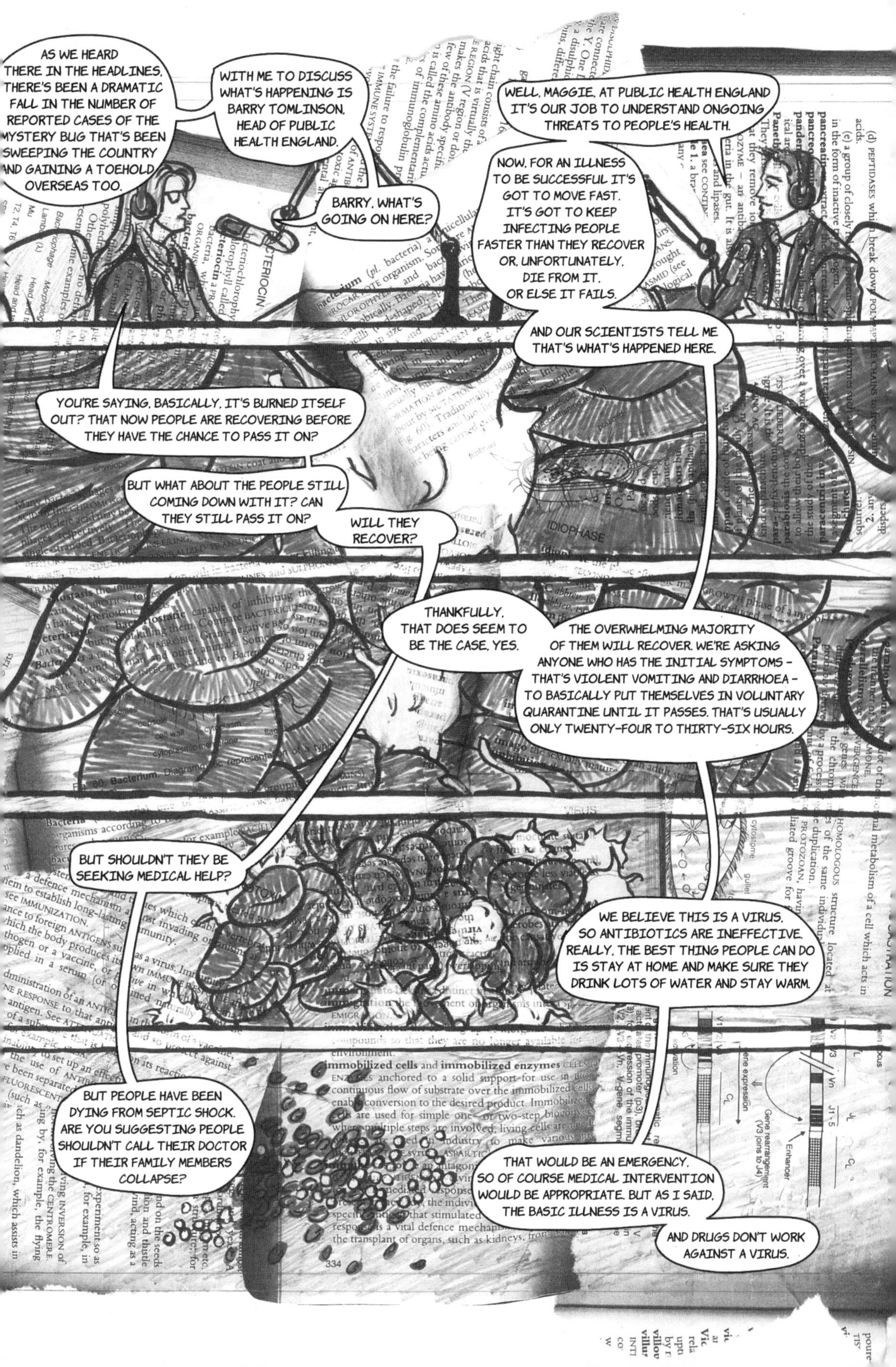
AS WE HEARD THERE IN THE HEADLINES, THERE'S BEEN A DRAMATIC FALL IN THE NUMBER OF REPORTED CASES OF THE MYSTERY BUG THAT'S BEEN SWEEPING THE COUNTRY AND GAINING A TOEHOLD OVERSEAS TOO.
WITH ME TO DISCUSS WHAT'S HAPPENING IS BARRY TOMLINSON, HEAD OF PUBLIC HEALTH ENGLAND.
BARRY, WHAT'S GOING ON HERE?
WELL, MAGGIE, AT PUBLIC HEALTH ENGLAND IT'S OUR JOB TO UNDERSTAND ONGOING THREATS TO PEOPLE'S HEALTH.
NOW, FOR AN ILLNESS TO BE SUCCESSFUL IT'S GOT TO MOVE FAST. IT'S GOT TO KEEP INFECTING PEOPLE FASTER THAN THEY RECOVER OR, UNFORTUNATELY, DIE FROM IT. OR ELSE IT FAILS.
AND OUR SCIENTISTS TELL ME THAT'S WHAT'S HAPPENED HERE.
YOU'RE SAYING, BASICALLY, IT'S BURNED ITSELF OUT? THAT NOW PEOPLE ARE RECOVERING BEFORE THEY HAVE THE CHANCE TO PASS IT ON?
BUT WHAT ABOUT THE PEOPLE STILL COMING DOWN WITH IT? CAN THEY STILL PASS IT ON?
WILL THEY RECOVER?
THANKFULLY, THAT DOES SEEM TO BE THE CASE, YES.
THE OVERWHELMING MAJORITY OF THEM WILL RECOVER. WE'RE ASKING ANYONE WHO HAS THE INITIAL SYMPTOMS – THAT'S VIOLENT VOMITING AND DIARRHOEA – TO BASICALLY PUT THEMSELVES IN VOLUNTARY QUARANTINE UNTIL IT PASSES. THAT'S USUALLY ONLY TWENTY-FOUR TO THIRTY-SIX HOURS.
BUT SHOULDN'T THEY BE SEEKING MEDICAL HELP?
WE BELIEVE THIS IS A VIRUS, SO ANTIBIOTICS ARE INEFFECTIVE. REALLY, THE BEST THING PEOPLE CAN DO IS STAY AT HOME AND MAKE SURE THEY DRINK LOTS OF WATER AND STAY WARM.
BUT PEOPLE HAVE BEEN DYING FROM SEPTIC SHOCK. ARE YOU SUGGESTING PEOPLE SHOULDN'T CALL THEIR DOCTOR IF THEIR FAMILY MEMBERS COLLAPSE?
THAT WOULD BE AN EMERGENCY, SO OF COURSE MEDICAL INTERVENTION WOULD BE APPROPRIATE. BUT AS I SAID, THE BASIC ILLNESS IS A VIRUS.
AND DRUGS DON'T WORK AGAINST A VIRUS.

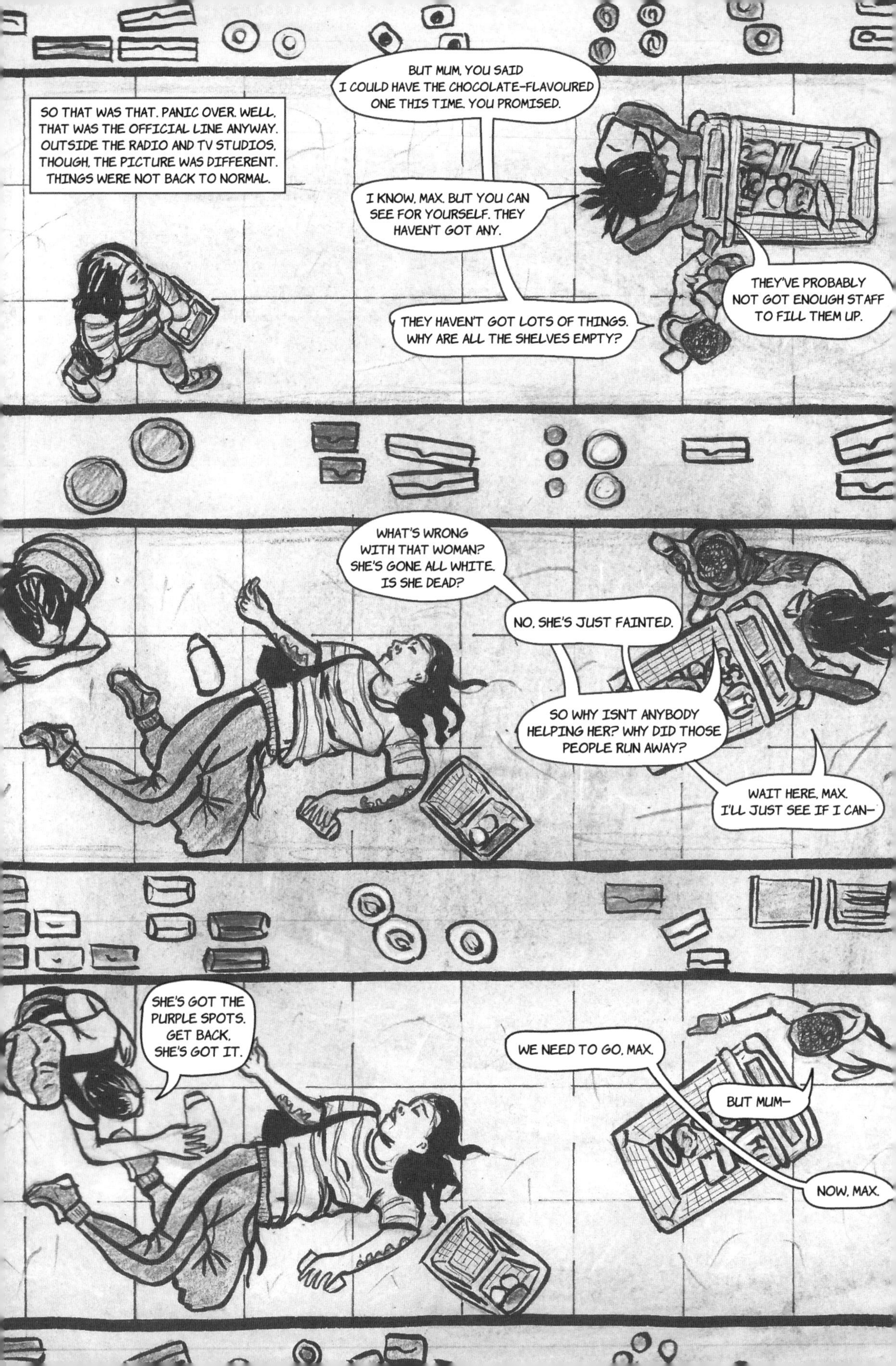
SO THAT WAS THAT. PANIC OVER. WELL, THAT WAS THE OFFICIAL LINE ANYWAY. OUTSIDE THE RADIO AND TV STUDIOS, THOUGH, THE PICTURE WAS DIFFERENT. THINGS WERE NOT BACK TO NORMAL.
BUT MUM, YOU SAID I COULD HAVE THE CHOCOLATE-FLAVOURED ONE THIS TIME. YOU PROMISED.
I KNOW, MAX. BUT YOU CAN SEE FOR YOURSELF. THEY HAVEN'T GOT ANY.
THEY HAVEN'T GOT LOTS OF THINGS. WHY ARE ALL THE SHELVES EMPTY?
THEY'VE PROBABLY NOT GOT ENOUGH STAFF TO FILL THEM UP.
WHAT'S WRONG WITH THAT WOMAN? SHE'S GONE ALL WHITE. IS SHE DEAD?
NO, SHE'S JUST FAINTED.
SO WHY ISN'T ANYBODY HELPING HER? WHY DID THOSE PEOPLE RUN AWAY?
WAIT HERE, MAX. I'LL JUST SEE IF I CAN–
SHE'S GOT THE PURPLE SPOTS. GET BACK, SHE'S GOT IT.
WE NEED TO GO, MAX.
BUT MUM–
NOW, MAX.

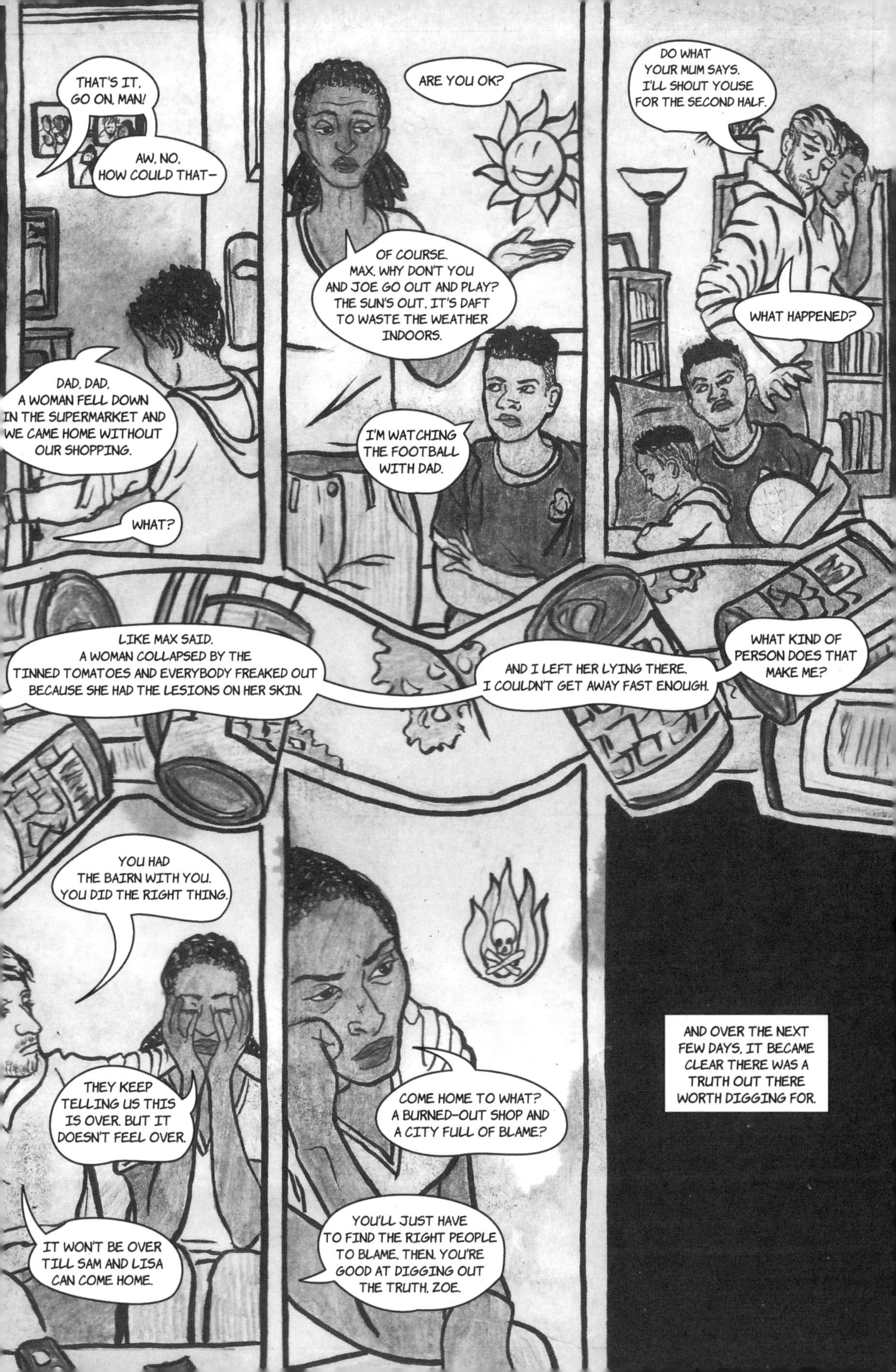
THAT'S IT. GO ON, MAN!
AW, NO. HOW COULD THAT—
DAD, DAD. A WOMAN FELL DOWN IN THE SUPERMARKET AND WE CAME HOME WITHOUT OUR SHOPPING.
WHAT?
ARE YOU OK?
OF COURSE. MAX, WHY DON'T YOU AND JOE GO OUT AND PLAY? THE SUN'S OUT. IT'S DAFT TO WASTE THE WEATHER INDOORS.
I'M WATCHING THE FOOTBALL WITH DAD.
DO WHAT YOUR MUM SAYS. I'LL SHOUT YOUSE FOR THE SECOND HALF.
WHAT HAPPENED?
LIKE MAX SAID. A WOMAN COLLAPSED BY THE TINNED TOMATOES AND EVERYBODY FREAKED OUT BECAUSE SHE HAD THE LESIONS ON HER SKIN.
AND I LEFT HER LYING THERE. I COULDN'T GET AWAY FAST ENOUGH.
WHAT KIND OF PERSON DOES THAT MAKE ME?
YOU HAD THE BAIRN WITH YOU. YOU DID THE RIGHT THING.
THEY KEEP TELLING US THIS IS OVER. BUT IT DOESN'T FEEL OVER.
IT WON'T BE OVER TILL SAM AND LISA CAN COME HOME.
COME HOME TO WHAT? A BURNED-OUT SHOP AND A CITY FULL OF BLAME?
YOU'LL JUST HAVE TO FIND THE RIGHT PEOPLE TO BLAME, THEN. YOU'RE GOOD AT DIGGING OUT THE TRUTH, ZOE.
AND OVER THE NEXT FEW DAYS, IT BECAME CLEAR THERE WAS A TRUTH OUT THERE WORTH DIGGING FOR.

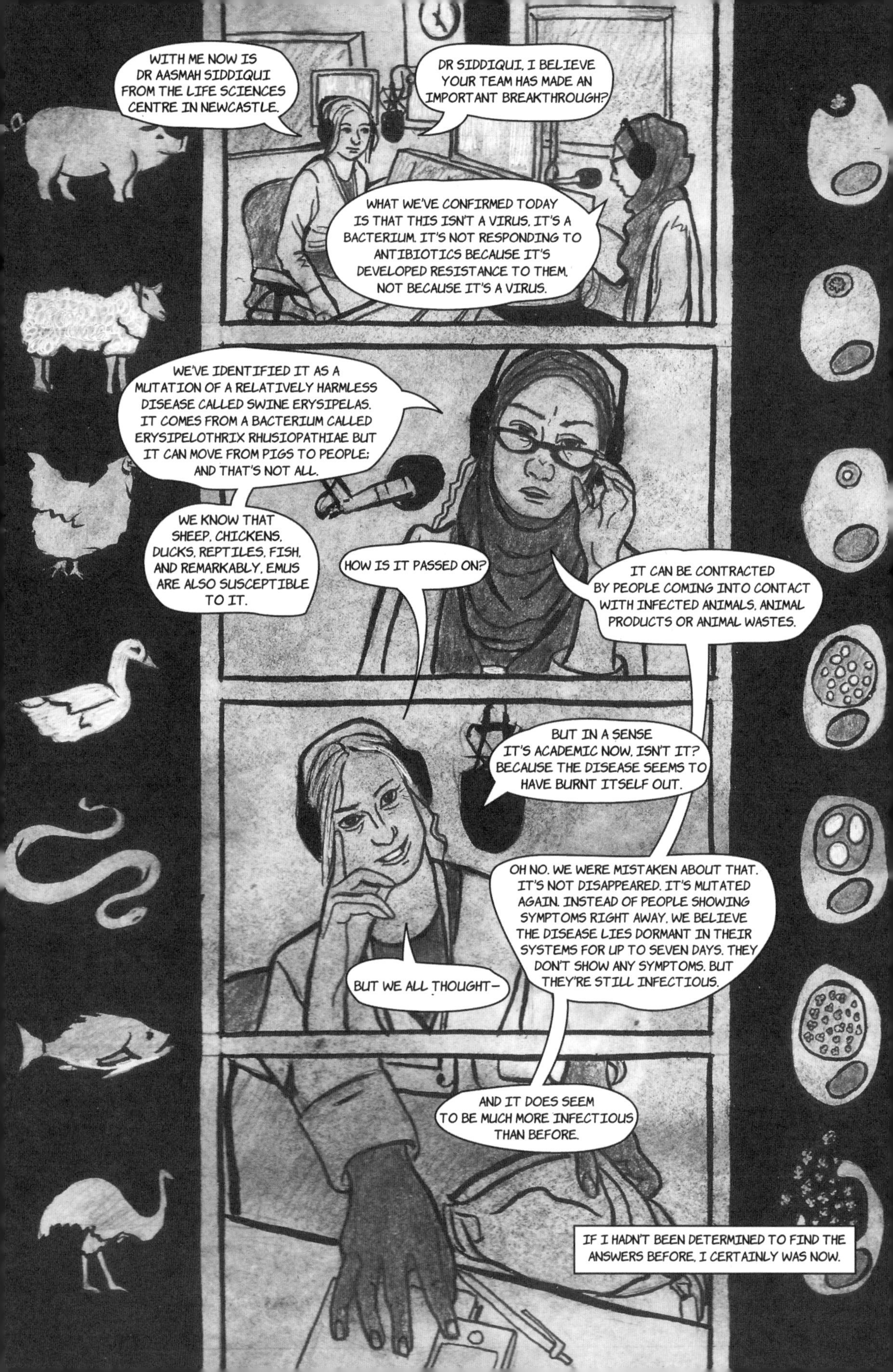
WITH ME NOW IS DR AASMAH SIDDIQUI FROM THE LIFE SCIENCES CENTRE IN NEWCASTLE.
DR SIDDIQUI, I BELIEVE YOUR TEAM HAS MADE AN IMPORTANT BREAKTHROUGH?
WHAT WE'VE CONFIRMED TODAY IS THAT THIS ISN'T A VIRUS, IT'S A BACTERIUM. IT'S NOT RESPONDING TO ANTIBIOTICS BECAUSE IT'S DEVELOPED RESISTANCE TO THEM, NOT BECAUSE IT'S A VIRUS.
WE'VE IDENTIFIED IT AS A MUTATION OF A RELATIVELY HARMLESS DISEASE CALLED SWINE ERYSIPELAS. IT COMES FROM A BACTERIUM CALLED ERYSIPELOTHRIX RHUSIOPATHIAE BUT IT CAN MOVE FROM PIGS TO PEOPLE; AND THAT'S NOT ALL.
WE KNOW THAT SHEEP, CHICKENS, DUCKS, REPTILES, FISH, AND REMARKABLY, EMUS ARE ALSO SUSCEPTIBLE TO IT.
HOW IS IT PASSED ON?
IT CAN BE CONTRACTED BY PEOPLE COMING INTO CONTACT WITH INFECTED ANIMALS, ANIMAL PRODUCTS OR ANIMAL WASTES.
BUT IN A SENSE IT'S ACADEMIC NOW, ISN'T IT? BECAUSE THE DISEASE SEEMS TO HAVE BURNT ITSELF OUT.
OH NO. WE WERE MISTAKEN ABOUT THAT. IT'S NOT DISAPPEARED. IT'S MUTATED AGAIN. INSTEAD OF PEOPLE SHOWING SYMPTOMS RIGHT AWAY, WE BELIEVE THE DISEASE LIES DORMANT IN THEIR SYSTEMS FOR UP TO SEVEN DAYS. THEY DON'T SHOW ANY SYMPTOMS. BUT THEY'RE STILL INFECTIOUS.
BUT WE ALL THOUGHT–
AND IT DOES SEEM TO BE MUCH MORE INFECTIOUS THAN BEFORE.
IF I HADN'T BEEN DETERMINED TO FIND THE ANSWERS BEFORE, I CERTAINLY WAS NOW.

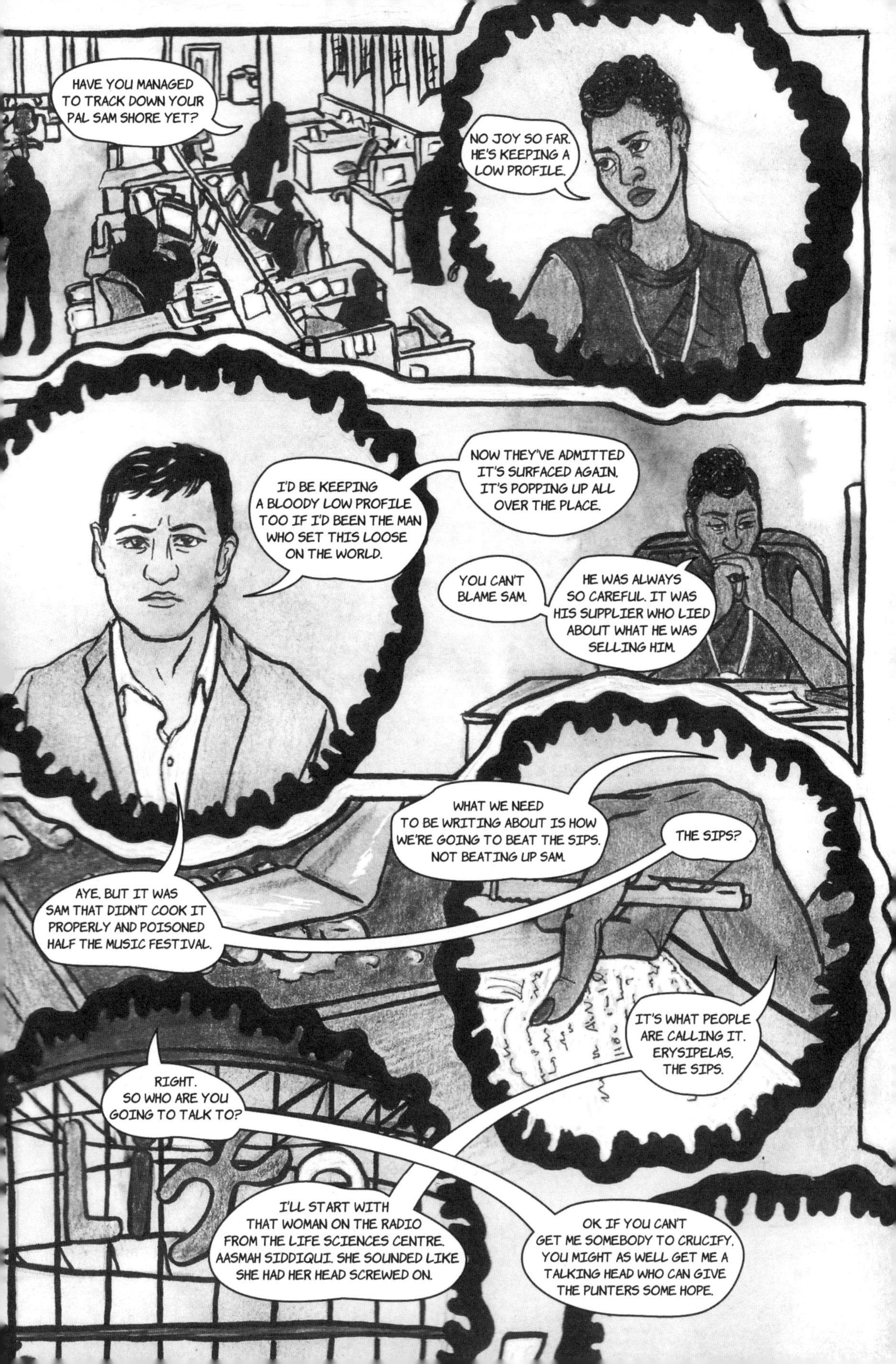
HAVE YOU MANAGED TO TRACK DOWN YOUR PAL SAM SHORE YET?
NO JOY SO FAR. HE'S KEEPING A LOW PROFILE.
I'D BE KEEPING A BLOODY LOW PROFILE TOO IF I'D BEEN THE MAN WHO SET THIS LOOSE ON THE WORLD.
NOW THEY'VE ADMITTED IT'S SURFACED AGAIN, IT'S POPPING UP ALL OVER THE PLACE.
YOU CAN'T BLAME SAM.
HE WAS ALWAYS SO CAREFUL. IT WAS HIS SUPPLIER WHO LIED ABOUT WHAT HE WAS SELLING HIM.
AYE, BUT IT WAS SAM THAT DIDN'T COOK IT PROPERLY AND POISONED HALF THE MUSIC FESTIVAL.
WHAT WE NEED TO BE WRITING ABOUT IS HOW WE'RE GOING TO BEAT THE SIPS. NOT BEATING UP SAM.
THE SIPS?
IT'S WHAT PEOPLE ARE CALLING IT. ERYSIPELAS, THE SIPS.
RIGHT. SO WHO ARE YOU GOING TO TALK TO?
I'LL START WITH THAT WOMAN ON THE RADIO FROM THE LIFE SCIENCES CENTRE. AASMAH SIDDIQUI. SHE SOUNDED LIKE SHE HAD HER HEAD SCREWED ON.
OK. IF YOU CAN'T GET ME SOMEBODY TO CRUCIFY, YOU MIGHT AS WELL GET ME A TALKING HEAD WHO CAN GIVE THE PUNTERS SOME HOPE.

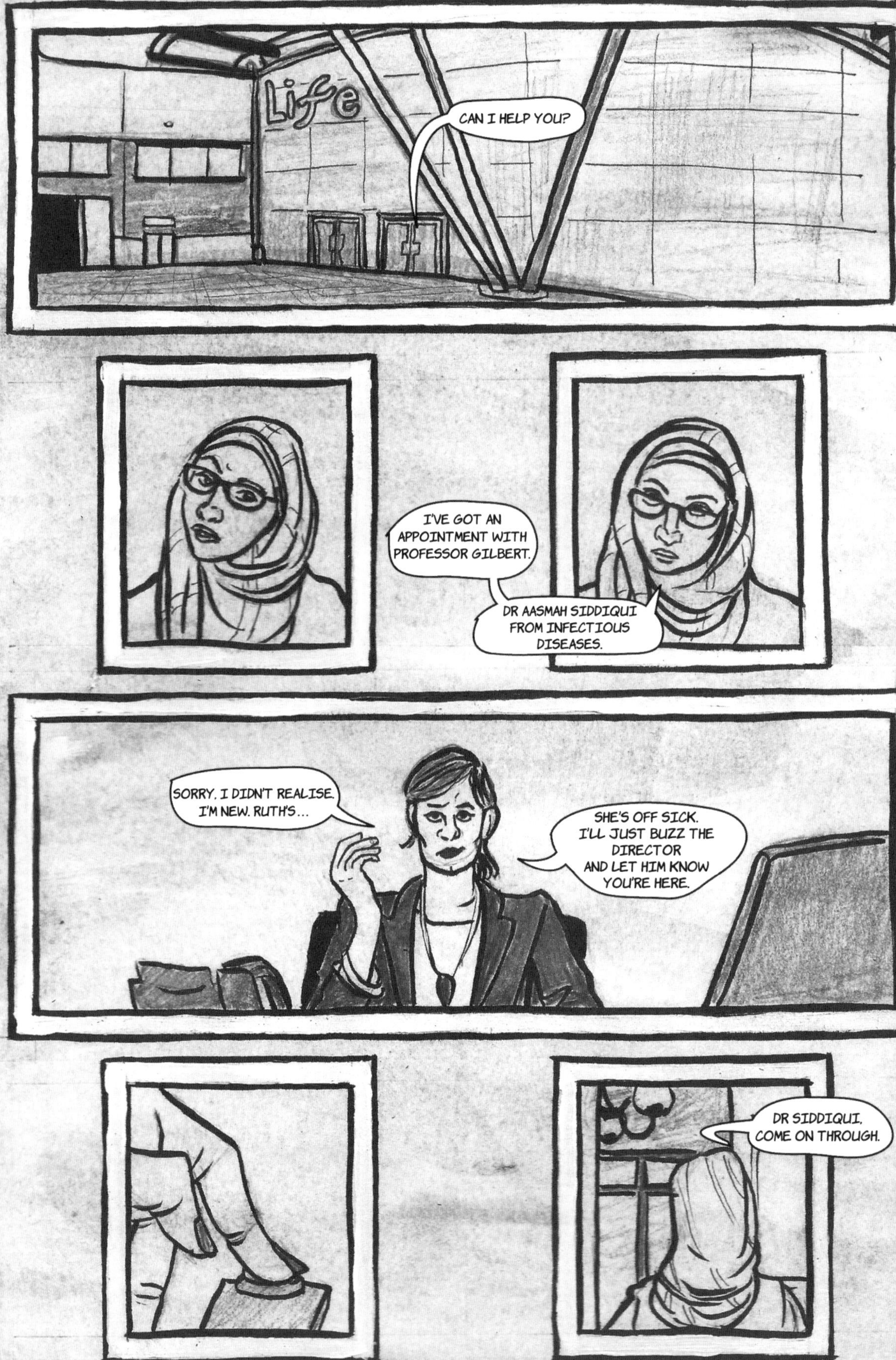
Life
CAN I HELP YOU?
I'VE GOT AN APPOINTMENT WITH PROFESSOR GILBERT.
DR AASMAH SIDDIQUI FROM INFECTIOUS DISEASES.
SORRY. I DIDN'T REALISE. I'M NEW. RUTH'S…
SHE'S OFF SICK. I'LL JUST BUZZ THE DIRECTOR AND LET HIM KNOW YOU'RE HERE.
DR SIDDIQUI, COME ON THROUGH.

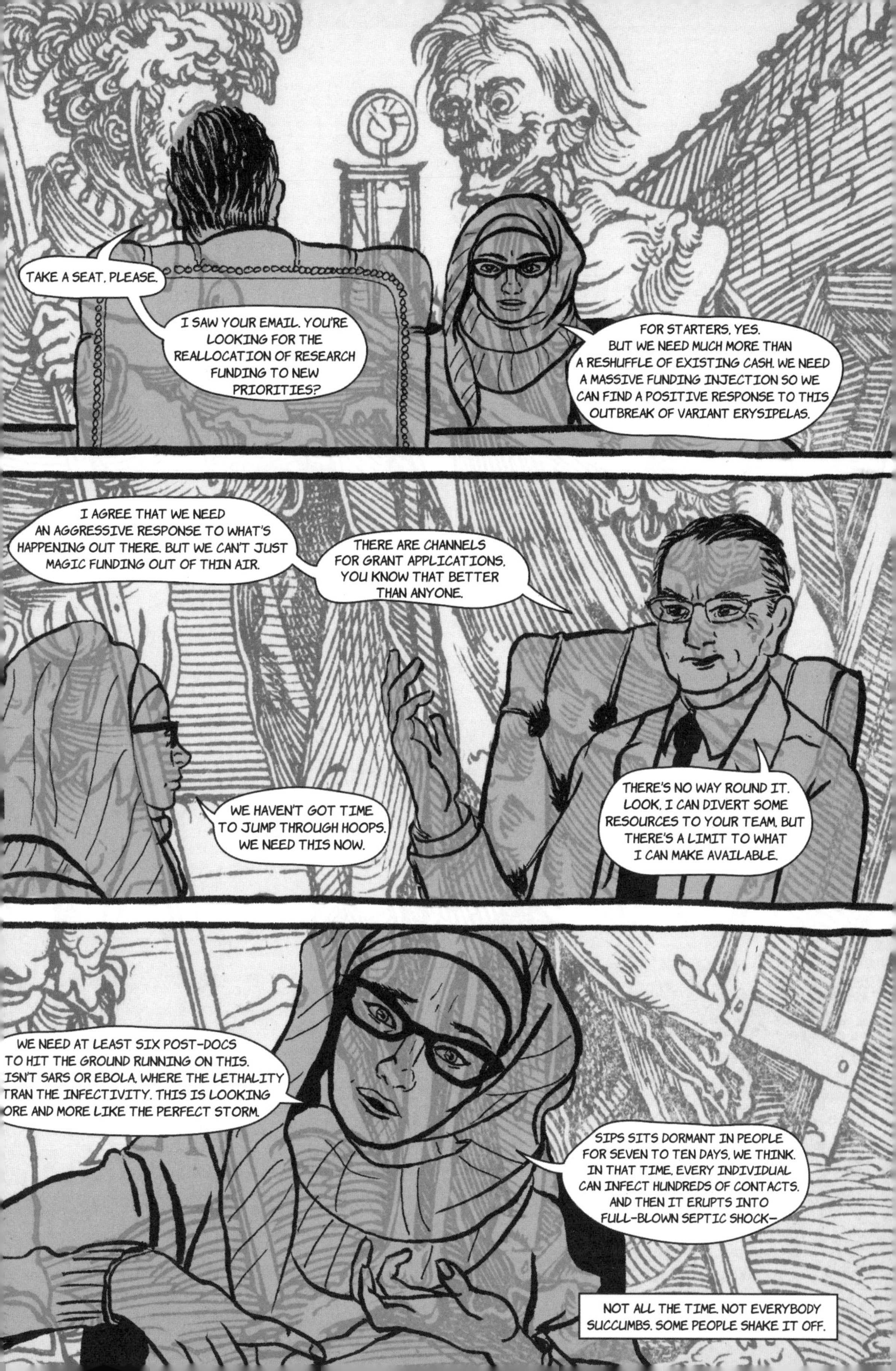

TAKE A SEAT, PLEASE.
I SAW YOUR EMAIL. YOU'RE LOOKING FOR THE REALLOCATION OF RESEARCH FUNDING TO NEW PRIORITIES?
FOR STARTERS, YES. BUT WE NEED MUCH MORE THAN A RESHUFFLE OF EXISTING CASH. WE NEED A MASSIVE FUNDING INJECTION SO WE CAN FIND A POSITIVE RESPONSE TO THIS OUTBREAK OF VARIANT ERYSIPELAS.
I AGREE THAT WE NEED AN AGGRESSIVE RESPONSE TO WHAT'S HAPPENING OUT THERE. BUT WE CAN'T JUST MAGIC FUNDING OUT OF THIN AIR.
THERE ARE CHANNELS FOR GRANT APPLICATIONS, YOU KNOW THAT BETTER THAN ANYONE.
WE HAVEN'T GOT TIME TO JUMP THROUGH HOOPS. WE NEED THIS NOW.
THERE'S NO WAY ROUND IT. LOOK, I CAN DIVERT SOME RESOURCES TO YOUR TEAM, BUT THERE'S A LIMIT TO WHAT I CAN MAKE AVAILABLE.
WE NEED AT LEAST SIX POST-DOCS TO HIT THE GROUND RUNNING ON THIS. ISN'T SARS OR EBOLA, WHERE THE LETHALITY TRAN THE INFECTIVITY. THIS IS LOOKING ORE AND MORE LIKE THE PERFECT STORM.
SIPS SITS DORMANT IN PEOPLE FOR SEVEN TO TEN DAYS, WE THINK. IN THAT TIME, EVERY INDIVIDUAL CAN INFECT HUNDREDS OF CONTACTS. AND THEN IT ERUPTS INTO FULL-BLOWN SEPTIC SHOCK—
NOT ALL THE TIME. NOT EVERYBODY SUCCUMBS. SOME PEOPLE SHAKE IT OFF.

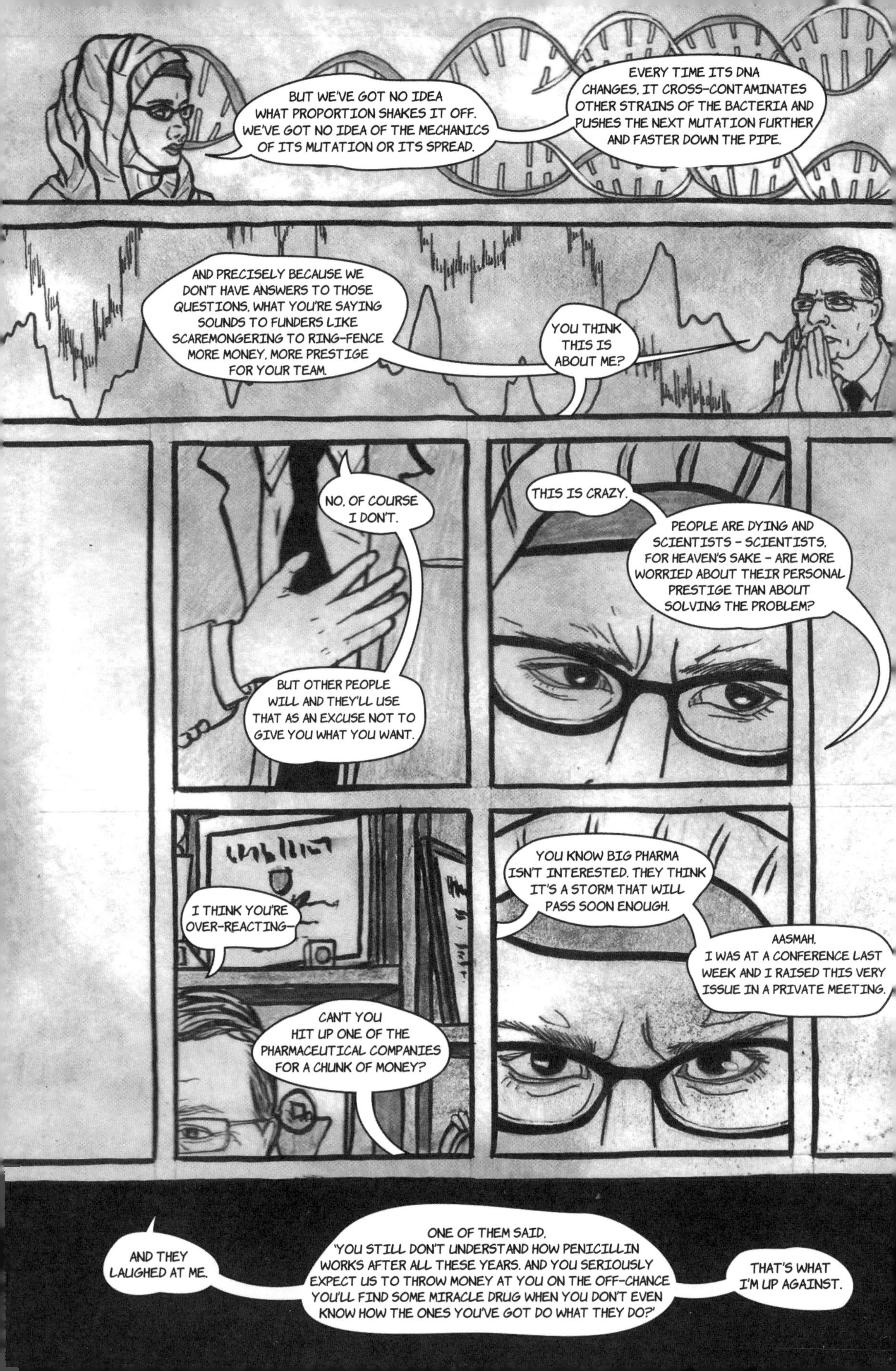

BUT WE'VE GOT NO IDEA WHAT PROPORTION SHAKES IT OFF. WE'VE GOT NO IDEA OF THE MECHANICS OF ITS MUTATION OR ITS SPREAD.
EVERY TIME ITS DNA CHANGES, IT CROSS-CONTAMINATES OTHER STRAINS OF THE BACTERIA AND PUSHES THE NEXT MUTATION FURTHER AND FASTER DOWN THE PIPE.
AND PRECISELY BECAUSE WE DON'T HAVE ANSWERS TO THOSE QUESTIONS, WHAT YOU'RE SAYING SOUNDS TO FUNDERS LIKE SCAREMONGERING TO RING-FENCE MORE MONEY, MORE PRESTIGE FOR YOUR TEAM.
YOU THINK THIS IS ABOUT ME?
NO, OF COURSE I DON'T.
BUT OTHER PEOPLE WILL AND THEY'LL USE THAT AS AN EXCUSE NOT TO GIVE YOU WHAT YOU WANT.
THIS IS CRAZY.
PEOPLE ARE DYING AND SCIENTISTS - SCIENTISTS, FOR HEAVEN'S SAKE - ARE MORE WORRIED ABOUT THEIR PERSONAL PRESTIGE THAN ABOUT SOLVING THE PROBLEM?
I THINK YOU'RE OVER-REACTING-
CAN'T YOU HIT UP ONE OF THE PHARMACEUTICAL COMPANIES FOR A CHUNK OF MONEY?
YOU KNOW BIG PHARMA ISN'T INTERESTED. THEY THINK IT'S A STORM THAT WILL PASS SOON ENOUGH.
AASMAH, I WAS AT A CONFERENCE LAST WEEK AND I RAISED THIS VERY ISSUE IN A PRIVATE MEETING.
AND THEY LAUGHED AT ME.
ONE OF THEM SAID, 'YOU STILL DON'T UNDERSTAND HOW PENICILLIN WORKS AFTER ALL THESE YEARS. AND YOU SERIOUSLY EXPECT US TO THROW MONEY AT YOU ON THE OFF-CHANCE YOU'LL FIND SOME MIRACLE DRUG WHEN YOU DON'T EVEN KNOW HOW THE ONES YOU'VE GOT DO WHAT THEY DO?'
THAT'S WHAT I'M UP AGAINST.

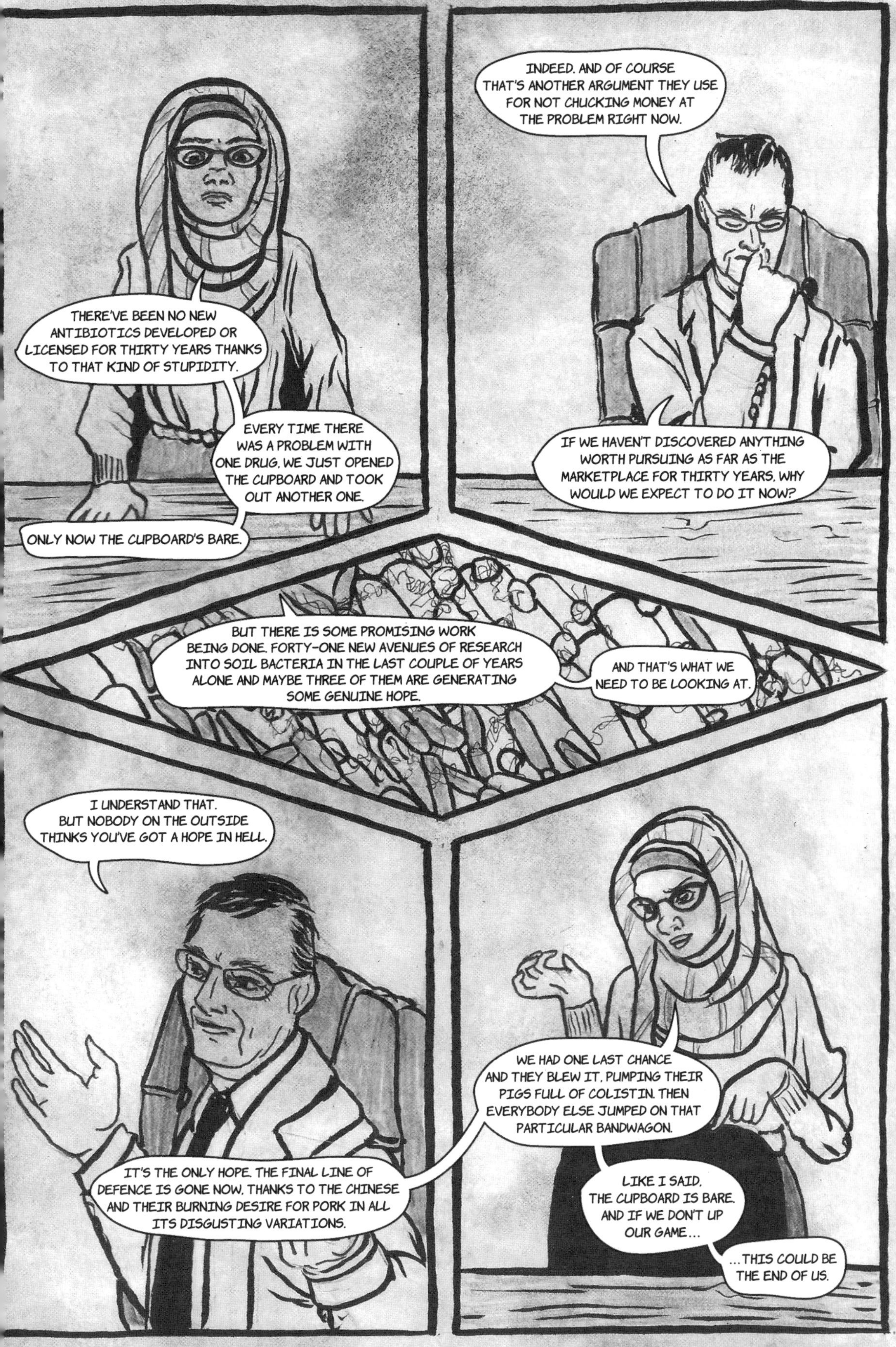
THERE'VE BEEN NO NEW ANTIBIOTICS DEVELOPED OR LICENSED FOR THIRTY YEARS THANKS TO THAT KIND OF STUPIDITY.
EVERY TIME THERE WAS A PROBLEM WITH ONE DRUG, WE JUST OPENED THE CUPBOARD AND TOOK OUT ANOTHER ONE.
ONLY NOW THE CUPBOARD'S BARE.
INDEED. AND OF COURSE THAT'S ANOTHER ARGUMENT THEY USE FOR NOT CHUCKING MONEY AT THE PROBLEM RIGHT NOW.
IF WE HAVEN'T DISCOVERED ANYTHING WORTH PURSUING AS FAR AS THE MARKETPLACE FOR THIRTY YEARS, WHY WOULD WE EXPECT TO DO IT NOW?
BUT THERE IS SOME PROMISING WORK BEING DONE. FORTY-ONE NEW AVENUES OF RESEARCH INTO SOIL BACTERIA IN THE LAST COUPLE OF YEARS ALONE AND MAYBE THREE OF THEM ARE GENERATING SOME GENUINE HOPE.
AND THAT'S WHAT WE NEED TO BE LOOKING AT.
I UNDERSTAND THAT. BUT NOBODY ON THE OUTSIDE THINKS YOU'VE GOT A HOPE IN HELL.
IT'S THE ONLY HOPE. THE FINAL LINE OF DEFENCE IS GONE NOW, THANKS TO THE CHINESE AND THEIR BURNING DESIRE FOR PORK IN ALL ITS DISGUSTING VARIATIONS.
WE HAD ONE LAST CHANCE AND THEY BLEW IT, PUMPING THEIR PIGS FULL OF COLISTIN. THEN EVERYBODY ELSE JUMPED ON THAT PARTICULAR BANDWAGON.
LIKE I SAID, THE CUPBOARD IS BARE. AND IF WE DON'T UP OUR GAME…
…THIS COULD BE THE END OF US.

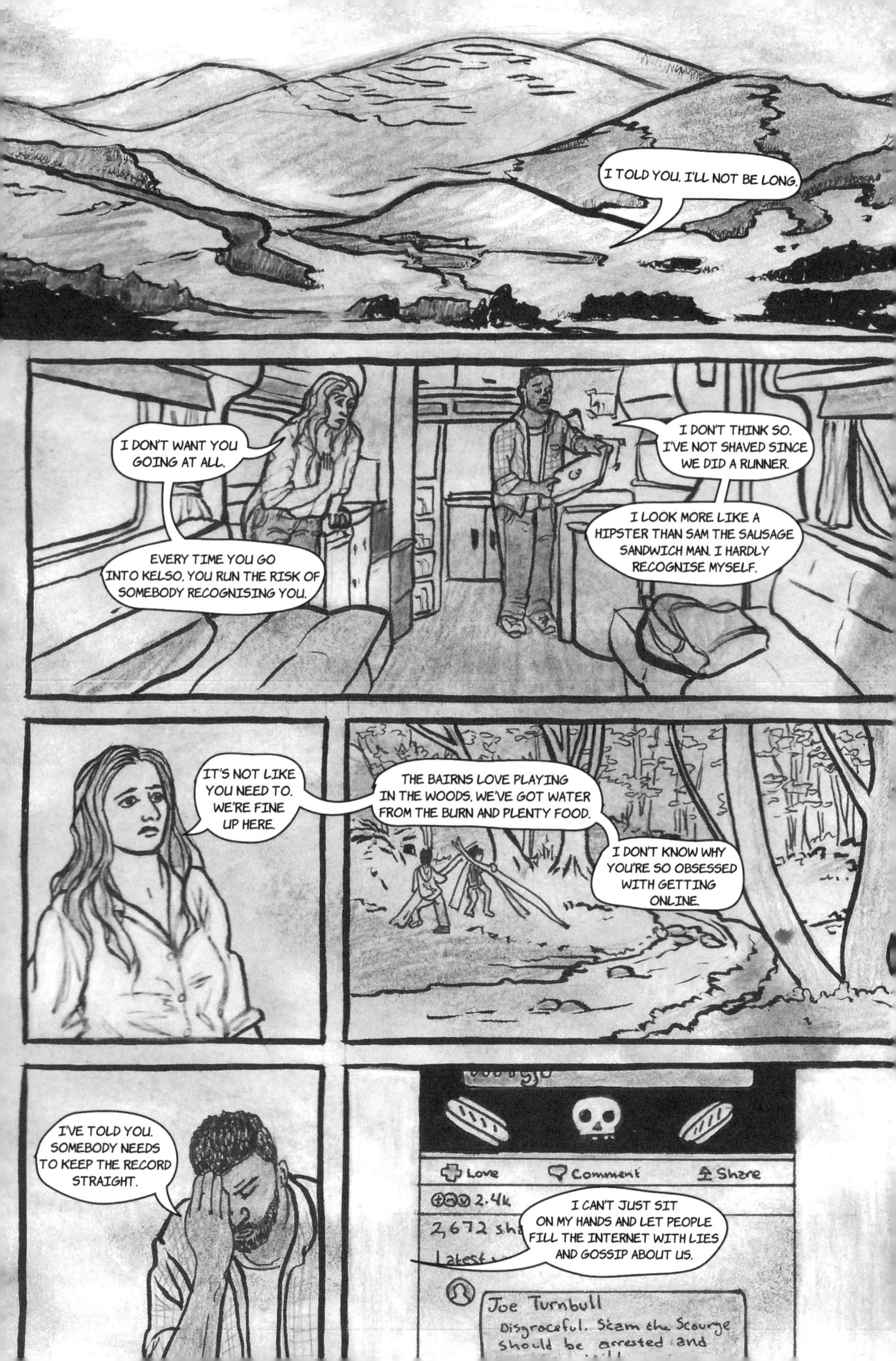
I TOLD YOU. I'LL NOT BE LONG.
I DON'T WANT YOU GOING AT ALL.
EVERY TIME YOU GO INTO KELSO, YOU RUN THE RISK OF SOMEBODY RECOGNISING YOU.
I DON'T THINK SO. I'VE NOT SHAVED SINCE WE DID A RUNNER.
I LOOK MORE LIKE A HIPSTER THAN SAM THE SAUSAGE SANDWICH MAN. I HARDLY RECOGNISE MYSELF.
IT'S NOT LIKE YOU NEED TO. WE'RE FINE UP HERE.
THE BAIRNS LOVE PLAYING IN THE WOODS, WE'VE GOT WATER FROM THE BURN AND PLENTY FOOD.
I DON'T KNOW WHY YOU'RE SO OBSESSED WITH GETTING ONLINE.
I'VE TOLD YOU. SOMEBODY NEEDS TO KEEP THE RECORD STRAIGHT.
Love
Comment
Share
2.4k
I CAN'T JUST SIT ON MY HANDS AND LET PEOPLE FILL THE INTERNET WITH LIES AND GOSSIP ABOUT US.
Joe Turnbull
Disgraceful. Scam the Scourge should be arrested and

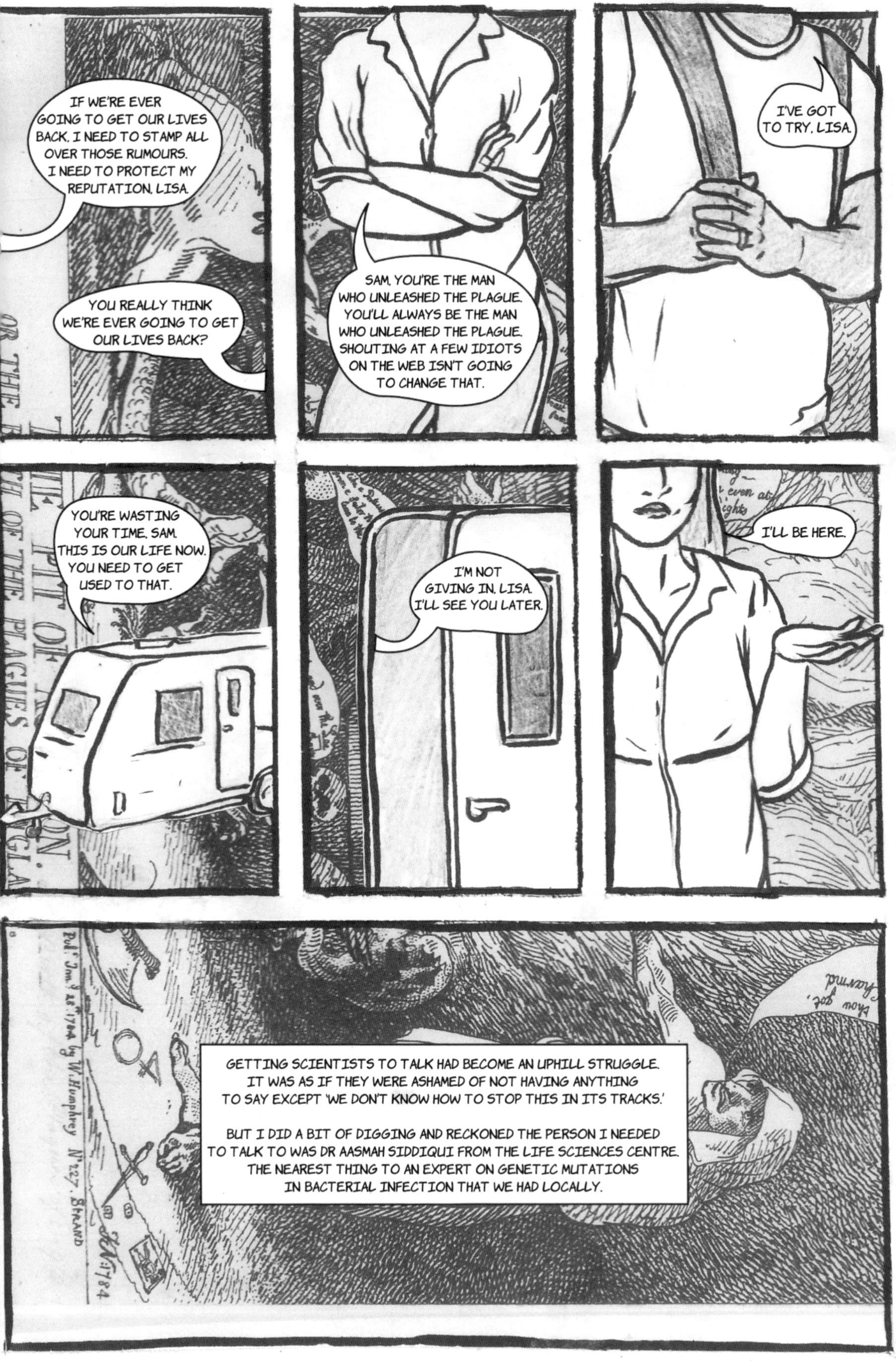
IF WE'RE EVER GOING TO GET OUR LIVES BACK, I NEED TO STAMP ALL OVER THOSE RUMOURS. I NEED TO PROTECT MY REPUTATION, LISA.
YOU REALLY THINK WE'RE EVER GOING TO GET OUR LIVES BACK?
SAM, YOU'RE THE MAN WHO UNLEASHED THE PLAGUE. YOU'LL ALWAYS BE THE MAN WHO UNLEASHED THE PLAGUE. SHOUTING AT A FEW IDIOTS ON THE WEB ISN'T GOING TO CHANGE THAT.
I'VE GOT TO TRY, LISA.
YOU'RE WASTING YOUR TIME, SAM. THIS IS OUR LIFE NOW. YOU NEED TO GET USED TO THAT.
I'M NOT GIVING IN, LISA. I'LL SEE YOU LATER.
I'LL BE HERE.
GETTING SCIENTISTS TO TALK HAD BECOME AN UPHILL STRUGGLE. IT WAS AS IF THEY WERE ASHAMED OF NOT HAVING ANYTHING TO SAY EXCEPT 'WE DON'T KNOW HOW TO STOP THIS IN ITS TRACKS.'
BUT I DID A BIT OF DIGGING AND RECKONED THE PERSON I NEEDED TO TALK TO WAS DR AASMAH SIDDIQUI FROM THE LIFE SCIENCES CENTRE. THE NEAREST THING TO AN EXPERT ON GENETIC MUTATIONS IN BACTERIAL INFECTION THAT WE HAD LOCALLY.

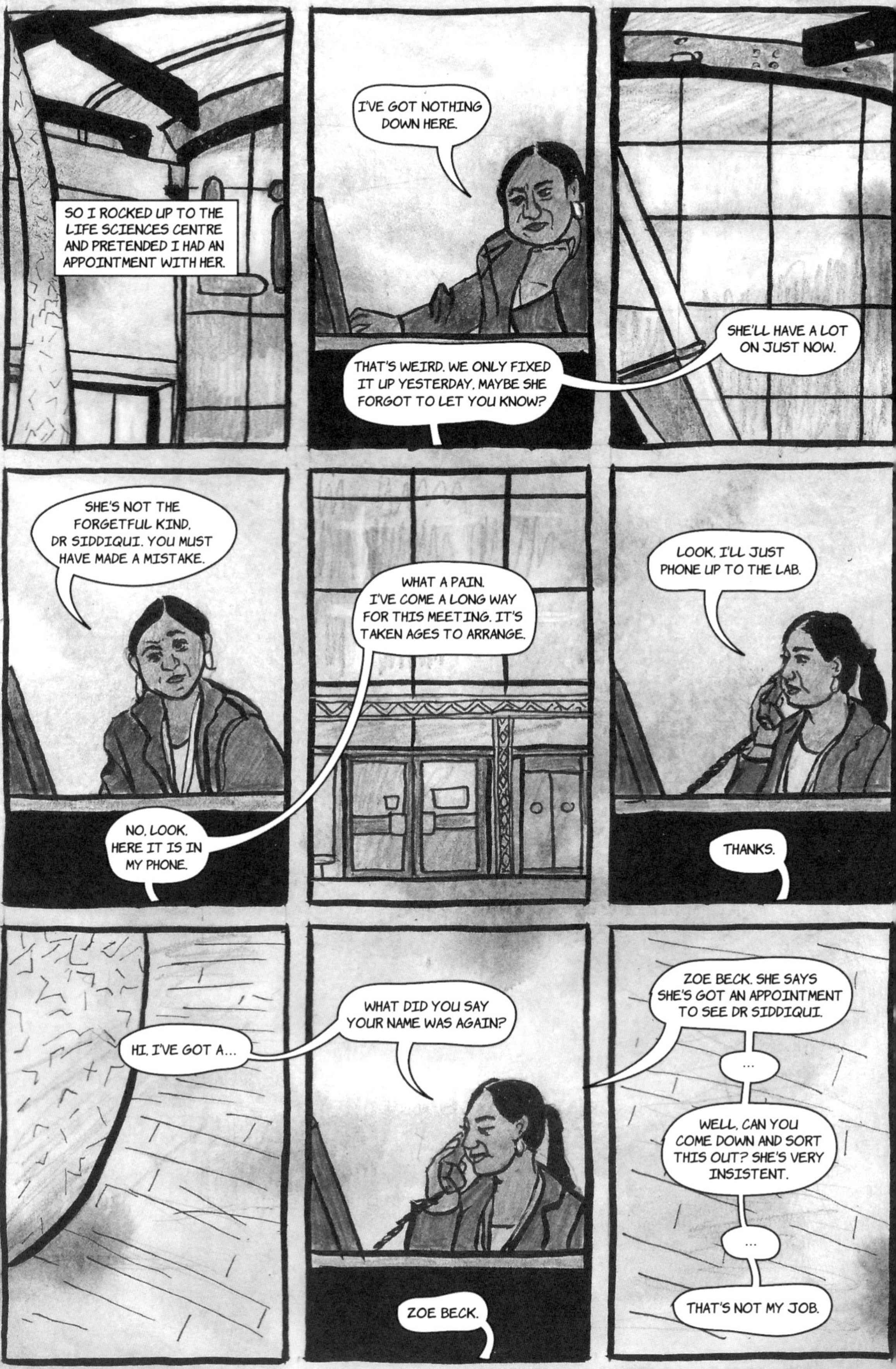
SO I ROCKED UP TO THE LIFE SCIENCES CENTRE AND PRETENDED I HAD AN APPOINTMENT WITH HER.
I'VE GOT NOTHING DOWN HERE.
THAT'S WEIRD. WE ONLY FIXED IT UP YESTERDAY. MAYBE SHE FORGOT TO LET YOU KNOW?
SHE'LL HAVE A LOT ON JUST NOW.
SHE'S NOT THE FORGETFUL KIND, DR SIDDIQUI. YOU MUST HAVE MADE A MISTAKE.
NO, LOOK, HERE IT IS IN MY PHONE.
WHAT A PAIN. I'VE COME A LONG WAY FOR THIS MEETING. IT'S TAKEN AGES TO ARRANGE.
LOOK, I'LL JUST PHONE UP TO THE LAB.
THANKS.
HI, I'VE GOT A…
WHAT DID YOU SAY YOUR NAME WAS AGAIN?
ZOE BECK.
ZOE BECK. SHE SAYS SHE'S GOT AN APPOINTMENT TO SEE DR SIDDIQUI.
…
WELL, CAN YOU COME DOWN AND SORT THIS OUT? SHE'S VERY INSISTENT.
…
THAT'S NOT MY JOB.

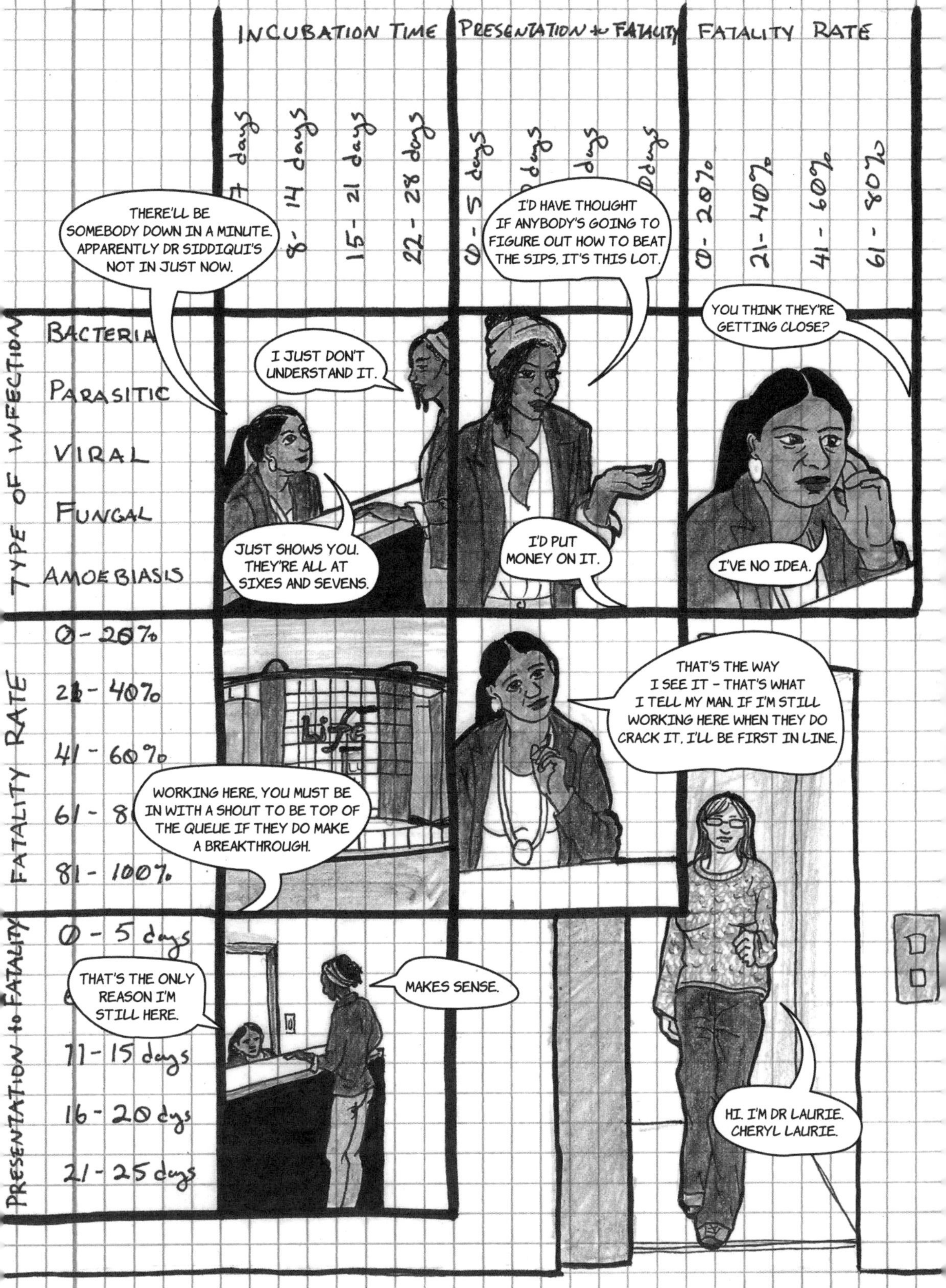
INCUBATION TIME
PRESENTATION to FATALITY
FATALITY RATE
8 - 14 days
15 - 21 days
22 - 28 days
0 - 5 days
0 - 20%
21 - 40%
41 - 60%
61 - 80%
TYPE OF INFECTION
BACTERIA
PARASITIC
VIRAL
FUNGAL
AMOEBIASIS
THERE'LL BE SOMEBODY DOWN IN A MINUTE. APPARENTLY DR SIDDIQUI'S NOT IN JUST NOW.
I JUST DON'T UNDERSTAND IT.
JUST SHOWS YOU. THEY'RE ALL AT SIXES AND SEVENS.
I'D HAVE THOUGHT IF ANYBODY'S GOING TO FIGURE OUT HOW TO BEAT THE SIPS, IT'S THIS LOT.
I'D PUT MONEY ON IT.
YOU THINK THEY'RE GETTING CLOSE?
I'VE NO IDEA.
FATALITY RATE
0 - 20%
21 - 40%
41 - 60%
81 - 100%
Life
WORKING HERE, YOU MUST BE IN WITH A SHOUT TO BE TOP OF THE QUEUE IF THEY DO MAKE A BREAKTHROUGH.
THAT'S THE WAY I SEE IT – THAT'S WHAT I TELL MY MAN. IF I'M STILL WORKING HERE WHEN THEY DO CRACK IT, I'LL BE FIRST IN LINE.
PRESENTATION to FATALITY
0 - 5 days
11 - 15 days
16 - 20 days
21 - 25 days
THAT'S THE ONLY REASON I'M STILL HERE.
MAKES SENSE.
HI. I'M DR LAURIE. CHERYL LAURIE.

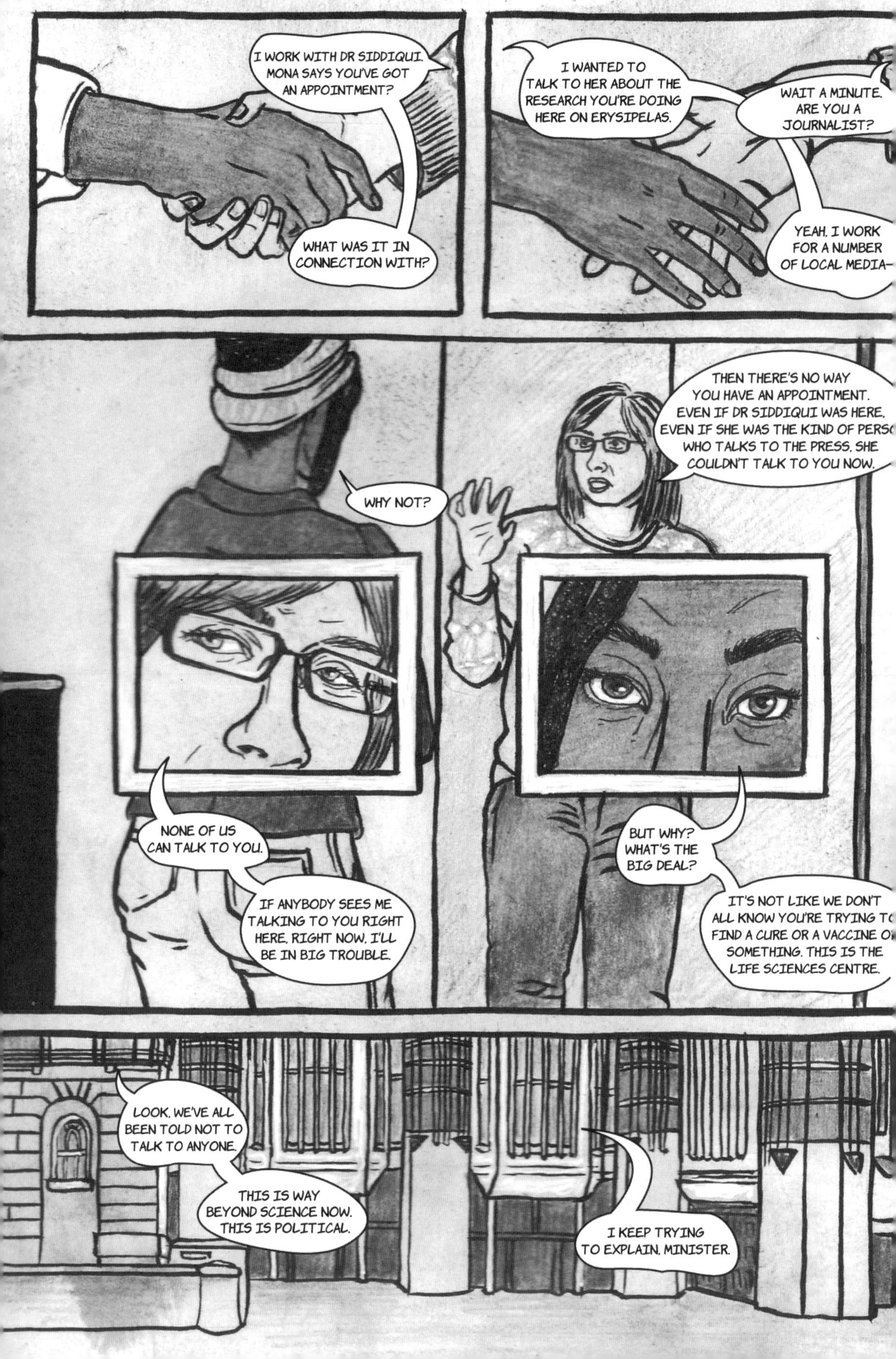
I WORK WITH DR SIDDIQUI. MONA SAYS YOU'VE GOT AN APPOINTMENT?
WHAT WAS IT IN CONNECTION WITH?
I WANTED TO TALK TO HER ABOUT THE RESEARCH YOU'RE DOING HERE ON ERYSIPELAS.
WAIT A MINUTE. ARE YOU A JOURNALIST?
YEAH. I WORK FOR A NUMBER OF LOCAL MEDIA—
THEN THERE'S NO WAY YOU HAVE AN APPOINTMENT. EVEN IF DR SIDDIQUI WAS HERE, EVEN IF SHE WAS THE KIND OF PERSO WHO TALKS TO THE PRESS, SHE COULDN'T TALK TO YOU NOW.
WHY NOT?
NONE OF US CAN TALK TO YOU.
IF ANYBODY SEES ME TALKING TO YOU RIGHT HERE, RIGHT NOW, I'LL BE IN BIG TROUBLE.
BUT WHY? WHAT'S THE BIG DEAL?
IT'S NOT LIKE WE DON'T ALL KNOW YOU'RE TRYING TO FIND A CURE OR A VACCINE OR SOMETHING. THIS IS THE LIFE SCIENCES CENTRE.
LOOK, WE'VE ALL BEEN TOLD NOT TO TALK TO ANYONE.
THIS IS WAY BEYOND SCIENCE NOW. THIS IS POLITICAL.
I KEEP TRYING TO EXPLAIN, MINISTER.

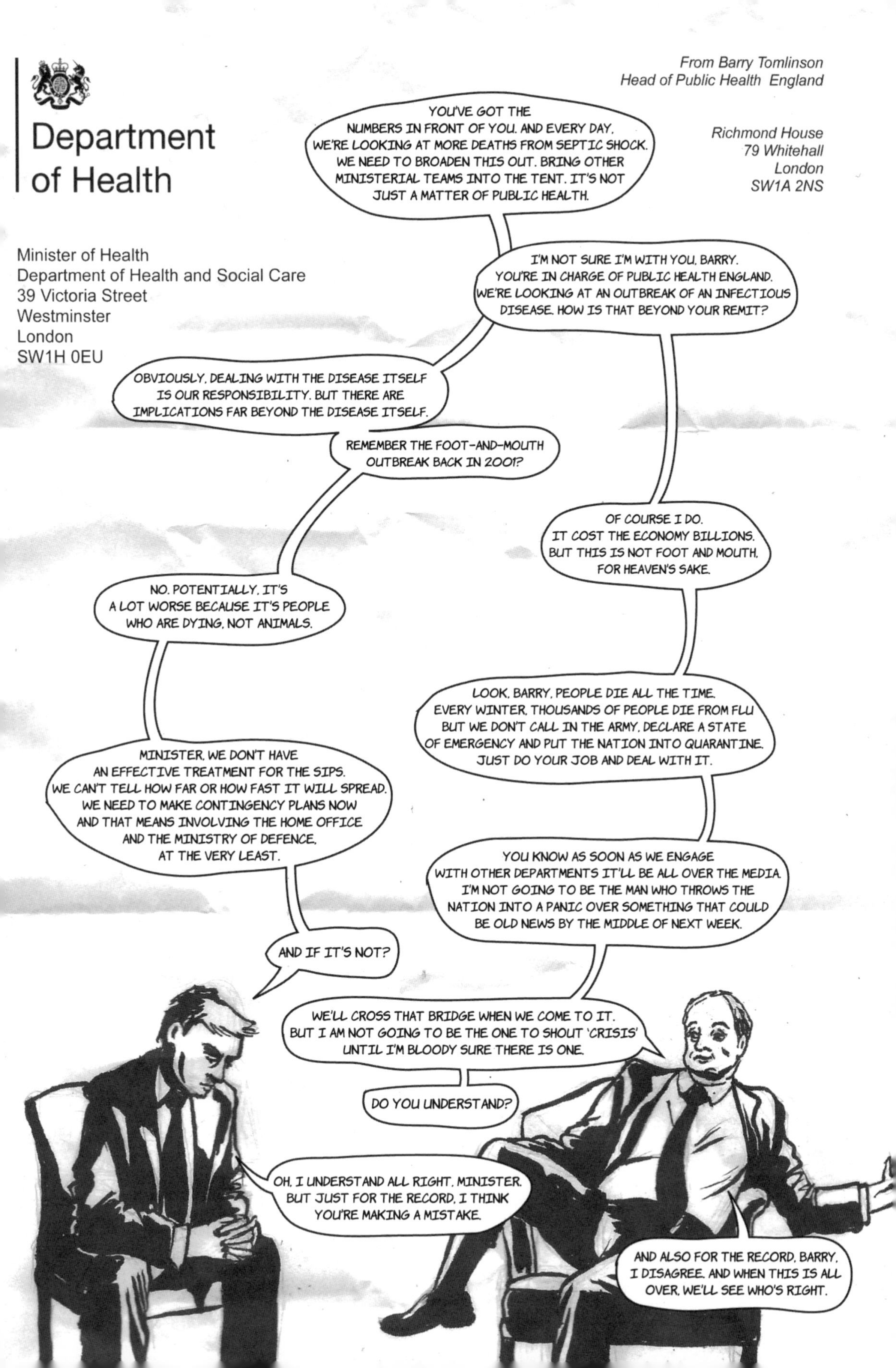
Department of Health
From Barry Tomlinson
Head of Public Health England
Richmond House
79 Whitehall
London
SW1A 2NS
Minister of Health
Department of Health and Social Care
39 Victoria Street
Westminster
London
SW1H 0EU
YOU'VE GOT THE NUMBERS IN FRONT OF YOU. AND EVERY DAY, WE'RE LOOKING AT MORE DEATHS FROM SEPTIC SHOCK. WE NEED TO BROADEN THIS OUT. BRING OTHER MINISTERIAL TEAMS INTO THE TENT. IT'S NOT JUST A MATTER OF PUBLIC HEALTH.
I'M NOT SURE I'M WITH YOU, BARRY. YOU'RE IN CHARGE OF PUBLIC HEALTH ENGLAND. WE'RE LOOKING AT AN OUTBREAK OF AN INFECTIOUS DISEASE. HOW IS THAT BEYOND YOUR REMIT?
OBVIOUSLY, DEALING WITH THE DISEASE ITSELF IS OUR RESPONSIBILITY. BUT THERE ARE IMPLICATIONS FAR BEYOND THE DISEASE ITSELF.
REMEMBER THE FOOT-AND-MOUTH OUTBREAK BACK IN 2001?
OF COURSE I DO. IT COST THE ECONOMY BILLIONS. BUT THIS IS NOT FOOT AND MOUTH, FOR HEAVEN'S SAKE.
NO. POTENTIALLY, IT'S A LOT WORSE BECAUSE IT'S PEOPLE WHO ARE DYING, NOT ANIMALS.
LOOK, BARRY, PEOPLE DIE ALL THE TIME. EVERY WINTER, THOUSANDS OF PEOPLE DIE FROM FLU BUT WE DON'T CALL IN THE ARMY, DECLARE A STATE OF EMERGENCY AND PUT THE NATION INTO QUARANTINE. JUST DO YOUR JOB AND DEAL WITH IT.
MINISTER, WE DON'T HAVE AN EFFECTIVE TREATMENT FOR THE SIPS. WE CAN'T TELL HOW FAR OR HOW FAST IT WILL SPREAD. WE NEED TO MAKE CONTINGENCY PLANS NOW AND THAT MEANS INVOLVING THE HOME OFFICE AND THE MINISTRY OF DEFENCE, AT THE VERY LEAST.
YOU KNOW AS SOON AS WE ENGAGE WITH OTHER DEPARTMENTS IT'LL BE ALL OVER THE MEDIA. I'M NOT GOING TO BE THE MAN WHO THROWS THE NATION INTO A PANIC OVER SOMETHING THAT COULD BE OLD NEWS BY THE MIDDLE OF NEXT WEEK.
AND IF IT'S NOT?
WE'LL CROSS THAT BRIDGE WHEN WE COME TO IT. BUT I AM NOT GOING TO BE THE ONE TO SHOUT 'CRISIS' UNTIL I'M BLOODY SURE THERE IS ONE.
DO YOU UNDERSTAND?
OH, I UNDERSTAND ALL RIGHT, MINISTER. BUT JUST FOR THE RECORD, I THINK YOU'RE MAKING A MISTAKE.
AND ALSO FOR THE RECORD, BARRY, I DISAGREE. AND WHEN THIS IS ALL OVER, WE'LL SEE WHO'S RIGHT.

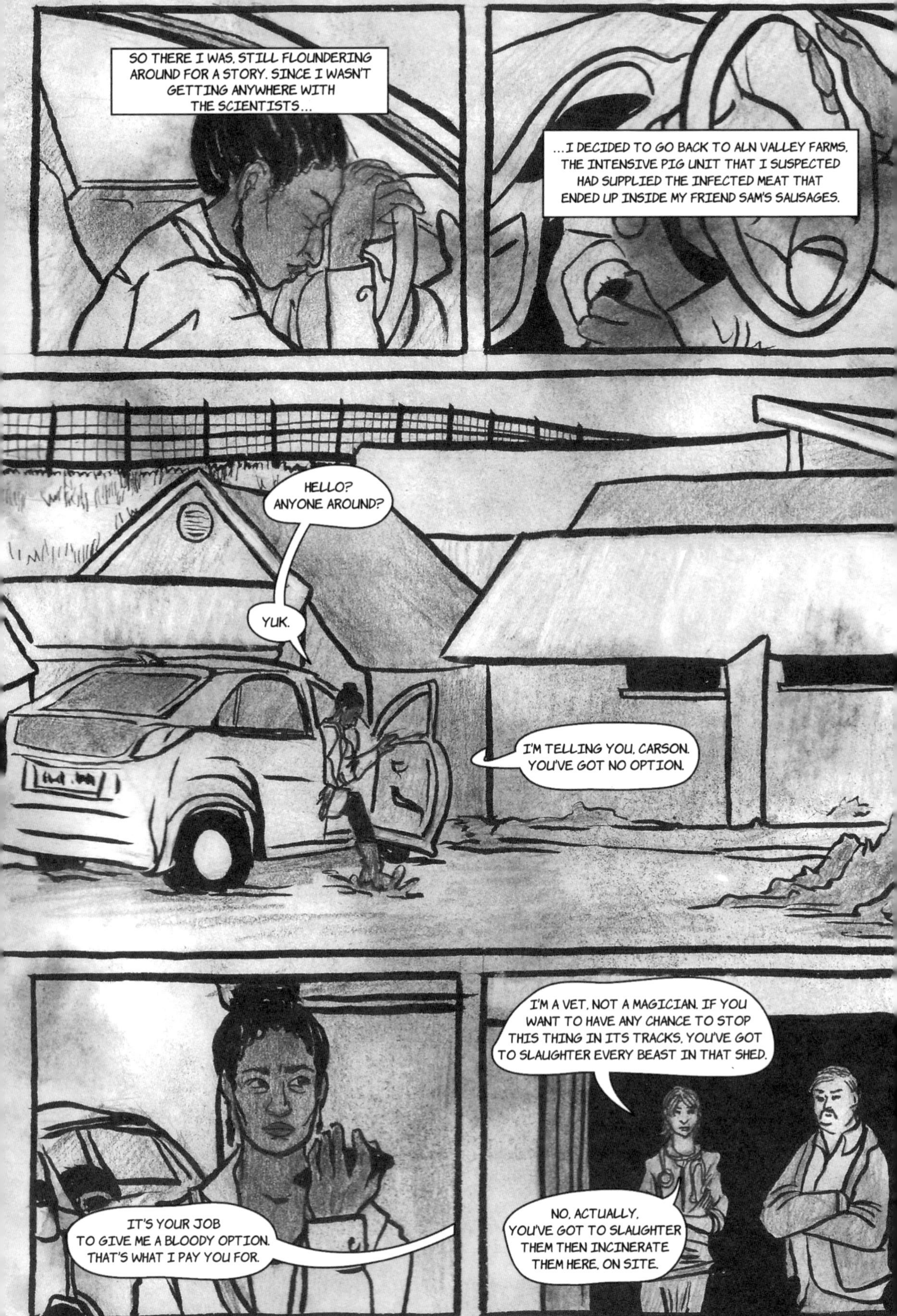
SO THERE I WAS, STILL FLOUNDERING AROUND FOR A STORY. SINCE I WASN'T GETTING ANYWHERE WITH THE SCIENTISTS...
...I DECIDED TO GO BACK TO ALN VALLEY FARMS, THE INTENSIVE PIG UNIT THAT I SUSPECTED HAD SUPPLIED THE INFECTED MEAT THAT ENDED UP INSIDE MY FRIEND SAM'S SAUSAGES.
HELLO? ANYONE AROUND?
YUK.
I'M TELLING YOU, CARSON. YOU'VE GOT NO OPTION.
IT'S YOUR JOB TO GIVE ME A BLOODY OPTION. THAT'S WHAT I PAY YOU FOR.
I'M A VET, NOT A MAGICIAN. IF YOU WANT TO HAVE ANY CHANCE TO STOP THIS THING IN ITS TRACKS, YOU'VE GOT TO SLAUGHTER EVERY BEAST IN THAT SHED.
NO, ACTUALLY, YOU'VE GOT TO SLAUGHTER THEM THEN INCINERATE THEM HERE, ON SITE.

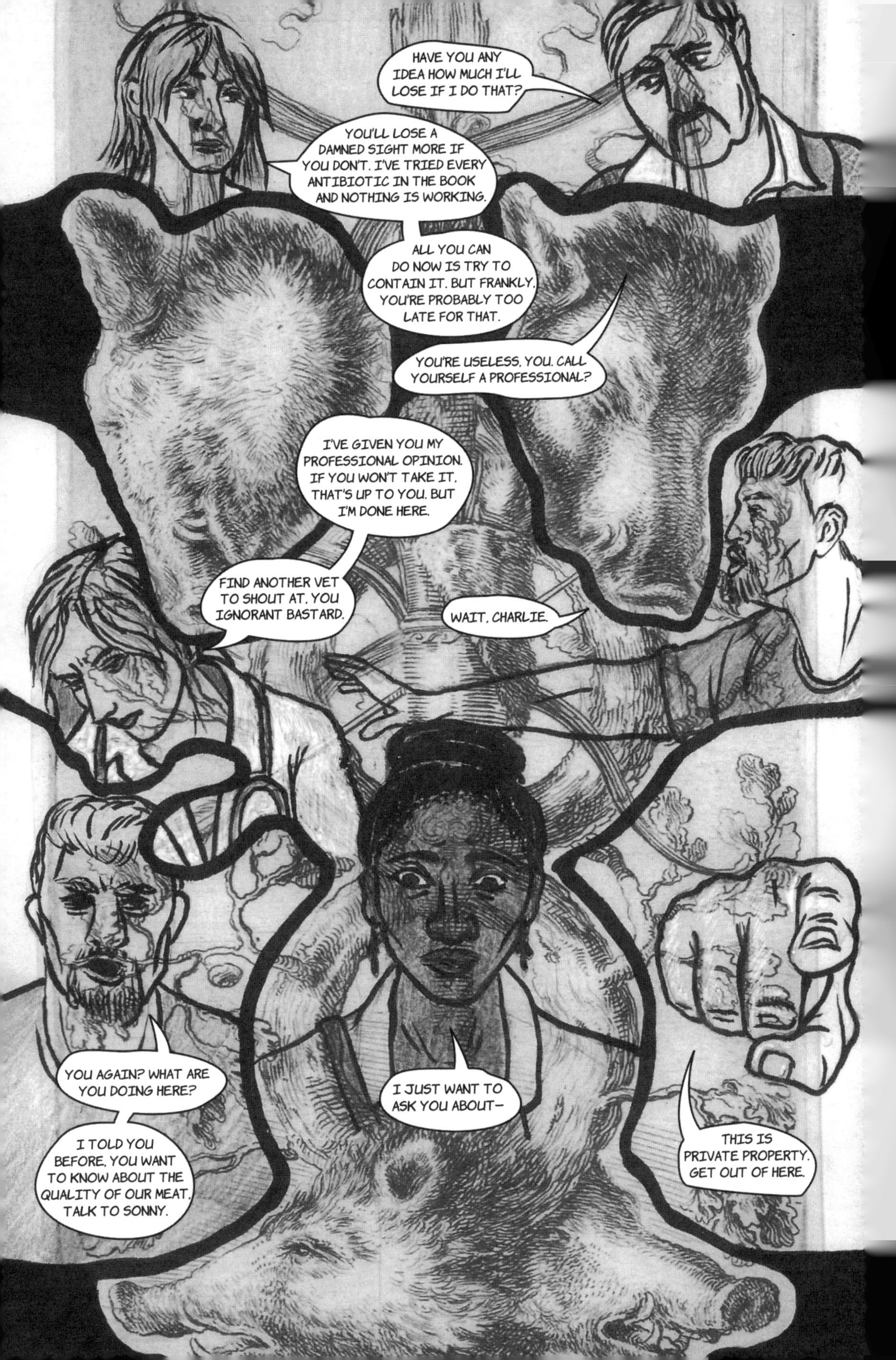
HAVE YOU ANY IDEA HOW MUCH I'LL LOSE IF I DO THAT?
YOU'LL LOSE A DAMNED SIGHT MORE IF YOU DON'T. I'VE TRIED EVERY ANTIBIOTIC IN THE BOOK AND NOTHING IS WORKING.
ALL YOU CAN DO NOW IS TRY TO CONTAIN IT. BUT FRANKLY, YOU'RE PROBABLY TOO LATE FOR THAT.
YOU'RE USELESS, YOU. CALL YOURSELF A PROFESSIONAL?
I'VE GIVEN YOU MY PROFESSIONAL OPINION. IF YOU WON'T TAKE IT, THAT'S UP TO YOU. BUT I'M DONE HERE.
FIND ANOTHER VET TO SHOUT AT, YOU IGNORANT BASTARD.
WAIT, CHARLIE.
YOU AGAIN? WHAT ARE YOU DOING HERE?
I TOLD YOU BEFORE, YOU WANT TO KNOW ABOUT THE QUALITY OF OUR MEAT, TALK TO SONNY.
I JUST WANT TO ASK YOU ABOUT—
THIS IS PRIVATE PROPERTY. GET OUT OF HERE.

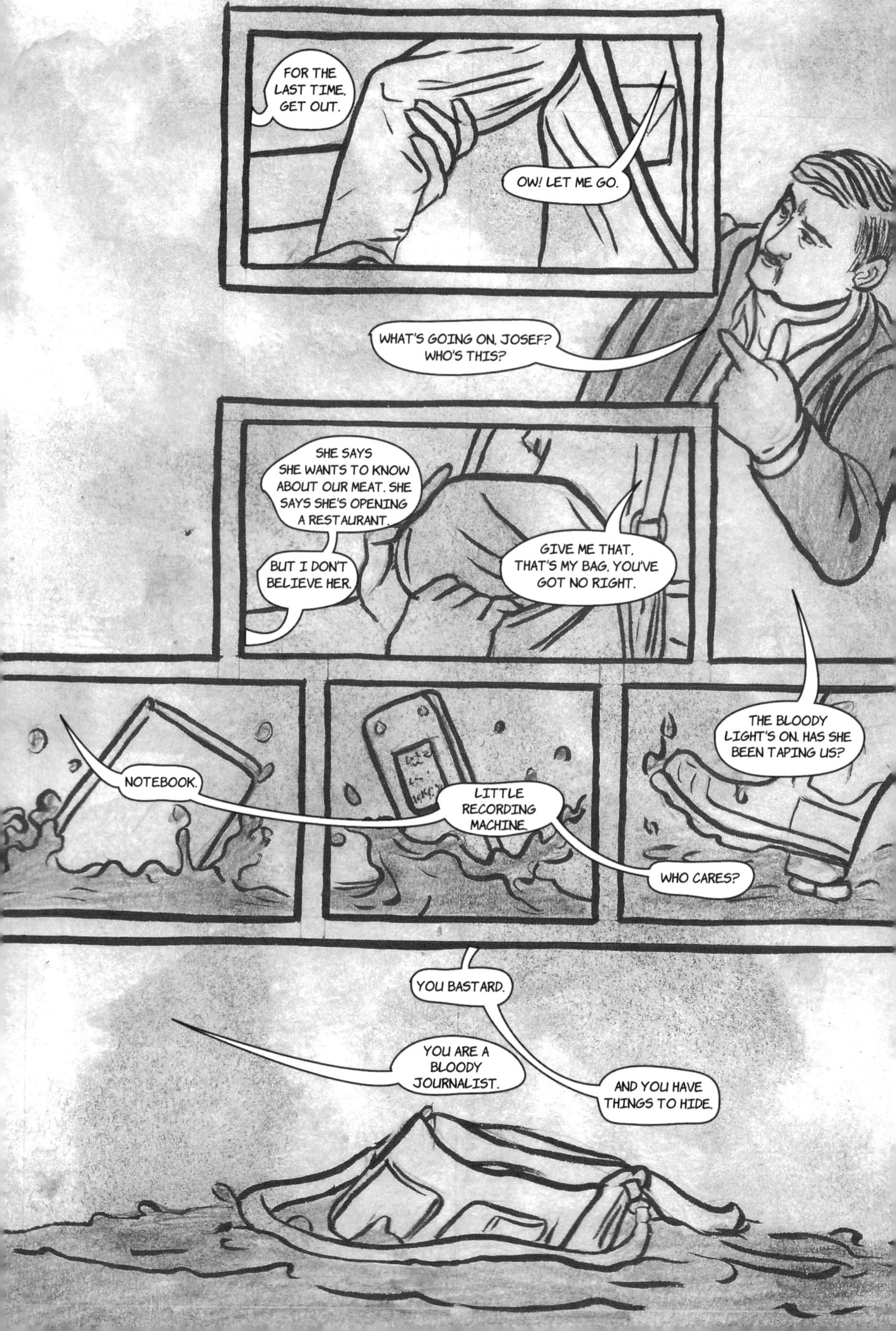
FOR THE LAST TIME. GET OUT.
OW! LET ME GO.
WHAT'S GOING ON, JOSEF? WHO'S THIS?
SHE SAYS SHE WANTS TO KNOW ABOUT OUR MEAT. SHE SAYS SHE'S OPENING A RESTAURANT.
BUT I DON'T BELIEVE HER.
GIVE ME THAT. THAT'S MY BAG. YOU'VE GOT NO RIGHT.
NOTEBOOK.
LITTLE RECORDING MACHINE.
THE BLOODY LIGHT'S ON. HAS SHE BEEN TAPING US?
WHO CARES?
YOU BASTARD.
YOU ARE A BLOODY JOURNALIST.
AND YOU HAVE THINGS TO HIDE.

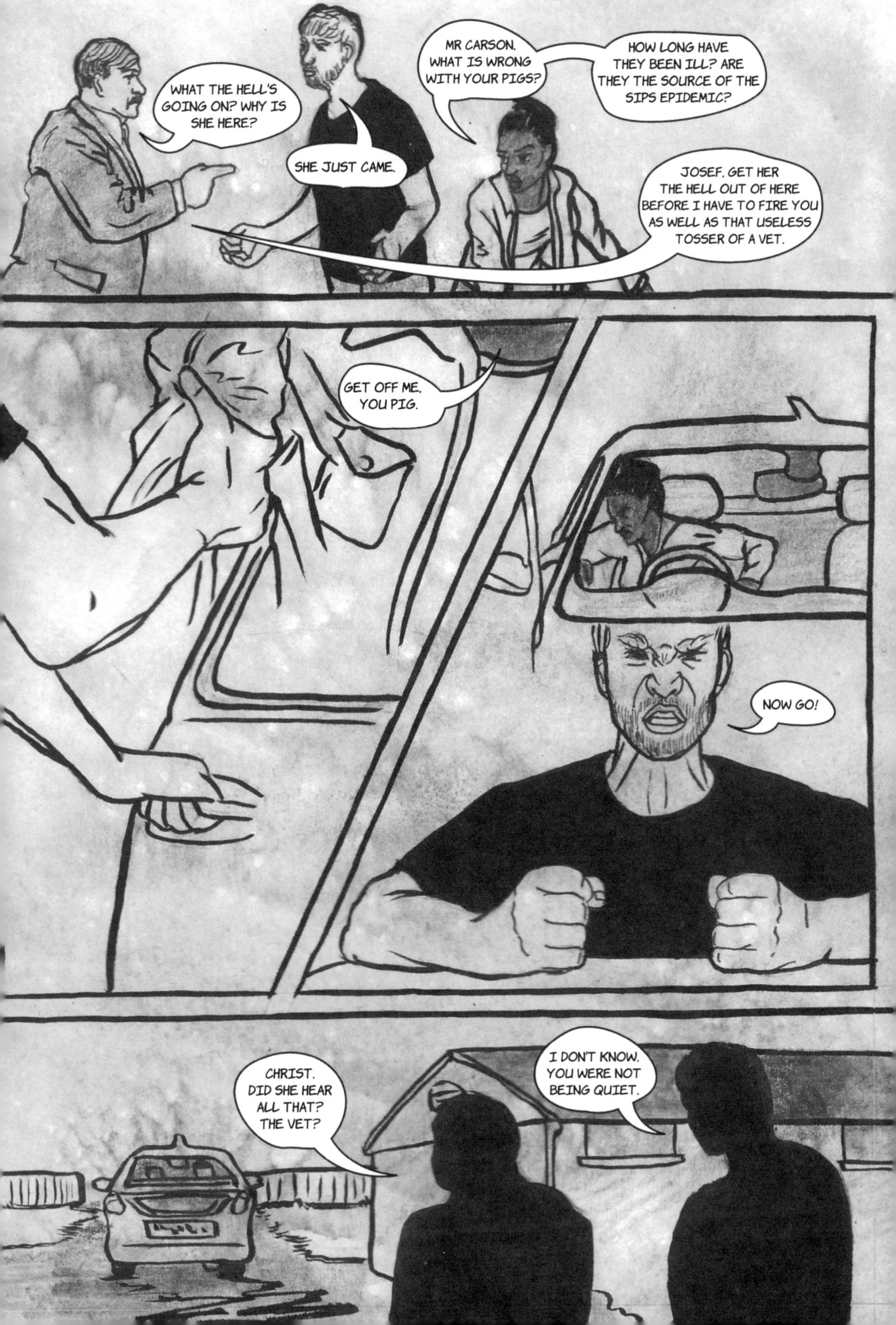
WHAT THE HELL'S GOING ON? WHY IS SHE HERE?
SHE JUST CAME.
MR CARSON, WHAT IS WRONG WITH YOUR PIGS?
HOW LONG HAVE THEY BEEN ILL? ARE THEY THE SOURCE OF THE SIPS EPIDEMIC?
JOSEF, GET HER THE HELL OUT OF HERE BEFORE I HAVE TO FIRE YOU AS WELL AS THAT USELESS TOSSER OF A VET.
GET OFF ME, YOU PIG.
NOW GO!
CHRIST. DID SHE HEAR ALL THAT? THE VET?
I DON'T KNOW. YOU WERE NOT BEING QUIET.

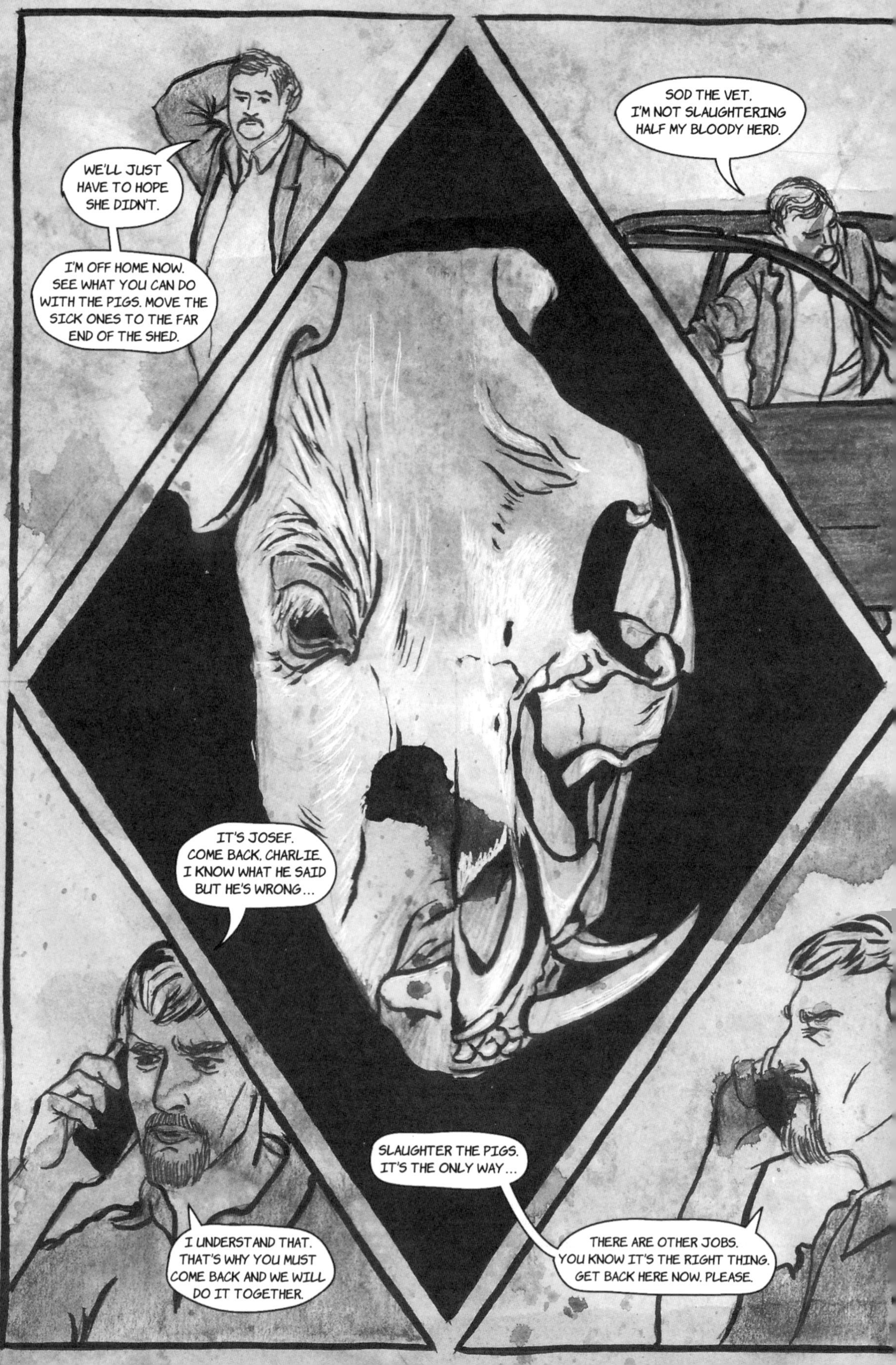
WE'LL JUST HAVE TO HOPE SHE DIDN'T.
I'M OFF HOME NOW. SEE WHAT YOU CAN DO WITH THE PIGS. MOVE THE SICK ONES TO THE FAR END OF THE SHED.
SOD THE VET. I'M NOT SLAUGHTERING HALF MY BLOODY HERD.
IT'S JOSEF. COME BACK, CHARLIE. I KNOW WHAT HE SAID BUT HE'S WRONG...
SLAUGHTER THE PIGS. IT'S THE ONLY WAY...
I UNDERSTAND THAT. THAT'S WHY YOU MUST COME BACK AND WE WILL DO IT TOGETHER.
THERE ARE OTHER JOBS. YOU KNOW IT'S THE RIGHT THING. GET BACK HERE NOW. PLEASE.

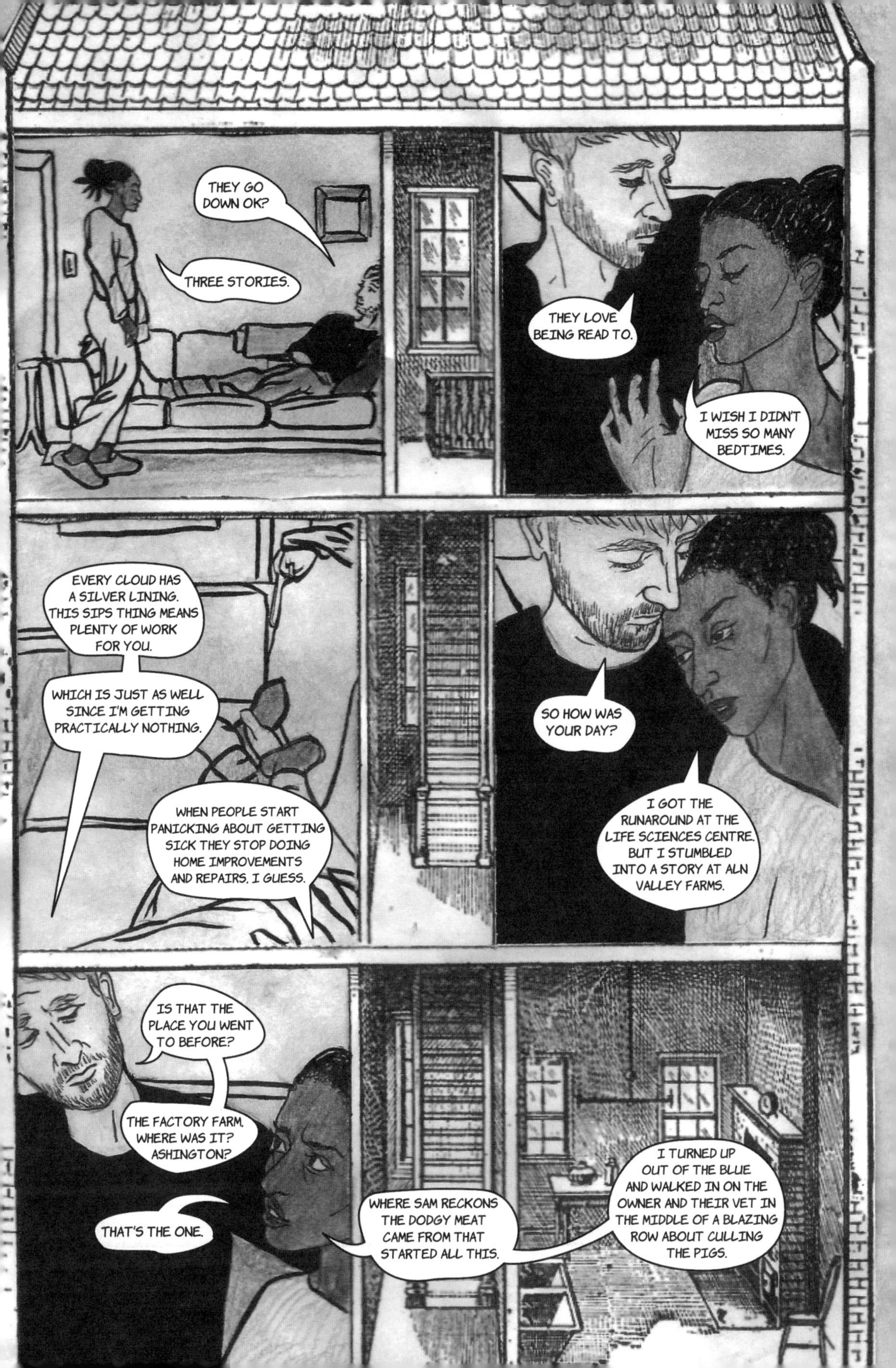
THEY GO DOWN OK?
THREE STORIES.
THEY LOVE BEING READ TO.
I WISH I DIDN'T MISS SO MANY BEDTIMES.
EVERY CLOUD HAS A SILVER LINING. THIS SIPS THING MEANS PLENTY OF WORK FOR YOU.
WHICH IS JUST AS WELL SINCE I'M GETTING PRACTICALLY NOTHING.
WHEN PEOPLE START PANICKING ABOUT GETTING SICK THEY STOP DOING HOME IMPROVEMENTS AND REPAIRS, I GUESS.
SO HOW WAS YOUR DAY?
I GOT THE RUNAROUND AT THE LIFE SCIENCES CENTRE. BUT I STUMBLED INTO A STORY AT ALN VALLEY FARMS.
IS THAT THE PLACE YOU WENT TO BEFORE?
THE FACTORY FARM, WHERE WAS IT? ASHINGTON?
THAT'S THE ONE.
WHERE SAM RECKONS THE DODGY MEAT CAME FROM THAT STARTED ALL THIS.
I TURNED UP OUT OF THE BLUE AND WALKED IN ON THE OWNER AND THEIR VET IN THE MIDDLE OF A BLAZING ROW ABOUT CULLING THE PIGS.

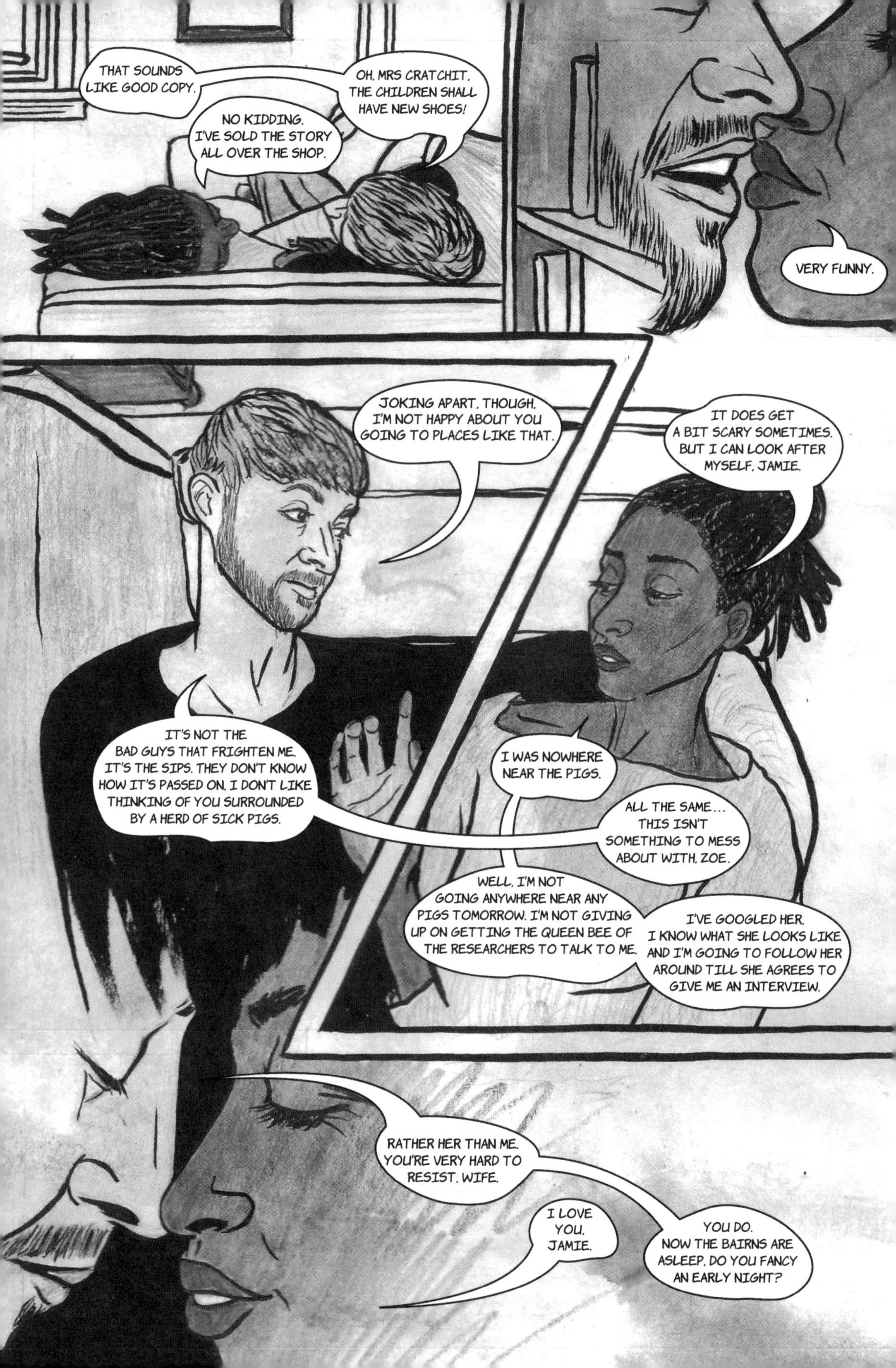
THAT SOUNDS LIKE GOOD COPY.
OH, MRS CRATCHIT, THE CHILDREN SHALL HAVE NEW SHOES!
NO KIDDING. I'VE SOLD THE STORY ALL OVER THE SHOP.
VERY FUNNY.
JOKING APART, THOUGH, I'M NOT HAPPY ABOUT YOU GOING TO PLACES LIKE THAT.
IT DOES GET A BIT SCARY SOMETIMES. BUT I CAN LOOK AFTER MYSELF, JAMIE.
IT'S NOT THE BAD GUYS THAT FRIGHTEN ME. IT'S THE SIPS. THEY DON'T KNOW HOW IT'S PASSED ON. I DON'T LIKE THINKING OF YOU SURROUNDED BY A HERD OF SICK PIGS.
I WAS NOWHERE NEAR THE PIGS.
ALL THE SAME… THIS ISN'T SOMETHING TO MESS ABOUT WITH, ZOE.
WELL, I'M NOT GOING ANYWHERE NEAR ANY PIGS TOMORROW. I'M NOT GIVING UP ON GETTING THE QUEEN BEE OF THE RESEARCHERS TO TALK TO ME.
I'VE GOOGLED HER. I KNOW WHAT SHE LOOKS LIKE AND I'M GOING TO FOLLOW HER AROUND TILL SHE AGREES TO GIVE ME AN INTERVIEW.
RATHER HER THAN ME. YOU'RE VERY HARD TO RESIST, WIFE.
I LOVE YOU, JAMIE.
YOU DO. NOW THE BAIRNS ARE ASLEEP, DO YOU FANCY AN EARLY NIGHT?

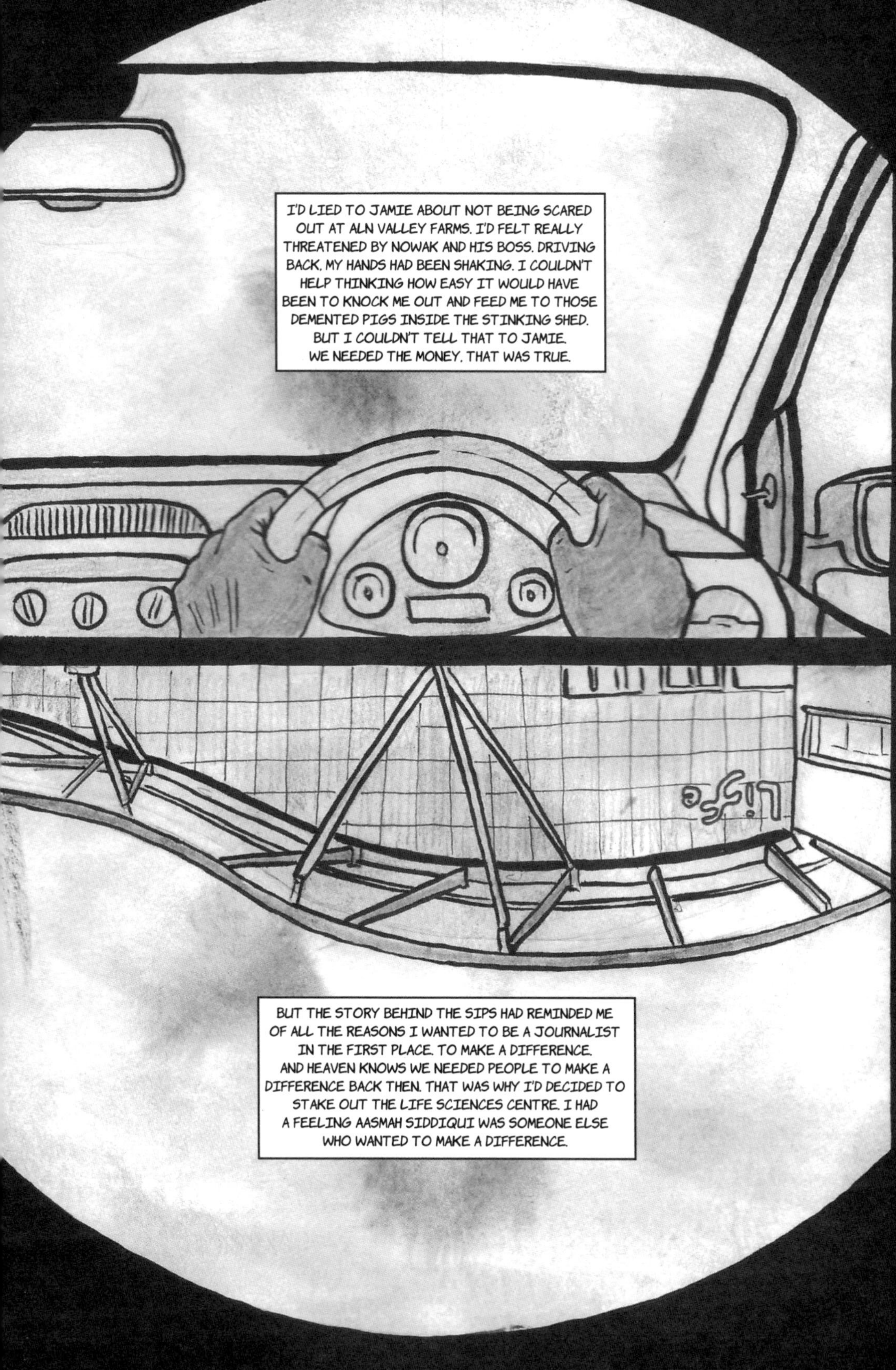
I'D LIED TO JAMIE ABOUT NOT BEING SCARED OUT AT ALN VALLEY FARMS. I'D FELT REALLY THREATENED BY NOWAK AND HIS BOSS. DRIVING BACK, MY HANDS HAD BEEN SHAKING. I COULDN'T HELP THINKING HOW EASY IT WOULD HAVE BEEN TO KNOCK ME OUT AND FEED ME TO THOSE DEMENTED PIGS INSIDE THE STINKING SHED. BUT I COULDN'T TELL THAT TO JAMIE. WE NEEDED THE MONEY, THAT WAS TRUE.
BUT THE STORY BEHIND THE SIPS HAD REMINDED ME OF ALL THE REASONS I WANTED TO BE A JOURNALIST IN THE FIRST PLACE. TO MAKE A DIFFERENCE. AND HEAVEN KNOWS WE NEEDED PEOPLE TO MAKE A DIFFERENCE BACK THEN. THAT WAS WHY I'D DECIDED TO STAKE OUT THE LIFE SCIENCES CENTRE. I HAD A FEELING AASMAH SIDDIQUI WAS SOMEONE ELSE WHO WANTED TO MAKE A DIFFERENCE.

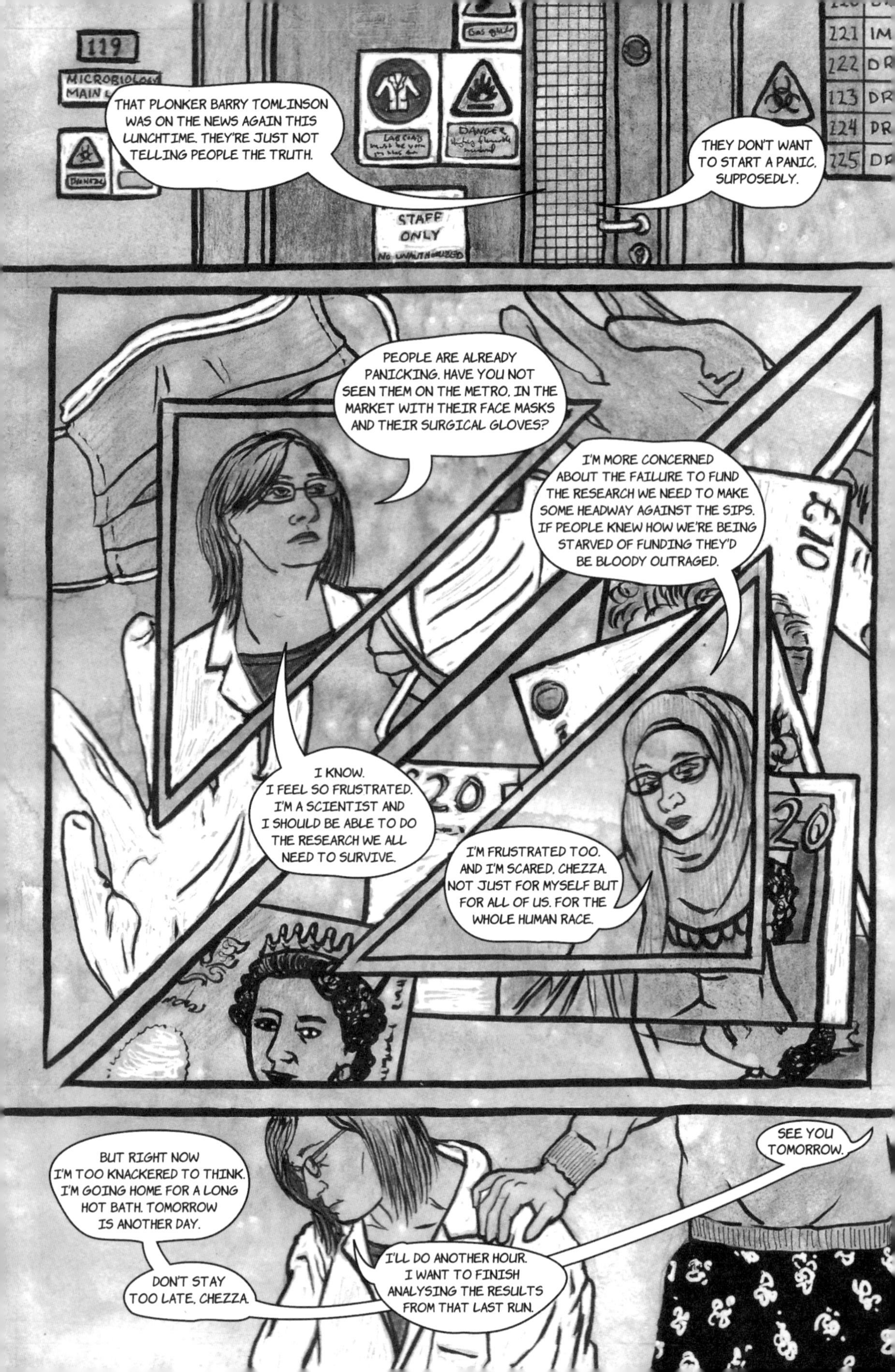
119
DANGER
STAFF ONLY
THAT PLONKER BARRY TOMLINSON WAS ON THE NEWS AGAIN THIS LUNCHTIME. THEY'RE JUST NOT TELLING PEOPLE THE TRUTH.
THEY DON'T WANT TO START A PANIC, SUPPOSEDLY.
PEOPLE ARE ALREADY PANICKING. HAVE YOU NOT SEEN THEM ON THE METRO, IN THE MARKET WITH THEIR FACE MASKS AND THEIR SURGICAL GLOVES?
I'M MORE CONCERNED ABOUT THE FAILURE TO FUND THE RESEARCH WE NEED TO MAKE SOME HEADWAY AGAINST THE SIPS. IF PEOPLE KNEW HOW WE'RE BEING STARVED OF FUNDING THEY'D BE BLOODY OUTRAGED.
I KNOW. I FEEL SO FRUSTRATED. I'M A SCIENTIST AND I SHOULD BE ABLE TO DO THE RESEARCH WE ALL NEED TO SURVIVE.
I'M FRUSTRATED TOO. AND I'M SCARED, CHEZZA. NOT JUST FOR MYSELF BUT FOR ALL OF US. FOR THE WHOLE HUMAN RACE.
BUT RIGHT NOW I'M TOO KNACKERED TO THINK. I'M GOING HOME FOR A LONG HOT BATH. TOMORROW IS ANOTHER DAY.
DON'T STAY TOO LATE, CHEZZA.
I'LL DO ANOTHER HOUR. I WANT TO FINISH ANALYSING THE RESULTS FROM THAT LAST RUN.
SEE YOU TOMORROW.

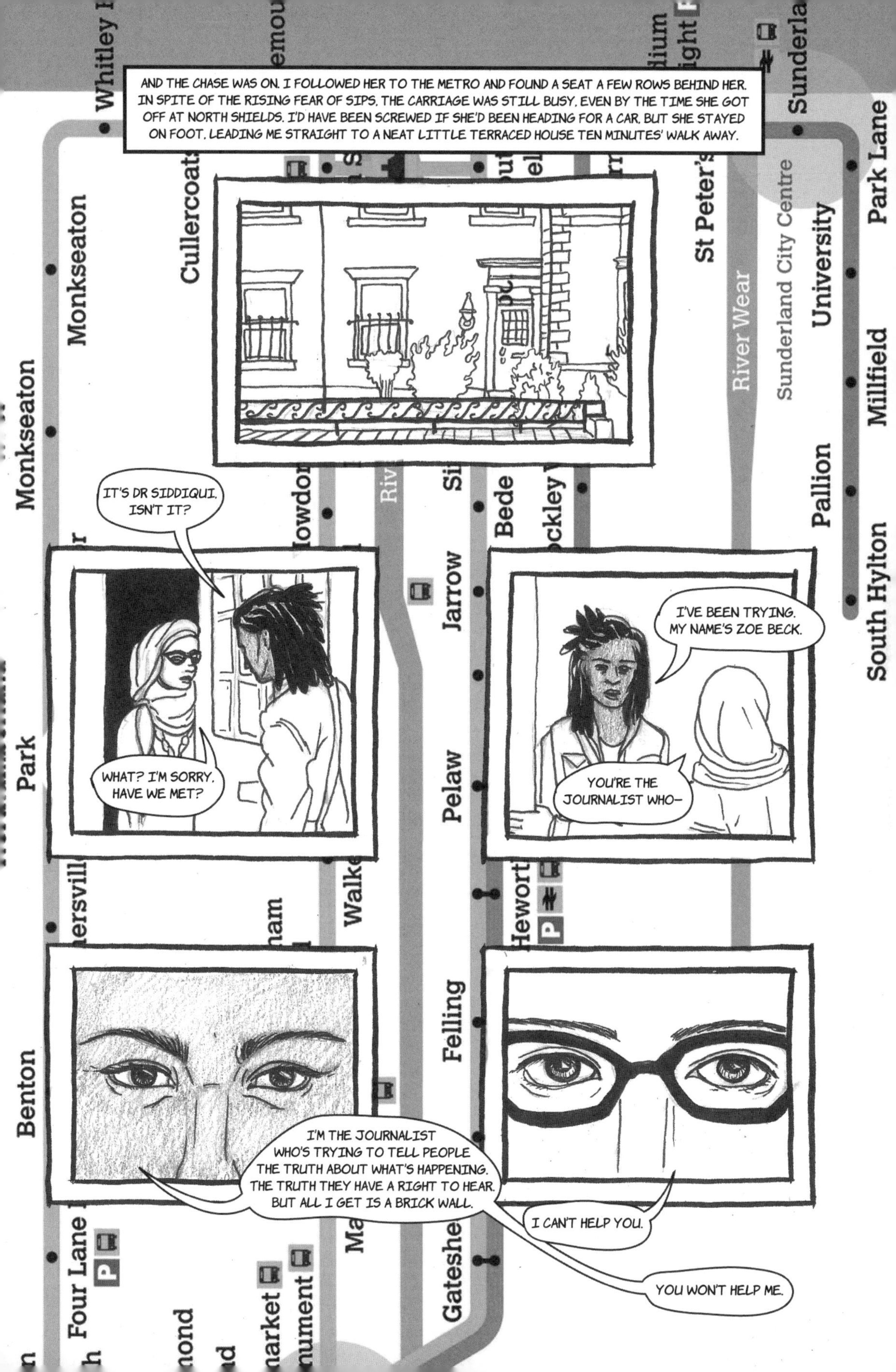
AND THE CHASE WAS ON. I FOLLOWED HER TO THE METRO AND FOUND A SEAT A FEW ROWS BEHIND HER. IN SPITE OF THE RISING FEAR OF SIPS, THE CARRIAGE WAS STILL BUSY, EVEN BY THE TIME SHE GOT OFF AT NORTH SHIELDS. I'D HAVE BEEN SCREWED IF SHE'D BEEN HEADING FOR A CAR, BUT SHE STAYED ON FOOT, LEADING ME STRAIGHT TO A NEAT LITTLE TERRACED HOUSE TEN MINUTES' WALK AWAY.
IT'S DR SIDDIQUI, ISN'T IT?
WHAT? I'M SORRY, HAVE WE MET?
I'VE BEEN TRYING. MY NAME'S ZOE BECK.
YOU'RE THE JOURNALIST WHO–
I'M THE JOURNALIST WHO'S TRYING TO TELL PEOPLE THE TRUTH ABOUT WHAT'S HAPPENING. THE TRUTH THEY HAVE A RIGHT TO HEAR. BUT ALL I GET IS A BRICK WALL.
I CAN'T HELP YOU.
YOU WON'T HELP ME.

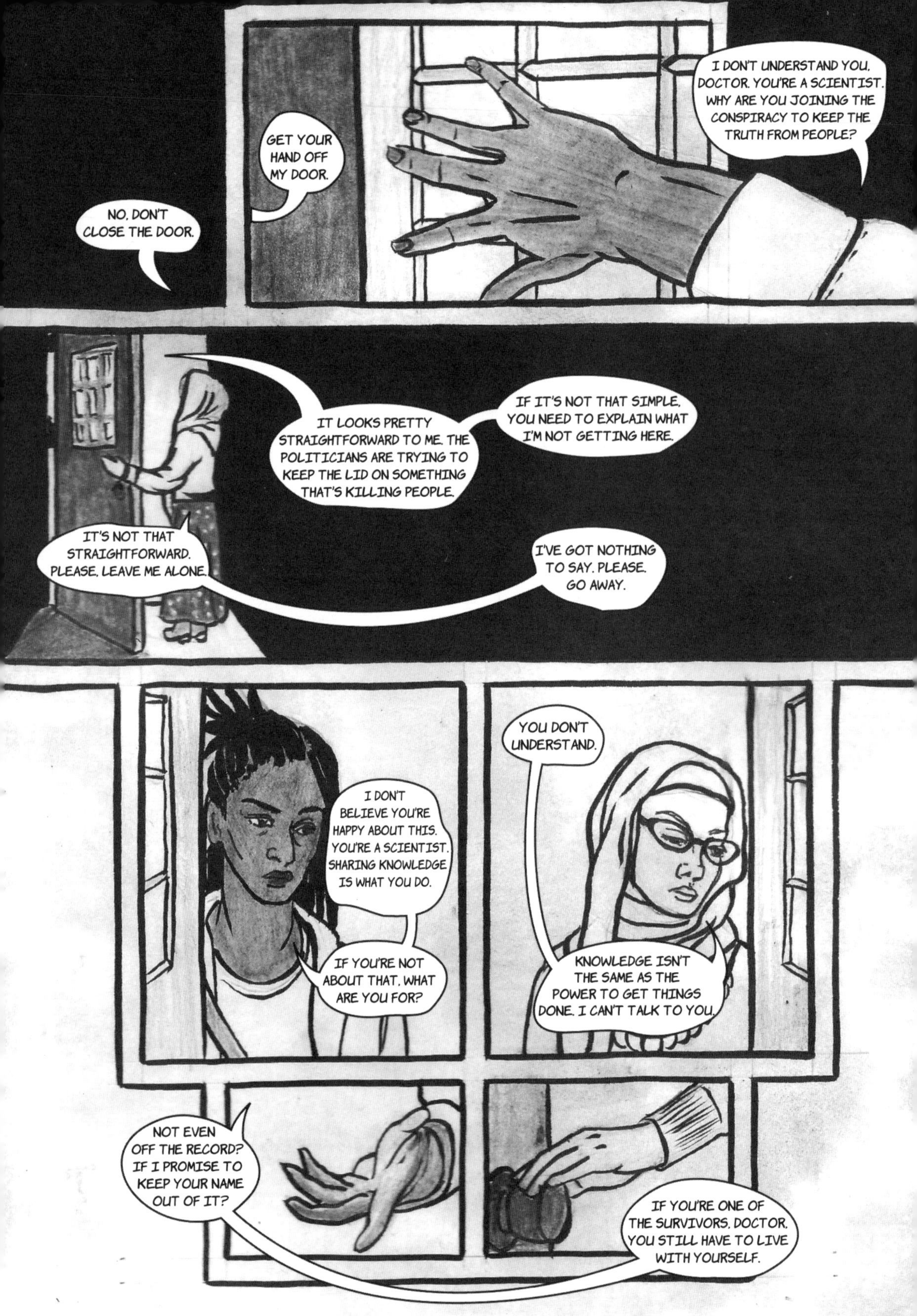
NO, DON'T CLOSE THE DOOR.
GET YOUR HAND OFF MY DOOR.
I DON'T UNDERSTAND YOU, DOCTOR. YOU'RE A SCIENTIST. WHY ARE YOU JOINING THE CONSPIRACY TO KEEP THE TRUTH FROM PEOPLE?
IT LOOKS PRETTY STRAIGHTFORWARD TO ME. THE POLITICIANS ARE TRYING TO KEEP THE LID ON SOMETHING THAT'S KILLING PEOPLE.
IF IT'S NOT THAT SIMPLE, YOU NEED TO EXPLAIN WHAT I'M NOT GETTING HERE.
IT'S NOT THAT STRAIGHTFORWARD. PLEASE, LEAVE ME ALONE.
I'VE GOT NOTHING TO SAY. PLEASE. GO AWAY.
I DON'T BELIEVE YOU'RE HAPPY ABOUT THIS. YOU'RE A SCIENTIST. SHARING KNOWLEDGE IS WHAT YOU DO.
IF YOU'RE NOT ABOUT THAT, WHAT ARE YOU FOR?
YOU DON'T UNDERSTAND.
KNOWLEDGE ISN'T THE SAME AS THE POWER TO GET THINGS DONE. I CAN'T TALK TO YOU.
NOT EVEN OFF THE RECORD? IF I PROMISE TO KEEP YOUR NAME OUT OF IT?
IF YOU'RE ONE OF THE SURVIVORS, DOCTOR, YOU STILL HAVE TO LIVE WITH YOURSELF.

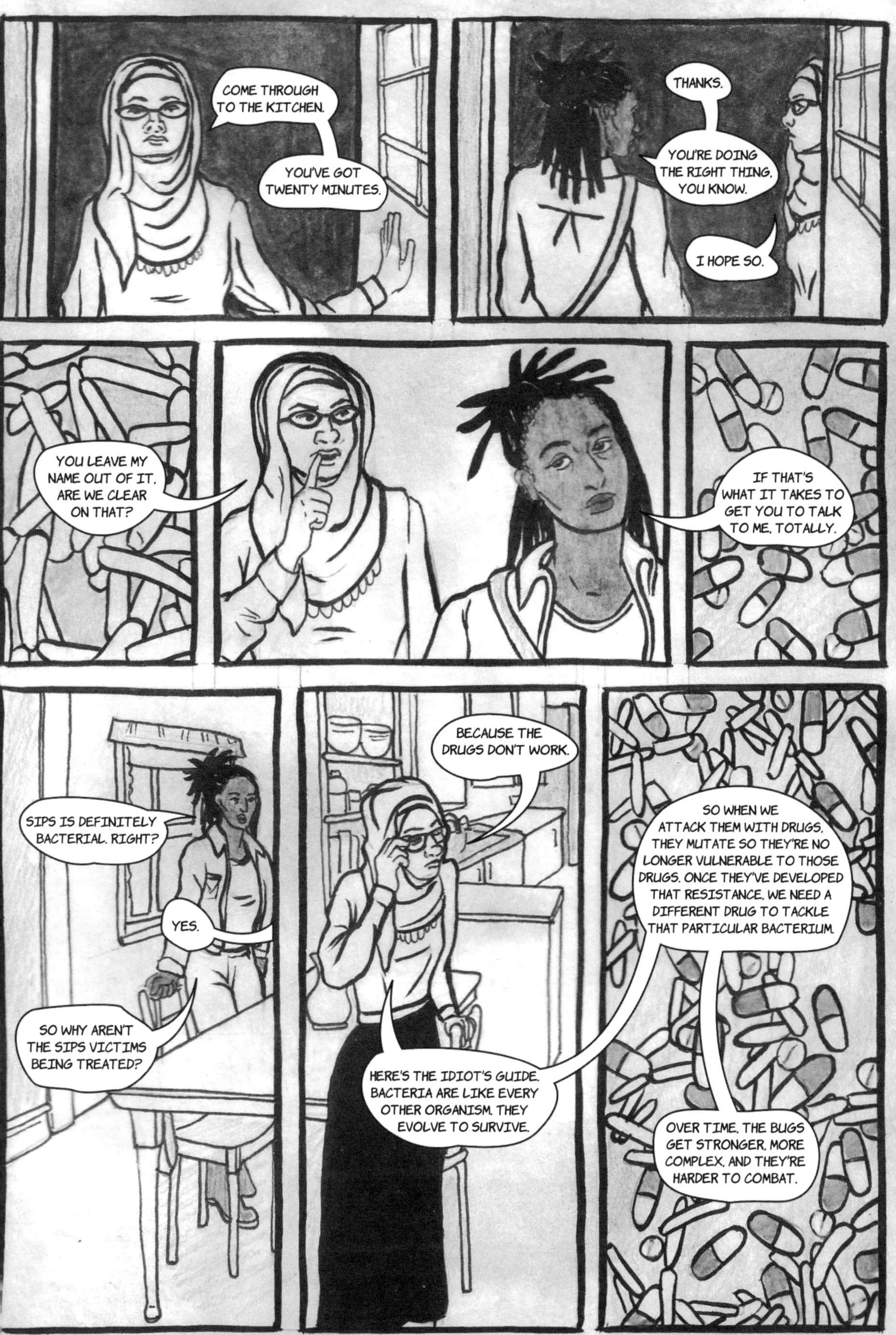
COME THROUGH TO THE KITCHEN.
YOU'VE GOT TWENTY MINUTES.
THANKS.
YOU'RE DOING THE RIGHT THING, YOU KNOW.
I HOPE SO.
YOU LEAVE MY NAME OUT OF IT. ARE WE CLEAR ON THAT?
IF THAT'S WHAT IT TAKES TO GET YOU TO TALK TO ME, TOTALLY.
SIPS IS DEFINITELY BACTERIAL. RIGHT?
YES.
SO WHY AREN'T THE SIPS VICTIMS BEING TREATED?
BECAUSE THE DRUGS DON'T WORK.
HERE'S THE IDIOT'S GUIDE. BACTERIA ARE LIKE EVERY OTHER ORGANISM. THEY EVOLVE TO SURVIVE.
SO WHEN WE ATTACK THEM WITH DRUGS, THEY MUTATE SO THEY'RE NO LONGER VULNERABLE TO THOSE DRUGS. ONCE THEY'VE DEVELOPED THAT RESISTANCE, WE NEED A DIFFERENT DRUG TO TACKLE THAT PARTICULAR BACTERIUM.
OVER TIME, THE BUGS GET STRONGER, MORE COMPLEX, AND THEY'RE HARDER TO COMBAT.

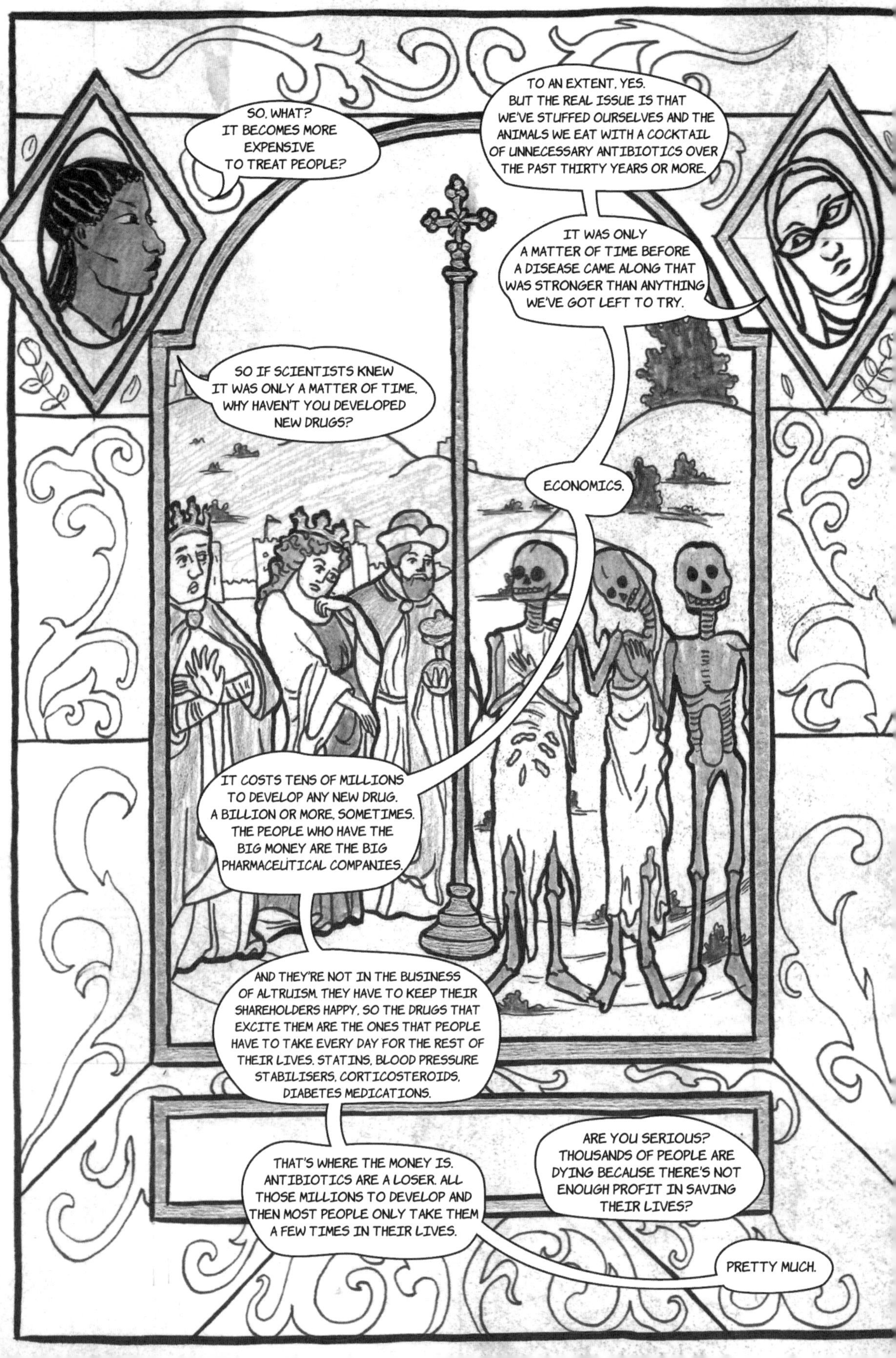
SO, WHAT? IT BECOMES MORE EXPENSIVE TO TREAT PEOPLE?
TO AN EXTENT, YES. BUT THE REAL ISSUE IS THAT WE'VE STUFFED OURSELVES AND THE ANIMALS WE EAT WITH A COCKTAIL OF UNNECESSARY ANTIBIOTICS OVER THE PAST THIRTY YEARS OR MORE.
IT WAS ONLY A MATTER OF TIME BEFORE A DISEASE CAME ALONG THAT WAS STRONGER THAN ANYTHING WE'VE GOT LEFT TO TRY.
SO IF SCIENTISTS KNEW IT WAS ONLY A MATTER OF TIME, WHY HAVEN'T YOU DEVELOPED NEW DRUGS?
ECONOMICS.
IT COSTS TENS OF MILLIONS TO DEVELOP ANY NEW DRUG. A BILLION OR MORE, SOMETIMES. THE PEOPLE WHO HAVE THE BIG MONEY ARE THE BIG PHARMACEUTICAL COMPANIES.
AND THEY'RE NOT IN THE BUSINESS OF ALTRUISM. THEY HAVE TO KEEP THEIR SHAREHOLDERS HAPPY, SO THE DRUGS THAT EXCITE THEM ARE THE ONES THAT PEOPLE HAVE TO TAKE EVERY DAY FOR THE REST OF THEIR LIVES. STATINS, BLOOD PRESSURE STABILISERS, CORTICOSTEROIDS, DIABETES MEDICATIONS.
THAT'S WHERE THE MONEY IS. ANTIBIOTICS ARE A LOSER. ALL THOSE MILLIONS TO DEVELOP AND THEN MOST PEOPLE ONLY TAKE THEM A FEW TIMES IN THEIR LIVES.
ARE YOU SERIOUS? THOUSANDS OF PEOPLE ARE DYING BECAUSE THERE'S NOT ENOUGH PROFIT IN SAVING THEIR LIVES?
PRETTY MUCH.

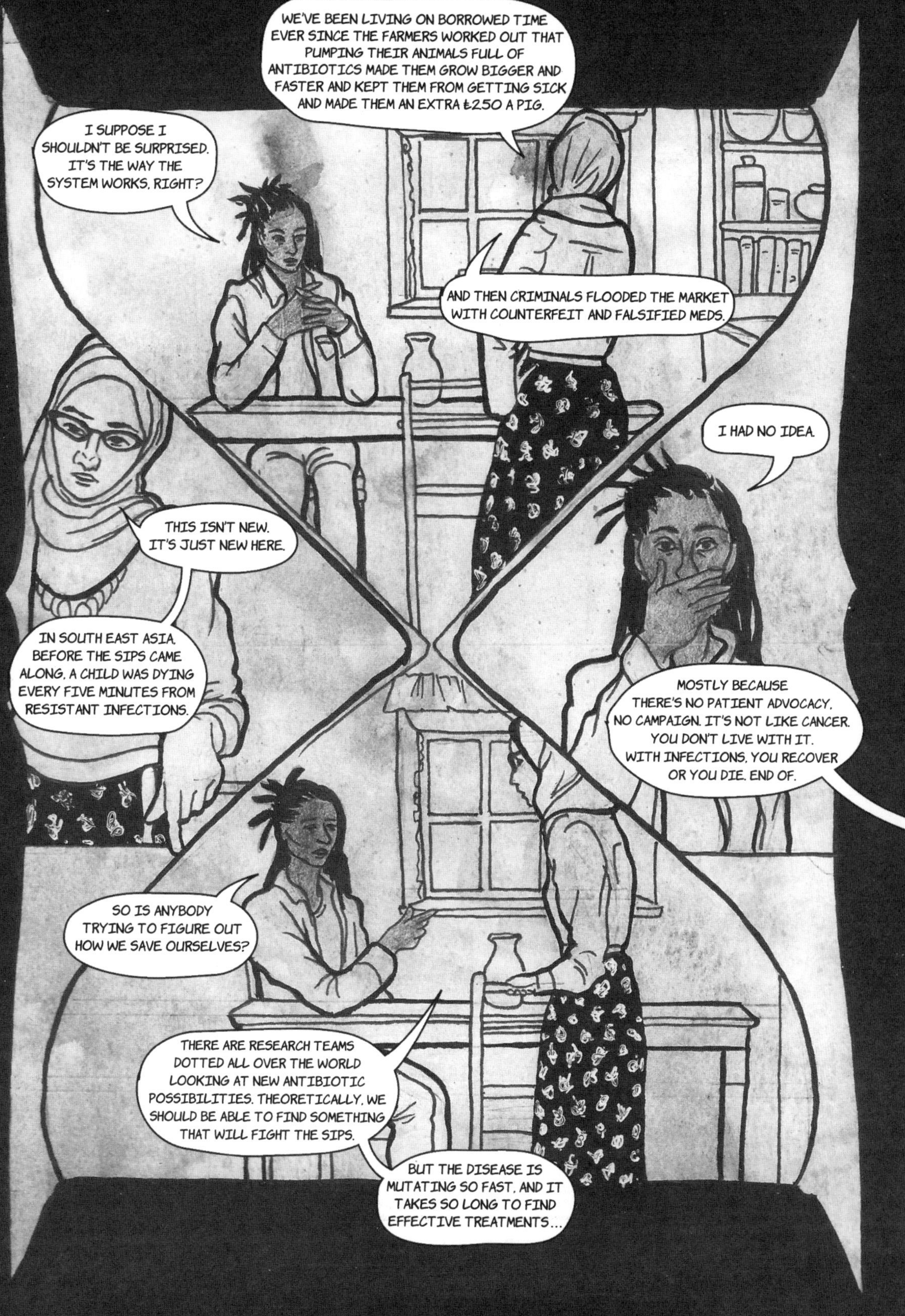
WE'VE BEEN LIVING ON BORROWED TIME EVER SINCE THE FARMERS WORKED OUT THAT PUMPING THEIR ANIMALS FULL OF ANTIBIOTICS MADE THEM GROW BIGGER AND FASTER AND KEPT THEM FROM GETTING SICK AND MADE THEM AN EXTRA ₺250 A PIG.
I SUPPOSE I SHOULDN'T BE SURPRISED. IT'S THE WAY THE SYSTEM WORKS, RIGHT?
AND THEN CRIMINALS FLOODED THE MARKET WITH COUNTERFEIT AND FALSIFIED MEDS.
THIS ISN'T NEW. IT'S JUST NEW HERE.
IN SOUTH EAST ASIA, BEFORE THE SIPS CAME ALONG, A CHILD WAS DYING EVERY FIVE MINUTES FROM RESISTANT INFECTIONS.
I HAD NO IDEA.
MOSTLY BECAUSE THERE'S NO PATIENT ADVOCACY, NO CAMPAIGN. IT'S NOT LIKE CANCER. YOU DON'T LIVE WITH IT. WITH INFECTIONS, YOU RECOVER OR YOU DIE. END OF.
SO IS ANYBODY TRYING TO FIGURE OUT HOW WE SAVE OURSELVES?
THERE ARE RESEARCH TEAMS DOTTED ALL OVER THE WORLD LOOKING AT NEW ANTIBIOTIC POSSIBILITIES. THEORETICALLY, WE SHOULD BE ABLE TO FIND SOMETHING THAT WILL FIGHT THE SIPS.
BUT THE DISEASE IS MUTATING SO FAST, AND IT TAKES SO LONG TO FIND EFFECTIVE TREATMENTS…

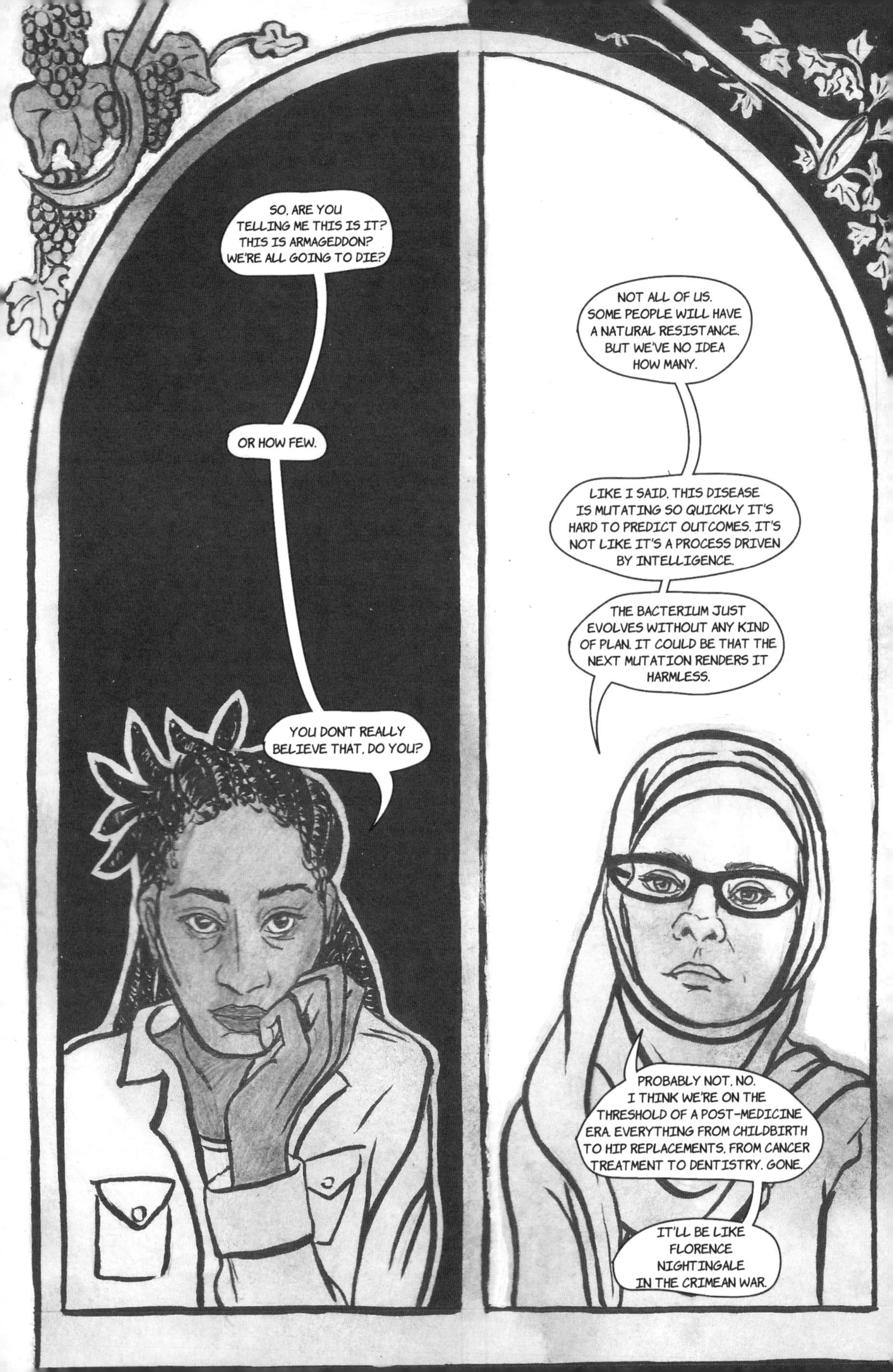
SO, ARE YOU TELLING ME THIS IS IT? THIS IS ARMAGEDDON? WE'RE ALL GOING TO DIE?
NOT ALL OF US. SOME PEOPLE WILL HAVE A NATURAL RESISTANCE. BUT WE'VE NO IDEA HOW MANY.
OR HOW FEW.
LIKE I SAID, THIS DISEASE IS MUTATING SO QUICKLY IT'S HARD TO PREDICT OUTCOMES. IT'S NOT LIKE IT'S A PROCESS DRIVEN BY INTELLIGENCE.
THE BACTERIUM JUST EVOLVES WITHOUT ANY KIND OF PLAN. IT COULD BE THAT THE NEXT MUTATION RENDERS IT HARMLESS.
YOU DON'T REALLY BELIEVE THAT, DO YOU?
PROBABLY NOT, NO. I THINK WE'RE ON THE THRESHOLD OF A POST-MEDICINE ERA. EVERYTHING FROM CHILDBIRTH TO HIP REPLACEMENTS, FROM CANCER TREATMENT TO DENTISTRY. GONE.
IT'LL BE LIKE FLORENCE NIGHTINGALE IN THE CRIMEAN WAR.

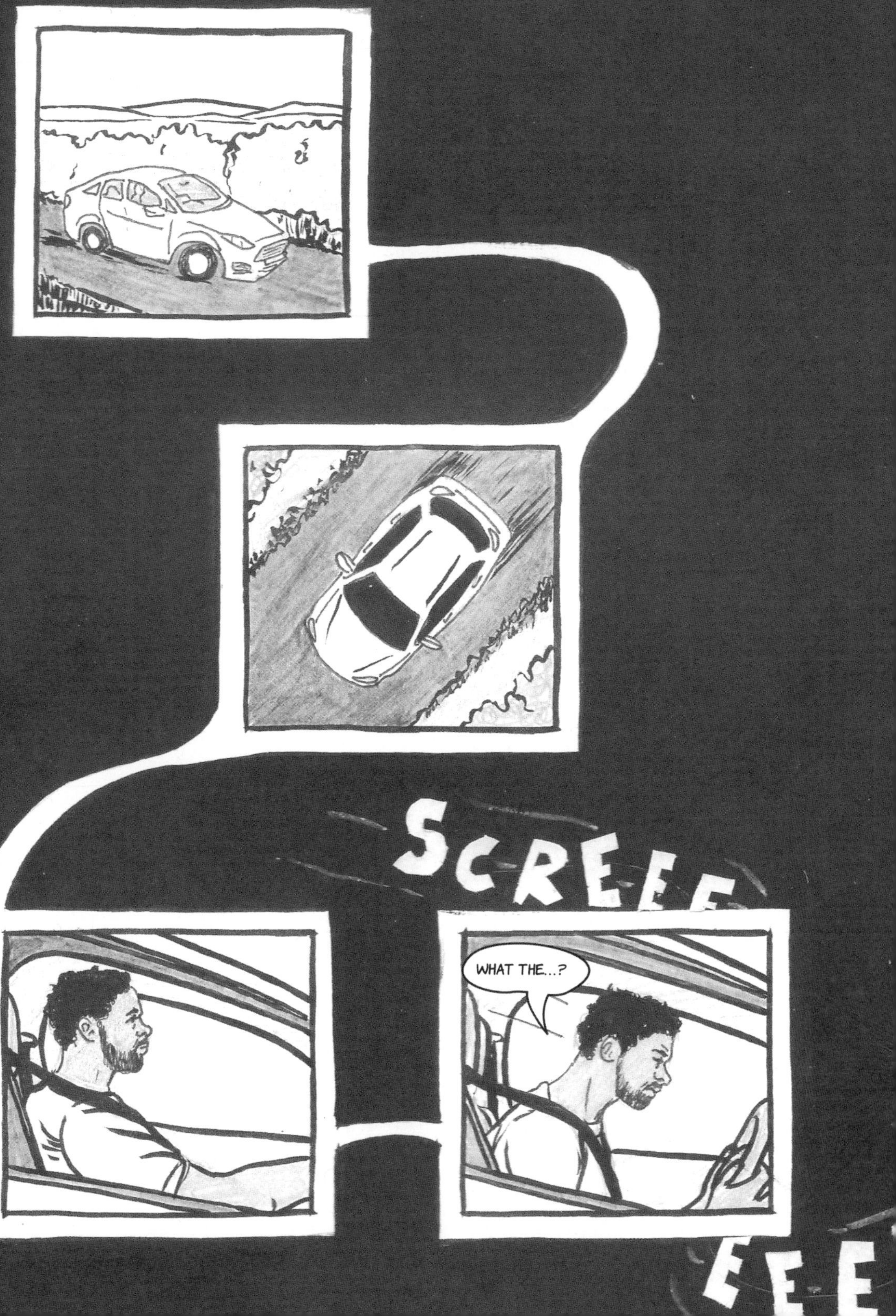
SCREEE
WHAT THE...?
EEE

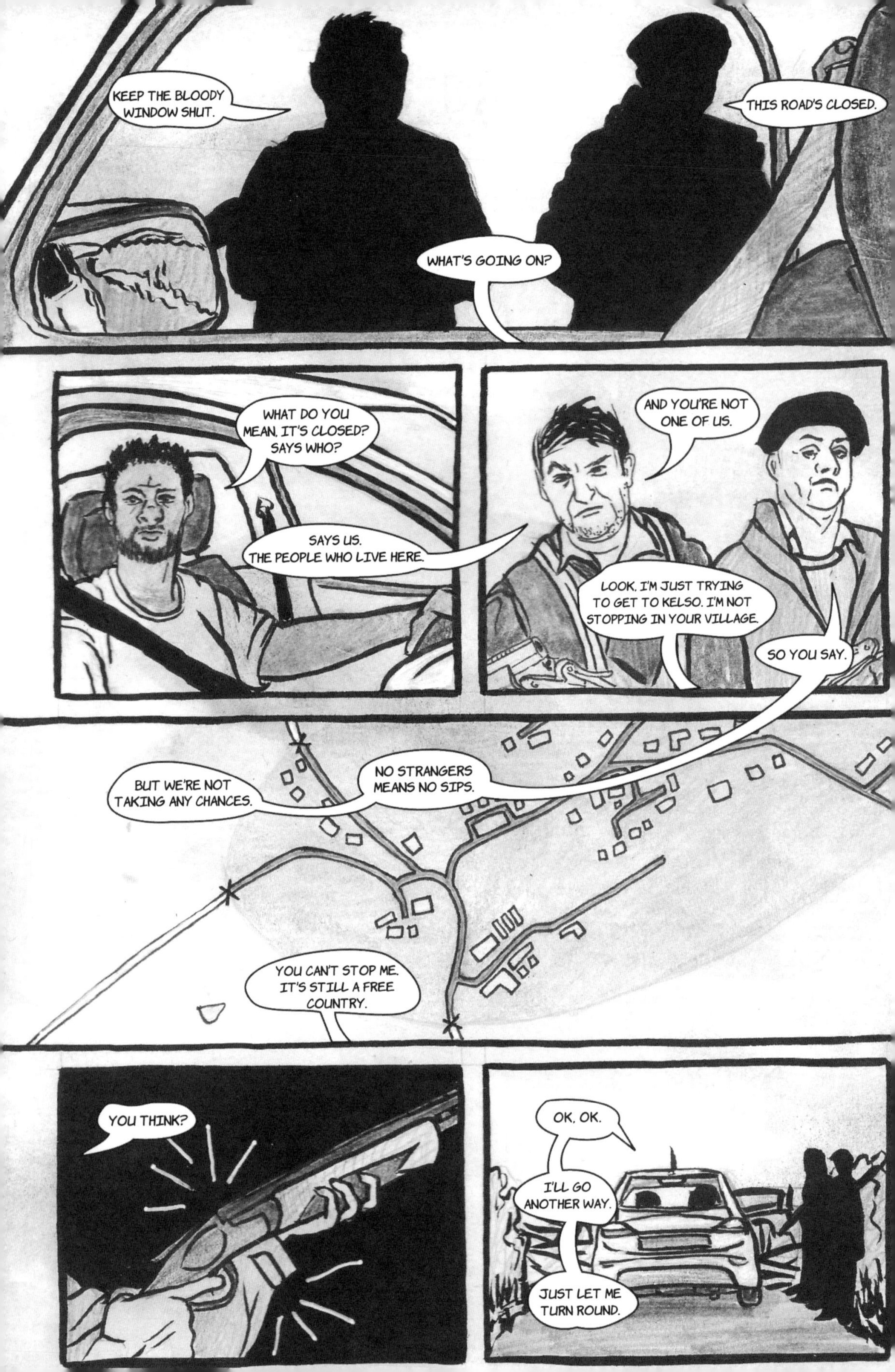
KEEP THE BLOODY WINDOW SHUT.
THIS ROAD'S CLOSED.
WHAT'S GOING ON?
WHAT DO YOU MEAN, IT'S CLOSED? SAYS WHO?
SAYS US. THE PEOPLE WHO LIVE HERE.
AND YOU'RE NOT ONE OF US.
LOOK, I'M JUST TRYING TO GET TO KELSO. I'M NOT STOPPING IN YOUR VILLAGE.
SO YOU SAY.
BUT WE'RE NOT TAKING ANY CHANCES.
NO STRANGERS MEANS NO SIPS.
YOU CAN'T STOP ME. IT'S STILL A FREE COUNTRY.
YOU THINK?
OK, OK.
I'LL GO ANOTHER WAY.
JUST LET ME TURN ROUND.

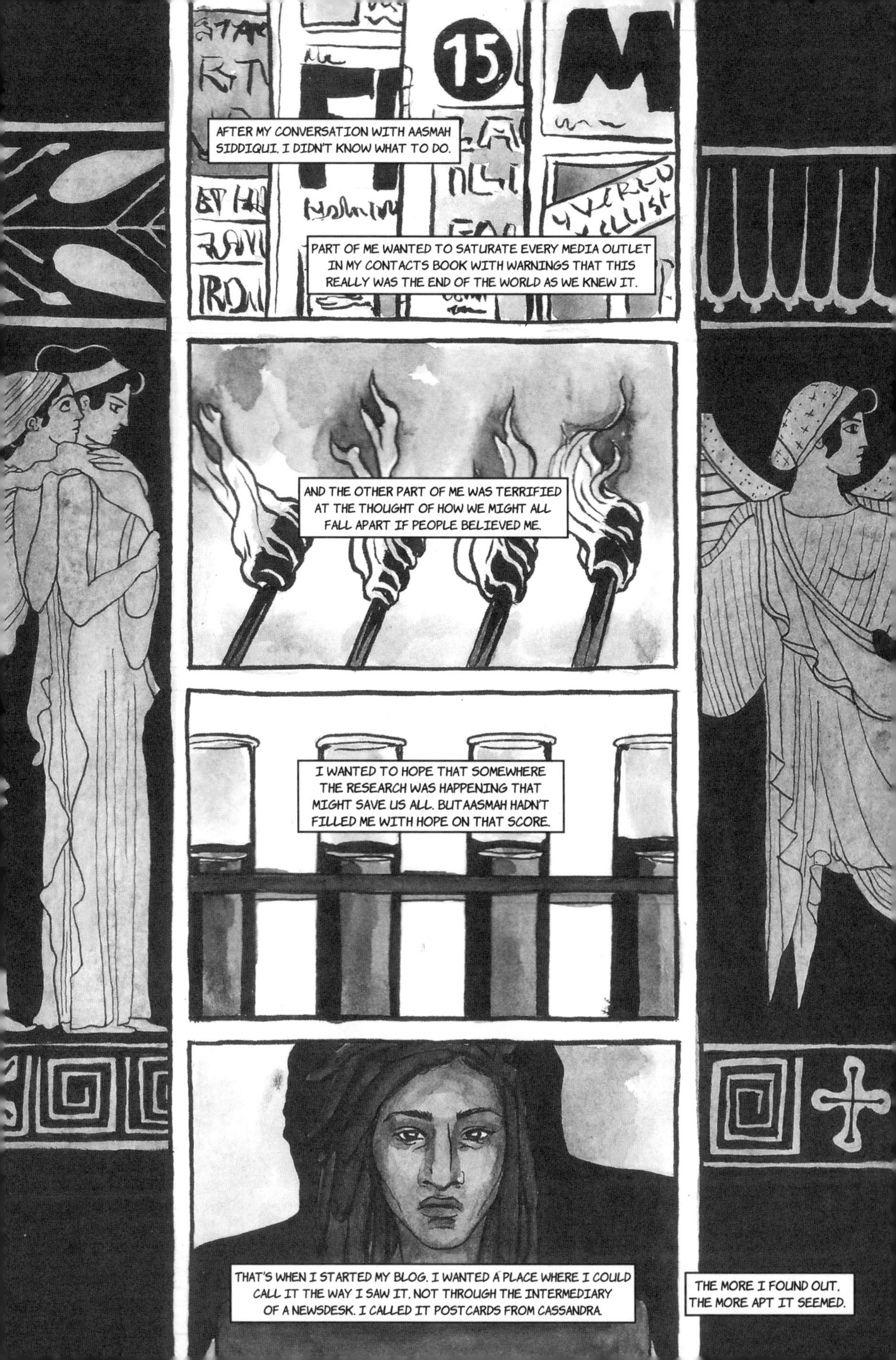
AFTER MY CONVERSATION WITH AASMAH SIDDIQUI, I DIDN'T KNOW WHAT TO DO.
PART OF ME WANTED TO SATURATE EVERY MEDIA OUTLET IN MY CONTACTS BOOK WITH WARNINGS THAT THIS REALLY WAS THE END OF THE WORLD AS WE KNEW IT.
AND THE OTHER PART OF ME WAS TERRIFIED AT THE THOUGHT OF HOW WE MIGHT ALL FALL APART IF PEOPLE BELIEVED ME.
I WANTED TO HOPE THAT SOMEWHERE THE RESEARCH WAS HAPPENING THAT MIGHT SAVE US ALL. BUT AASMAH HADN'T FILLED ME WITH HOPE ON THAT SCORE.
THAT'S WHEN I STARTED MY BLOG. I WANTED A PLACE WHERE I COULD CALL IT THE WAY I SAW IT, NOT THROUGH THE INTERMEDIARY OF A NEWSDESK. I CALLED IT POSTCARDS FROM CASSANDRA.
THE MORE I FOUND OUT, THE MORE APT IT SEEMED.

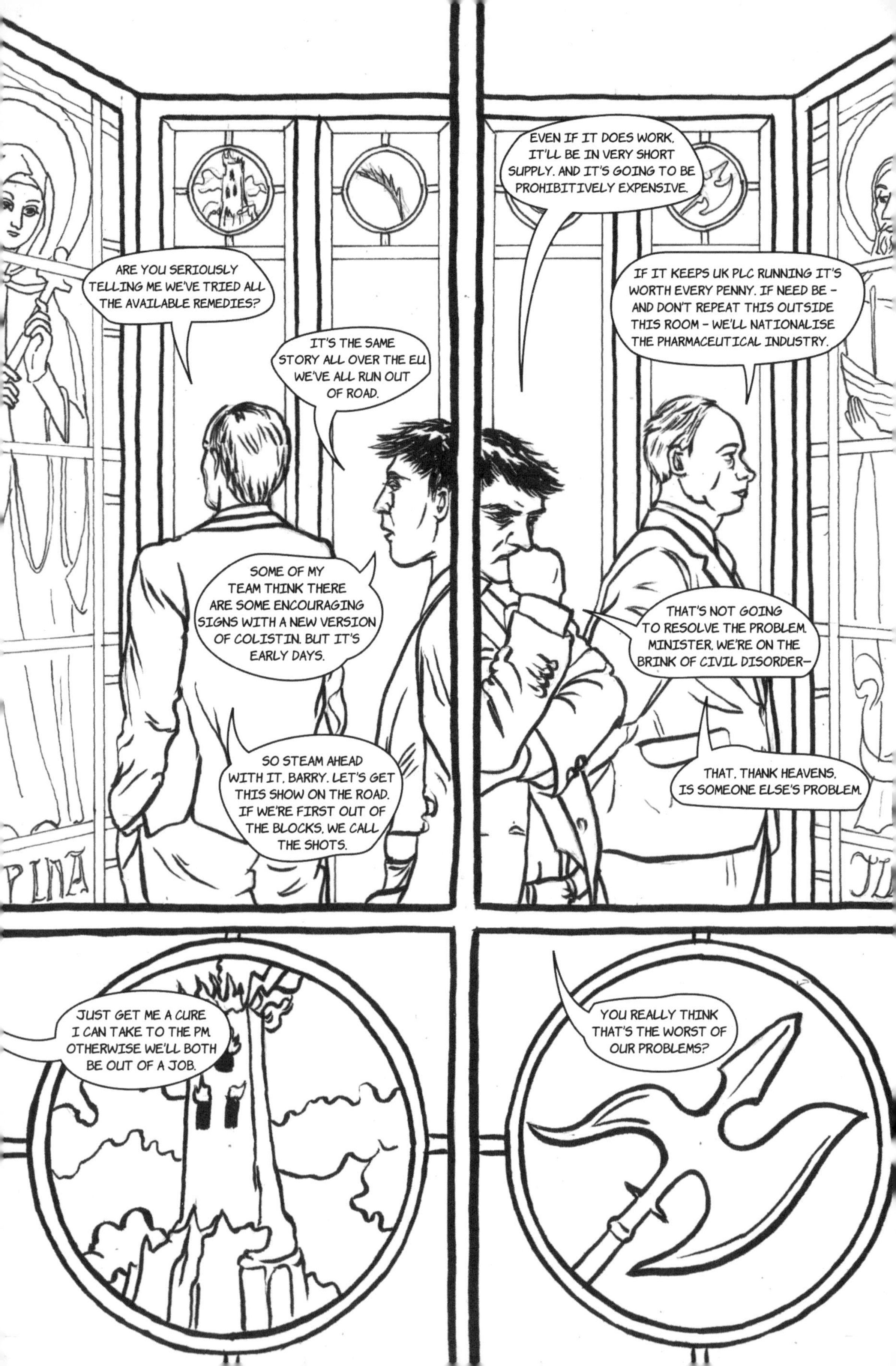
ARE YOU SERIOUSLY TELLING ME WE'VE TRIED ALL THE AVAILABLE REMEDIES?
IT'S THE SAME STORY ALL OVER THE EU. WE'VE ALL RUN OUT OF ROAD.
SOME OF MY TEAM THINK THERE ARE SOME ENCOURAGING SIGNS WITH A NEW VERSION OF COLISTIN. BUT IT'S EARLY DAYS.
SO STEAM AHEAD WITH IT, BARRY. LET'S GET THIS SHOW ON THE ROAD. IF WE'RE FIRST OUT OF THE BLOCKS, WE CALL THE SHOTS.
EVEN IF IT DOES WORK, IT'LL BE IN VERY SHORT SUPPLY. AND IT'S GOING TO BE PROHIBITIVELY EXPENSIVE.
IF IT KEEPS UK PLC RUNNING IT'S WORTH EVERY PENNY. IF NEED BE – AND DON'T REPEAT THIS OUTSIDE THIS ROOM – WE'LL NATIONALISE THE PHARMACEUTICAL INDUSTRY.
THAT'S NOT GOING TO RESOLVE THE PROBLEM, MINISTER. WE'RE ON THE BRINK OF CIVIL DISORDER–
THAT, THANK HEAVENS, IS SOMEONE ELSE'S PROBLEM.
JUST GET ME A CURE I CAN TAKE TO THE PM. OTHERWISE WE'LL BOTH BE OUT OF A JOB.
YOU REALLY THINK THAT'S THE WORST OF OUR PROBLEMS?

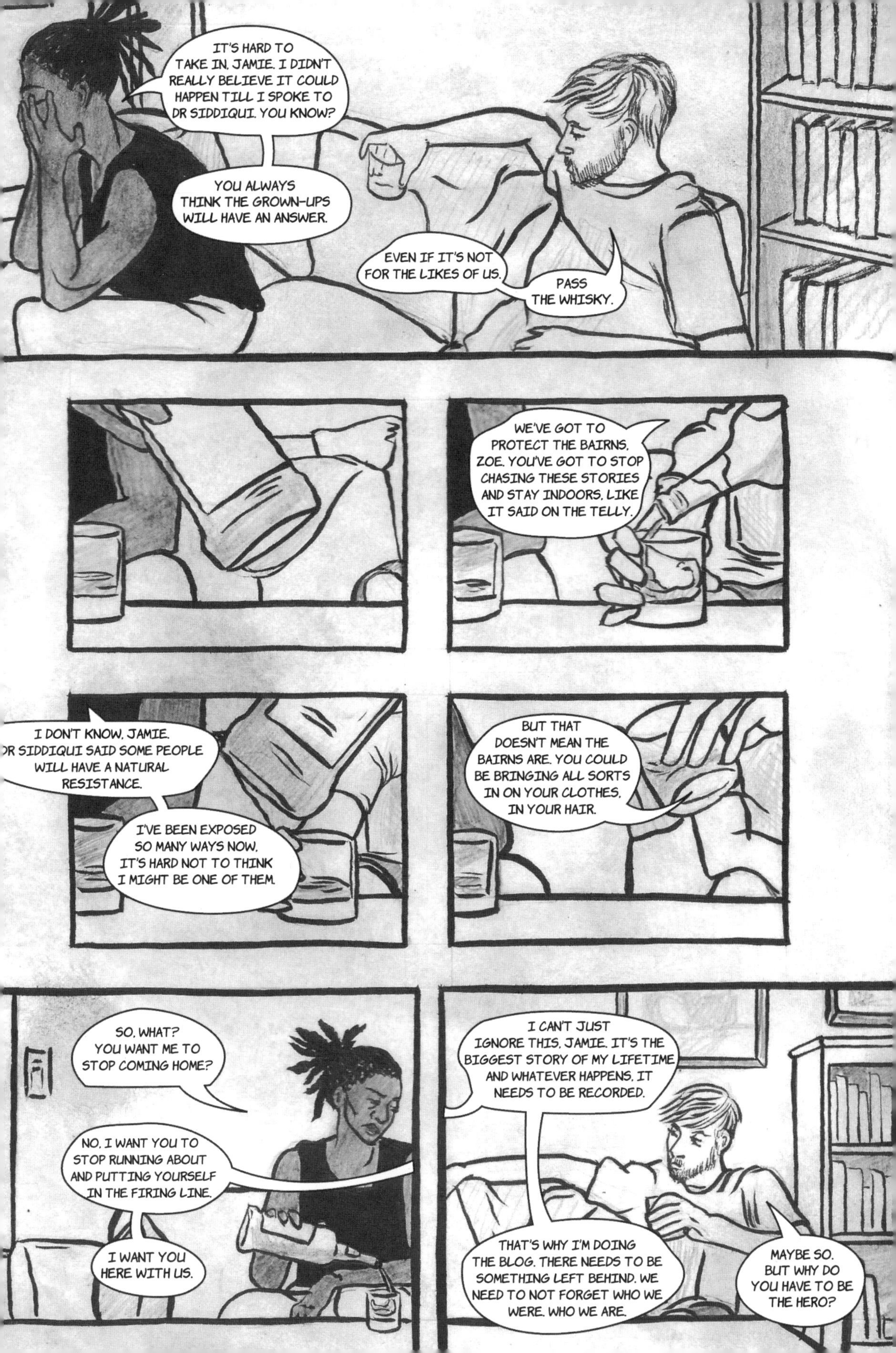
IT'S HARD TO TAKE IN, JAMIE. I DIDN'T REALLY BELIEVE IT COULD HAPPEN TILL I SPOKE TO DR SIDDIQUI. YOU KNOW?
YOU ALWAYS THINK THE GROWN-UPS WILL HAVE AN ANSWER.
EVEN IF IT'S NOT FOR THE LIKES OF US.
PASS THE WHISKY.
WE'VE GOT TO PROTECT THE BAIRNS, ZOE. YOU'VE GOT TO STOP CHASING THESE STORIES AND STAY INDOORS, LIKE IT SAID ON THE TELLY.
I DON'T KNOW, JAMIE. DR SIDDIQUI SAID SOME PEOPLE WILL HAVE A NATURAL RESISTANCE.
I'VE BEEN EXPOSED SO MANY WAYS NOW, IT'S HARD NOT TO THINK I MIGHT BE ONE OF THEM.
BUT THAT DOESN'T MEAN THE BAIRNS ARE. YOU COULD BE BRINGING ALL SORTS IN ON YOUR CLOTHES, IN YOUR HAIR.
SO, WHAT? YOU WANT ME TO STOP COMING HOME?
NO, I WANT YOU TO STOP RUNNING ABOUT AND PUTTING YOURSELF IN THE FIRING LINE.
I WANT YOU HERE WITH US.
I CAN'T JUST IGNORE THIS, JAMIE. IT'S THE BIGGEST STORY OF MY LIFETIME AND WHATEVER HAPPENS, IT NEEDS TO BE RECORDED.
THAT'S WHY I'M DOING THE BLOG. THERE NEEDS TO BE SOMETHING LEFT BEHIND. WE NEED TO NOT FORGET WHO WE WERE. WHO WE ARE.
MAYBE SO. BUT WHY DO YOU HAVE TO BE THE HERO?

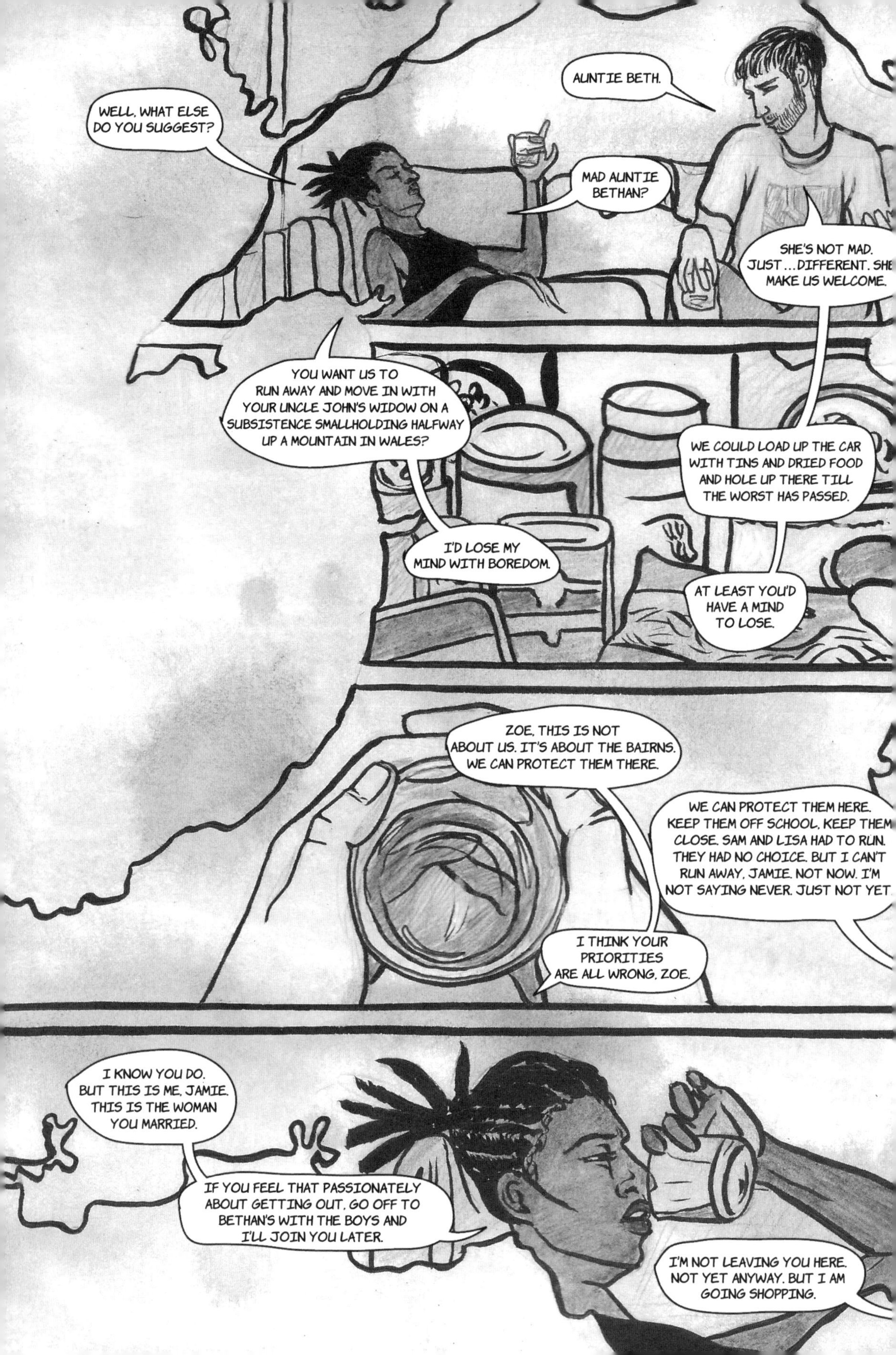
AUNTIE BETH.
WELL, WHAT ELSE DO YOU SUGGEST?
MAD AUNTIE BETHAN?
SHE'S NOT MAD. JUST ... DIFFERENT. SHE MAKE US WELCOME.
YOU WANT US TO RUN AWAY AND MOVE IN WITH YOUR UNCLE JOHN'S WIDOW ON A SUBSISTENCE SMALLHOLDING HALFWAY UP A MOUNTAIN IN WALES?
WE COULD LOAD UP THE CAR WITH TINS AND DRIED FOOD AND HOLE UP THERE TILL THE WORST HAS PASSED.
I'D LOSE MY MIND WITH BOREDOM.
AT LEAST YOU'D HAVE A MIND TO LOSE.
ZOE, THIS IS NOT ABOUT US. IT'S ABOUT THE BAIRNS. WE CAN PROTECT THEM THERE.
WE CAN PROTECT THEM HERE. KEEP THEM OFF SCHOOL, KEEP THEM CLOSE. SAM AND LISA HAD TO RUN. THEY HAD NO CHOICE. BUT I CAN'T RUN AWAY, JAMIE. NOT NOW. I'M NOT SAYING NEVER. JUST NOT YET.
I THINK YOUR PRIORITIES ARE ALL WRONG, ZOE.
I KNOW YOU DO. BUT THIS IS ME, JAMIE. THIS IS THE WOMAN YOU MARRIED.
IF YOU FEEL THAT PASSIONATELY ABOUT GETTING OUT, GO OFF TO BETHAN'S WITH THE BOYS AND I'LL JOIN YOU LATER.
I'M NOT LEAVING YOU HERE. NOT YET ANYWAY. BUT I AM GOING SHOPPING.

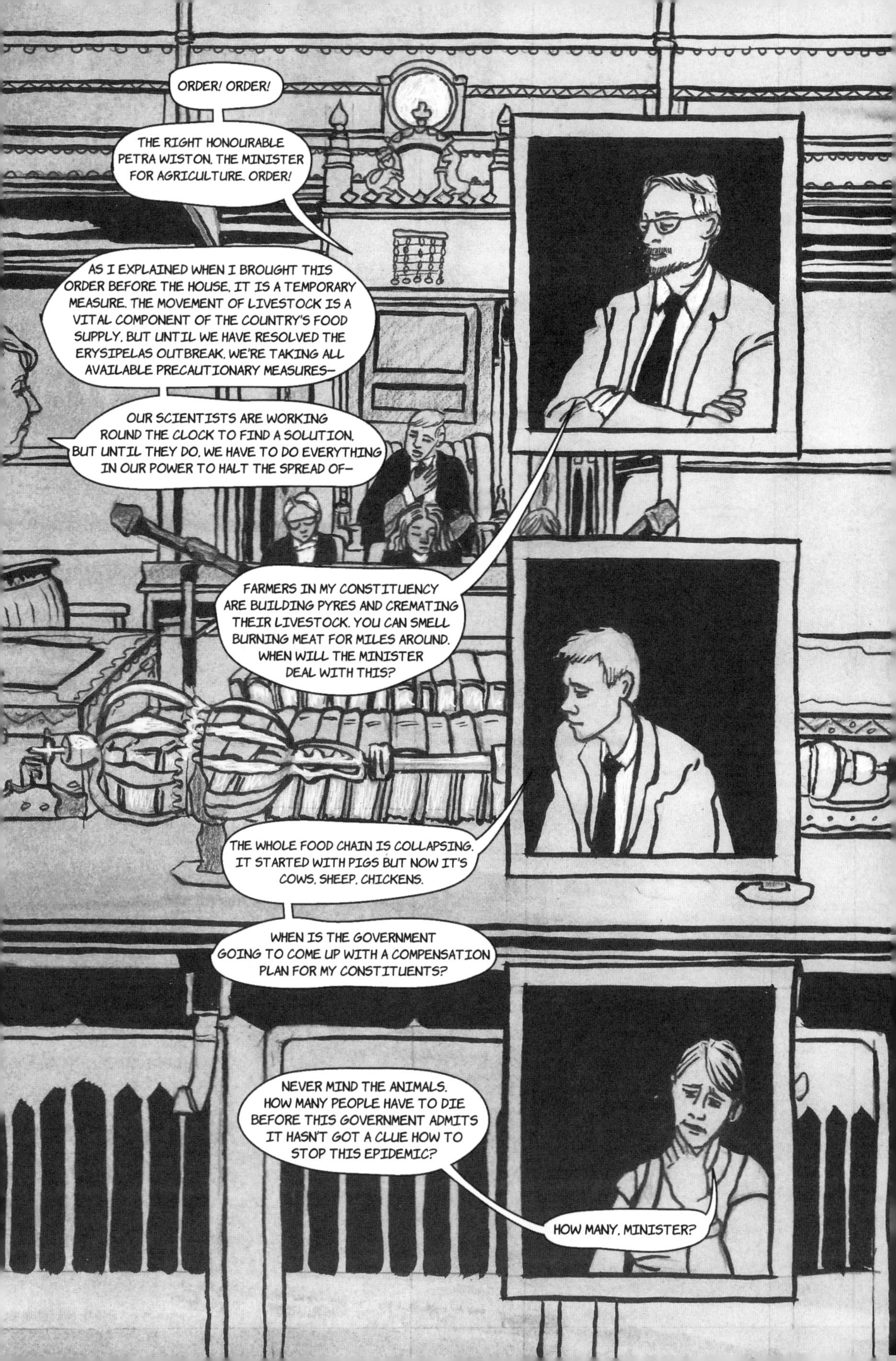
ORDER! ORDER!
THE RIGHT HONOURABLE PETRA WISTON, THE MINISTER FOR AGRICULTURE. ORDER!
AS I EXPLAINED WHEN I BROUGHT THIS ORDER BEFORE THE HOUSE, IT IS A TEMPORARY MEASURE. THE MOVEMENT OF LIVESTOCK IS A VITAL COMPONENT OF THE COUNTRY'S FOOD SUPPLY, BUT UNTIL WE HAVE RESOLVED THE ERYSIPELAS OUTBREAK, WE'RE TAKING ALL AVAILABLE PRECAUTIONARY MEASURES—
OUR SCIENTISTS ARE WORKING ROUND THE CLOCK TO FIND A SOLUTION, BUT UNTIL THEY DO, WE HAVE TO DO EVERYTHING IN OUR POWER TO HALT THE SPREAD OF—
FARMERS IN MY CONSTITUENCY ARE BUILDING PYRES AND CREMATING THEIR LIVESTOCK. YOU CAN SMELL BURNING MEAT FOR MILES AROUND. WHEN WILL THE MINISTER DEAL WITH THIS?
THE WHOLE FOOD CHAIN IS COLLAPSING. IT STARTED WITH PIGS BUT NOW IT'S COWS, SHEEP, CHICKENS.
WHEN IS THE GOVERNMENT GOING TO COME UP WITH A COMPENSATION PLAN FOR MY CONSTITUENTS?
NEVER MIND THE ANIMALS. HOW MANY PEOPLE HAVE TO DIE BEFORE THIS GOVERNMENT ADMITS IT HASN'T GOT A CLUE HOW TO STOP THIS EPIDEMIC?
HOW MANY, MINISTER?

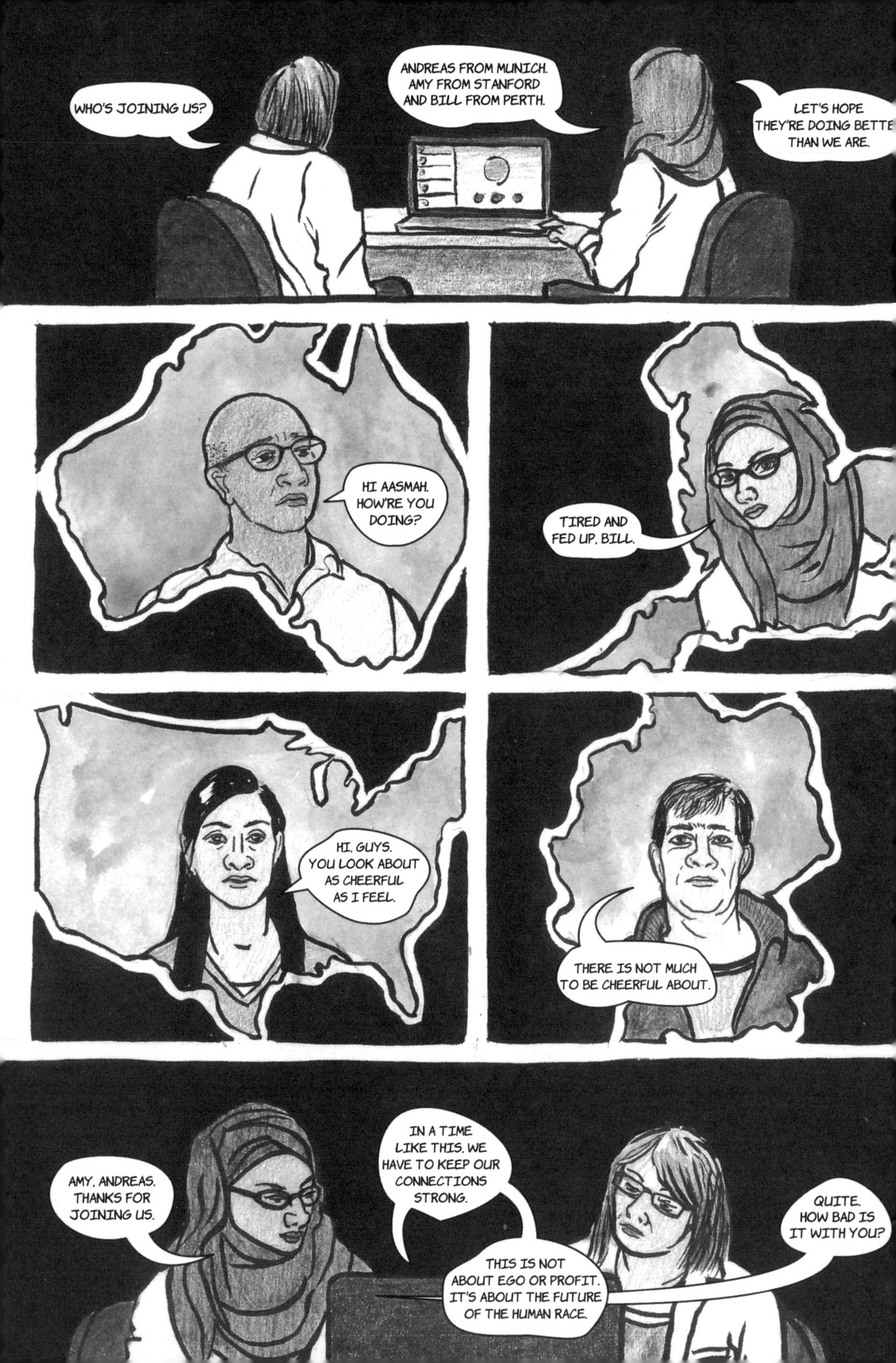
WHO'S JOINING US?
ANDREAS FROM MUNICH. AMY FROM STANFORD AND BILL FROM PERTH.
LET'S HOPE THEY'RE DOING BETTE THAN WE ARE.
HI AASMAH. HOW'RE YOU DOING?
TIRED AND FED UP, BILL.
HI, GUYS. YOU LOOK ABOUT AS CHEERFUL AS I FEEL.
THERE IS NOT MUCH TO BE CHEERFUL ABOUT.
AMY, ANDREAS. THANKS FOR JOINING US.
IN A TIME LIKE THIS, WE HAVE TO KEEP OUR CONNECTIONS STRONG.
THIS IS NOT ABOUT EGO OR PROFIT. IT'S ABOUT THE FUTURE OF THE HUMAN RACE.
QUITE. HOW BAD IS IT WITH YOU?

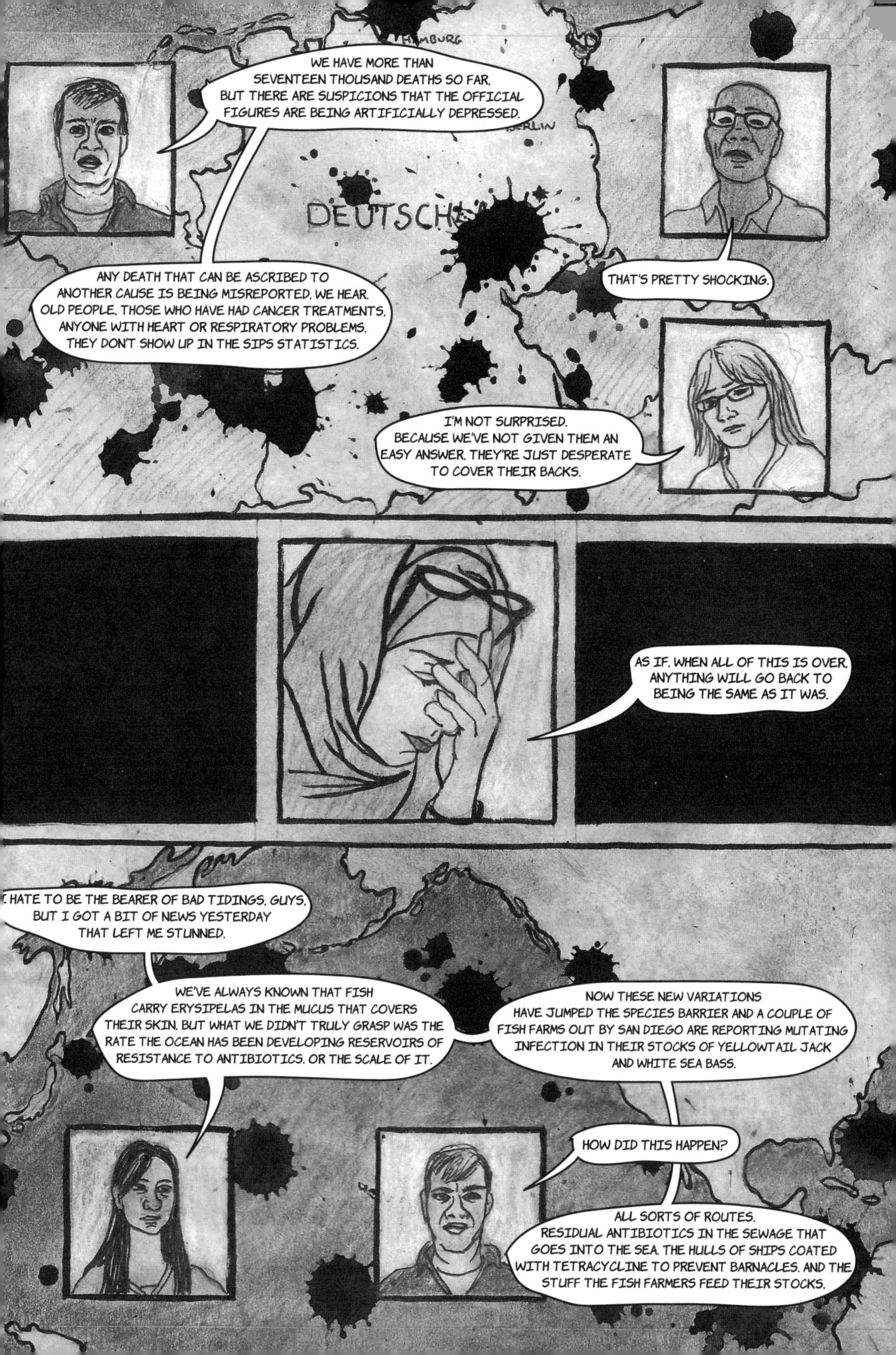
WE HAVE MORE THAN SEVENTEEN THOUSAND DEATHS SO FAR, BUT THERE ARE SUSPICIONS THAT THE OFFICIAL FIGURES ARE BEING ARTIFICIALLY DEPRESSED.
DEUTSCH
ANY DEATH THAT CAN BE ASCRIBED TO ANOTHER CAUSE IS BEING MISREPORTED, WE HEAR. OLD PEOPLE, THOSE WHO HAVE HAD CANCER TREATMENTS, ANYONE WITH HEART OR RESPIRATORY PROBLEMS. THEY DON'T SHOW UP IN THE SIPS STATISTICS.
THAT'S PRETTY SHOCKING.
I'M NOT SURPRISED. BECAUSE WE'VE NOT GIVEN THEM AN EASY ANSWER, THEY'RE JUST DESPERATE TO COVER THEIR BACKS.
AS IF, WHEN ALL OF THIS IS OVER, ANYTHING WILL GO BACK TO BEING THE SAME AS IT WAS.
I HATE TO BE THE BEARER OF BAD TIDINGS, GUYS, BUT I GOT A BIT OF NEWS YESTERDAY THAT LEFT ME STUNNED.
WE'VE ALWAYS KNOWN THAT FISH CARRY ERYSIPELAS IN THE MUCUS THAT COVERS THEIR SKIN, BUT WHAT WE DIDN'T TRULY GRASP WAS THE RATE THE OCEAN HAS BEEN DEVELOPING RESERVOIRS OF RESISTANCE TO ANTIBIOTICS. OR THE SCALE OF IT.
NOW THESE NEW VARIATIONS HAVE JUMPED THE SPECIES BARRIER AND A COUPLE OF FISH FARMS OUT BY SAN DIEGO ARE REPORTING MUTATING INFECTION IN THEIR STOCKS OF YELLOWTAIL JACK AND WHITE SEA BASS.
HOW DID THIS HAPPEN?
ALL SORTS OF ROUTES. RESIDUAL ANTIBIOTICS IN THE SEWAGE THAT GOES INTO THE SEA. THE HULLS OF SHIPS COATED WITH TETRACYCLINE TO PREVENT BARNACLES. AND THE STUFF THE FISH FARMERS FEED THEIR STOCKS.

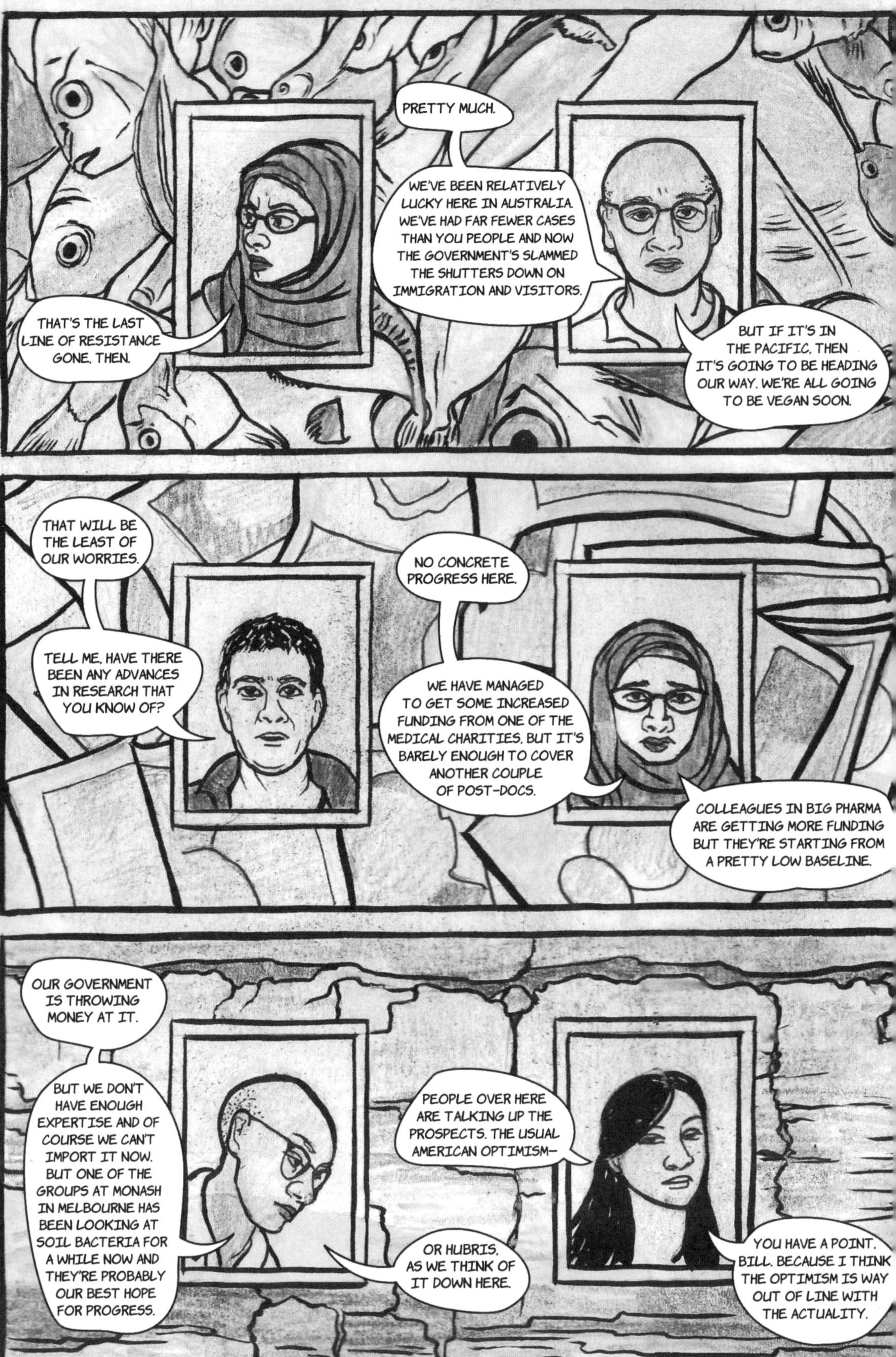

THAT'S THE LAST LINE OF RESISTANCE GONE, THEN.
PRETTY MUCH.
WE'VE BEEN RELATIVELY LUCKY HERE IN AUSTRALIA. WE'VE HAD FAR FEWER CASES THAN YOU PEOPLE AND NOW THE GOVERNMENT'S SLAMMED THE SHUTTERS DOWN ON IMMIGRATION AND VISITORS.
BUT IF IT'S IN THE PACIFIC, THEN IT'S GOING TO BE HEADING OUR WAY. WE'RE ALL GOING TO BE VEGAN SOON.
THAT WILL BE THE LEAST OF OUR WORRIES.
TELL ME, HAVE THERE BEEN ANY ADVANCES IN RESEARCH THAT YOU KNOW OF?
NO CONCRETE PROGRESS HERE.
WE HAVE MANAGED TO GET SOME INCREASED FUNDING FROM ONE OF THE MEDICAL CHARITIES, BUT IT'S BARELY ENOUGH TO COVER ANOTHER COUPLE OF POST-DOCS.
COLLEAGUES IN BIG PHARMA ARE GETTING MORE FUNDING BUT THEY'RE STARTING FROM A PRETTY LOW BASELINE.
OUR GOVERNMENT IS THROWING MONEY AT IT.
BUT WE DON'T HAVE ENOUGH EXPERTISE AND OF COURSE WE CAN'T IMPORT IT NOW. BUT ONE OF THE GROUPS AT MONASH IN MELBOURNE HAS BEEN LOOKING AT SOIL BACTERIA FOR A WHILE NOW AND THEY'RE PROBABLY OUR BEST HOPE FOR PROGRESS.
PEOPLE OVER HERE ARE TALKING UP THE PROSPECTS. THE USUAL AMERICAN OPTIMISM—
OR HUBRIS, AS WE THINK OF IT DOWN HERE.
YOU HAVE A POINT, BILL. BECAUSE I THINK THE OPTIMISM IS WAY OUT OF LINE WITH THE ACTUALITY.

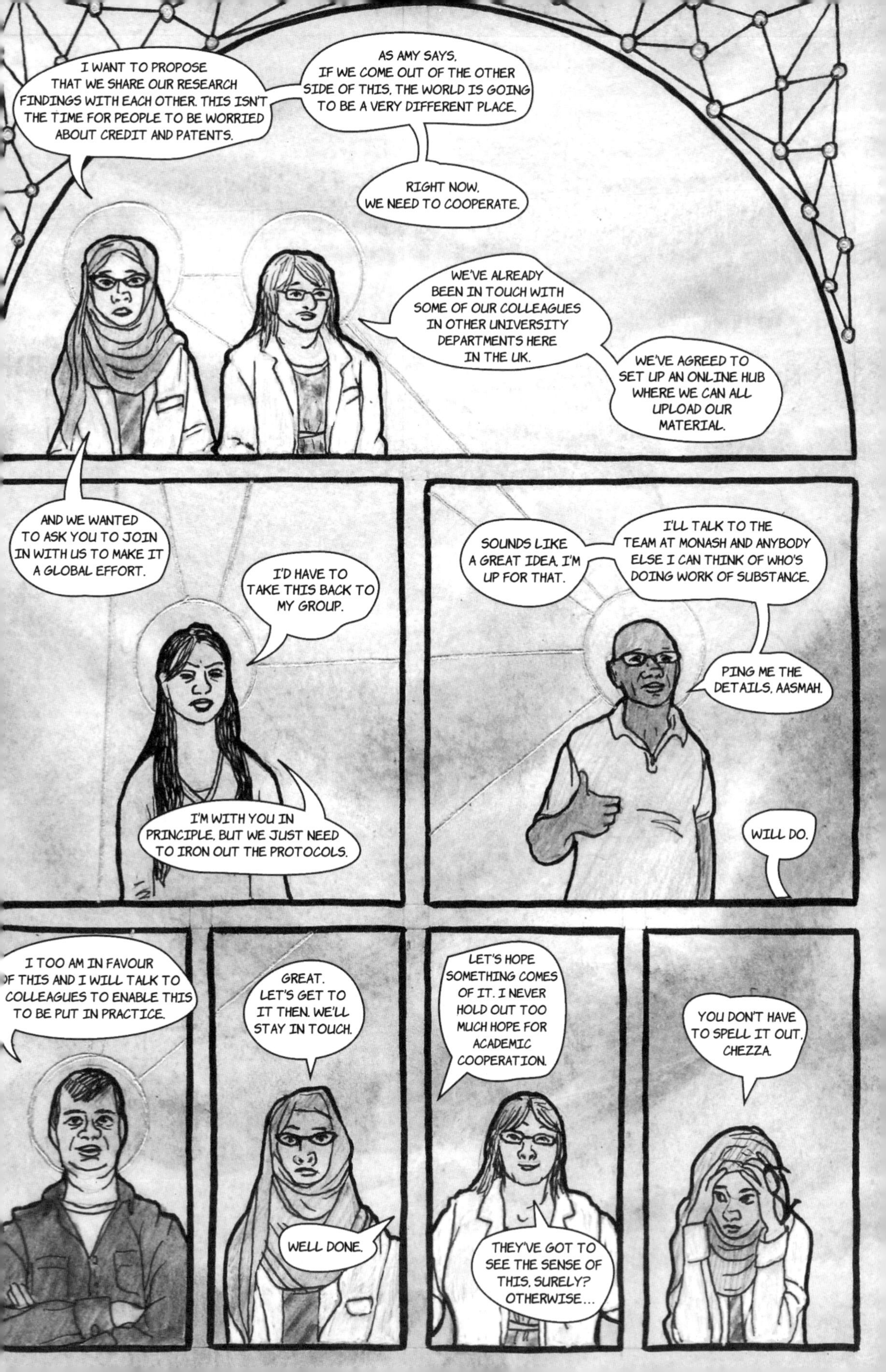

I WANT TO PROPOSE THAT WE SHARE OUR RESEARCH FINDINGS WITH EACH OTHER. THIS ISN'T THE TIME FOR PEOPLE TO BE WORRIED ABOUT CREDIT AND PATENTS.
AS AMY SAYS, IF WE COME OUT OF THE OTHER SIDE OF THIS, THE WORLD IS GOING TO BE A VERY DIFFERENT PLACE.
RIGHT NOW, WE NEED TO COOPERATE.
WE'VE ALREADY BEEN IN TOUCH WITH SOME OF OUR COLLEAGUES IN OTHER UNIVERSITY DEPARTMENTS HERE IN THE UK.
WE'VE AGREED TO SET UP AN ONLINE HUB WHERE WE CAN ALL UPLOAD OUR MATERIAL.
AND WE WANTED TO ASK YOU TO JOIN IN WITH US TO MAKE IT A GLOBAL EFFORT.
I'D HAVE TO TAKE THIS BACK TO MY GROUP.
I'M WITH YOU IN PRINCIPLE, BUT WE JUST NEED TO IRON OUT THE PROTOCOLS.
SOUNDS LIKE A GREAT IDEA, I'M UP FOR THAT.
I'LL TALK TO THE TEAM AT MONASH AND ANYBODY ELSE I CAN THINK OF WHO'S DOING WORK OF SUBSTANCE.
PING ME THE DETAILS, AASMAH.
WILL DO.
I TOO AM IN FAVOUR OF THIS AND I WILL TALK TO COLLEAGUES TO ENABLE THIS TO BE PUT IN PRACTICE.
GREAT. LET'S GET TO IT THEN. WE'LL STAY IN TOUCH.
WELL DONE.
LET'S HOPE SOMETHING COMES OF IT. I NEVER HOLD OUT TOO MUCH HOPE FOR ACADEMIC COOPERATION.
THEY'VE GOT TO SEE THE SENSE OF THIS, SURELY? OTHERWISE…
YOU DON'T HAVE TO SPELL IT OUT, CHEZZA.

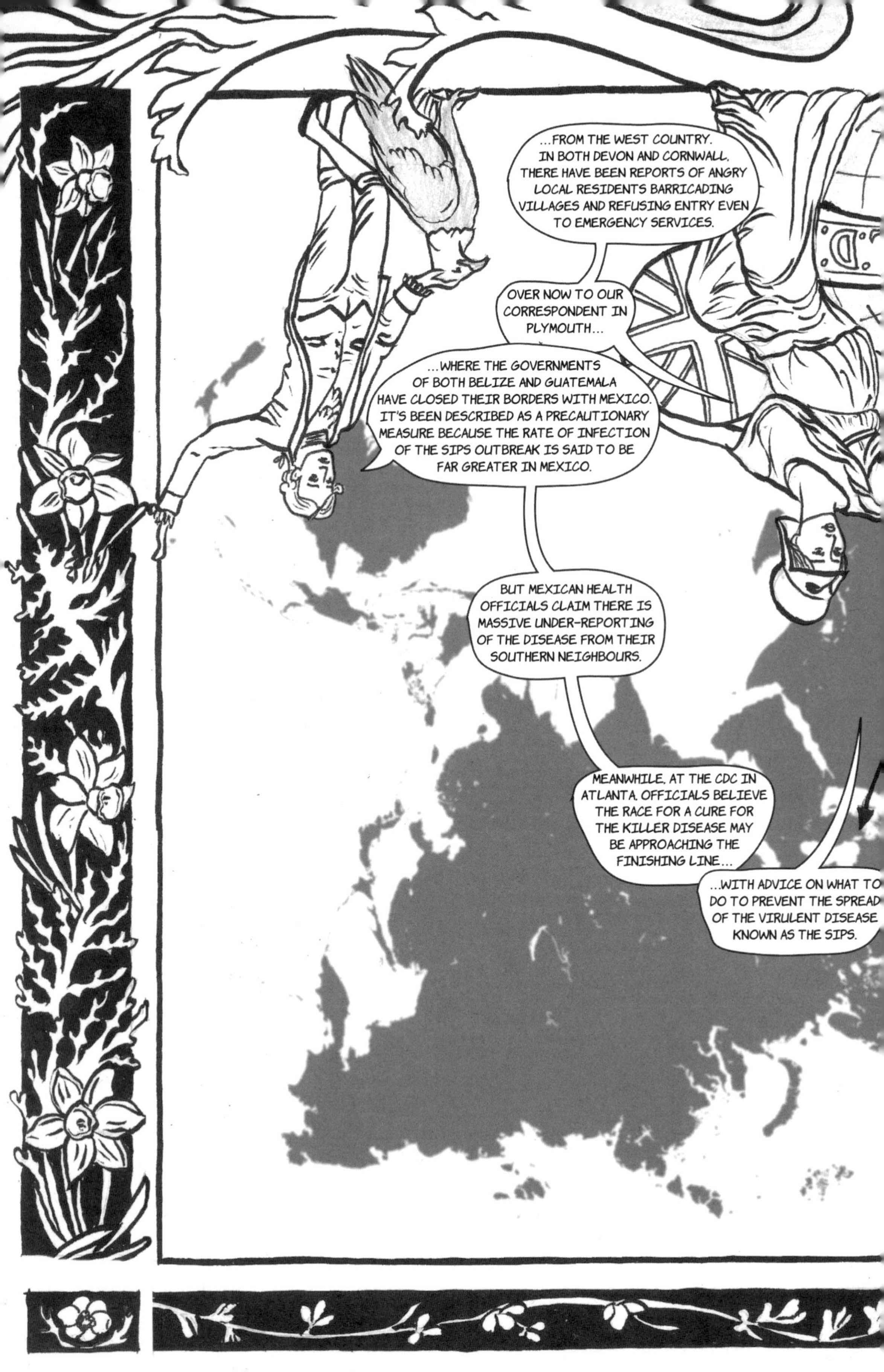

...FROM THE WEST COUNTRY. IN BOTH DEVON AND CORNWALL, THERE HAVE BEEN REPORTS OF ANGRY LOCAL RESIDENTS BARRICADING VILLAGES AND REFUSING ENTRY EVEN TO EMERGENCY SERVICES.
OVER NOW TO OUR CORRESPONDENT IN PLYMOUTH...
...WHERE THE GOVERNMENTS OF BOTH BELIZE AND GUATEMALA HAVE CLOSED THEIR BORDERS WITH MEXICO. IT'S BEEN DESCRIBED AS A PRECAUTIONARY MEASURE BECAUSE THE RATE OF INFECTION OF THE SIPS OUTBREAK IS SAID TO BE FAR GREATER IN MEXICO.
BUT MEXICAN HEALTH OFFICIALS CLAIM THERE IS MASSIVE UNDER-REPORTING OF THE DISEASE FROM THEIR SOUTHERN NEIGHBOURS.
MEANWHILE, AT THE CDC IN ATLANTA, OFFICIALS BELIEVE THE RACE FOR A CURE FOR THE KILLER DISEASE MAY BE APPROACHING THE FINISHING LINE...
...WITH ADVICE ON WHAT TO DO TO PREVENT THE SPREAD OF THE VIRULENT DISEASE KNOWN AS THE SIPS.

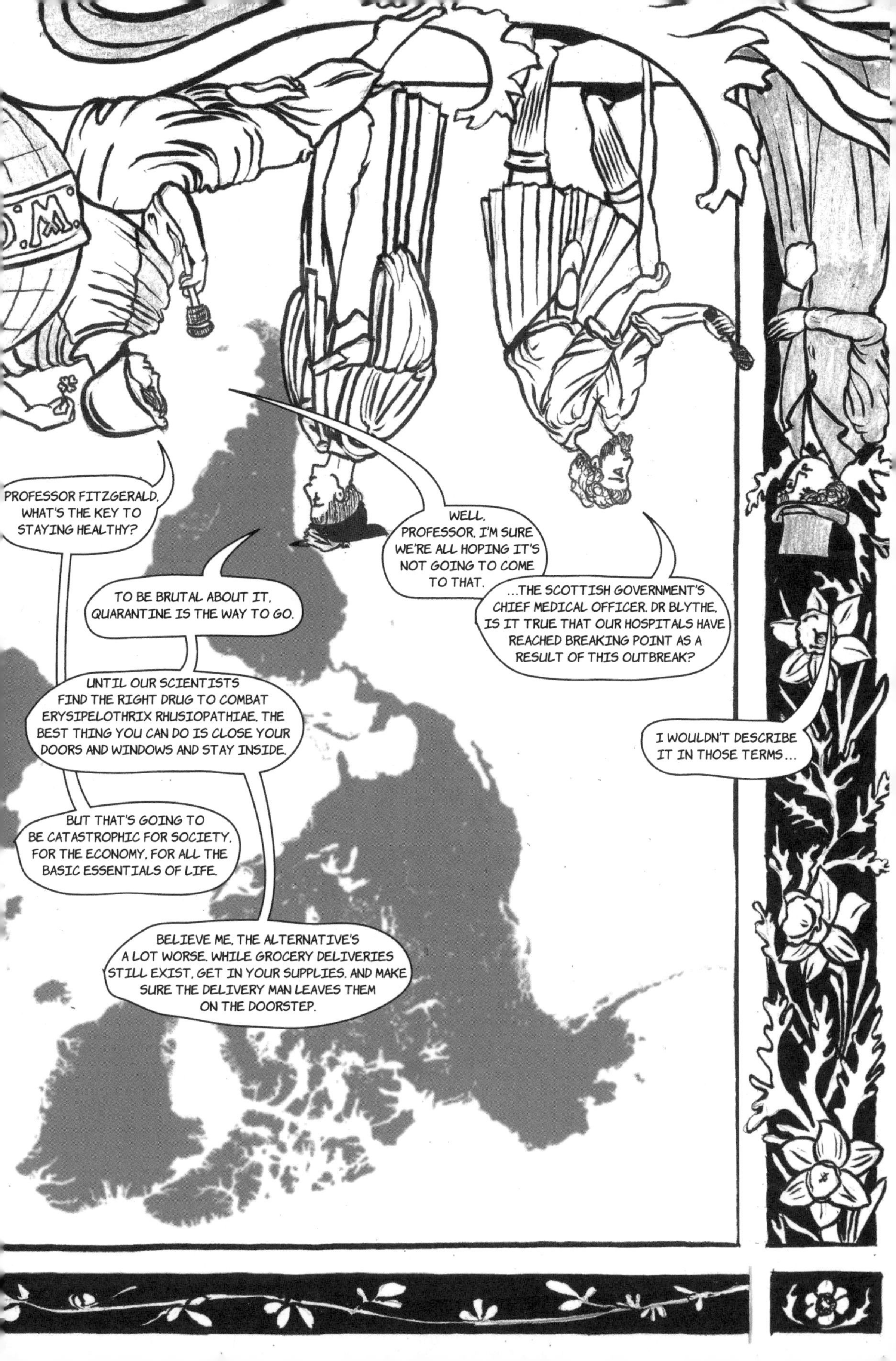
WELL, PROFESSOR, I'M SURE WE'RE ALL HOPING IT'S NOT GOING TO COME TO THAT.
...THE SCOTTISH GOVERNMENT'S CHIEF MEDICAL OFFICER, DR BLYTHE, IS IT TRUE THAT OUR HOSPITALS HAVE REACHED BREAKING POINT AS A RESULT OF THIS OUTBREAK?
I WOULDN'T DESCRIBE IT IN THOSE TERMS...
PROFESSOR FITZGERALD, WHAT'S THE KEY TO STAYING HEALTHY?
TO BE BRUTAL ABOUT IT, QUARANTINE IS THE WAY TO GO.
UNTIL OUR SCIENTISTS FIND THE RIGHT DRUG TO COMBAT ERYSIPELOTHRIX RHUSIOPATHIAE, THE BEST THING YOU CAN DO IS CLOSE YOUR DOORS AND WINDOWS AND STAY INSIDE.
BUT THAT'S GOING TO BE CATASTROPHIC FOR SOCIETY, FOR THE ECONOMY, FOR ALL THE BASIC ESSENTIALS OF LIFE.
BELIEVE ME, THE ALTERNATIVE'S A LOT WORSE. WHILE GROCERY DELIVERIES STILL EXIST, GET IN YOUR SUPPLIES, AND MAKE SURE THE DELIVERY MAN LEAVES THEM ON THE DOORSTEP.

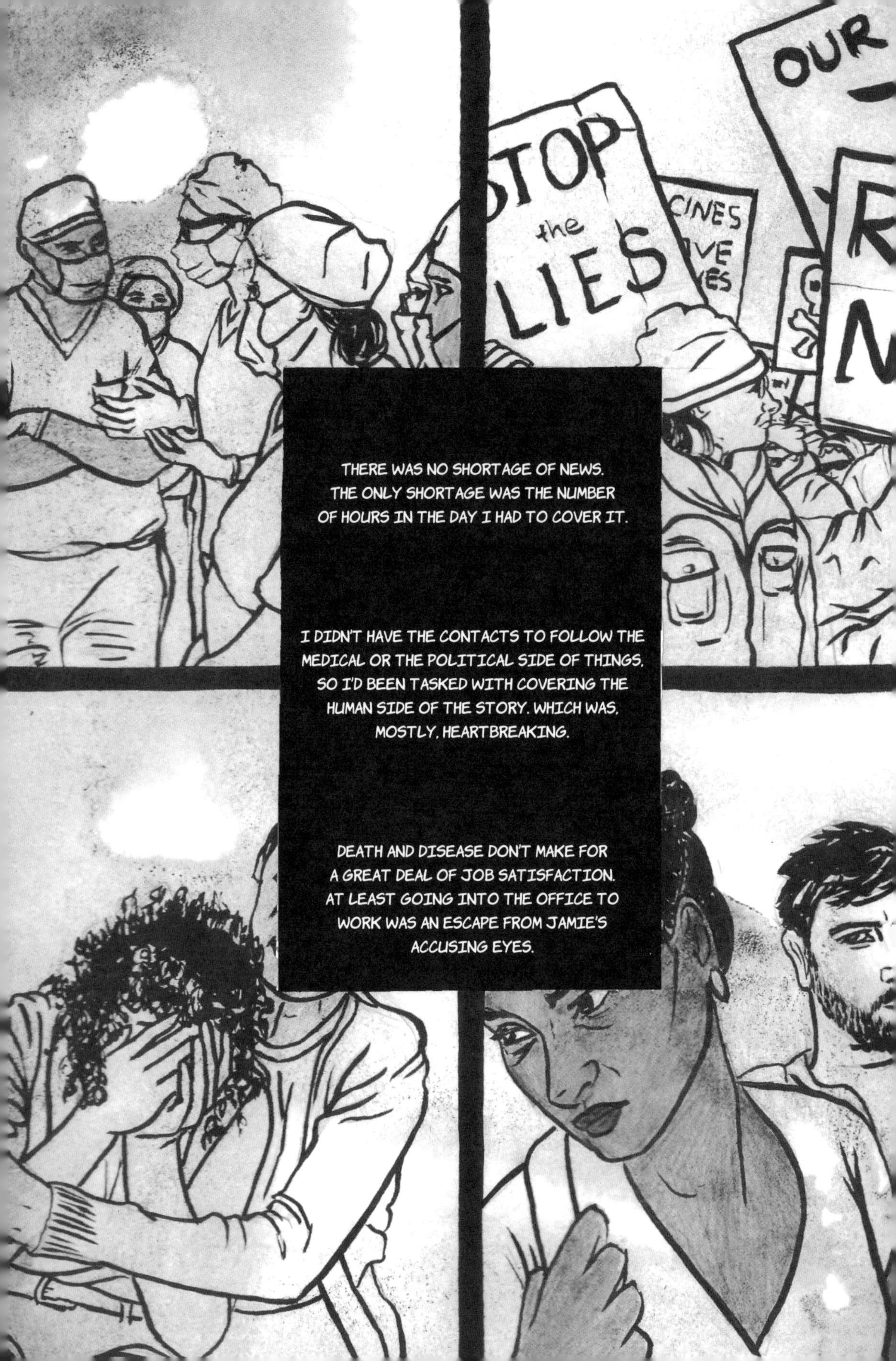
TOP the LIES
CINES
OUR
THERE WAS NO SHORTAGE OF NEWS. THE ONLY SHORTAGE WAS THE NUMBER OF HOURS IN THE DAY I HAD TO COVER IT.
I DIDN'T HAVE THE CONTACTS TO FOLLOW THE MEDICAL OR THE POLITICAL SIDE OF THINGS, SO I'D BEEN TASKED WITH COVERING THE HUMAN SIDE OF THE STORY. WHICH WAS, MOSTLY, HEARTBREAKING.
DEATH AND DISEASE DON'T MAKE FOR A GREAT DEAL OF JOB SATISFACTION. AT LEAST GOING INTO THE OFFICE TO WORK WAS AN ESCAPE FROM JAMIE'S ACCUSING EYES.

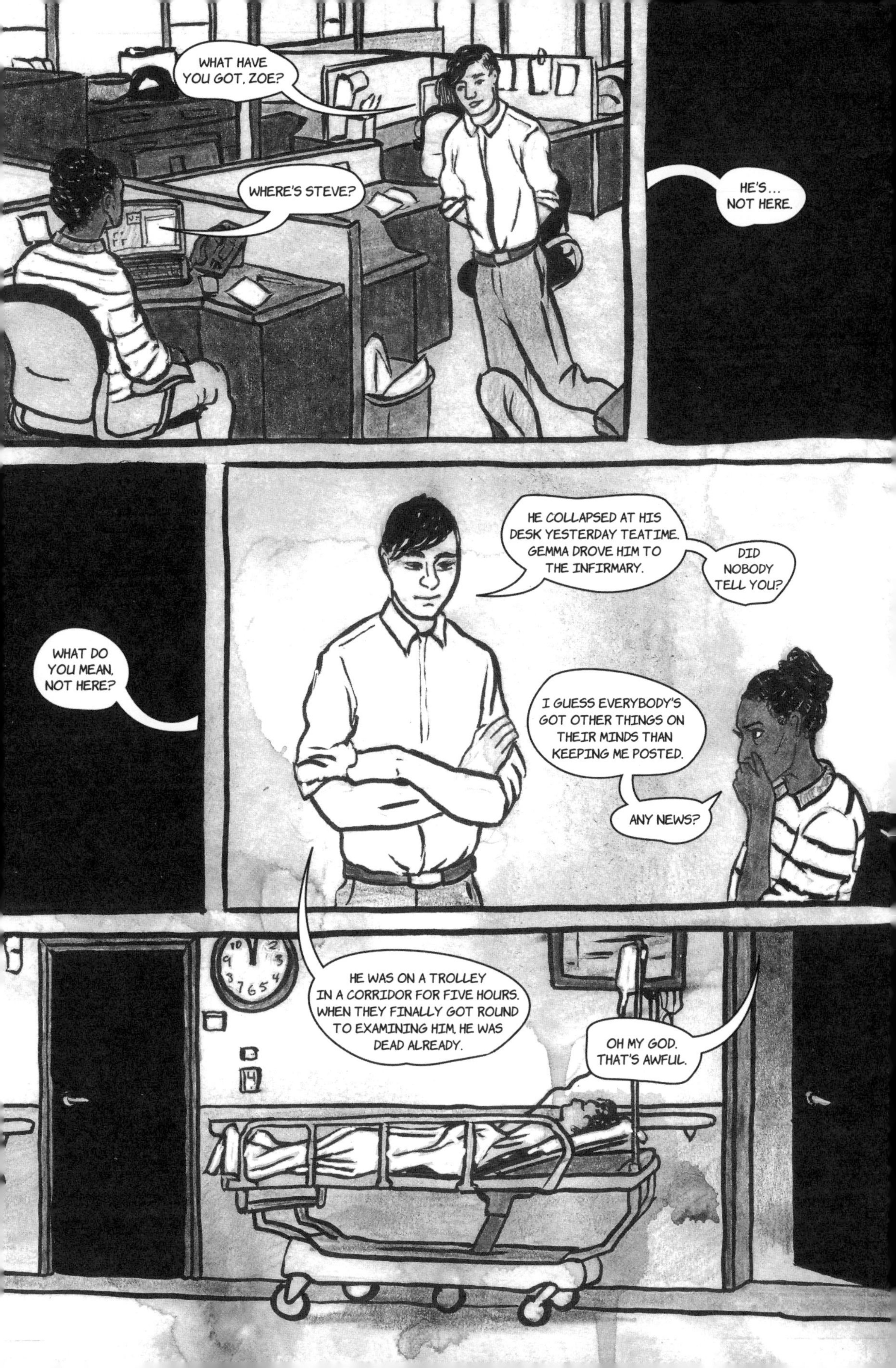
WHAT HAVE YOU GOT, ZOE?
WHERE'S STEVE?
HE'S... NOT HERE.
WHAT DO YOU MEAN, NOT HERE?
HE COLLAPSED AT HIS DESK YESTERDAY TEATIME. GEMMA DROVE HIM TO THE INFIRMARY.
DID NOBODY TELL YOU?
I GUESS EVERYBODY'S GOT OTHER THINGS ON THEIR MINDS THAN KEEPING ME POSTED.
ANY NEWS?
HE WAS ON A TROLLEY IN A CORRIDOR FOR FIVE HOURS. WHEN THEY FINALLY GOT ROUND TO EXAMINING HIM, HE WAS DEAD ALREADY.
OH MY GOD. THAT'S AWFUL.

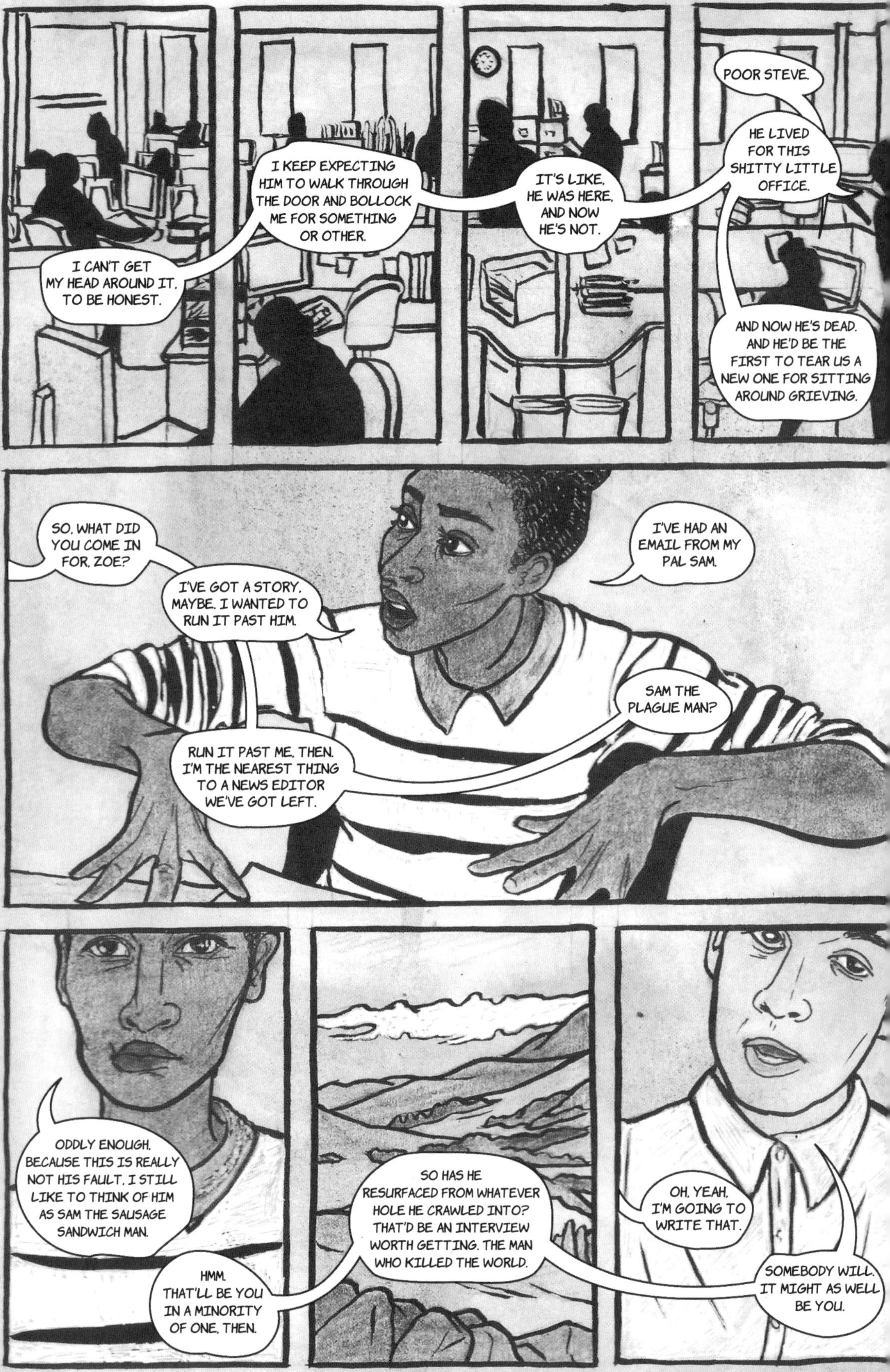
I CAN'T GET MY HEAD AROUND IT, TO BE HONEST.
I KEEP EXPECTING HIM TO WALK THROUGH THE DOOR AND BOLLOCK ME FOR SOMETHING OR OTHER.
IT'S LIKE, HE WAS HERE, AND NOW HE'S NOT.
POOR STEVE.
HE LIVED FOR THIS SHITTY LITTLE OFFICE.
AND NOW HE'S DEAD. AND HE'D BE THE FIRST TO TEAR US A NEW ONE FOR SITTING AROUND GRIEVING.
SO, WHAT DID YOU COME IN FOR, ZOE?
I'VE GOT A STORY, MAYBE. I WANTED TO RUN IT PAST HIM.
I'VE HAD AN EMAIL FROM MY PAL SAM.
RUN IT PAST ME, THEN. I'M THE NEAREST THING TO A NEWS EDITOR WE'VE GOT LEFT.
SAM THE PLAGUE MAN?
ODDLY ENOUGH, BECAUSE THIS IS REALLY NOT HIS FAULT, I STILL LIKE TO THINK OF HIM AS SAM THE SAUSAGE SANDWICH MAN.
HMM. THAT'LL BE YOU IN A MINORITY OF ONE, THEN.
SO HAS HE RESURFACED FROM WHATEVER HOLE HE CRAWLED INTO? THAT'D BE AN INTERVIEW WORTH GETTING. THE MAN WHO KILLED THE WORLD.
OH, YEAH, I'M GOING TO WRITE THAT.
SOMEBODY WILL. IT MIGHT AS WELL BE YOU.

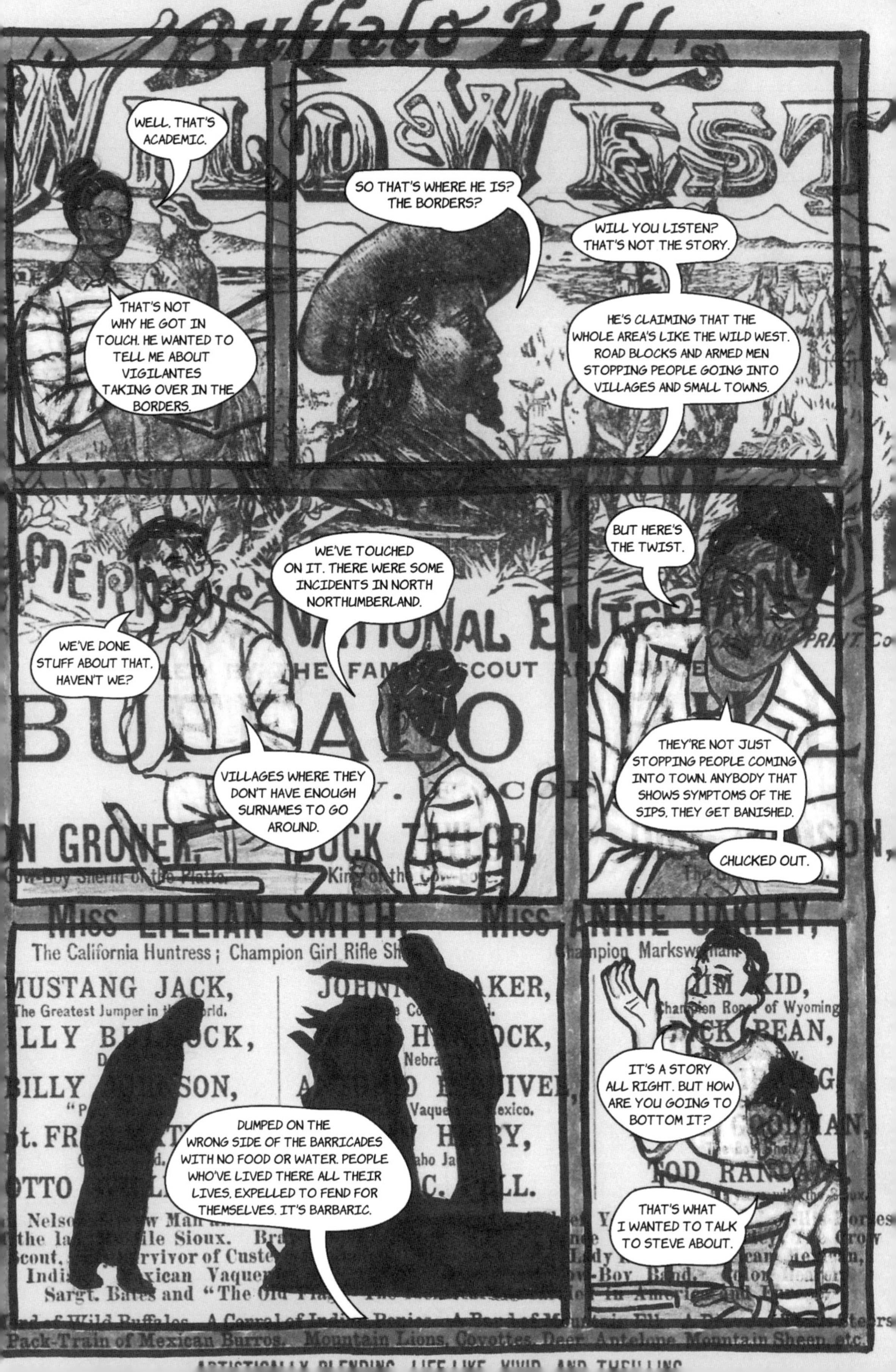
WELL, THAT'S ACADEMIC.
THAT'S NOT WHY HE GOT IN TOUCH. HE WANTED TO TELL ME ABOUT VIGILANTES TAKING OVER IN THE BORDERS.
SO THAT'S WHERE HE IS? THE BORDERS?
WILL YOU LISTEN? THAT'S NOT THE STORY.
HE'S CLAIMING THAT THE WHOLE AREA'S LIKE THE WILD WEST. ROAD BLOCKS AND ARMED MEN STOPPING PEOPLE GOING INTO VILLAGES AND SMALL TOWNS.
WE'VE DONE STUFF ABOUT THAT, HAVEN'T WE?
WE'VE TOUCHED ON IT. THERE WERE SOME INCIDENTS IN NORTH NORTHUMBERLAND.
VILLAGES WHERE THEY DON'T HAVE ENOUGH SURNAMES TO GO AROUND.
BUT HERE'S THE TWIST.
THEY'RE NOT JUST STOPPING PEOPLE COMING INTO TOWN. ANYBODY THAT SHOWS SYMPTOMS OF THE SIPS, THEY GET BANISHED.
CHUCKED OUT.
DUMPED ON THE WRONG SIDE OF THE BARRICADES WITH NO FOOD OR WATER. PEOPLE WHO'VE LIVED THERE ALL THEIR LIVES, EXPELLED TO FEND FOR THEMSELVES. IT'S BARBARIC.
IT'S A STORY ALL RIGHT. BUT HOW ARE YOU GOING TO BOTTOM IT?
THAT'S WHAT I WANTED TO TALK TO STEVE ABOUT.

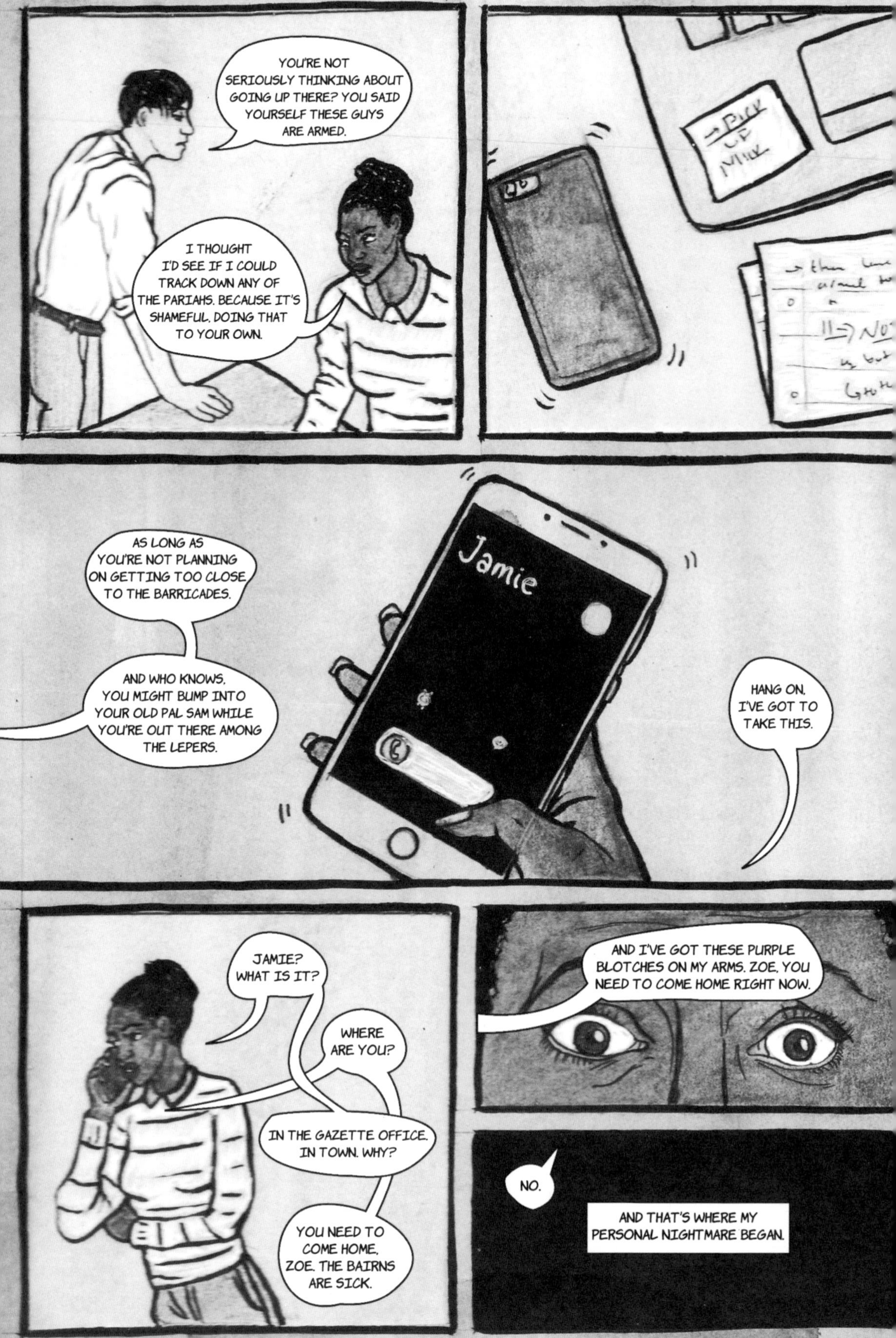

YOU'RE NOT SERIOUSLY THINKING ABOUT GOING UP THERE? YOU SAID YOURSELF THESE GUYS ARE ARMED.
I THOUGHT I'D SEE IF I COULD TRACK DOWN ANY OF THE PARIAHS. BECAUSE IT'S SHAMEFUL, DOING THAT TO YOUR OWN.
Jamie
AS LONG AS YOU'RE NOT PLANNING ON GETTING TOO CLOSE TO THE BARRICADES.
AND WHO KNOWS, YOU MIGHT BUMP INTO YOUR OLD PAL SAM WHILE YOU'RE OUT THERE AMONG THE LEPERS.
HANG ON. I'VE GOT TO TAKE THIS.
JAMIE? WHAT IS IT?
WHERE ARE YOU?
IN THE GAZETTE OFFICE. IN TOWN. WHY?
YOU NEED TO COME HOME, ZOE. THE BAIRNS ARE SICK.
AND I'VE GOT THESE PURPLE BLOTCHES ON MY ARMS. ZOE, YOU NEED TO COME HOME RIGHT NOW.
NO.
AND THAT'S WHERE MY PERSONAL NIGHTMARE BEGAN.

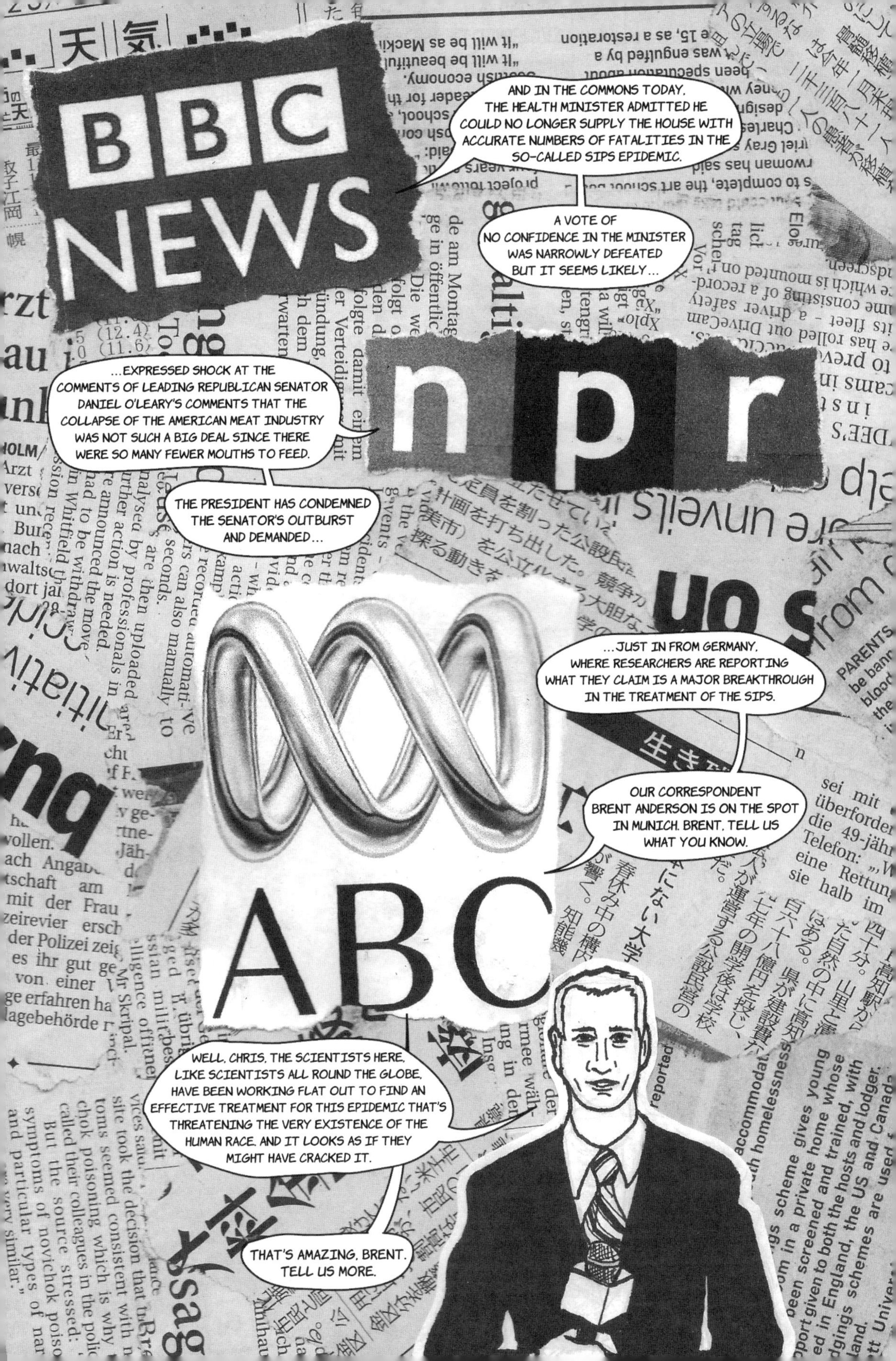
BBC NEWS
AND IN THE COMMONS TODAY, THE HEALTH MINISTER ADMITTED HE COULD NO LONGER SUPPLY THE HOUSE WITH ACCURATE NUMBERS OF FATALITIES IN THE SO-CALLED SIPS EPIDEMIC.
A VOTE OF NO CONFIDENCE IN THE MINISTER WAS NARROWLY DEFEATED BUT IT SEEMS LIKELY…
npr
…EXPRESSED SHOCK AT THE COMMENTS OF LEADING REPUBLICAN SENATOR DANIEL O'LEARY'S COMMENTS THAT THE COLLAPSE OF THE AMERICAN MEAT INDUSTRY WAS NOT SUCH A BIG DEAL SINCE THERE WERE SO MANY FEWER MOUTHS TO FEED.
THE PRESIDENT HAS CONDEMNED THE SENATOR'S OUTBURST AND DEMANDED…
ABC
…JUST IN FROM GERMANY, WHERE RESEARCHERS ARE REPORTING WHAT THEY CLAIM IS A MAJOR BREAKTHROUGH IN THE TREATMENT OF THE SIPS.
OUR CORRESPONDENT BRENT ANDERSON IS ON THE SPOT IN MUNICH. BRENT, TELL US WHAT YOU KNOW.
WELL, CHRIS, THE SCIENTISTS HERE, LIKE SCIENTISTS ALL ROUND THE GLOBE, HAVE BEEN WORKING FLAT OUT TO FIND AN EFFECTIVE TREATMENT FOR THIS EPIDEMIC THAT'S THREATENING THE VERY EXISTENCE OF THE HUMAN RACE. AND IT LOOKS AS IF THEY MIGHT HAVE CRACKED IT.
THAT'S AMAZING, BRENT. TELL US MORE.

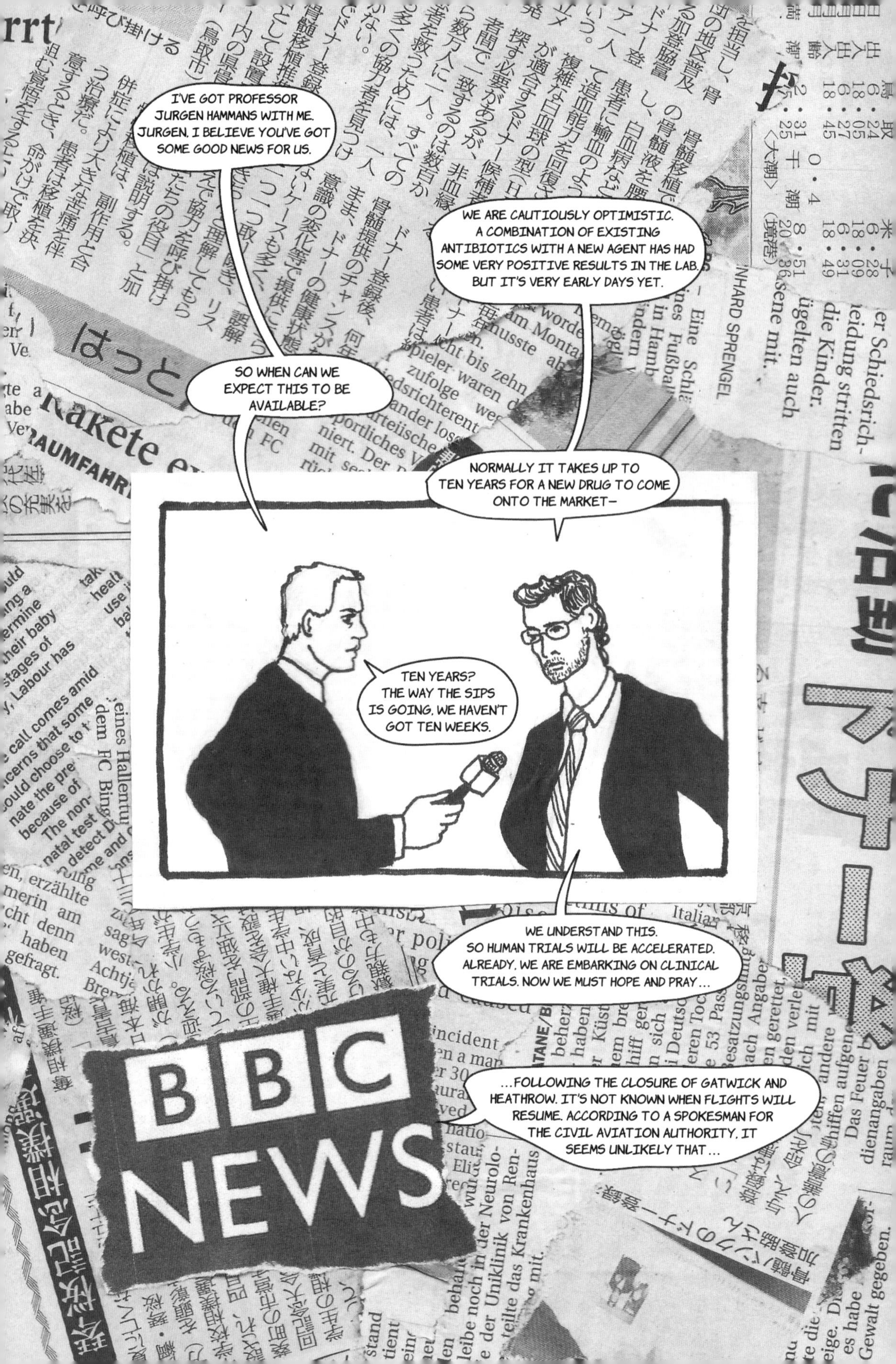
I'VE GOT PROFESSOR JURGEN HAMMANS WITH ME. JURGEN, I BELIEVE YOU'VE GOT SOME GOOD NEWS FOR US.
WE ARE CAUTIOUSLY OPTIMISTIC. A COMBINATION OF EXISTING ANTIBIOTICS WITH A NEW AGENT HAS HAD SOME VERY POSITIVE RESULTS IN THE LAB. BUT IT'S VERY EARLY DAYS YET.
SO WHEN CAN WE EXPECT THIS TO BE AVAILABLE?
NORMALLY IT TAKES UP TO TEN YEARS FOR A NEW DRUG TO COME ONTO THE MARKET–
TEN YEARS? THE WAY THE SIPS IS GOING, WE HAVEN'T GOT TEN WEEKS.
WE UNDERSTAND THIS. SO HUMAN TRIALS WILL BE ACCELERATED. ALREADY, WE ARE EMBARKING ON CLINICAL TRIALS. NOW WE MUST HOPE AND PRAY…
BBC NEWS
…FOLLOWING THE CLOSURE OF GATWICK AND HEATHROW. IT'S NOT KNOWN WHEN FLIGHTS WILL RESUME. ACCORDING TO A SPOKESMAN FOR THE CIVIL AVIATION AUTHORITY, IT SEEMS UNLIKELY THAT…

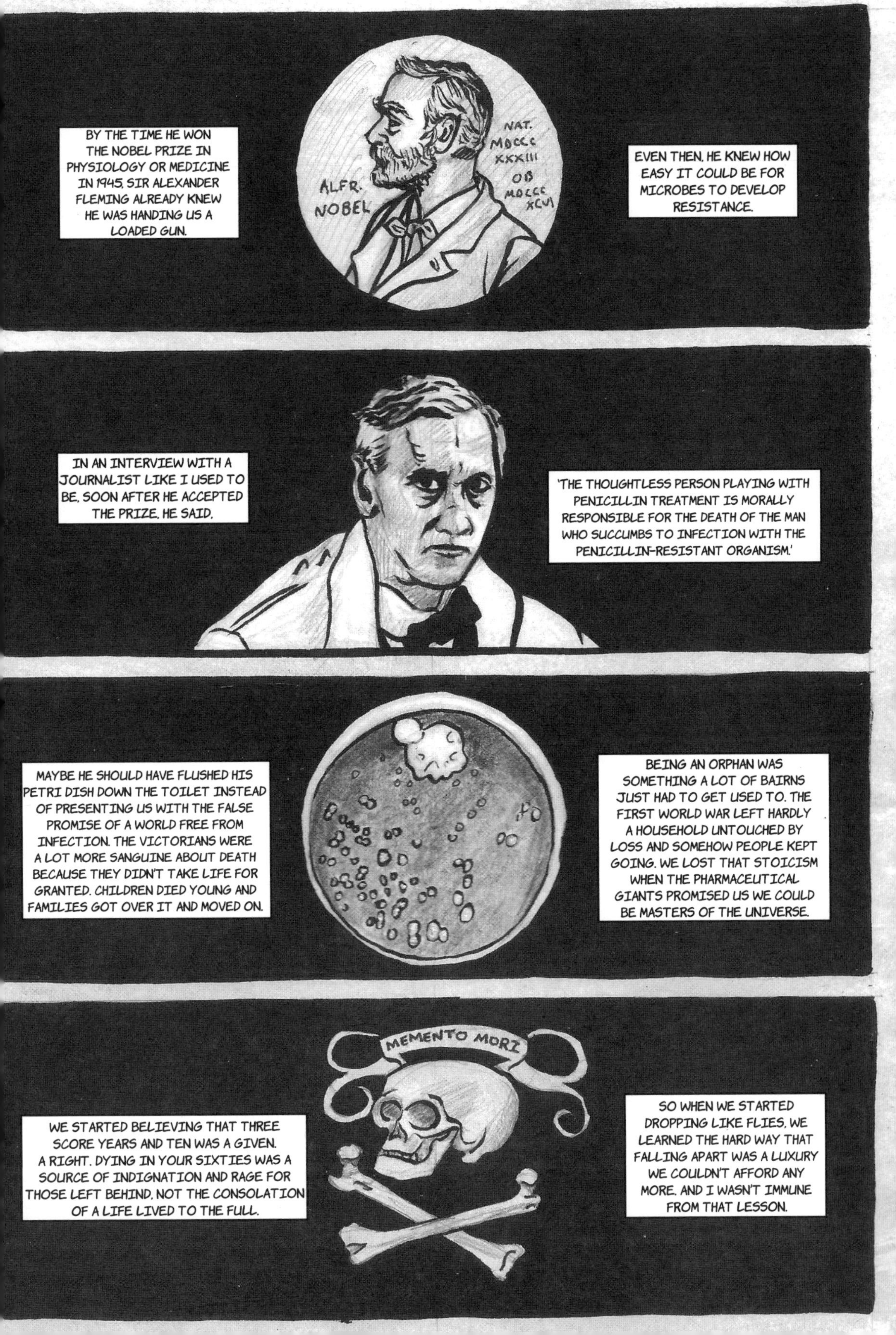
BY THE TIME HE WON THE NOBEL PRIZE IN PHYSIOLOGY OR MEDICINE IN 1945, SIR ALEXANDER FLEMING ALREADY KNEW HE WAS HANDING US A LOADED GUN.
ALFR. NOBEL
NAT. MDCCC XXXIII
OB MDCCC XCVI
EVEN THEN, HE KNEW HOW EASY IT COULD BE FOR MICROBES TO DEVELOP RESISTANCE.
IN AN INTERVIEW WITH A JOURNALIST LIKE I USED TO BE, SOON AFTER HE ACCEPTED THE PRIZE, HE SAID,
'THE THOUGHTLESS PERSON PLAYING WITH PENICILLIN TREATMENT IS MORALLY RESPONSIBLE FOR THE DEATH OF THE MAN WHO SUCCUMBS TO INFECTION WITH THE PENICILLIN-RESISTANT ORGANISM.'
MAYBE HE SHOULD HAVE FLUSHED HIS PETRI DISH DOWN THE TOILET INSTEAD OF PRESENTING US WITH THE FALSE PROMISE OF A WORLD FREE FROM INFECTION. THE VICTORIANS WERE A LOT MORE SANGUINE ABOUT DEATH BECAUSE THEY DIDN'T TAKE LIFE FOR GRANTED. CHILDREN DIED YOUNG AND FAMILIES GOT OVER IT AND MOVED ON.
BEING AN ORPHAN WAS SOMETHING A LOT OF BAIRNS JUST HAD TO GET USED TO. THE FIRST WORLD WAR LEFT HARDLY A HOUSEHOLD UNTOUCHED BY LOSS AND SOMEHOW PEOPLE KEPT GOING. WE LOST THAT STOICISM WHEN THE PHARMACEUTICAL GIANTS PROMISED US WE COULD BE MASTERS OF THE UNIVERSE.
MEMENTO MORI
WE STARTED BELIEVING THAT THREE SCORE YEARS AND TEN WAS A GIVEN. A RIGHT. DYING IN YOUR SIXTIES WAS A SOURCE OF INDIGNATION AND RAGE FOR THOSE LEFT BEHIND, NOT THE CONSOLATION OF A LIFE LIVED TO THE FULL.
SO WHEN WE STARTED DROPPING LIKE FLIES, WE LEARNED THE HARD WAY THAT FALLING APART WAS A LUXURY WE COULDN'T AFFORD ANY MORE. AND I WASN'T IMMUNE FROM THAT LESSON.

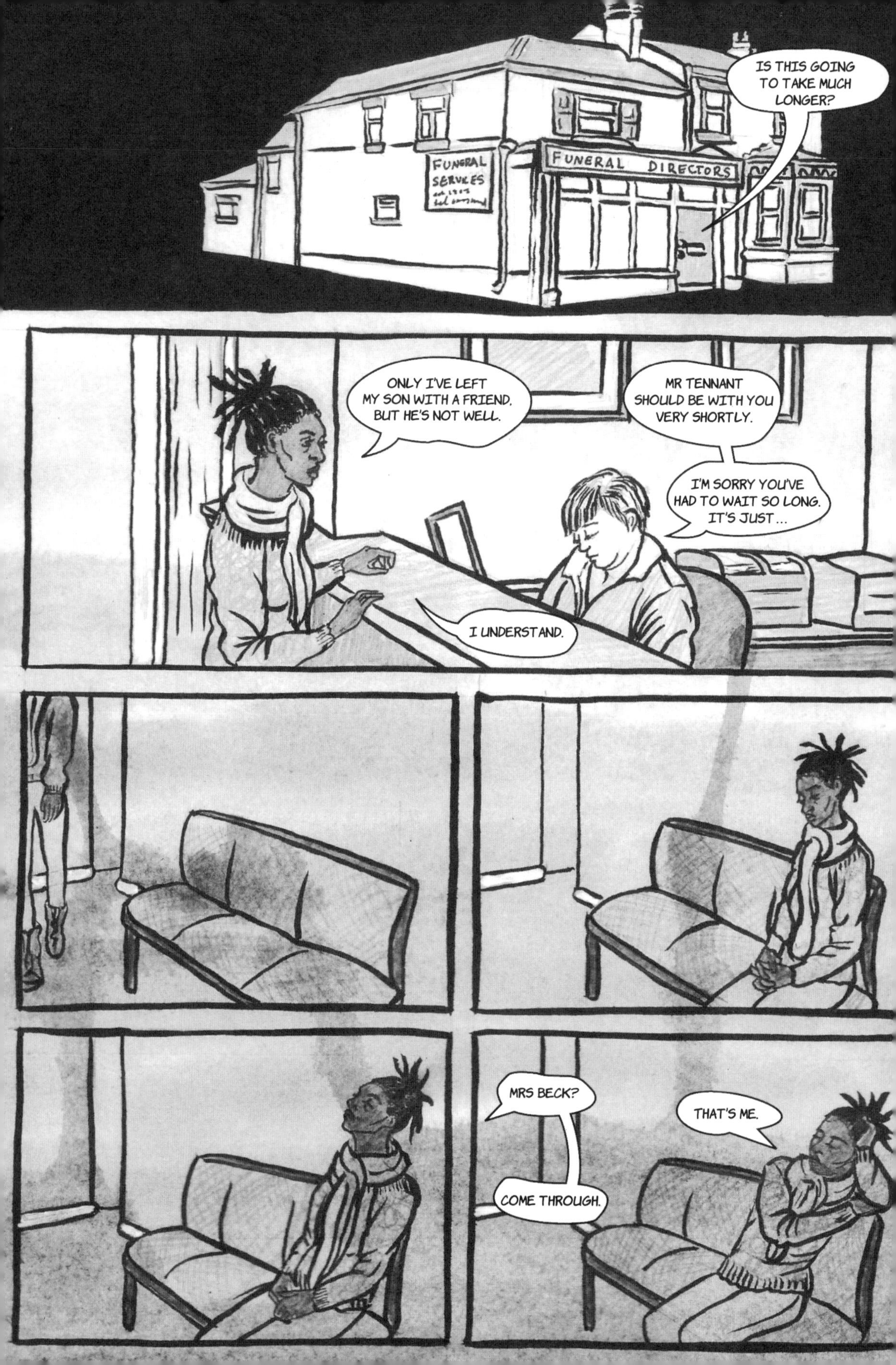
FUNERAL SERVICES
FUNERAL DIRECTORS
IS THIS GOING TO TAKE MUCH LONGER?
ONLY I'VE LEFT MY SON WITH A FRIEND, BUT HE'S NOT WELL.
MR TENNANT SHOULD BE WITH YOU VERY SHORTLY.
I'M SORRY YOU'VE HAD TO WAIT SO LONG. IT'S JUST...
I UNDERSTAND.
MRS BECK?
COME THROUGH.
THAT'S ME.

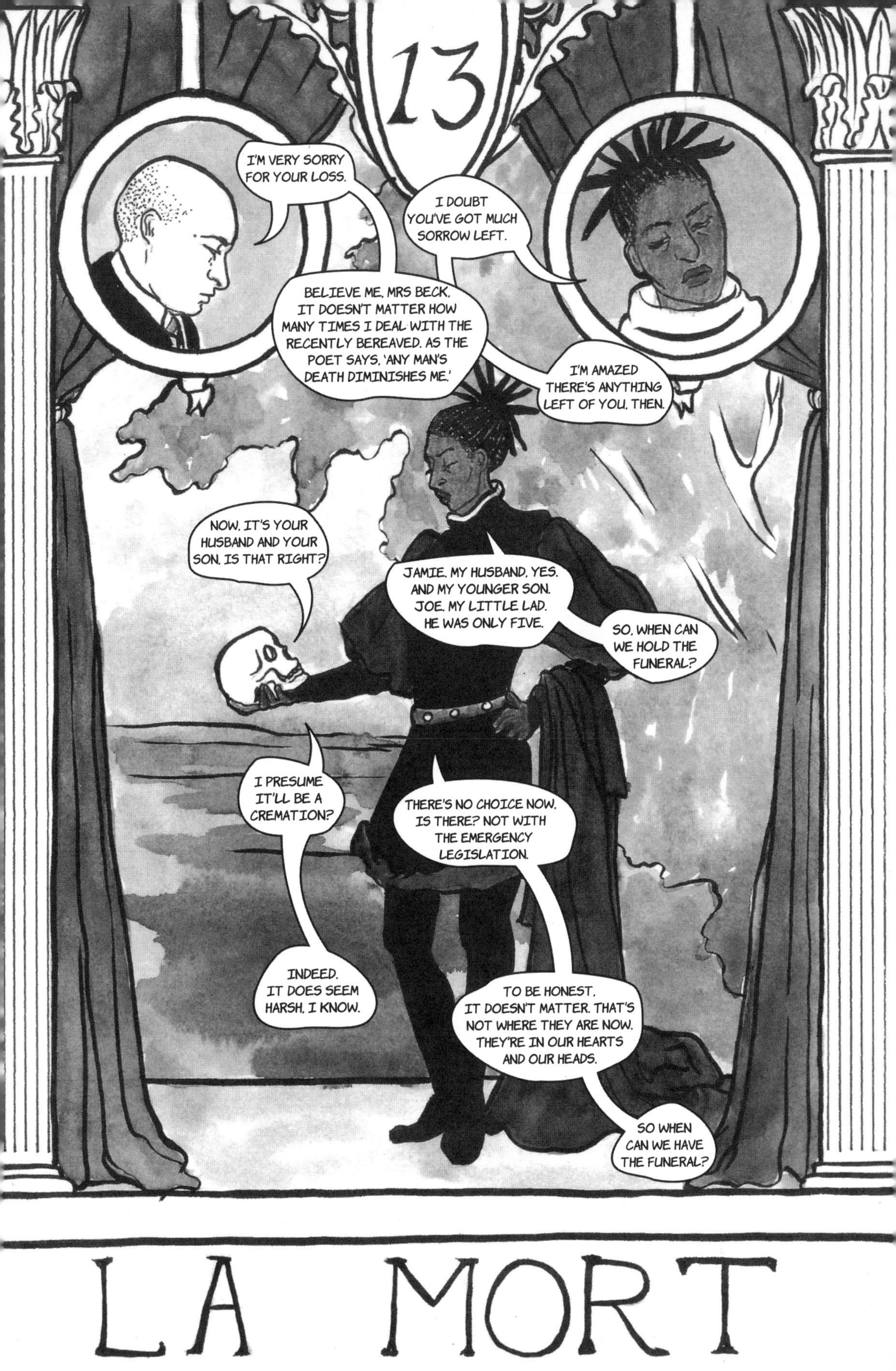
13
I'M VERY SORRY FOR YOUR LOSS.
I DOUBT YOU'VE GOT MUCH SORROW LEFT.
BELIEVE ME, MRS BECK, IT DOESN'T MATTER HOW MANY TIMES I DEAL WITH THE RECENTLY BEREAVED. AS THE POET SAYS, 'ANY MAN'S DEATH DIMINISHES ME.'
I'M AMAZED THERE'S ANYTHING LEFT OF YOU, THEN.
NOW, IT'S YOUR HUSBAND AND YOUR SON, IS THAT RIGHT?
JAMIE, MY HUSBAND, YES. AND MY YOUNGER SON. JOE. MY LITTLE LAD. HE WAS ONLY FIVE.
SO, WHEN CAN WE HOLD THE FUNERAL?
I PRESUME IT'LL BE A CREMATION?
THERE'S NO CHOICE NOW, IS THERE? NOT WITH THE EMERGENCY LEGISLATION.
INDEED. IT DOES SEEM HARSH, I KNOW.
TO BE HONEST, IT DOESN'T MATTER. THAT'S NOT WHERE THEY ARE NOW. THEY'RE IN OUR HEARTS AND OUR HEADS.
SO WHEN CAN WE HAVE THE FUNERAL?
LA MORT

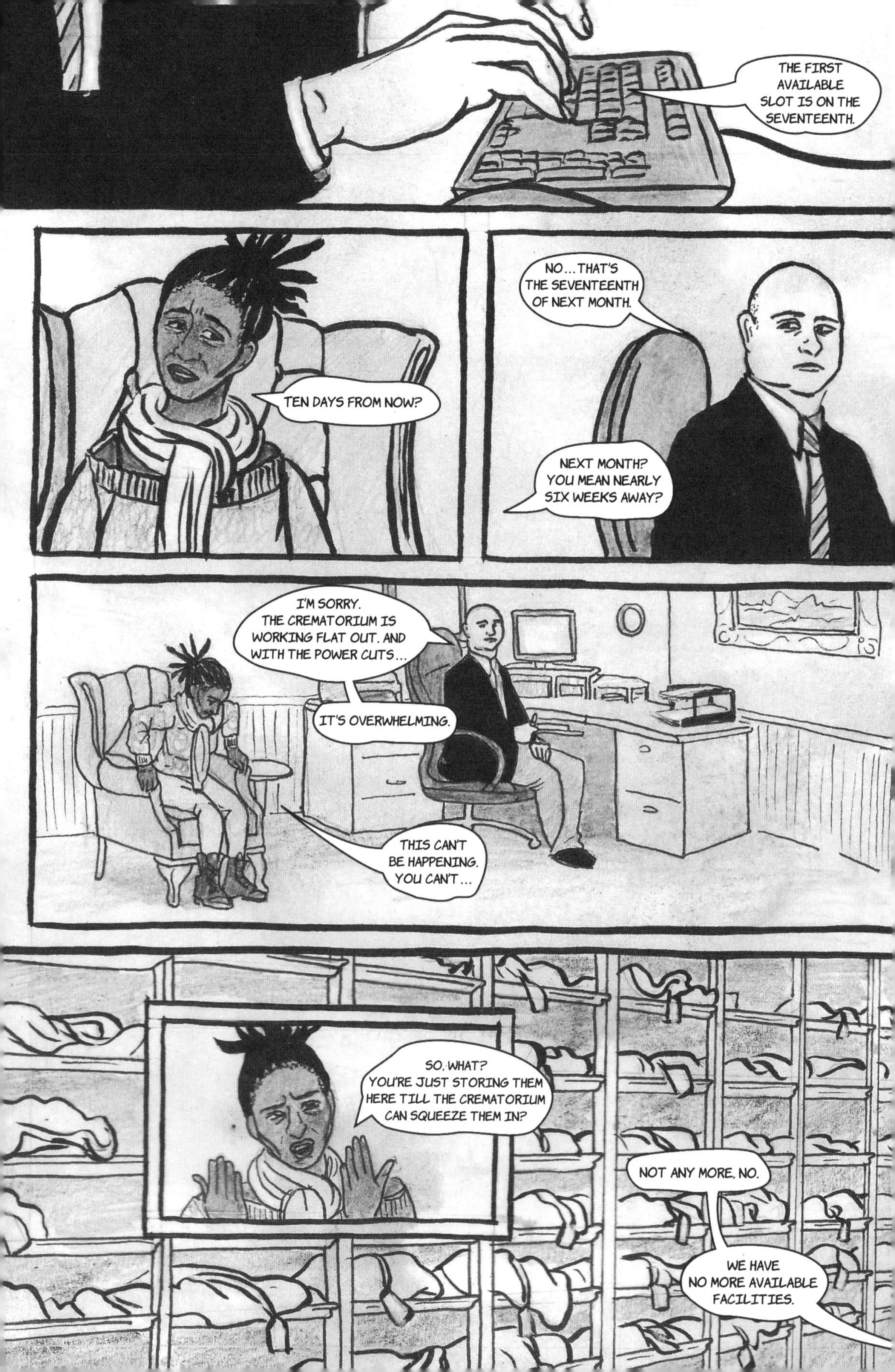
THE FIRST AVAILABLE SLOT IS ON THE SEVENTEENTH.
TEN DAYS FROM NOW?
NO... THAT'S THE SEVENTEENTH OF NEXT MONTH.
NEXT MONTH? YOU MEAN NEARLY SIX WEEKS AWAY?
I'M SORRY. THE CREMATORIUM IS WORKING FLAT OUT. AND WITH THE POWER CUTS...
IT'S OVERWHELMING.
THIS CAN'T BE HAPPENING. YOU CAN'T...
SO, WHAT? YOU'RE JUST STORING THEM HERE TILL THE CREMATORIUM CAN SQUEEZE THEM IN?
NOT ANY MORE, NO.
WE HAVE NO MORE AVAILABLE FACILITIES.

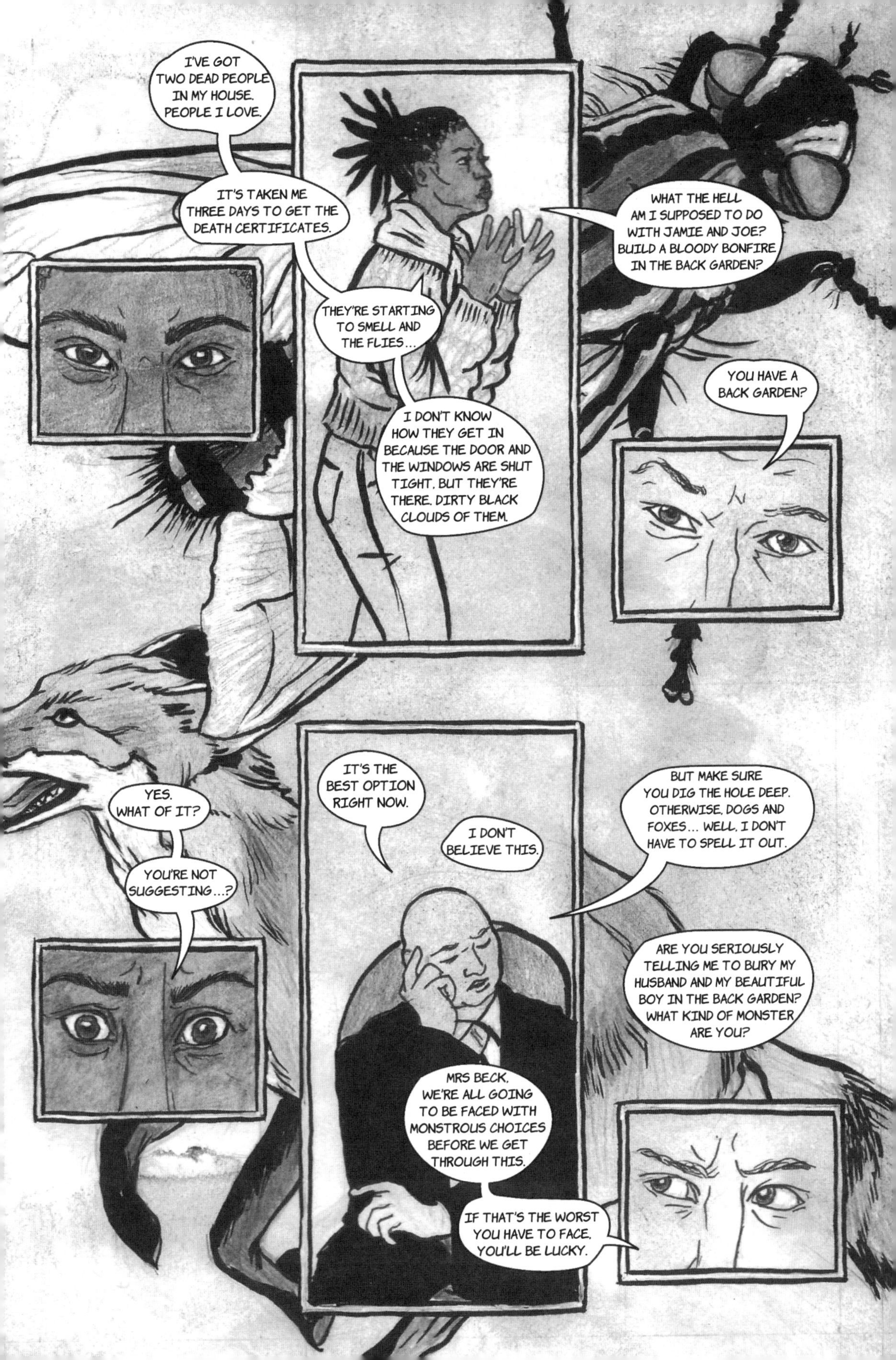
I'VE GOT TWO DEAD PEOPLE IN MY HOUSE. PEOPLE I LOVE.
IT'S TAKEN ME THREE DAYS TO GET THE DEATH CERTIFICATES.
THEY'RE STARTING TO SMELL AND THE FLIES…
I DON'T KNOW HOW THEY GET IN BECAUSE THE DOOR AND THE WINDOWS ARE SHUT TIGHT, BUT THEY'RE THERE. DIRTY BLACK CLOUDS OF THEM.
WHAT THE HELL AM I SUPPOSED TO DO WITH JAMIE AND JOE? BUILD A BLOODY BONFIRE IN THE BACK GARDEN?
YOU HAVE A BACK GARDEN?
YES. WHAT OF IT?
YOU'RE NOT SUGGESTING…?
IT'S THE BEST OPTION RIGHT NOW.
I DON'T BELIEVE THIS.
BUT MAKE SURE YOU DIG THE HOLE DEEP. OTHERWISE, DOGS AND FOXES… WELL, I DON'T HAVE TO SPELL IT OUT.
ARE YOU SERIOUSLY TELLING ME TO BURY MY HUSBAND AND MY BEAUTIFUL BOY IN THE BACK GARDEN? WHAT KIND OF MONSTER ARE YOU?
MRS BECK, WE'RE ALL GOING TO BE FACED WITH MONSTROUS CHOICES BEFORE WE GET THROUGH THIS.
IF THAT'S THE WORST YOU HAVE TO FACE, YOU'LL BE LUCKY.

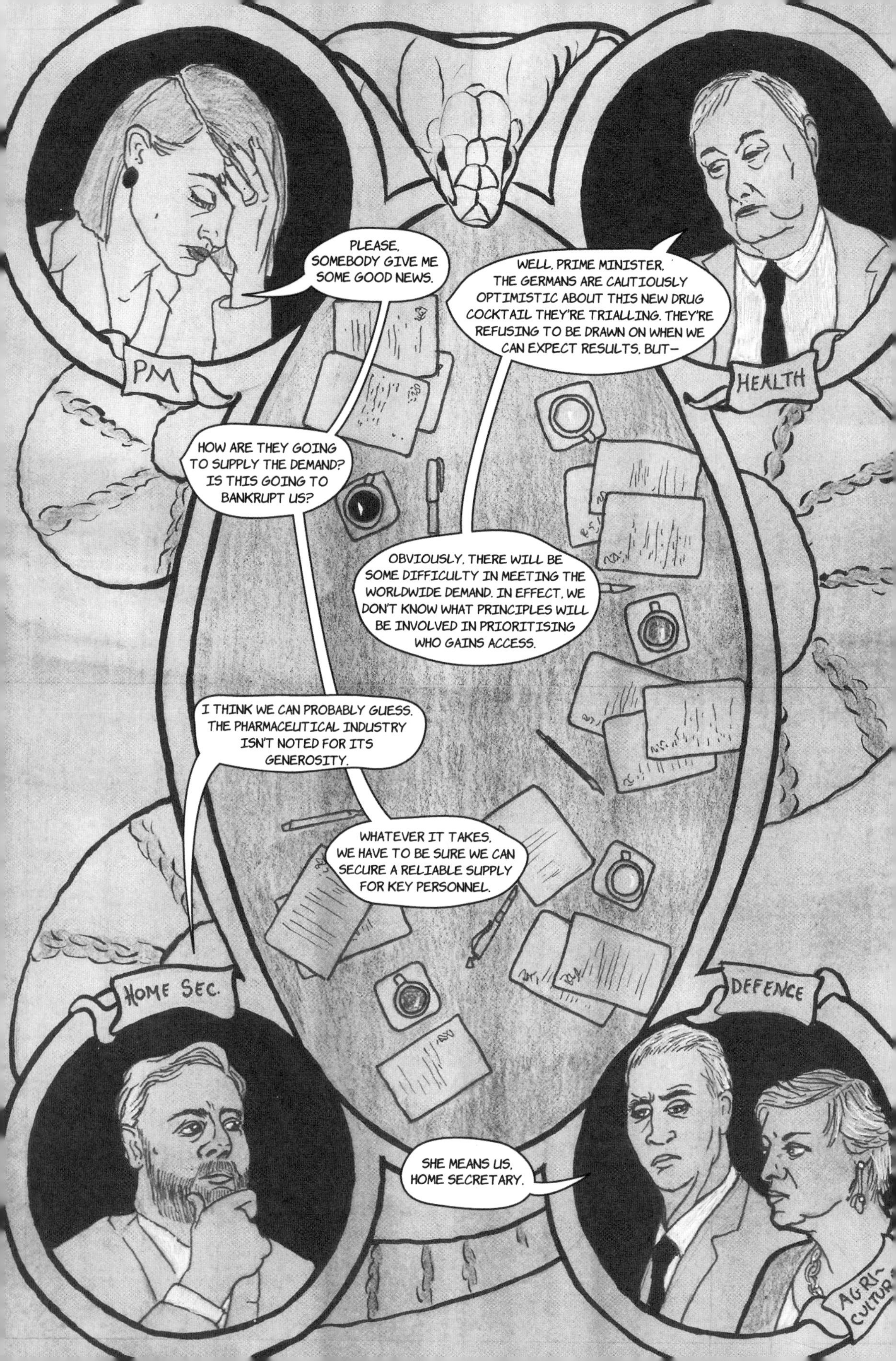
PM
HEALTH
PLEASE, SOMEBODY GIVE ME SOME GOOD NEWS.
WELL, PRIME MINISTER, THE GERMANS ARE CAUTIOUSLY OPTIMISTIC ABOUT THIS NEW DRUG COCKTAIL THEY'RE TRIALLING. THEY'RE REFUSING TO BE DRAWN ON WHEN WE CAN EXPECT RESULTS, BUT—
HOW ARE THEY GOING TO SUPPLY THE DEMAND? IS THIS GOING TO BANKRUPT US?
OBVIOUSLY, THERE WILL BE SOME DIFFICULTY IN MEETING THE WORLDWIDE DEMAND. IN EFFECT, WE DON'T KNOW WHAT PRINCIPLES WILL BE INVOLVED IN PRIORITISING WHO GAINS ACCESS.
I THINK WE CAN PROBABLY GUESS. THE PHARMACEUTICAL INDUSTRY ISN'T NOTED FOR ITS GENEROSITY.
WHATEVER IT TAKES, WE HAVE TO BE SURE WE CAN SECURE A RELIABLE SUPPLY FOR KEY PERSONNEL.
HOME SEC.
DEFENCE
SHE MEANS US, HOME SECRETARY.
AGRI-CULTURE

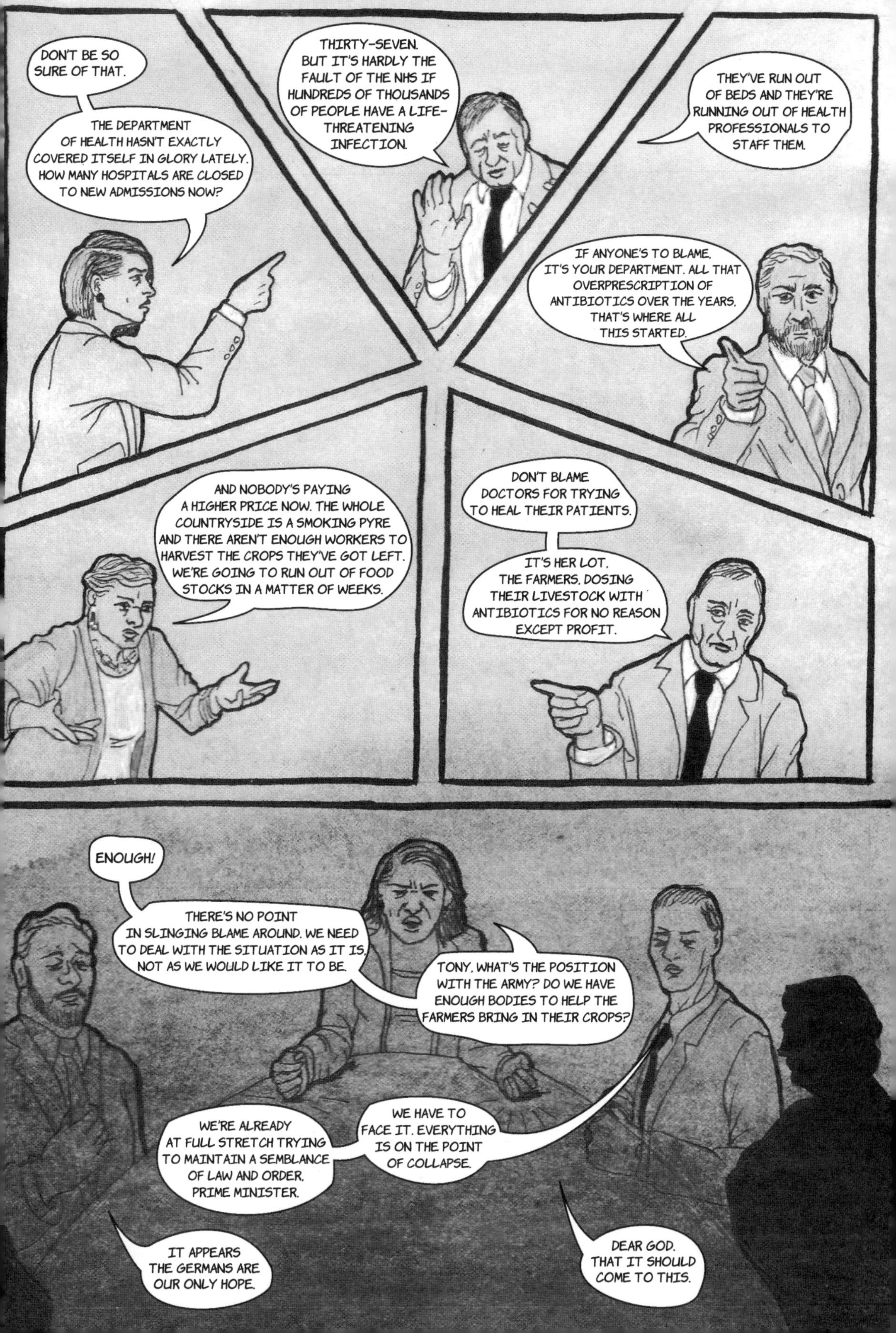
DON'T BE SO SURE OF THAT.
THE DEPARTMENT OF HEALTH HASN'T EXACTLY COVERED ITSELF IN GLORY LATELY. HOW MANY HOSPITALS ARE CLOSED TO NEW ADMISSIONS NOW?
THIRTY-SEVEN. BUT IT'S HARDLY THE FAULT OF THE NHS IF HUNDREDS OF THOUSANDS OF PEOPLE HAVE A LIFE-THREATENING INFECTION.
THEY'VE RUN OUT OF BEDS AND THEY'RE RUNNING OUT OF HEALTH PROFESSIONALS TO STAFF THEM.
IF ANYONE'S TO BLAME, IT'S YOUR DEPARTMENT. ALL THAT OVERPRESCRIPTION OF ANTIBIOTICS OVER THE YEARS, THAT'S WHERE ALL THIS STARTED.
AND NOBODY'S PAYING A HIGHER PRICE NOW. THE WHOLE COUNTRYSIDE IS A SMOKING PYRE AND THERE AREN'T ENOUGH WORKERS TO HARVEST THE CROPS THEY'VE GOT LEFT. WE'RE GOING TO RUN OUT OF FOOD STOCKS IN A MATTER OF WEEKS.
DON'T BLAME DOCTORS FOR TRYING TO HEAL THEIR PATIENTS.
IT'S HER LOT, THE FARMERS, DOSING THEIR LIVESTOCK WITH ANTIBIOTICS FOR NO REASON EXCEPT PROFIT.
ENOUGH!
THERE'S NO POINT IN SLINGING BLAME AROUND. WE NEED TO DEAL WITH THE SITUATION AS IT IS, NOT AS WE WOULD LIKE IT TO BE.
TONY, WHAT'S THE POSITION WITH THE ARMY? DO WE HAVE ENOUGH BODIES TO HELP THE FARMERS BRING IN THEIR CROPS?
WE'RE ALREADY AT FULL STRETCH TRYING TO MAINTAIN A SEMBLANCE OF LAW AND ORDER, PRIME MINISTER.
WE HAVE TO FACE IT. EVERYTHING IS ON THE POINT OF COLLAPSE.
IT APPEARS THE GERMANS ARE OUR ONLY HOPE.
DEAR GOD. THAT IT SHOULD COME TO THIS.

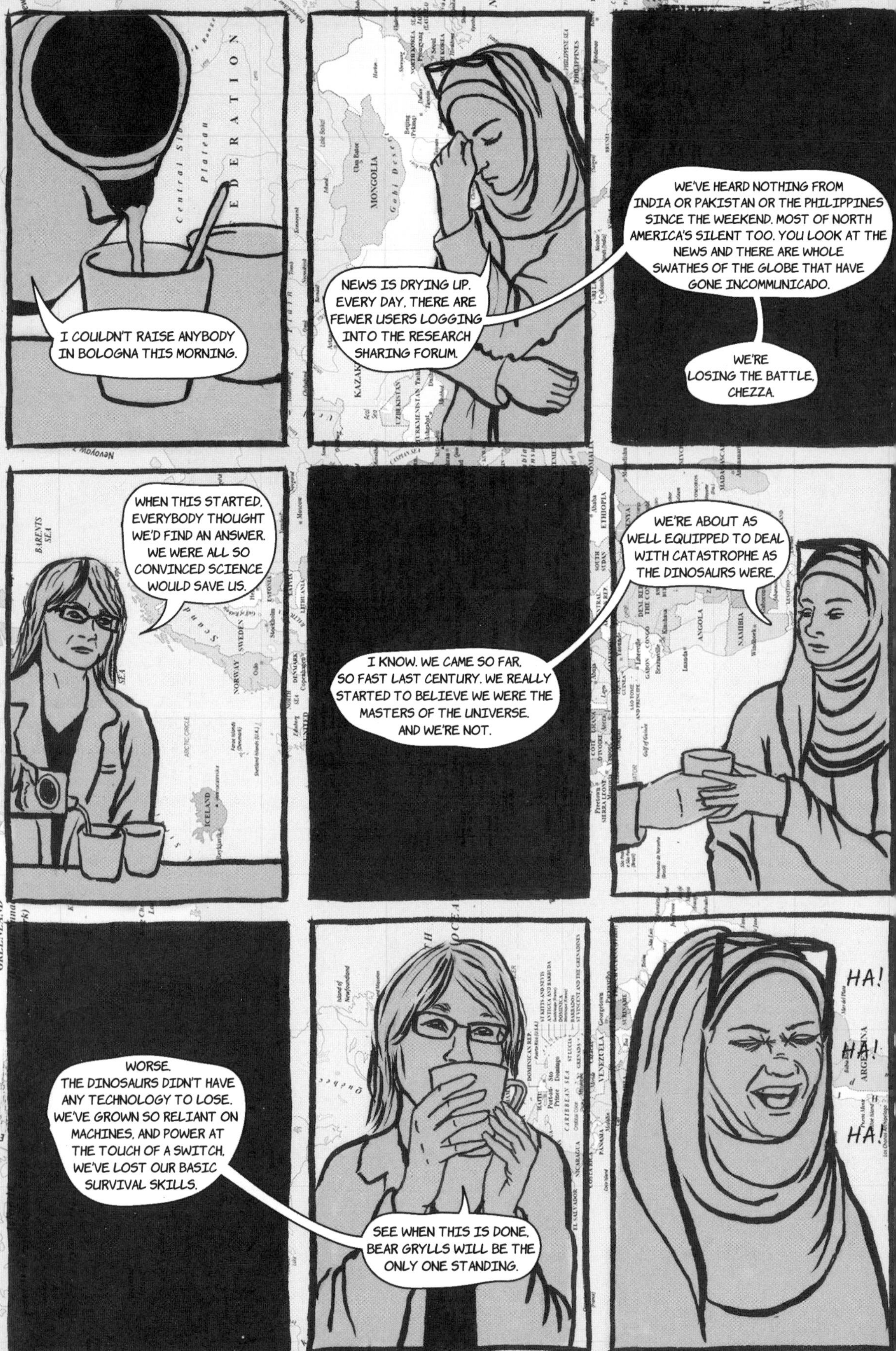
I COULDN'T RAISE ANYBODY IN BOLOGNA THIS MORNING.
NEWS IS DRYING UP. EVERY DAY, THERE ARE FEWER USERS LOGGING INTO THE RESEARCH SHARING FORUM.
WE'VE HEARD NOTHING FROM INDIA OR PAKISTAN OR THE PHILIPPINES SINCE THE WEEKEND. MOST OF NORTH AMERICA'S SILENT TOO. YOU LOOK AT THE NEWS AND THERE ARE WHOLE SWATHES OF THE GLOBE THAT HAVE GONE INCOMMUNICADO.
WE'RE LOSING THE BATTLE, CHEZZA.
WHEN THIS STARTED, EVERYBODY THOUGHT WE'D FIND AN ANSWER. WE WERE ALL SO CONVINCED SCIENCE WOULD SAVE US.
I KNOW. WE CAME SO FAR, SO FAST LAST CENTURY. WE REALLY STARTED TO BELIEVE WE WERE THE MASTERS OF THE UNIVERSE. AND WE'RE NOT.
WE'RE ABOUT AS WELL EQUIPPED TO DEAL WITH CATASTROPHE AS THE DINOSAURS WERE.
WORSE. THE DINOSAURS DIDN'T HAVE ANY TECHNOLOGY TO LOSE. WE'VE GROWN SO RELIANT ON MACHINES, AND POWER AT THE TOUCH OF A SWITCH, WE'VE LOST OUR BASIC SURVIVAL SKILLS.
SEE WHEN THIS IS DONE, BEAR GRYLLS WILL BE THE ONLY ONE STANDING.
HA!
HA!
HA!

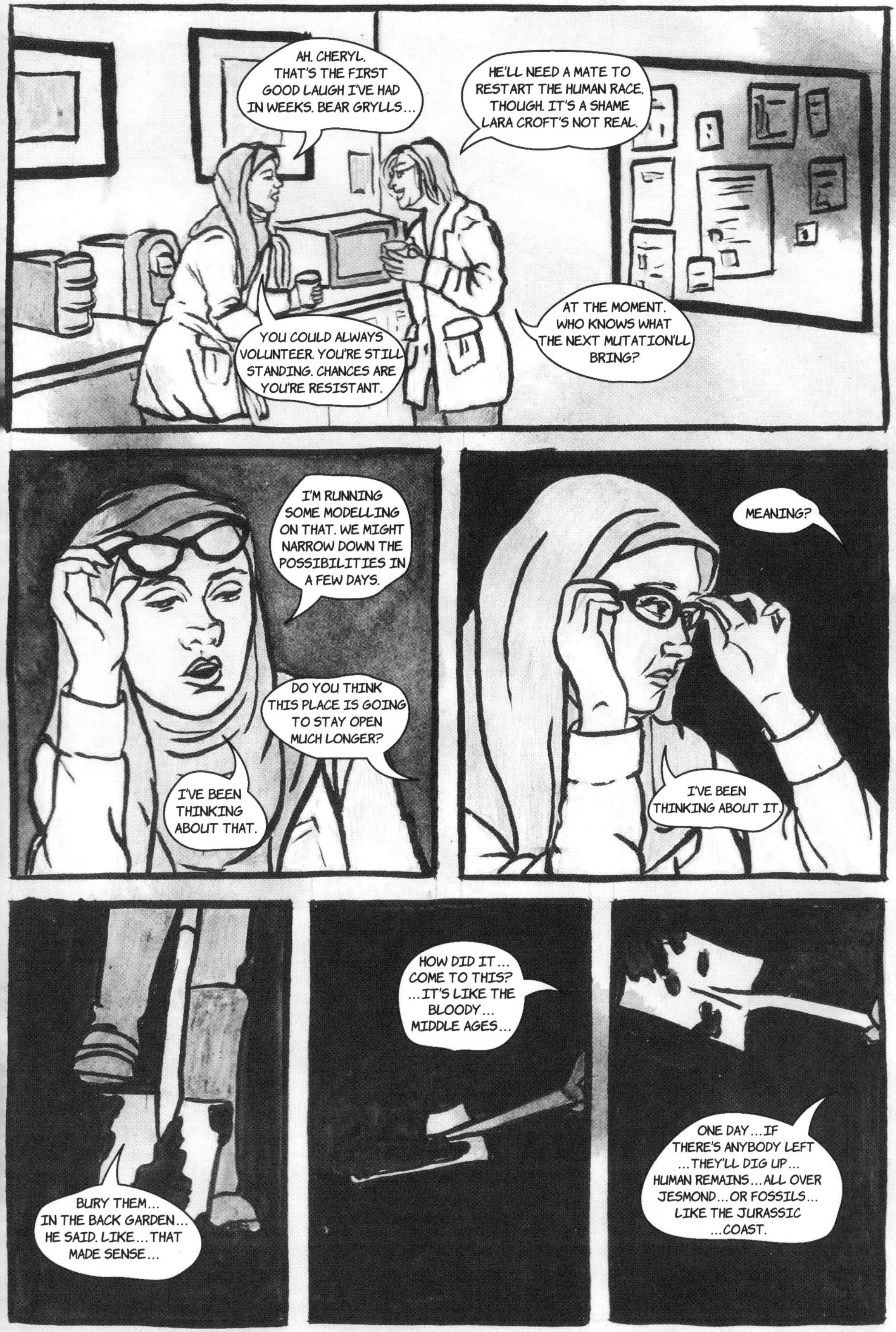
AH, CHERYL, THAT'S THE FIRST GOOD LAUGH I'VE HAD IN WEEKS. BEAR GRYLLS…
HE'LL NEED A MATE TO RESTART THE HUMAN RACE, THOUGH. IT'S A SHAME LARA CROFT'S NOT REAL.
YOU COULD ALWAYS VOLUNTEER. YOU'RE STILL STANDING. CHANCES ARE YOU'RE RESISTANT.
AT THE MOMENT. WHO KNOWS WHAT THE NEXT MUTATION'LL BRING?
I'M RUNNING SOME MODELLING ON THAT. WE MIGHT NARROW DOWN THE POSSIBILITIES IN A FEW DAYS.
DO YOU THINK THIS PLACE IS GOING TO STAY OPEN MUCH LONGER?
I'VE BEEN THINKING ABOUT THAT.
MEANING?
I'VE BEEN THINKING ABOUT IT.
BURY THEM… IN THE BACK GARDEN… HE SAID. LIKE… THAT MADE SENSE…
HOW DID IT… COME TO THIS? …IT'S LIKE THE BLOODY… MIDDLE AGES…
ONE DAY… IF THERE'S ANYBODY LEFT …THEY'LL DIG UP… HUMAN REMAINS… ALL OVER JESMOND… OR FOSSILS… LIKE THE JURASSIC …COAST.

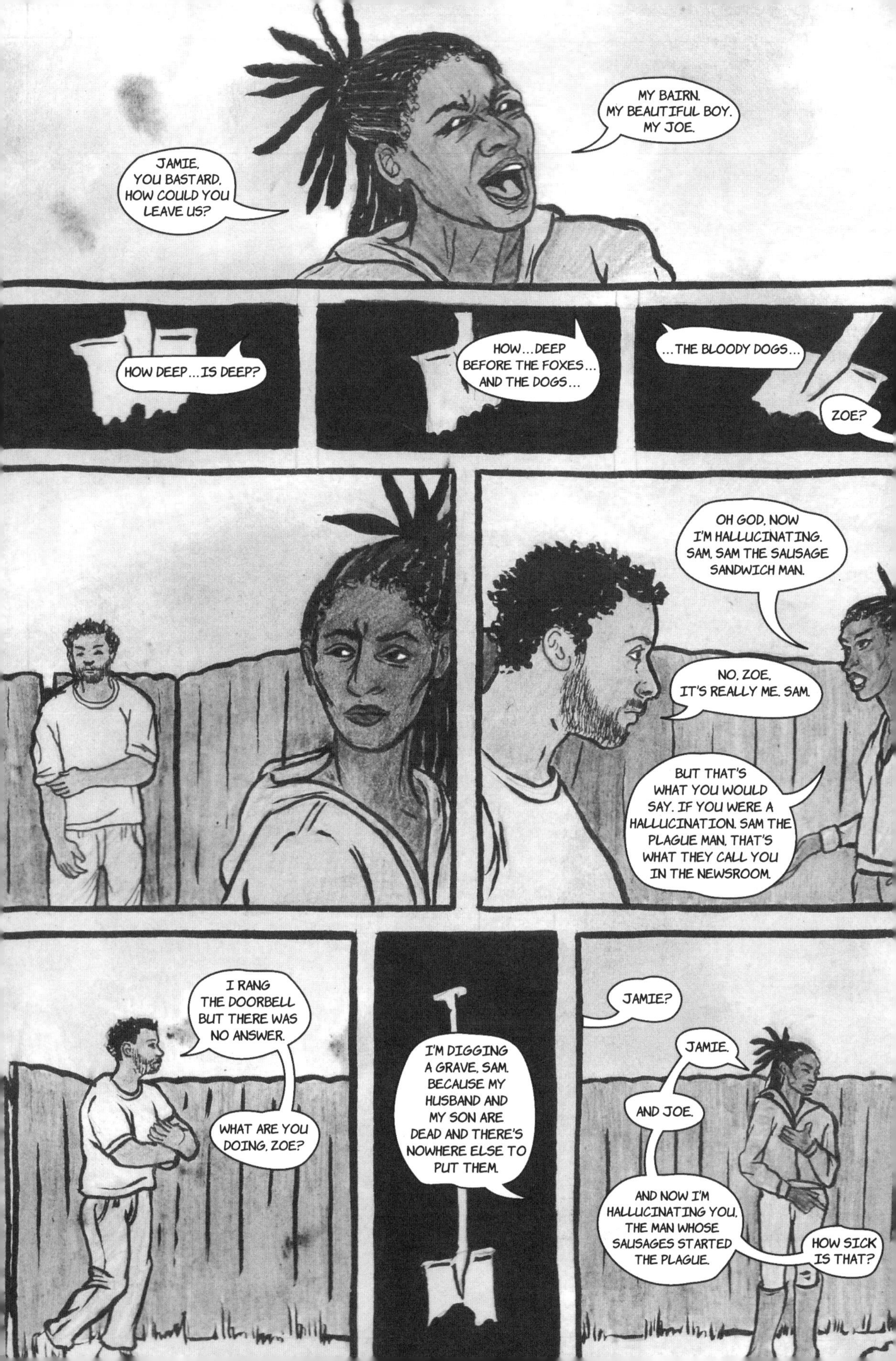
JAMIE. YOU BASTARD. HOW COULD YOU LEAVE US?
MY BAIRN. MY BEAUTIFUL BOY. MY JOE.
HOW DEEP…IS DEEP?
HOW…DEEP BEFORE THE FOXES… AND THE DOGS…
…THE BLOODY DOGS…
ZOE?
OH GOD. NOW I'M HALLUCINATING. SAM. SAM THE SAUSAGE SANDWICH MAN.
NO. ZOE. IT'S REALLY ME. SAM.
BUT THAT'S WHAT YOU WOULD SAY. IF YOU WERE A HALLUCINATION. SAM THE PLAGUE MAN. THAT'S WHAT THEY CALL YOU IN THE NEWSROOM.
I RANG THE DOORBELL BUT THERE WAS NO ANSWER.
WHAT ARE YOU DOING. ZOE?
I'M DIGGING A GRAVE. SAM. BECAUSE MY HUSBAND AND MY SON ARE DEAD AND THERE'S NOWHERE ELSE TO PUT THEM.
JAMIE?
JAMIE.
AND JOE.
AND NOW I'M HALLUCINATING YOU. THE MAN WHOSE SAUSAGES STARTED THE PLAGUE.
HOW SICK IS THAT?

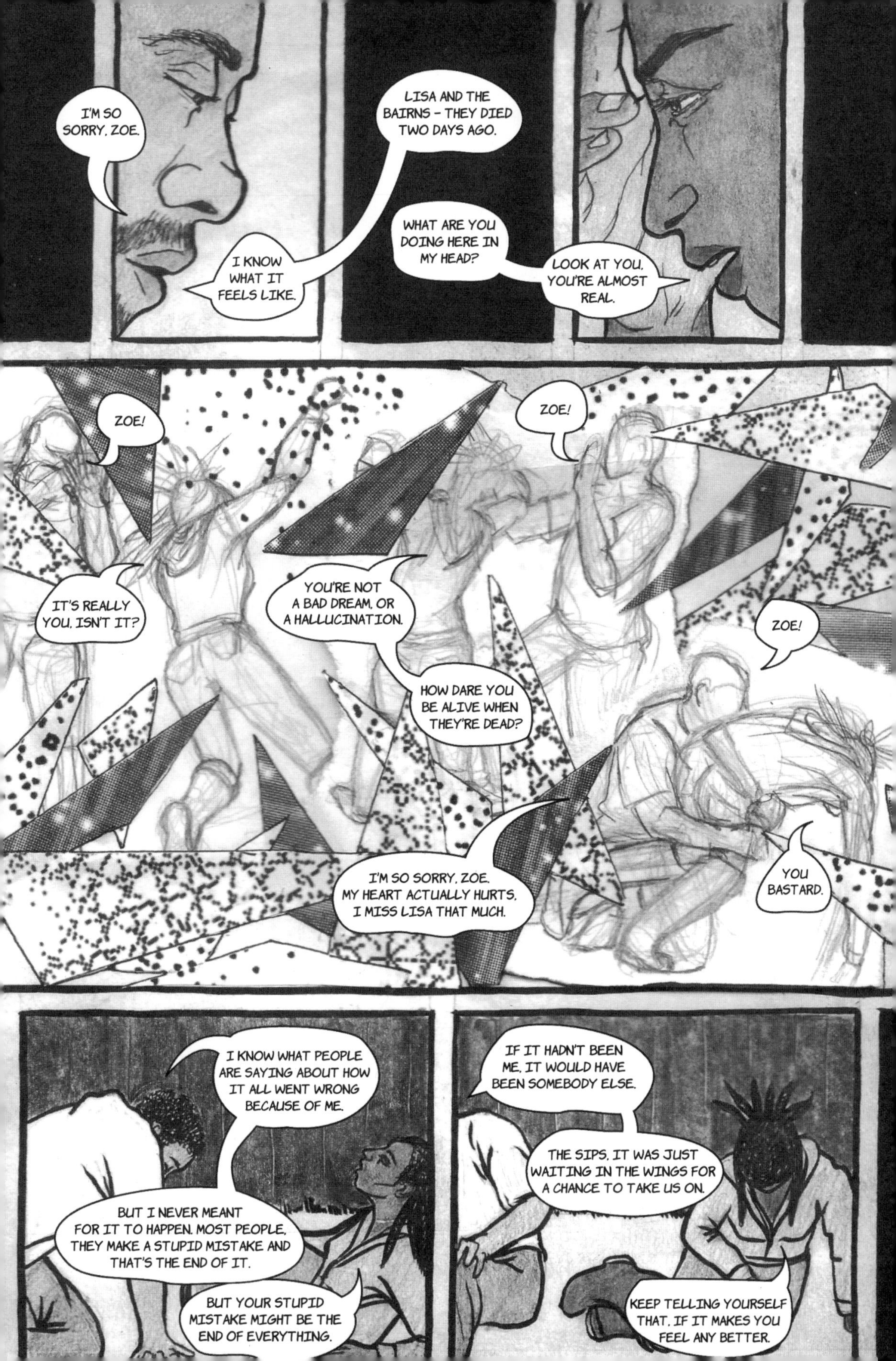
I'M SO SORRY, ZOE.
LISA AND THE BAIRNS – THEY DIED TWO DAYS AGO.
I KNOW WHAT IT FEELS LIKE.
WHAT ARE YOU DOING HERE IN MY HEAD?
LOOK AT YOU, YOU'RE ALMOST REAL.
ZOE!
IT'S REALLY YOU, ISN'T IT?
YOU'RE NOT A BAD DREAM, OR A HALLUCINATION.
HOW DARE YOU BE ALIVE WHEN THEY'RE DEAD?
ZOE!
ZOE!
I'M SO SORRY, ZOE. MY HEART ACTUALLY HURTS, I MISS LISA THAT MUCH.
YOU BASTARD.
I KNOW WHAT PEOPLE ARE SAYING ABOUT HOW IT ALL WENT WRONG BECAUSE OF ME.
BUT I NEVER MEANT FOR IT TO HAPPEN. MOST PEOPLE, THEY MAKE A STUPID MISTAKE AND THAT'S THE END OF IT.
BUT YOUR STUPID MISTAKE MIGHT BE THE END OF EVERYTHING.
IF IT HADN'T BEEN ME, IT WOULD HAVE BEEN SOMEBODY ELSE.
THE SIPS, IT WAS JUST WAITING IN THE WINGS FOR A CHANCE TO TAKE US ON.
KEEP TELLING YOURSELF THAT, IF IT MAKES YOU FEEL ANY BETTER.

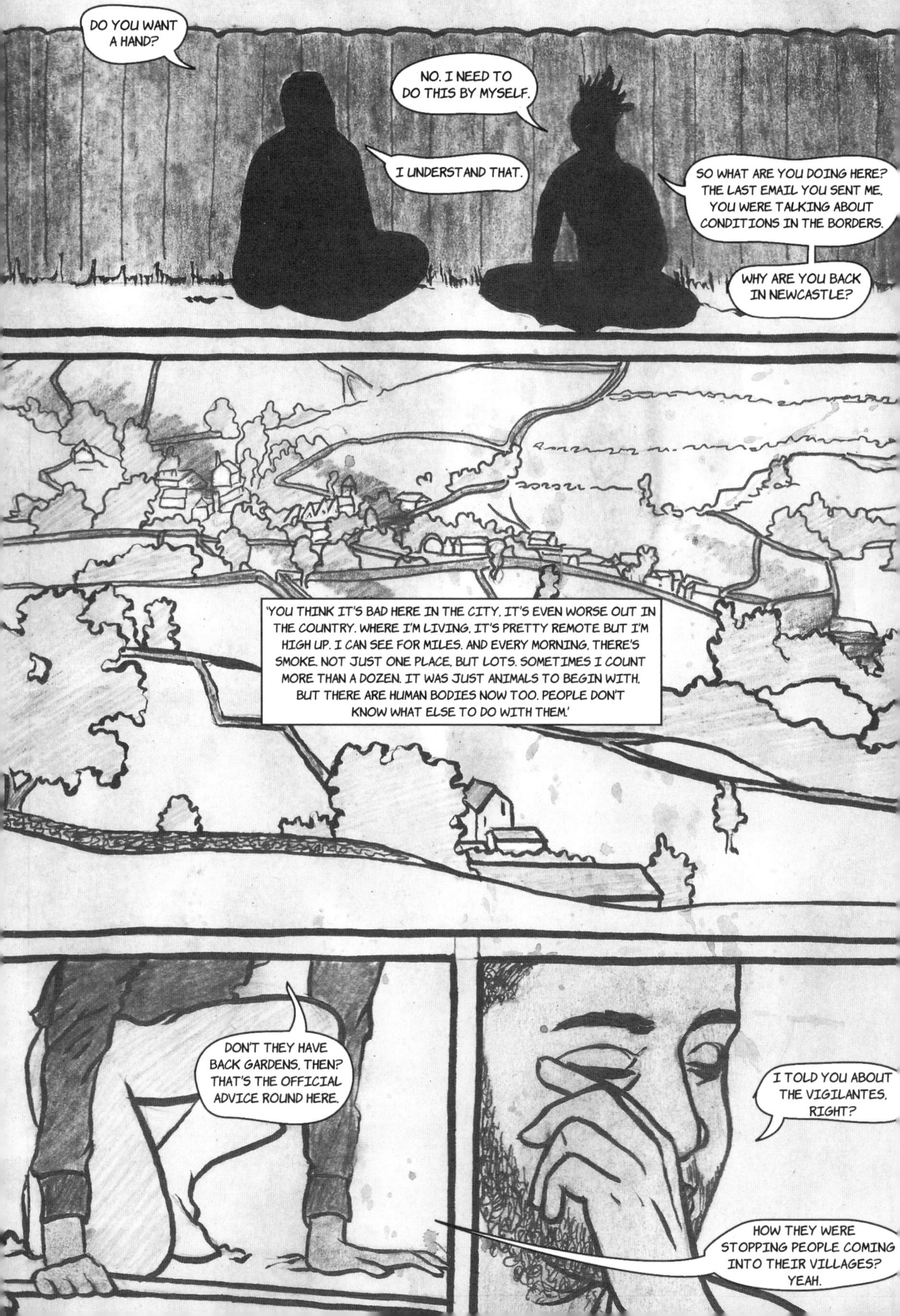
DO YOU WANT A HAND?
NO. I NEED TO DO THIS BY MYSELF.
I UNDERSTAND THAT.
SO WHAT ARE YOU DOING HERE? THE LAST EMAIL YOU SENT ME, YOU WERE TALKING ABOUT CONDITIONS IN THE BORDERS.
WHY ARE YOU BACK IN NEWCASTLE?
'YOU THINK IT'S BAD HERE IN THE CITY, IT'S EVEN WORSE OUT IN THE COUNTRY. WHERE I'M LIVING, IT'S PRETTY REMOTE BUT I'M HIGH UP. I CAN SEE FOR MILES. AND EVERY MORNING, THERE'S SMOKE. NOT JUST ONE PLACE, BUT LOTS. SOMETIMES I COUNT MORE THAN A DOZEN. IT WAS JUST ANIMALS TO BEGIN WITH, BUT THERE ARE HUMAN BODIES NOW TOO. PEOPLE DON'T KNOW WHAT ELSE TO DO WITH THEM.'
DON'T THEY HAVE BACK GARDENS, THEN? THAT'S THE OFFICIAL ADVICE ROUND HERE.
I TOLD YOU ABOUT THE VIGILANTES, RIGHT?
HOW THEY WERE STOPPING PEOPLE COMING INTO THEIR VILLAGES? YEAH.

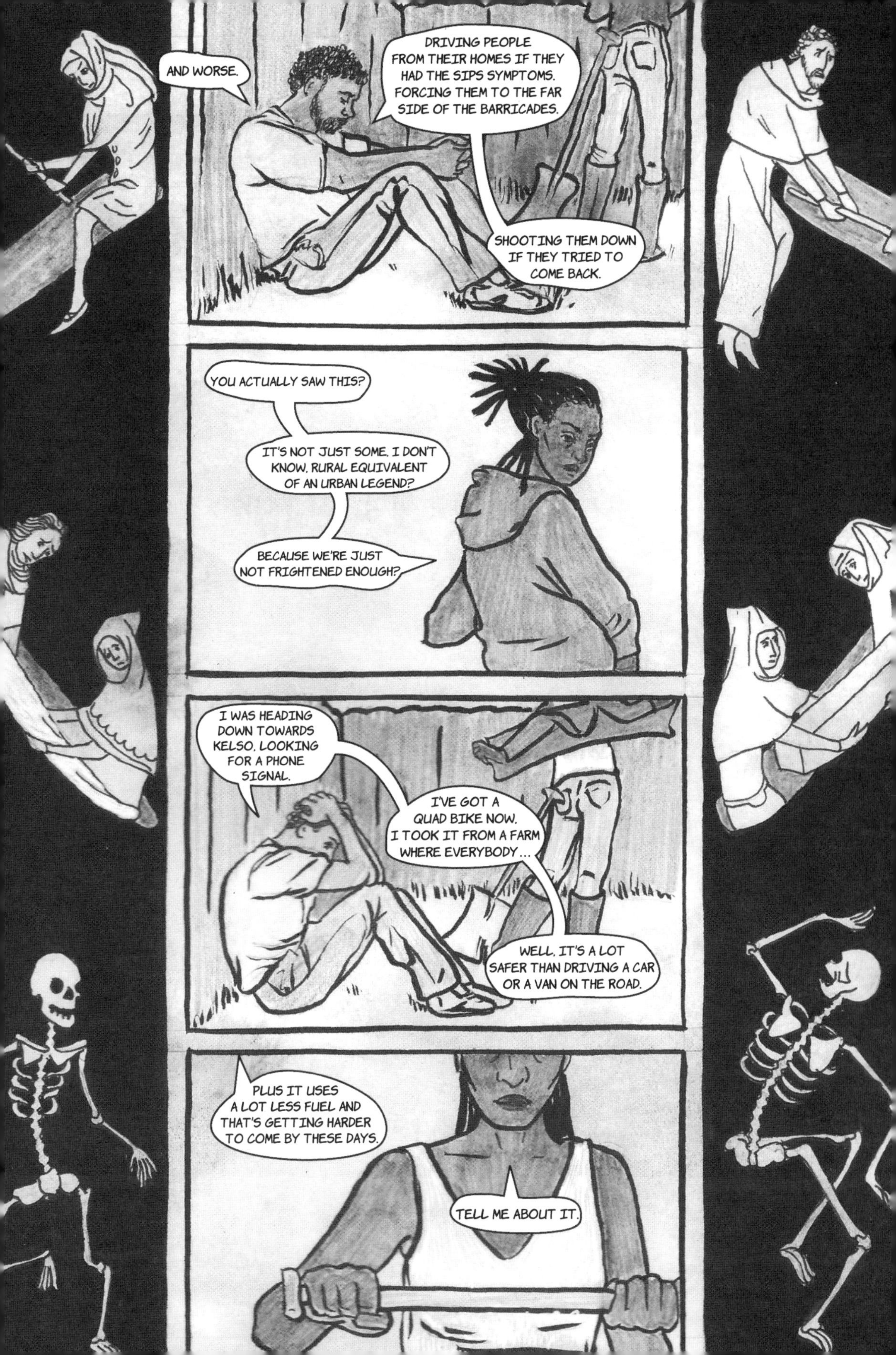
AND WORSE.
DRIVING PEOPLE FROM THEIR HOMES IF THEY HAD THE SIPS SYMPTOMS. FORCING THEM TO THE FAR SIDE OF THE BARRICADES.
SHOOTING THEM DOWN IF THEY TRIED TO COME BACK.
YOU ACTUALLY SAW THIS?
IT'S NOT JUST SOME, I DON'T KNOW, RURAL EQUIVALENT OF AN URBAN LEGEND?
BECAUSE WE'RE JUST NOT FRIGHTENED ENOUGH?
I WAS HEADING DOWN TOWARDS KELSO, LOOKING FOR A PHONE SIGNAL.
I'VE GOT A QUAD BIKE NOW. I TOOK IT FROM A FARM WHERE EVERYBODY...
WELL, IT'S A LOT SAFER THAN DRIVING A CAR OR A VAN ON THE ROAD.
PLUS IT USES A LOT LESS FUEL AND THAT'S GETTING HARDER TO COME BY THESE DAYS.
TELL ME ABOUT IT.

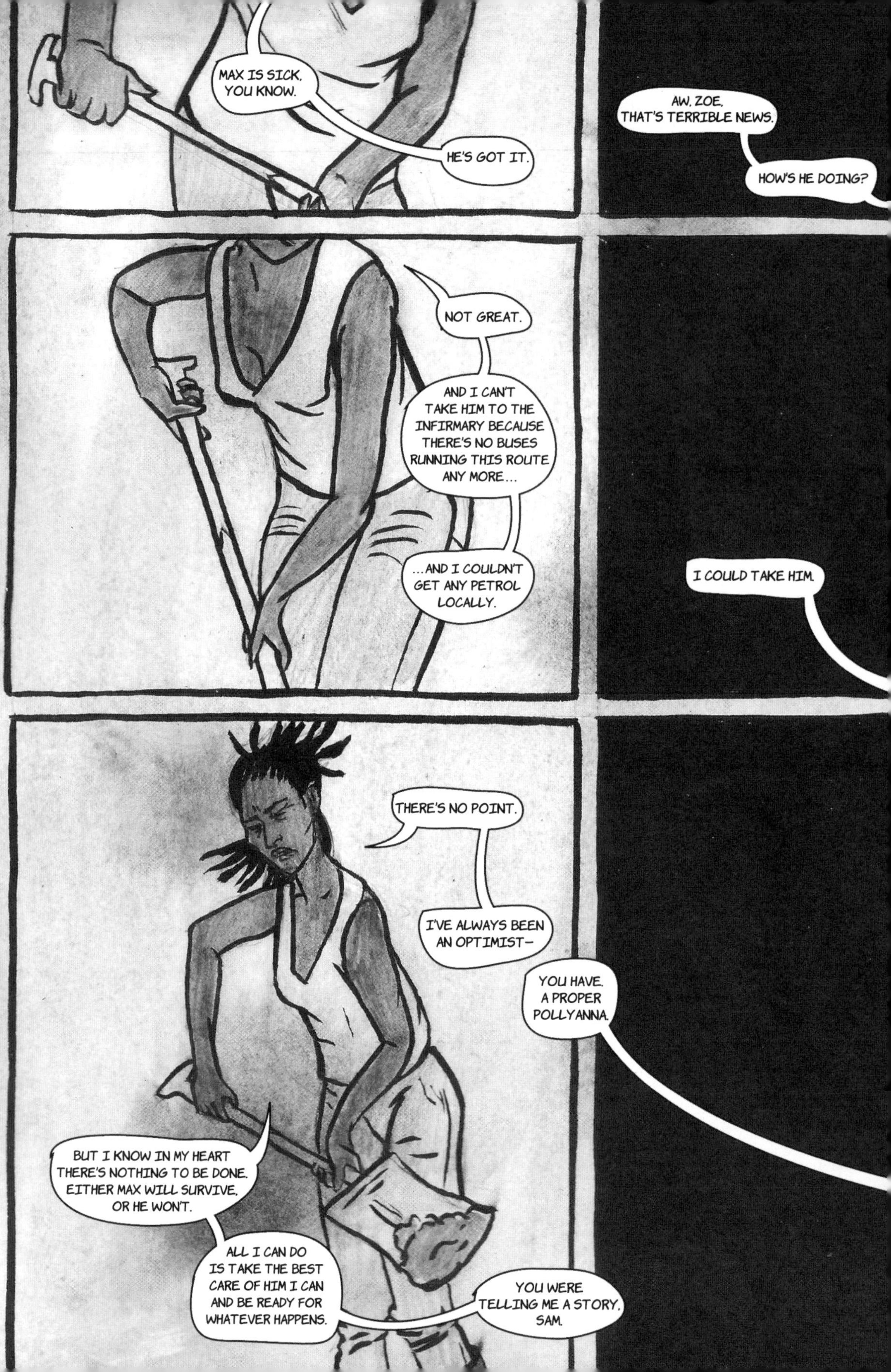
MAX IS SICK. YOU KNOW.
HE'S GOT IT.
AW, ZOE. THAT'S TERRIBLE NEWS.
HOW'S HE DOING?
NOT GREAT.
AND I CAN'T TAKE HIM TO THE INFIRMARY BECAUSE THERE'S NO BUSES RUNNING THIS ROUTE ANY MORE…
…AND I COULDN'T GET ANY PETROL LOCALLY.
I COULD TAKE HIM.
THERE'S NO POINT.
I'VE ALWAYS BEEN AN OPTIMIST–
YOU HAVE. A PROPER POLLYANNA.
BUT I KNOW IN MY HEART THERE'S NOTHING TO BE DONE. EITHER MAX WILL SURVIVE, OR HE WON'T.
ALL I CAN DO IS TAKE THE BEST CARE OF HIM I CAN AND BE READY FOR WHATEVER HAPPENS.
YOU WERE TELLING ME A STORY, SAM.

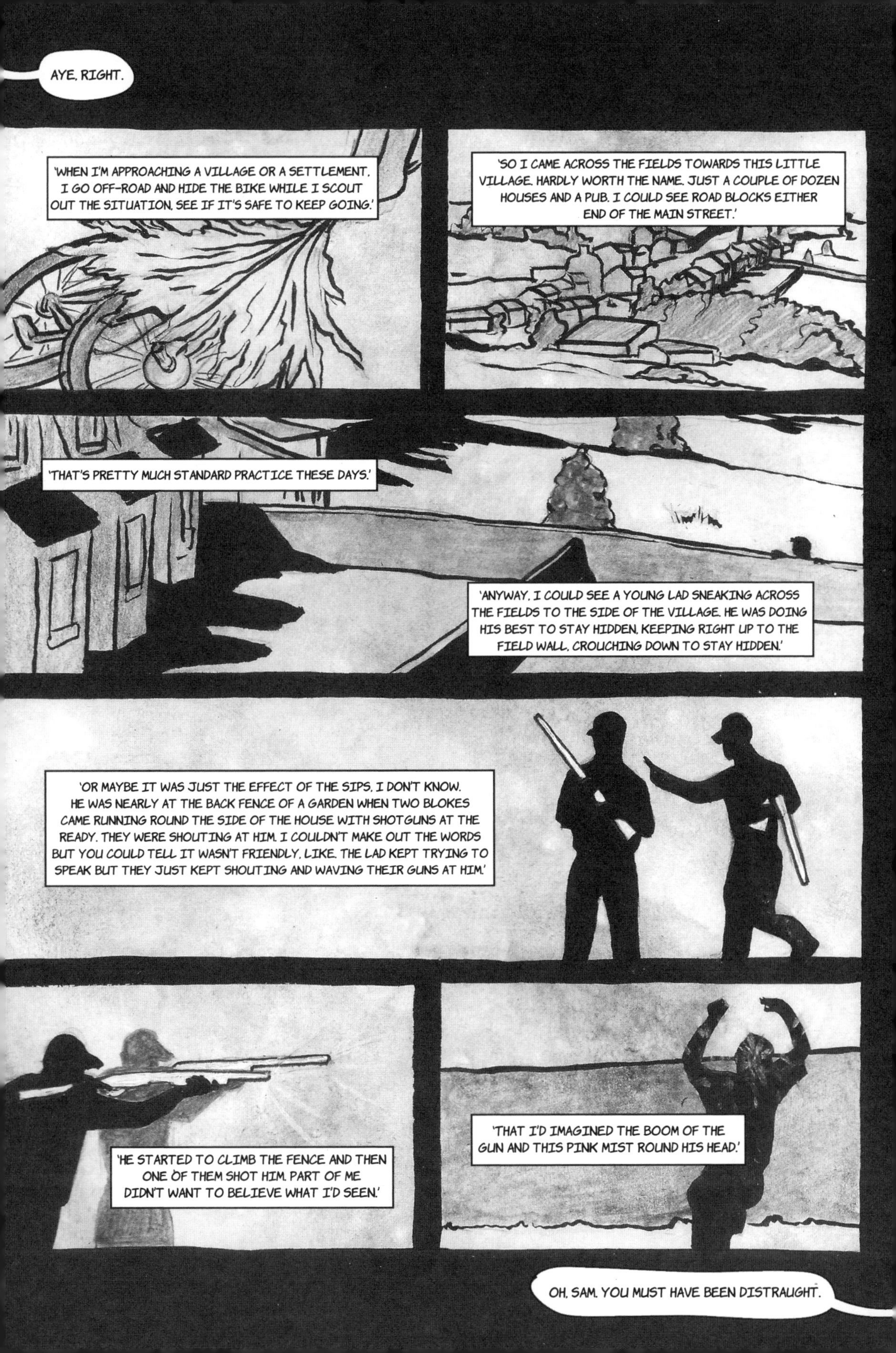
AYE, RIGHT.
'WHEN I'M APPROACHING A VILLAGE OR A SETTLEMENT, I GO OFF-ROAD AND HIDE THE BIKE WHILE I SCOUT OUT THE SITUATION, SEE IF IT'S SAFE TO KEEP GOING.'
'SO I CAME ACROSS THE FIELDS TOWARDS THIS LITTLE VILLAGE. HARDLY WORTH THE NAME. JUST A COUPLE OF DOZEN HOUSES AND A PUB. I COULD SEE ROAD BLOCKS EITHER END OF THE MAIN STREET.'
'THAT'S PRETTY MUCH STANDARD PRACTICE THESE DAYS.'
'ANYWAY, I COULD SEE A YOUNG LAD SNEAKING ACROSS THE FIELDS TO THE SIDE OF THE VILLAGE. HE WAS DOING HIS BEST TO STAY HIDDEN, KEEPING RIGHT UP TO THE FIELD WALL, CROUCHING DOWN TO STAY HIDDEN.'
'OR MAYBE IT WAS JUST THE EFFECT OF THE SIPS, I DON'T KNOW. HE WAS NEARLY AT THE BACK FENCE OF A GARDEN WHEN TWO BLOKES CAME RUNNING ROUND THE SIDE OF THE HOUSE WITH SHOTGUNS AT THE READY. THEY WERE SHOUTING AT HIM. I COULDN'T MAKE OUT THE WORDS BUT YOU COULD TELL IT WASN'T FRIENDLY, LIKE. THE LAD KEPT TRYING TO SPEAK BUT THEY JUST KEPT SHOUTING AND WAVING THEIR GUNS AT HIM.'
'HE STARTED TO CLIMB THE FENCE AND THEN ONE OF THEM SHOT HIM. PART OF ME DIDN'T WANT TO BELIEVE WHAT I'D SEEN.'
'THAT I'D IMAGINED THE BOOM OF THE GUN AND THIS PINK MIST ROUND HIS HEAD.'
OH, SAM. YOU MUST HAVE BEEN DISTRAUGHT.

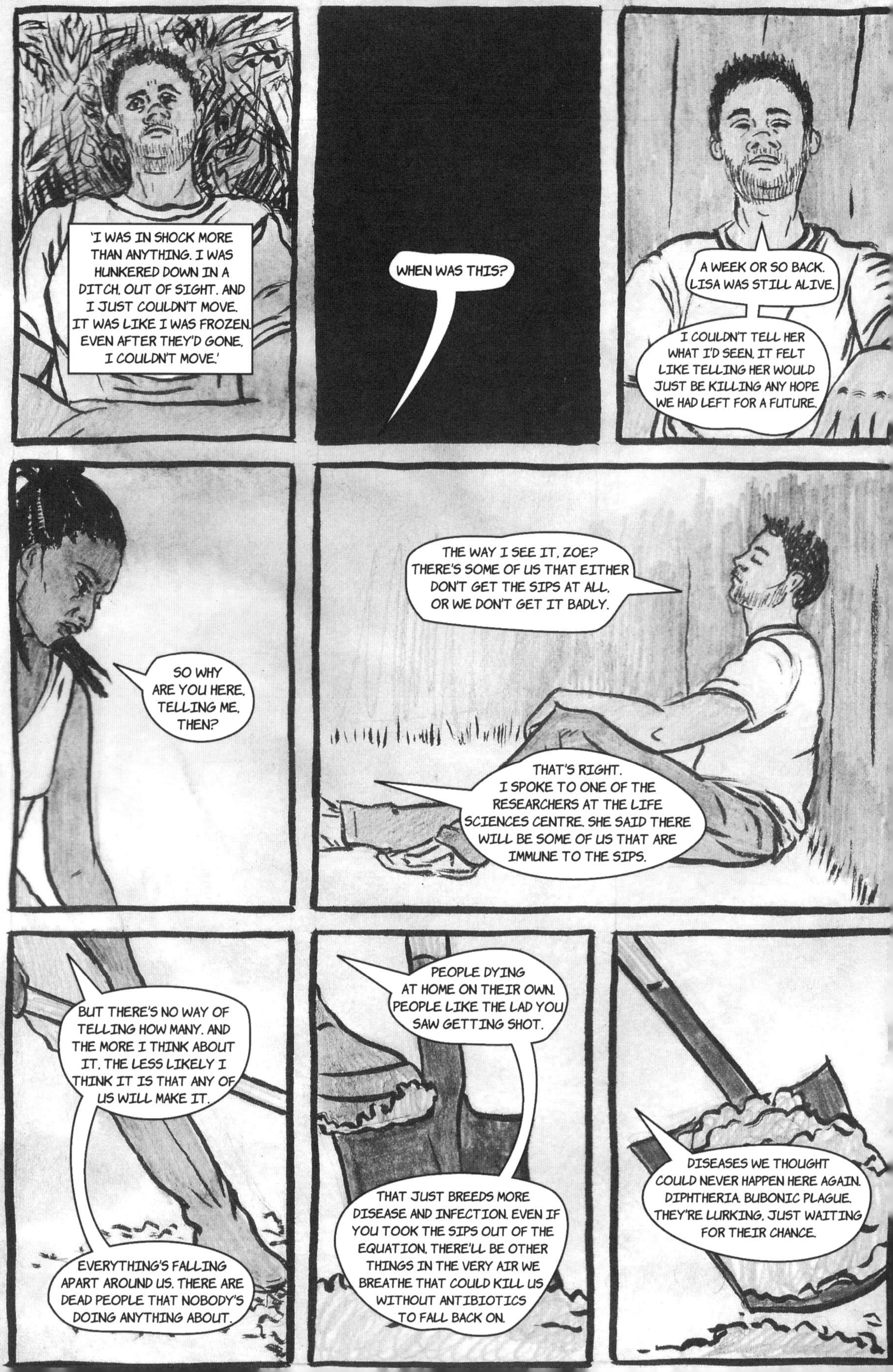
'I WAS IN SHOCK MORE THAN ANYTHING. I WAS HUNKERED DOWN IN A DITCH, OUT OF SIGHT. AND I JUST COULDN'T MOVE. IT WAS LIKE I WAS FROZEN. EVEN AFTER THEY'D GONE, I COULDN'T MOVE.'
WHEN WAS THIS?
A WEEK OR SO BACK. LISA WAS STILL ALIVE.
I COULDN'T TELL HER WHAT I'D SEEN. IT FELT LIKE TELLING HER WOULD JUST BE KILLING ANY HOPE WE HAD LEFT FOR A FUTURE.
SO WHY ARE YOU HERE, TELLING ME, THEN?
THE WAY I SEE IT, ZOE? THERE'S SOME OF US THAT EITHER DON'T GET THE SIPS AT ALL, OR WE DON'T GET IT BADLY.
THAT'S RIGHT. I SPOKE TO ONE OF THE RESEARCHERS AT THE LIFE SCIENCES CENTRE. SHE SAID THERE WILL BE SOME OF US THAT ARE IMMUNE TO THE SIPS.
BUT THERE'S NO WAY OF TELLING HOW MANY. AND THE MORE I THINK ABOUT IT, THE LESS LIKELY I THINK IT IS THAT ANY OF US WILL MAKE IT.
EVERYTHING'S FALLING APART AROUND US. THERE ARE DEAD PEOPLE THAT NOBODY'S DOING ANYTHING ABOUT.
PEOPLE DYING AT HOME ON THEIR OWN. PEOPLE LIKE THE LAD YOU SAW GETTING SHOT.
THAT JUST BREEDS MORE DISEASE AND INFECTION. EVEN IF YOU TOOK THE SIPS OUT OF THE EQUATION, THERE'LL BE OTHER THINGS IN THE VERY AIR WE BREATHE THAT COULD KILL US WITHOUT ANTIBIOTICS TO FALL BACK ON.
DISEASES WE THOUGHT COULD NEVER HAPPEN HERE AGAIN. DIPHTHERIA. BUBONIC PLAGUE. THEY'RE LURKING, JUST WAITING FOR THEIR CHANCE.

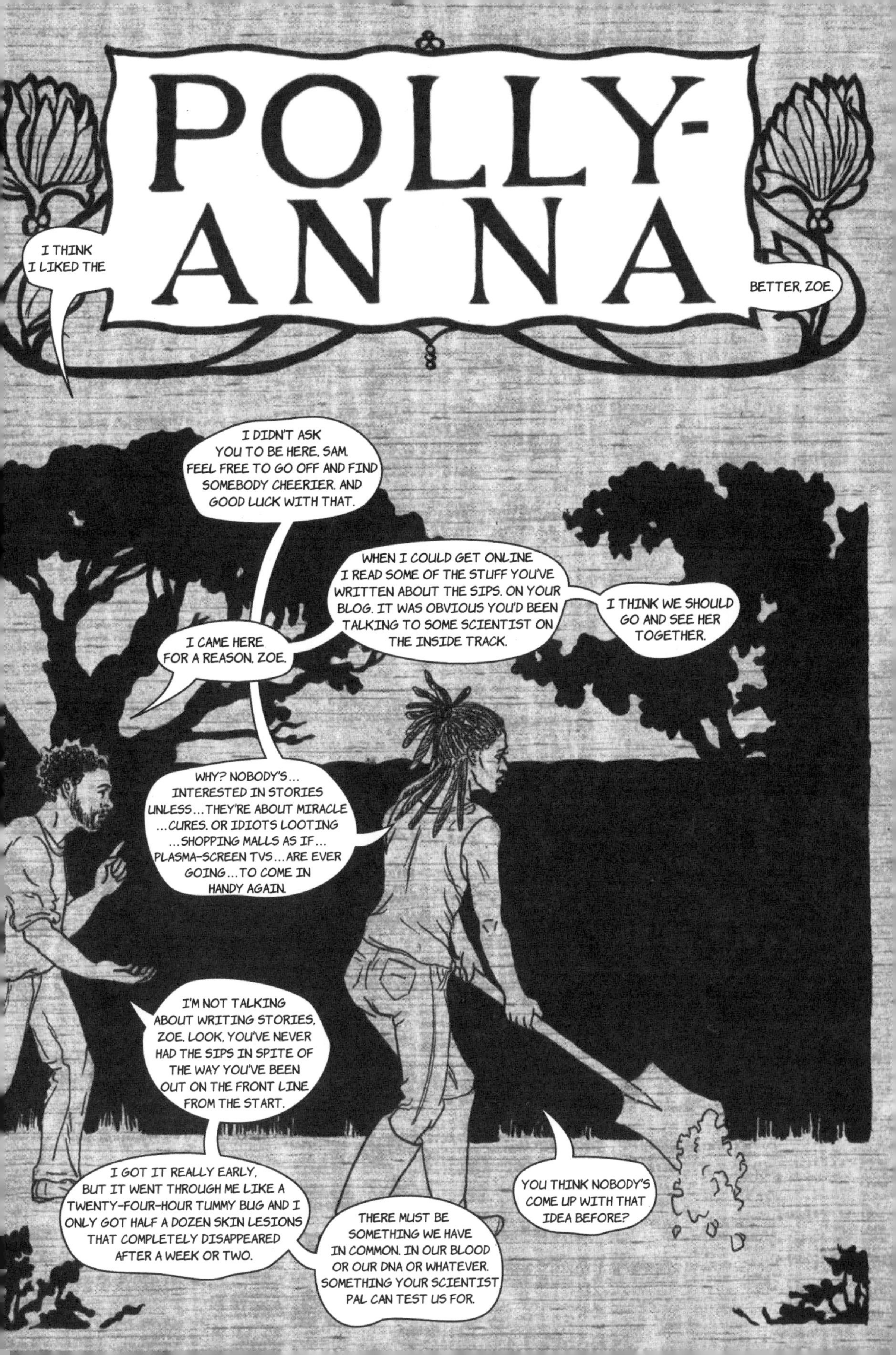
I THINK I LIKED THE
POLLY-ANNA
BETTER, ZOE.
I DIDN'T ASK YOU TO BE HERE, SAM. FEEL FREE TO GO OFF AND FIND SOMEBODY CHEERIER. AND GOOD LUCK WITH THAT.
I CAME HERE FOR A REASON, ZOE.
WHEN I COULD GET ONLINE I READ SOME OF THE STUFF YOU'VE WRITTEN ABOUT THE SIPS. ON YOUR BLOG. IT WAS OBVIOUS YOU'D BEEN TALKING TO SOME SCIENTIST ON THE INSIDE TRACK.
I THINK WE SHOULD GO AND SEE HER TOGETHER.
WHY? NOBODY'S... INTERESTED IN STORIES UNLESS... THEY'RE ABOUT MIRACLE ...CURES. OR IDIOTS LOOTING ...SHOPPING MALLS AS IF... PLASMA-SCREEN TVS... ARE EVER GOING... TO COME IN HANDY AGAIN.
I'M NOT TALKING ABOUT WRITING STORIES, ZOE. LOOK, YOU'VE NEVER HAD THE SIPS IN SPITE OF THE WAY YOU'VE BEEN OUT ON THE FRONT LINE FROM THE START.
I GOT IT REALLY EARLY, BUT IT WENT THROUGH ME LIKE A TWENTY-FOUR-HOUR TUMMY BUG AND I ONLY GOT HALF A DOZEN SKIN LESIONS THAT COMPLETELY DISAPPEARED AFTER A WEEK OR TWO.
THERE MUST BE SOMETHING WE HAVE IN COMMON. IN OUR BLOOD OR OUR DNA OR WHATEVER. SOMETHING YOUR SCIENTIST PAL CAN TEST US FOR.
YOU THINK NOBODY'S COME UP WITH THAT IDEA BEFORE?

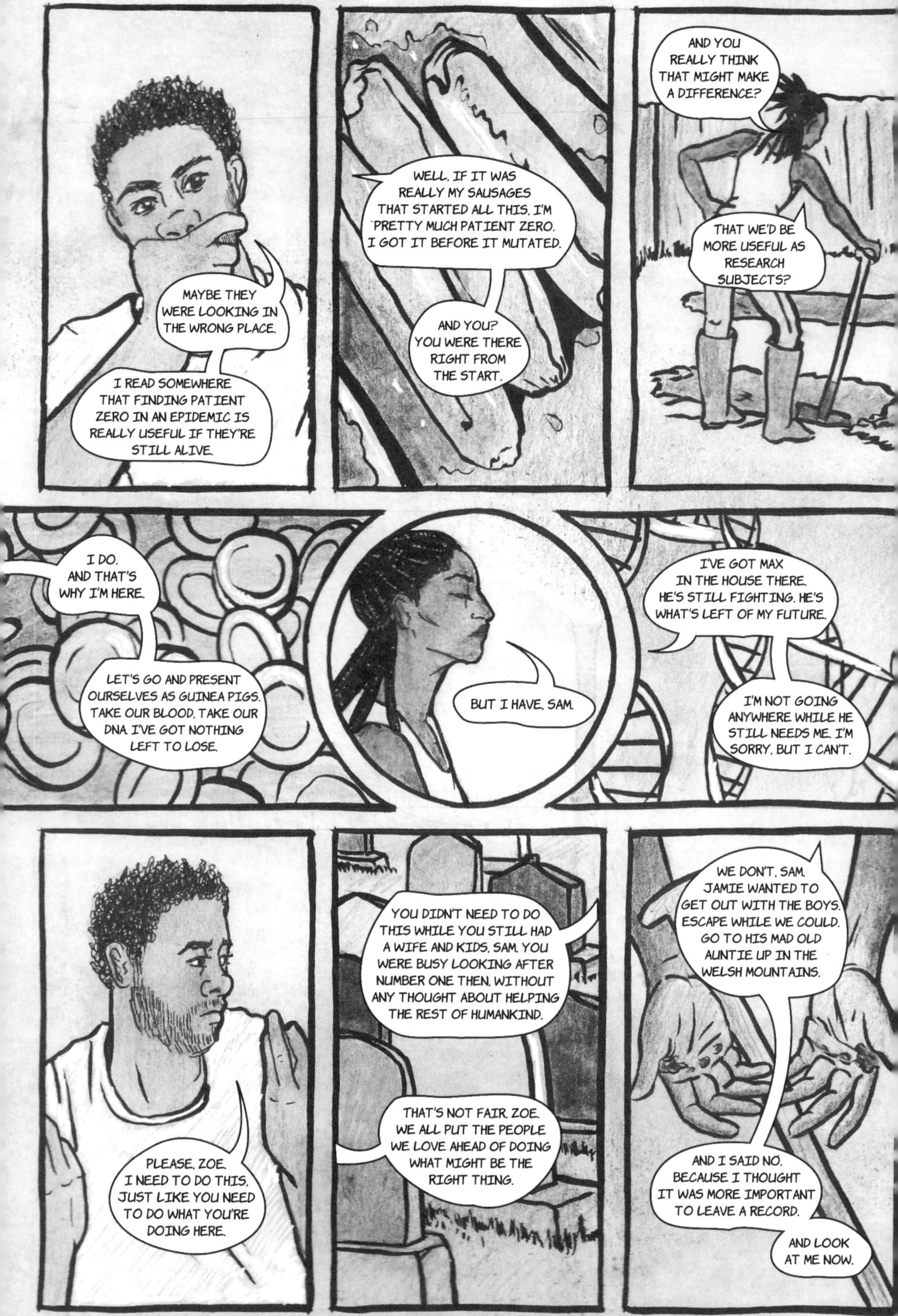
MAYBE THEY WERE LOOKING IN THE WRONG PLACE.
I READ SOMEWHERE THAT FINDING PATIENT ZERO IN AN EPIDEMIC IS REALLY USEFUL IF THEY'RE STILL ALIVE.
WELL, IF IT WAS REALLY MY SAUSAGES THAT STARTED ALL THIS, I'M PRETTY MUCH PATIENT ZERO. I GOT IT BEFORE IT MUTATED.
AND YOU? YOU WERE THERE RIGHT FROM THE START.
AND YOU REALLY THINK THAT MIGHT MAKE A DIFFERENCE?
THAT WE'D BE MORE USEFUL AS RESEARCH SUBJECTS?
I DO. AND THAT'S WHY I'M HERE.
LET'S GO AND PRESENT OURSELVES AS GUINEA PIGS. TAKE OUR BLOOD, TAKE OUR DNA. I'VE GOT NOTHING LEFT TO LOSE.
BUT I HAVE, SAM.
I'VE GOT MAX IN THE HOUSE THERE. HE'S STILL FIGHTING. HE'S WHAT'S LEFT OF MY FUTURE.
I'M NOT GOING ANYWHERE WHILE HE STILL NEEDS ME. I'M SORRY, BUT I CAN'T.
PLEASE, ZOE. I NEED TO DO THIS, JUST LIKE YOU NEED TO DO WHAT YOU'RE DOING HERE.
YOU DIDN'T NEED TO DO THIS WHILE YOU STILL HAD A WIFE AND KIDS, SAM. YOU WERE BUSY LOOKING AFTER NUMBER ONE THEN, WITHOUT ANY THOUGHT ABOUT HELPING THE REST OF HUMANKIND.
THAT'S NOT FAIR, ZOE. WE ALL PUT THE PEOPLE WE LOVE AHEAD OF DOING WHAT MIGHT BE THE RIGHT THING.
WE DON'T, SAM. JAMIE WANTED TO GET OUT WITH THE BOYS. ESCAPE WHILE WE COULD. GO TO HIS MAD OLD AUNTIE UP IN THE WELSH MOUNTAINS.
AND I SAID NO. BECAUSE I THOUGHT IT WAS MORE IMPORTANT TO LEAVE A RECORD.
AND LOOK AT ME NOW.

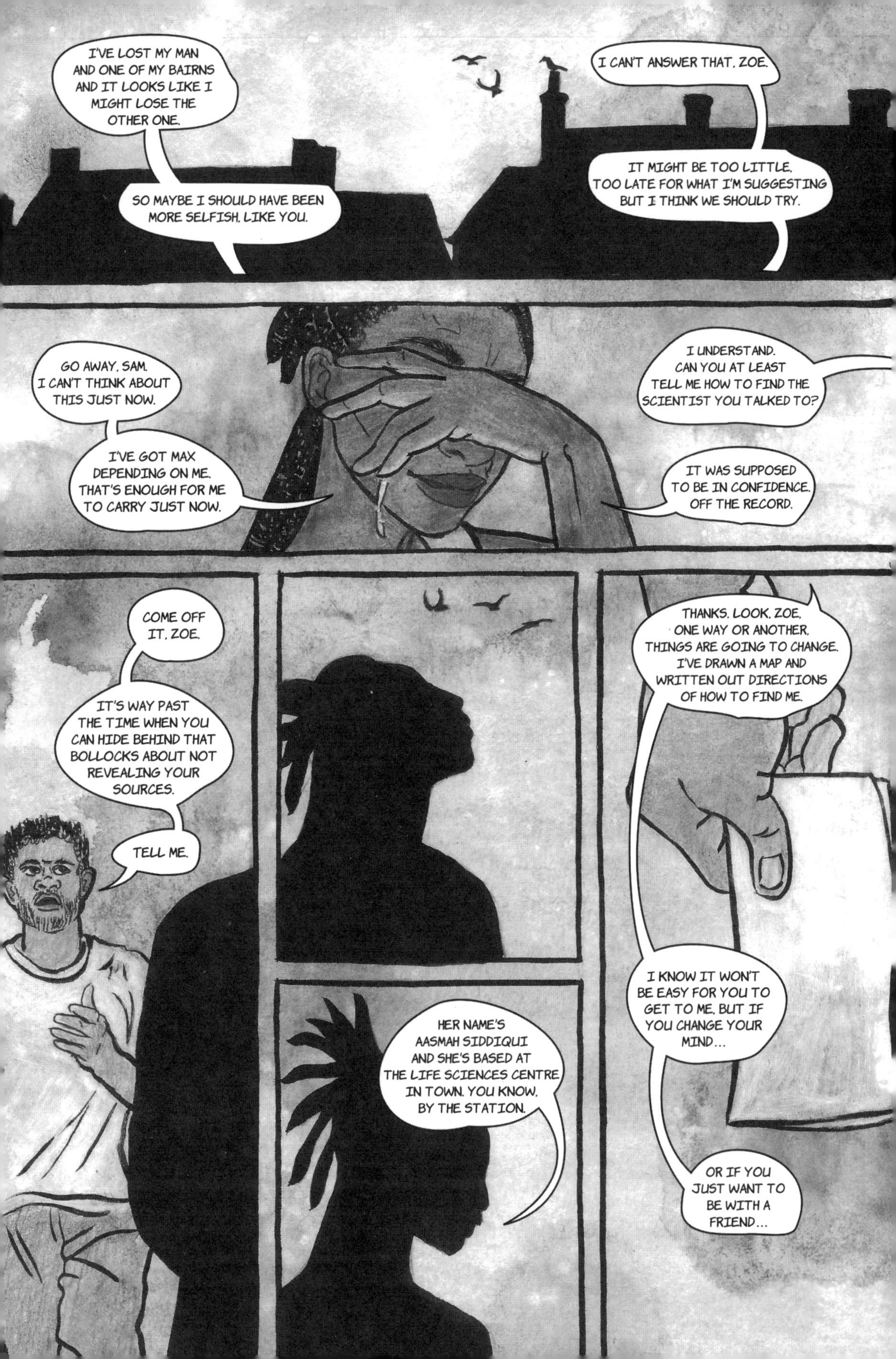
I'VE LOST MY MAN AND ONE OF MY BAIRNS AND IT LOOKS LIKE I MIGHT LOSE THE OTHER ONE.
SO MAYBE I SHOULD HAVE BEEN MORE SELFISH, LIKE YOU.
I CAN'T ANSWER THAT, ZOE.
IT MIGHT BE TOO LITTLE, TOO LATE FOR WHAT I'M SUGGESTING BUT I THINK WE SHOULD TRY.
GO AWAY, SAM. I CAN'T THINK ABOUT THIS JUST NOW.
I'VE GOT MAX DEPENDING ON ME. THAT'S ENOUGH FOR ME TO CARRY JUST NOW.
I UNDERSTAND. CAN YOU AT LEAST TELL ME HOW TO FIND THE SCIENTIST YOU TALKED TO?
IT WAS SUPPOSED TO BE IN CONFIDENCE. OFF THE RECORD.
COME OFF IT, ZOE.
IT'S WAY PAST THE TIME WHEN YOU CAN HIDE BEHIND THAT BOLLOCKS ABOUT NOT REVEALING YOUR SOURCES.
TELL ME.
HER NAME'S AASMAH SIDDIQUI AND SHE'S BASED AT THE LIFE SCIENCES CENTRE IN TOWN. YOU KNOW, BY THE STATION.
THANKS. LOOK, ZOE, ONE WAY OR ANOTHER, THINGS ARE GOING TO CHANGE. I'VE DRAWN A MAP AND WRITTEN OUT DIRECTIONS OF HOW TO FIND ME.
I KNOW IT WON'T BE EASY FOR YOU TO GET TO ME, BUT IF YOU CHANGE YOUR MIND…
OR IF YOU JUST WANT TO BE WITH A FRIEND…

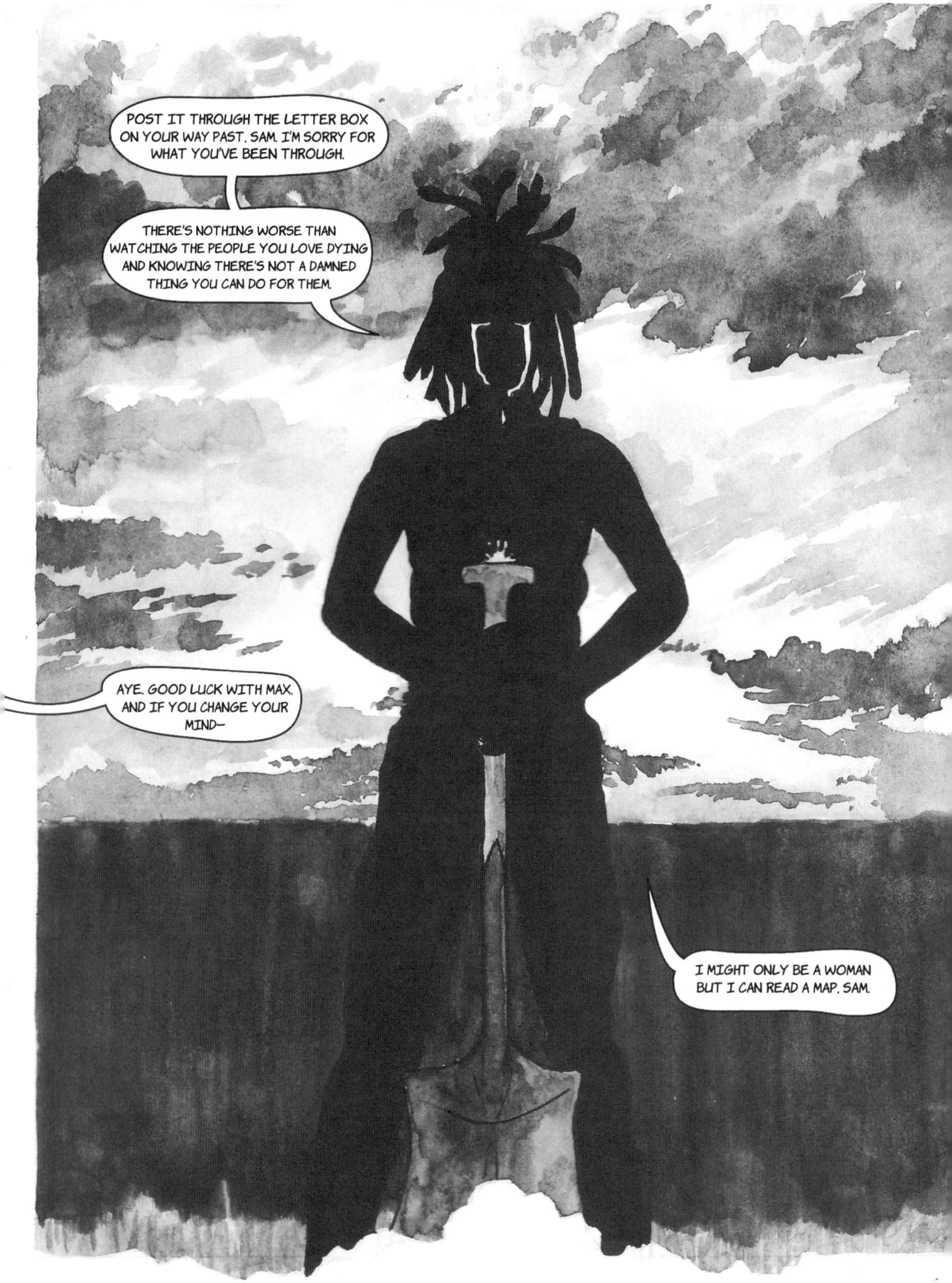
POST IT THROUGH THE LETTER BOX ON YOUR WAY PAST, SAM. I'M SORRY FOR WHAT YOU'VE BEEN THROUGH.
THERE'S NOTHING WORSE THAN WATCHING THE PEOPLE YOU LOVE DYING AND KNOWING THERE'S NOT A DAMNED THING YOU CAN DO FOR THEM.
AYE. GOOD LUCK WITH MAX. AND IF YOU CHANGE YOUR MIND–
I MIGHT ONLY BE A WOMAN BUT I CAN READ A MAP, SAM.

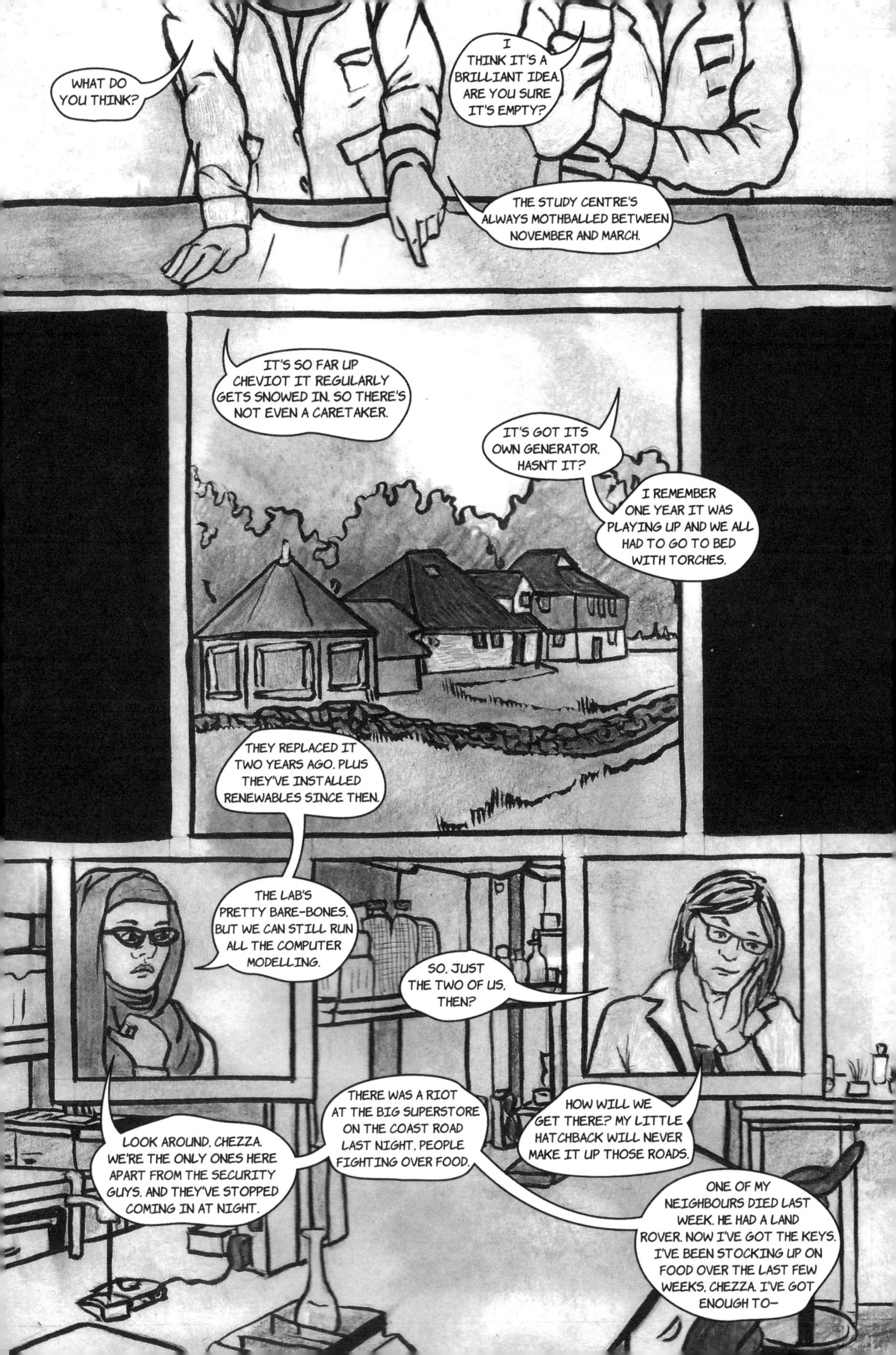

WHAT DO YOU THINK?
I THINK IT'S A BRILLIANT IDEA. ARE YOU SURE IT'S EMPTY?
THE STUDY CENTRE'S ALWAYS MOTHBALLED BETWEEN NOVEMBER AND MARCH.
IT'S SO FAR UP CHEVIOT IT REGULARLY GETS SNOWED IN. SO THERE'S NOT EVEN A CARETAKER.
IT'S GOT ITS OWN GENERATOR, HASN'T IT?
I REMEMBER ONE YEAR IT WAS PLAYING UP AND WE ALL HAD TO GO TO BED WITH TORCHES.
THEY REPLACED IT TWO YEARS AGO. PLUS THEY'VE INSTALLED RENEWABLES SINCE THEN.
THE LAB'S PRETTY BARE-BONES, BUT WE CAN STILL RUN ALL THE COMPUTER MODELLING.
SO, JUST THE TWO OF US, THEN?
LOOK AROUND, CHEZZA. WE'RE THE ONLY ONES HERE APART FROM THE SECURITY GUYS. AND THEY'VE STOPPED COMING IN AT NIGHT.
THERE WAS A RIOT AT THE BIG SUPERSTORE ON THE COAST ROAD LAST NIGHT. PEOPLE FIGHTING OVER FOOD.
HOW WILL WE GET THERE? MY LITTLE HATCHBACK WILL NEVER MAKE IT UP THOSE ROADS.
ONE OF MY NEIGHBOURS DIED LAST WEEK. HE HAD A LAND ROVER. NOW I'VE GOT THE KEYS. I'VE BEEN STOCKING UP ON FOOD OVER THE LAST FEW WEEKS, CHEZZA. I'VE GOT ENOUGH TO—

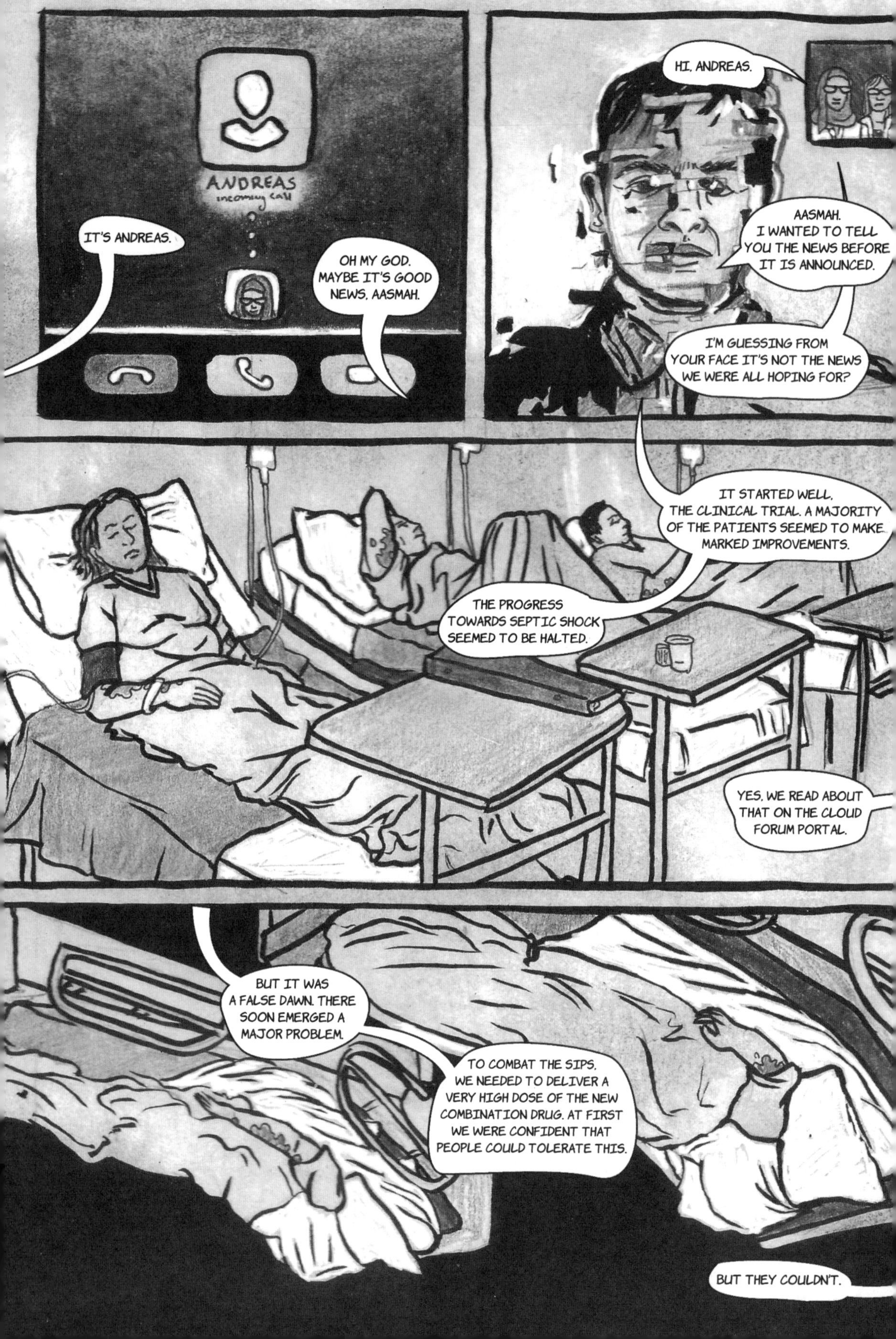

ANDREAS
incoming call
IT'S ANDREAS.
OH MY GOD. MAYBE IT'S GOOD NEWS, AASMAH.
HI, ANDREAS.
AASMAH. I WANTED TO TELL YOU THE NEWS BEFORE IT IS ANNOUNCED.
I'M GUESSING FROM YOUR FACE IT'S NOT THE NEWS WE WERE ALL HOPING FOR?
IT STARTED WELL, THE CLINICAL TRIAL. A MAJORITY OF THE PATIENTS SEEMED TO MAKE MARKED IMPROVEMENTS.
THE PROGRESS TOWARDS SEPTIC SHOCK SEEMED TO BE HALTED.
YES, WE READ ABOUT THAT ON THE CLOUD FORUM PORTAL.
BUT IT WAS A FALSE DAWN. THERE SOON EMERGED A MAJOR PROBLEM.
TO COMBAT THE SIPS, WE NEEDED TO DELIVER A VERY HIGH DOSE OF THE NEW COMBINATION DRUG. AT FIRST WE WERE CONFIDENT THAT PEOPLE COULD TOLERATE THIS.
BUT THEY COULDN'T.

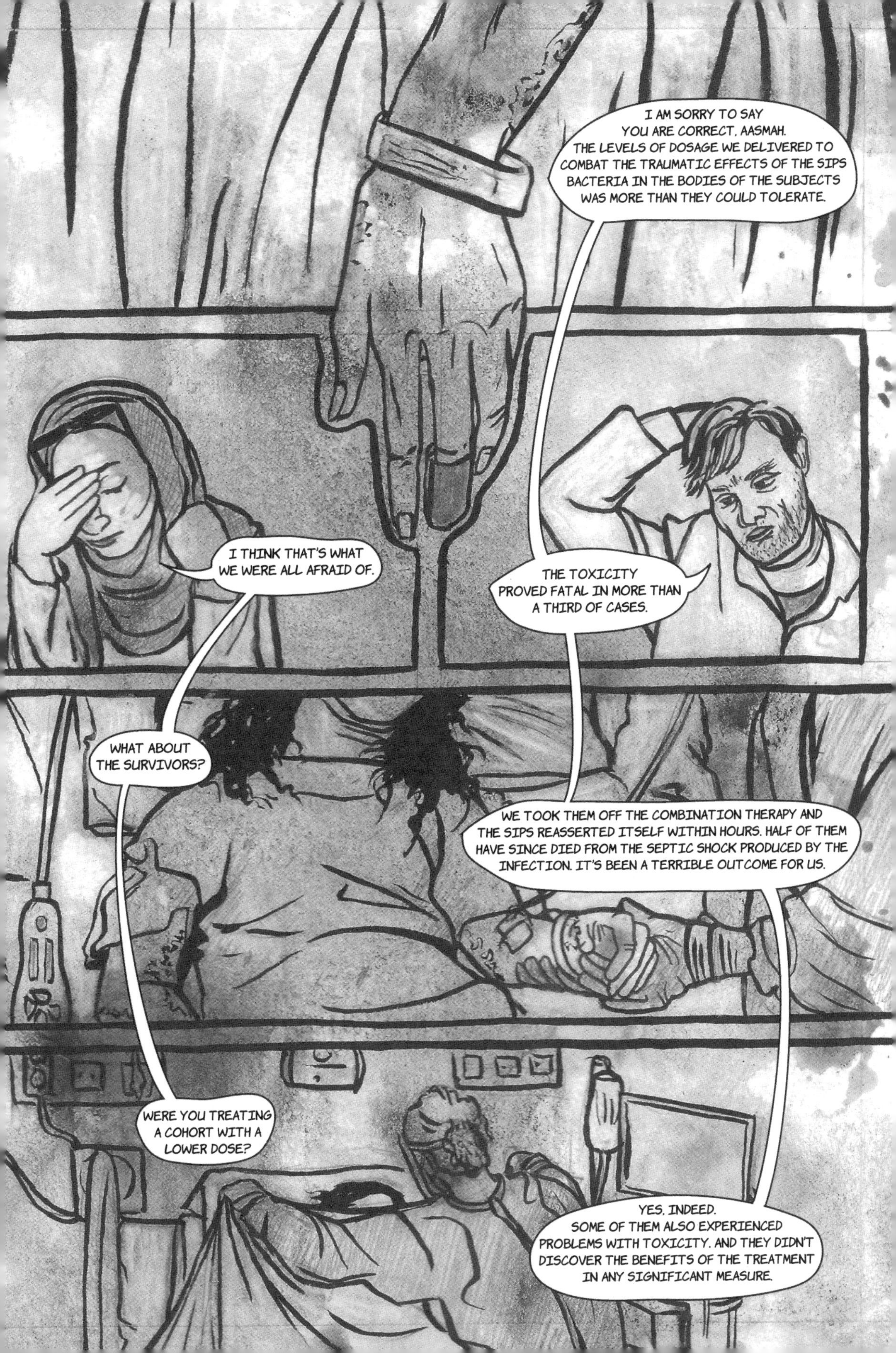
I AM SORRY TO SAY YOU ARE CORRECT, AASMAH. THE LEVELS OF DOSAGE WE DELIVERED TO COMBAT THE TRAUMATIC EFFECTS OF THE SIPS BACTERIA IN THE BODIES OF THE SUBJECTS WAS MORE THAN THEY COULD TOLERATE.
I THINK THAT'S WHAT WE WERE ALL AFRAID OF.
THE TOXICITY PROVED FATAL IN MORE THAN A THIRD OF CASES.
WHAT ABOUT THE SURVIVORS?
WE TOOK THEM OFF THE COMBINATION THERAPY AND THE SIPS REASSERTED ITSELF WITHIN HOURS. HALF OF THEM HAVE SINCE DIED FROM THE SEPTIC SHOCK PRODUCED BY THE INFECTION. IT'S BEEN A TERRIBLE OUTCOME FOR US.
WERE YOU TREATING A COHORT WITH A LOWER DOSE?
YES, INDEED. SOME OF THEM ALSO EXPERIENCED PROBLEMS WITH TOXICITY. AND THEY DIDN'T DISCOVER THE BENEFITS OF THE TREATMENT IN ANY SIGNIFICANT MEASURE.

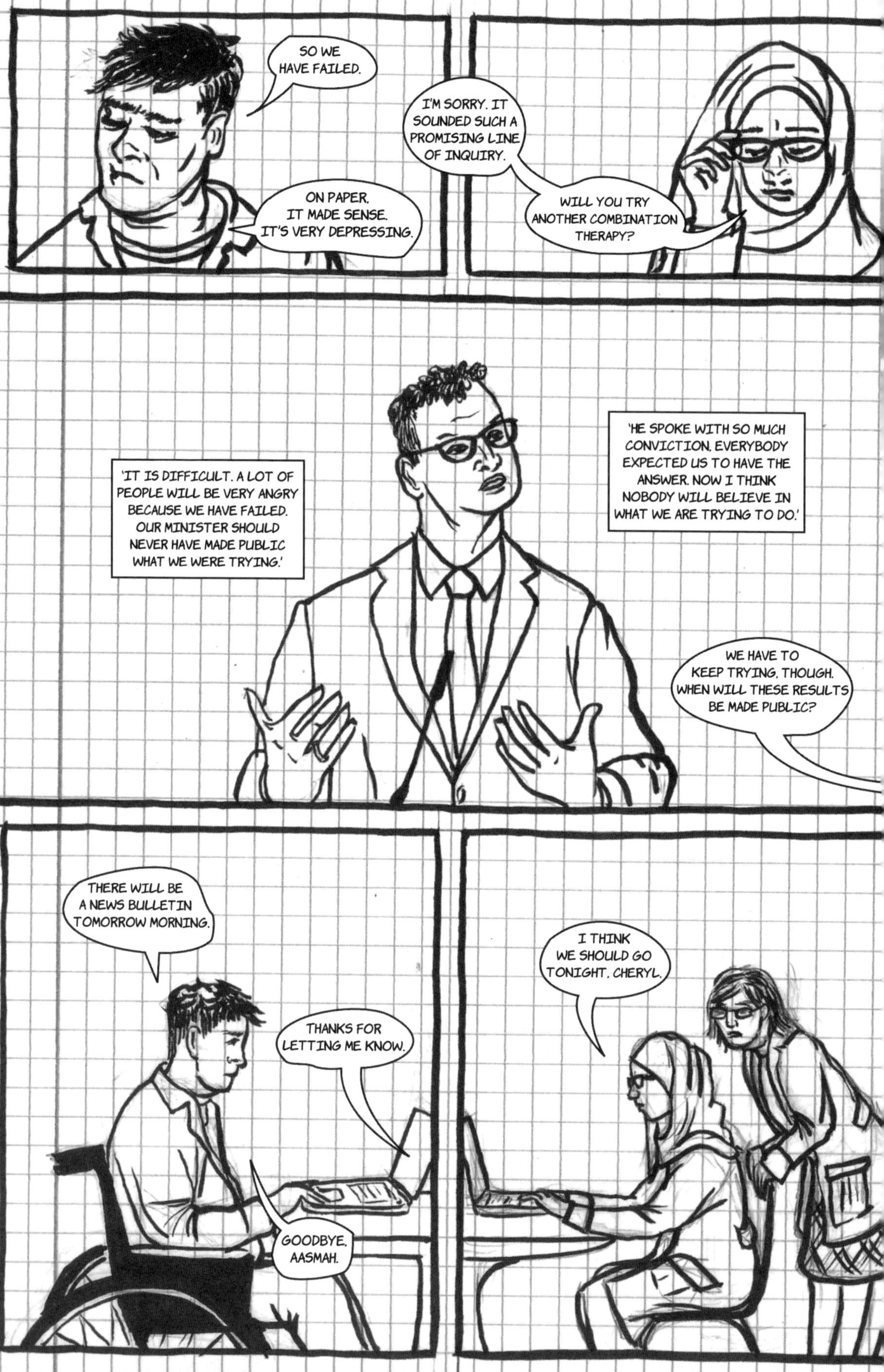
SO WE HAVE FAILED.
ON PAPER, IT MADE SENSE. IT'S VERY DEPRESSING.
I'M SORRY. IT SOUNDED SUCH A PROMISING LINE OF INQUIRY.
WILL YOU TRY ANOTHER COMBINATION THERAPY?
'IT IS DIFFICULT. A LOT OF PEOPLE WILL BE VERY ANGRY BECAUSE WE HAVE FAILED. OUR MINISTER SHOULD NEVER HAVE MADE PUBLIC WHAT WE WERE TRYING.'
'HE SPOKE WITH SO MUCH CONVICTION, EVERYBODY EXPECTED US TO HAVE THE ANSWER. NOW I THINK NOBODY WILL BELIEVE IN WHAT WE ARE TRYING TO DO.'
WE HAVE TO KEEP TRYING, THOUGH. WHEN WILL THESE RESULTS BE MADE PUBLIC?
THERE WILL BE A NEWS BULLETIN TOMORROW MORNING.
THANKS FOR LETTING ME KNOW.
GOODBYE, AASMAH.
I THINK WE SHOULD GO TONIGHT, CHERYL.

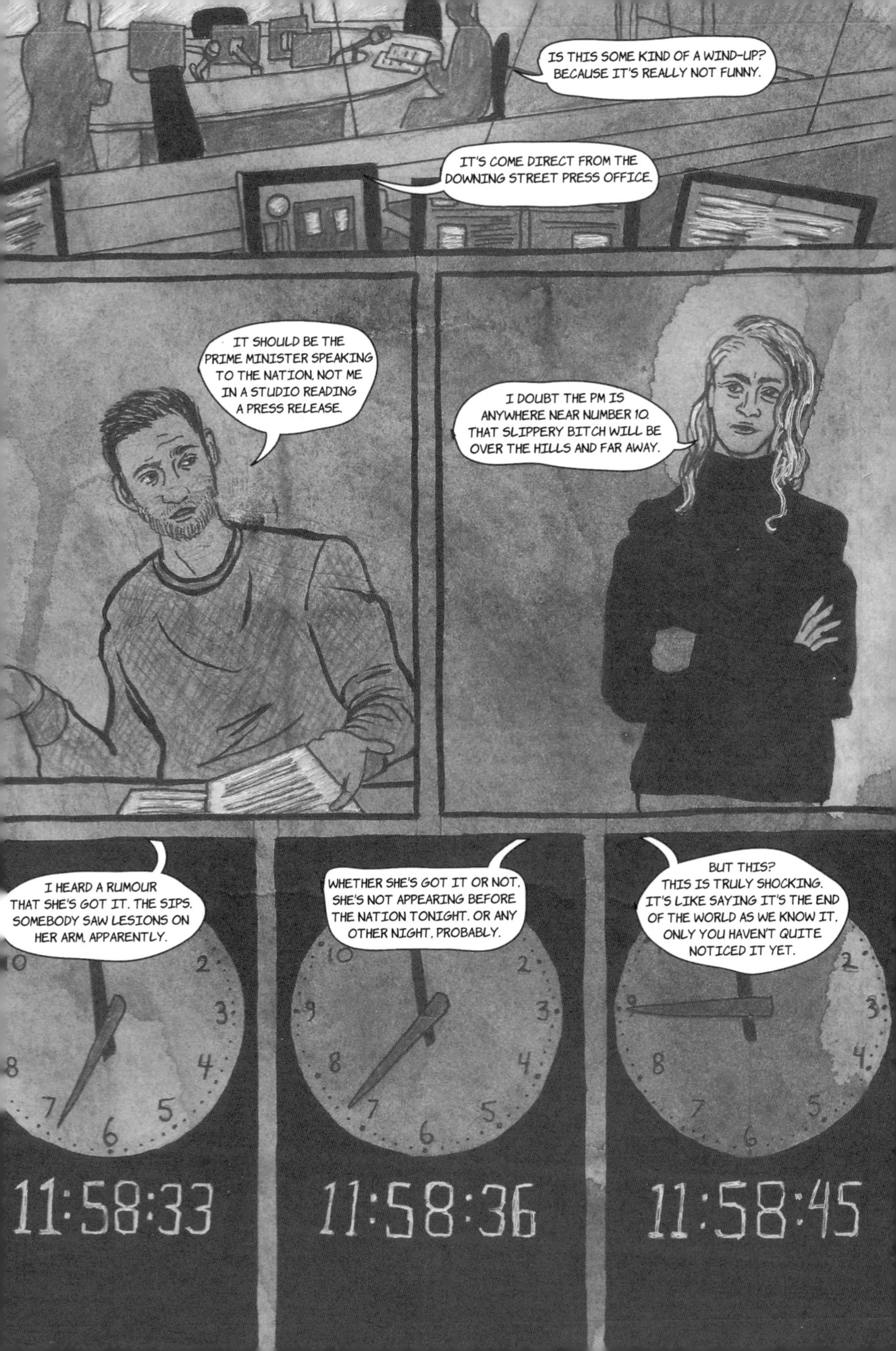
IS THIS SOME KIND OF A WIND-UP? BECAUSE IT'S REALLY NOT FUNNY.
IT'S COME DIRECT FROM THE DOWNING STREET PRESS OFFICE.
IT SHOULD BE THE PRIME MINISTER SPEAKING TO THE NATION, NOT ME IN A STUDIO READING A PRESS RELEASE.
I DOUBT THE PM IS ANYWHERE NEAR NUMBER 10. THAT SLIPPERY BITCH WILL BE OVER THE HILLS AND FAR AWAY.
I HEARD A RUMOUR THAT SHE'S GOT IT. THE SIPS. SOMEBODY SAW LESIONS ON HER ARM, APPARENTLY.
11:58:33
WHETHER SHE'S GOT IT OR NOT, SHE'S NOT APPEARING BEFORE THE NATION TONIGHT. OR ANY OTHER NIGHT, PROBABLY.
11:58:36
BUT THIS? THIS IS TRULY SHOCKING. IT'S LIKE SAYING IT'S THE END OF THE WORLD AS WE KNOW IT, ONLY YOU HAVEN'T QUITE NOTICED IT YET.
11:58:45

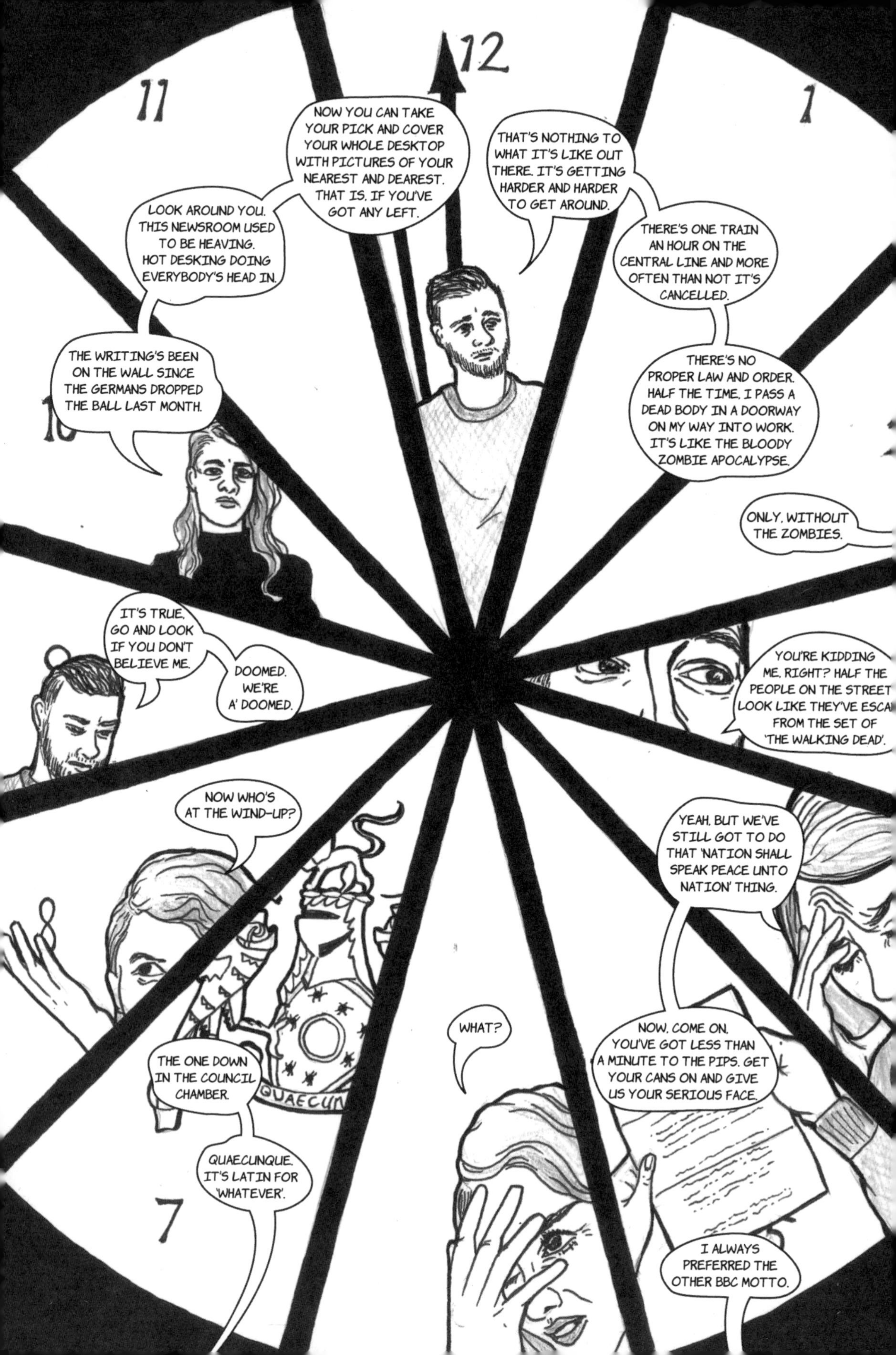
THE WRITING'S BEEN ON THE WALL SINCE THE GERMANS DROPPED THE BALL LAST MONTH.
LOOK AROUND YOU. THIS NEWSROOM USED TO BE HEAVING. HOT DESKING DOING EVERYBODY'S HEAD IN.
NOW YOU CAN TAKE YOUR PICK AND COVER YOUR WHOLE DESKTOP WITH PICTURES OF YOUR NEAREST AND DEAREST. THAT IS, IF YOU'VE GOT ANY LEFT.
THAT'S NOTHING TO WHAT IT'S LIKE OUT THERE. IT'S GETTING HARDER AND HARDER TO GET AROUND.
THERE'S ONE TRAIN AN HOUR ON THE CENTRAL LINE AND MORE OFTEN THAN NOT IT'S CANCELLED.
THERE'S NO PROPER LAW AND ORDER. HALF THE TIME, I PASS A DEAD BODY IN A DOORWAY ON MY WAY INTO WORK. IT'S LIKE THE BLOODY ZOMBIE APOCALYPSE.
ONLY, WITHOUT THE ZOMBIES.
YOU'RE KIDDING ME, RIGHT? HALF THE PEOPLE ON THE STREET LOOK LIKE THEY'VE ESCA FROM THE SET OF 'THE WALKING DEAD'.
IT'S TRUE. GO AND LOOK IF YOU DON'T BELIEVE ME.
DOOMED. WE'RE A' DOOMED.
NOW WHO'S AT THE WIND-UP?
THE ONE DOWN IN THE COUNCIL CHAMBER.
QUAECUNQUE. IT'S LATIN FOR 'WHATEVER'.
YEAH, BUT WE'VE STILL GOT TO DO THAT 'NATION SHALL SPEAK PEACE UNTO NATION' THING.
NOW, COME ON. YOU'VE GOT LESS THAN A MINUTE TO THE PIPS. GET YOUR CANS ON AND GIVE US YOUR SERIOUS FACE.
WHAT?
I ALWAYS PREFERRED THE OTHER BBC MOTTO.

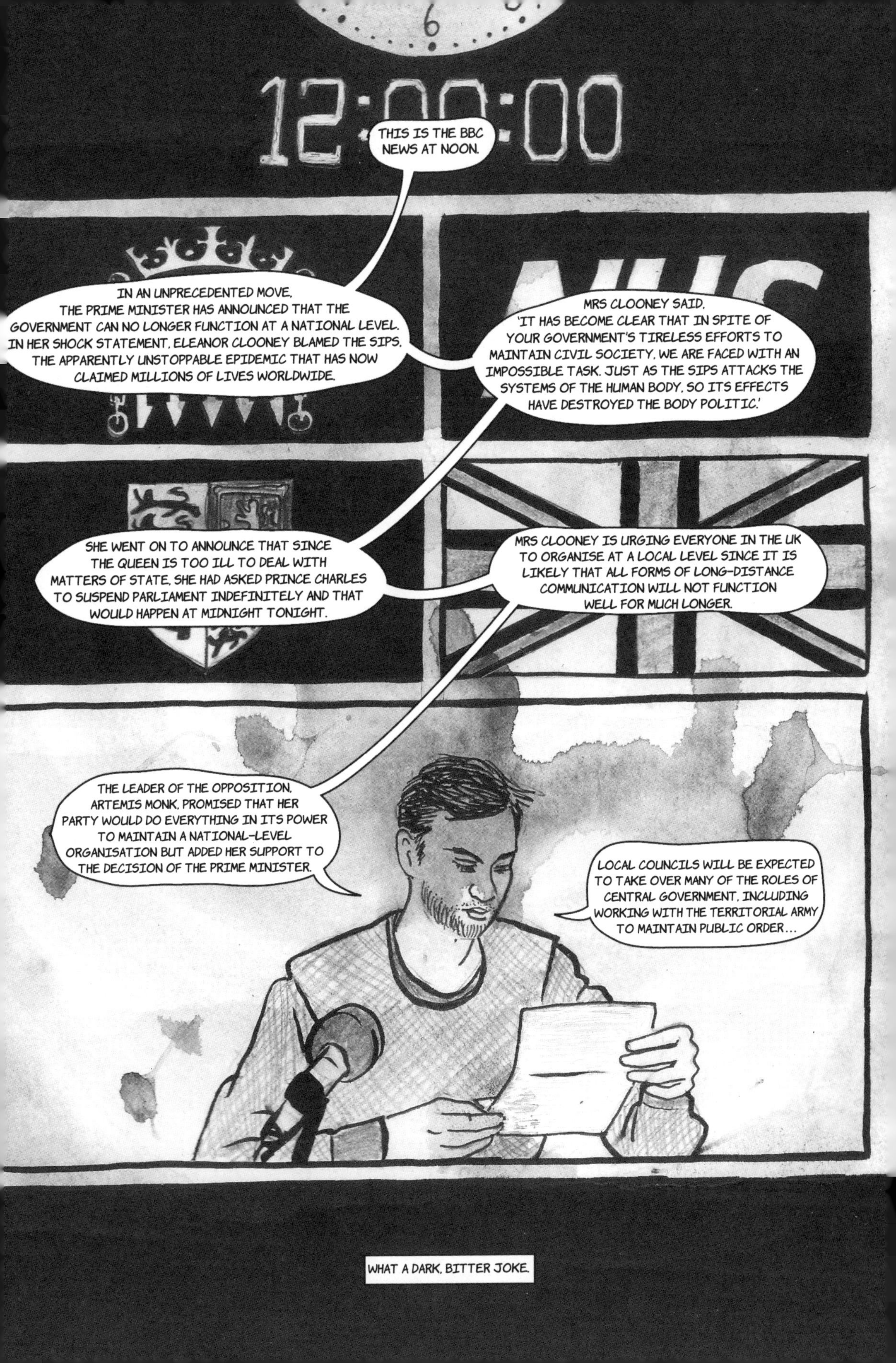
12:00:00
THIS IS THE BBC NEWS AT NOON.
IN AN UNPRECEDENTED MOVE, THE PRIME MINISTER HAS ANNOUNCED THAT THE GOVERNMENT CAN NO LONGER FUNCTION AT A NATIONAL LEVEL. IN HER SHOCK STATEMENT, ELEANOR CLOONEY BLAMED THE SIPS, THE APPARENTLY UNSTOPPABLE EPIDEMIC THAT HAS NOW CLAIMED MILLIONS OF LIVES WORLDWIDE.
MRS CLOONEY SAID, 'IT HAS BECOME CLEAR THAT IN SPITE OF YOUR GOVERNMENT'S TIRELESS EFFORTS TO MAINTAIN CIVIL SOCIETY, WE ARE FACED WITH AN IMPOSSIBLE TASK. JUST AS THE SIPS ATTACKS THE SYSTEMS OF THE HUMAN BODY, SO ITS EFFECTS HAVE DESTROYED THE BODY POLITIC.'
SHE WENT ON TO ANNOUNCE THAT SINCE THE QUEEN IS TOO ILL TO DEAL WITH MATTERS OF STATE, SHE HAD ASKED PRINCE CHARLES TO SUSPEND PARLIAMENT INDEFINITELY AND THAT WOULD HAPPEN AT MIDNIGHT TONIGHT.
MRS CLOONEY IS URGING EVERYONE IN THE UK TO ORGANISE AT A LOCAL LEVEL SINCE IT IS LIKELY THAT ALL FORMS OF LONG-DISTANCE COMMUNICATION WILL NOT FUNCTION WELL FOR MUCH LONGER.
THE LEADER OF THE OPPOSITION, ARTEMIS MONK, PROMISED THAT HER PARTY WOULD DO EVERYTHING IN ITS POWER TO MAINTAIN A NATIONAL-LEVEL ORGANISATION BUT ADDED HER SUPPORT TO THE DECISION OF THE PRIME MINISTER.
LOCAL COUNCILS WILL BE EXPECTED TO TAKE OVER MANY OF THE ROLES OF CENTRAL GOVERNMENT, INCLUDING WORKING WITH THE TERRITORIAL ARMY TO MAINTAIN PUBLIC ORDER...
WHAT A DARK, BITTER JOKE.

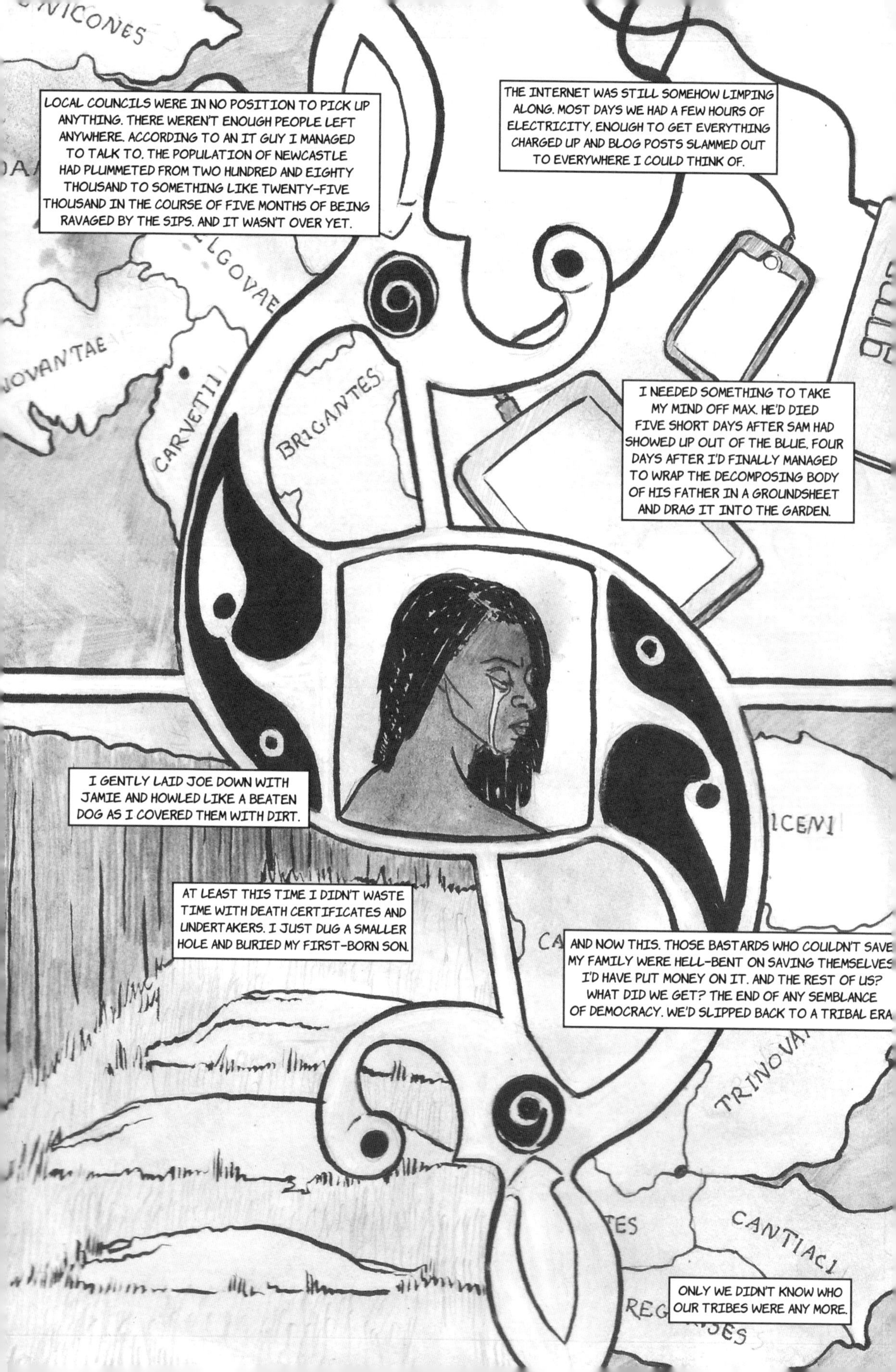
LOCAL COUNCILS WERE IN NO POSITION TO PICK UP ANYTHING. THERE WEREN'T ENOUGH PEOPLE LEFT ANYWHERE. ACCORDING TO AN IT GUY I MANAGED TO TALK TO, THE POPULATION OF NEWCASTLE HAD PLUMMETED FROM TWO HUNDRED AND EIGHTY THOUSAND TO SOMETHING LIKE TWENTY-FIVE THOUSAND IN THE COURSE OF FIVE MONTHS OF BEING RAVAGED BY THE SIPS. AND IT WASN'T OVER YET.
THE INTERNET WAS STILL SOMEHOW LIMPING ALONG. MOST DAYS WE HAD A FEW HOURS OF ELECTRICITY, ENOUGH TO GET EVERYTHING CHARGED UP AND BLOG POSTS SLAMMED OUT TO EVERYWHERE I COULD THINK OF.
CARVETII
BRIGANTES
I NEEDED SOMETHING TO TAKE MY MIND OFF MAX. HE'D DIED FIVE SHORT DAYS AFTER SAM HAD SHOWED UP OUT OF THE BLUE. FOUR DAYS AFTER I'D FINALLY MANAGED TO WRAP THE DECOMPOSING BODY OF HIS FATHER IN A GROUNDSHEET AND DRAG IT INTO THE GARDEN.
I GENTLY LAID JOE DOWN WITH JAMIE AND HOWLED LIKE A BEATEN DOG AS I COVERED THEM WITH DIRT.
ICENI
AT LEAST THIS TIME I DIDN'T WASTE TIME WITH DEATH CERTIFICATES AND UNDERTAKERS. I JUST DUG A SMALLER HOLE AND BURIED MY FIRST-BORN SON.
AND NOW THIS. THOSE BASTARDS WHO COULDN'T SAVE MY FAMILY WERE HELL-BENT ON SAVING THEMSELVES. I'D HAVE PUT MONEY ON IT. AND THE REST OF US? WHAT DID WE GET? THE END OF ANY SEMBLANCE OF DEMOCRACY. WE'D SLIPPED BACK TO A TRIBAL ERA.
CANTIACI
ONLY WE DIDN'T KNOW WHO OUR TRIBES WERE ANY MORE.

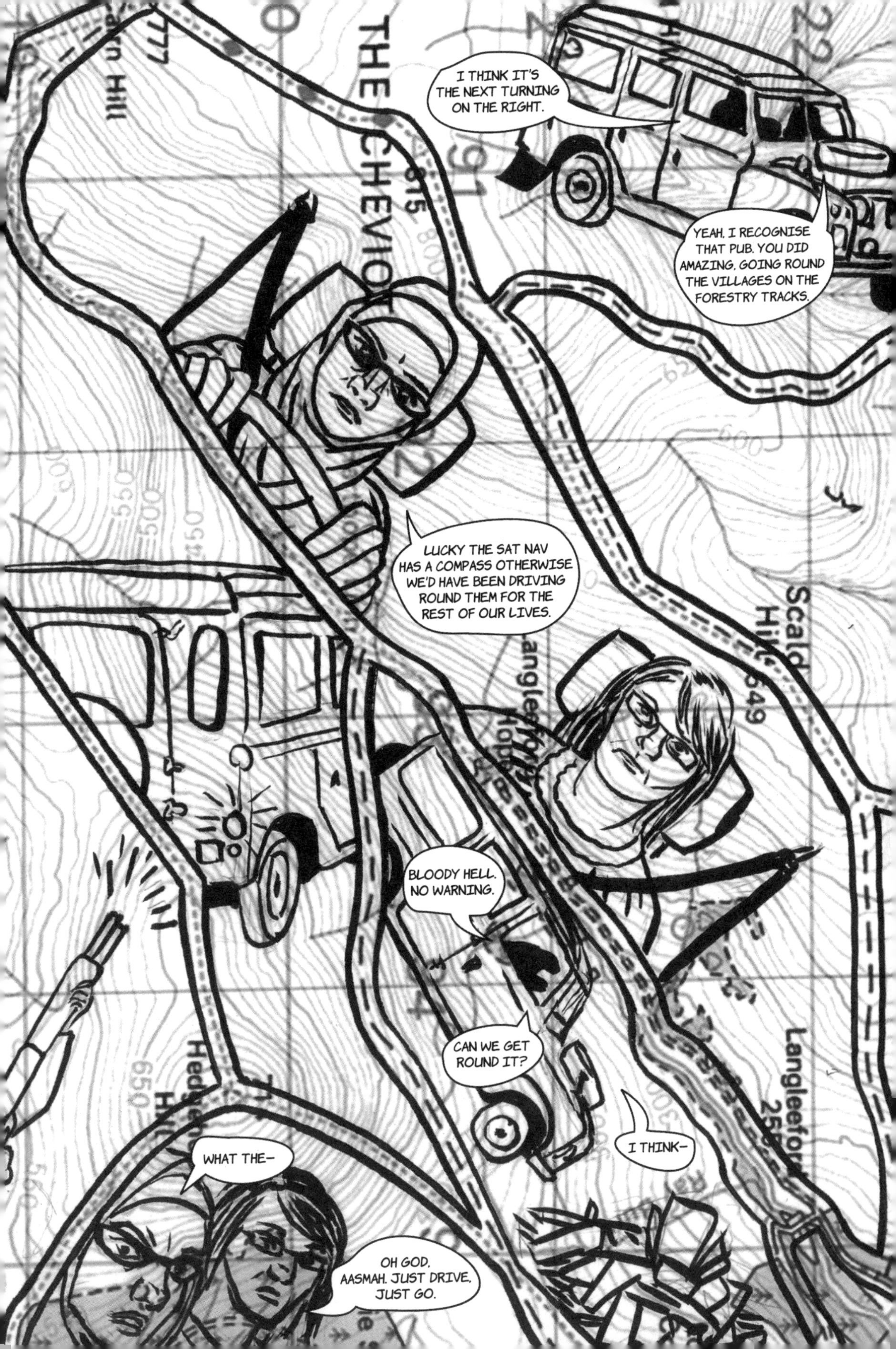
I THINK IT'S THE NEXT TURNING ON THE RIGHT.
YEAH, I RECOGNISE THAT PUB. YOU DID AMAZING, GOING ROUND THE VILLAGES ON THE FORESTRY TRACKS.
LUCKY THE SAT NAV HAS A COMPASS OTHERWISE WE'D HAVE BEEN DRIVING ROUND THEM FOR THE REST OF OUR LIVES.
BLOODY HELL. NO WARNING.
CAN WE GET ROUND IT?
I THINK–
WHAT THE–
OH GOD, AASMAH. JUST DRIVE, JUST GO.

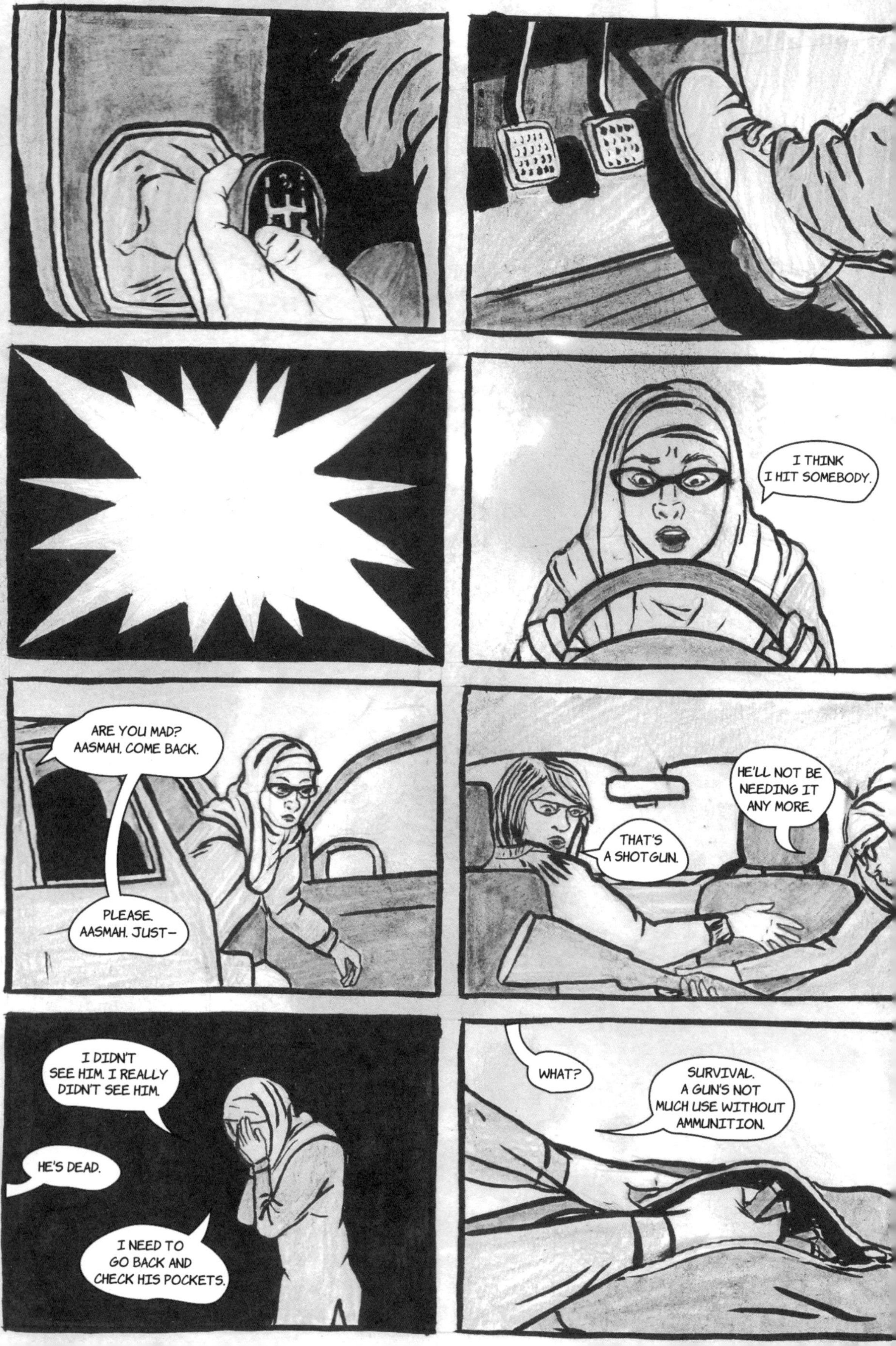
I THINK I HIT SOMEBODY.
ARE YOU MAD? AASMAH. COME BACK.
PLEASE. AASMAH. JUST—
HE'LL NOT BE NEEDING IT ANY MORE.
THAT'S A SHOTGUN.
I DIDN'T SEE HIM. I REALLY DIDN'T SEE HIM.
HE'S DEAD.
I NEED TO GO BACK AND CHECK HIS POCKETS.
WHAT?
SURVIVAL. A GUN'S NOT MUCH USE WITHOUT AMMUNITION.

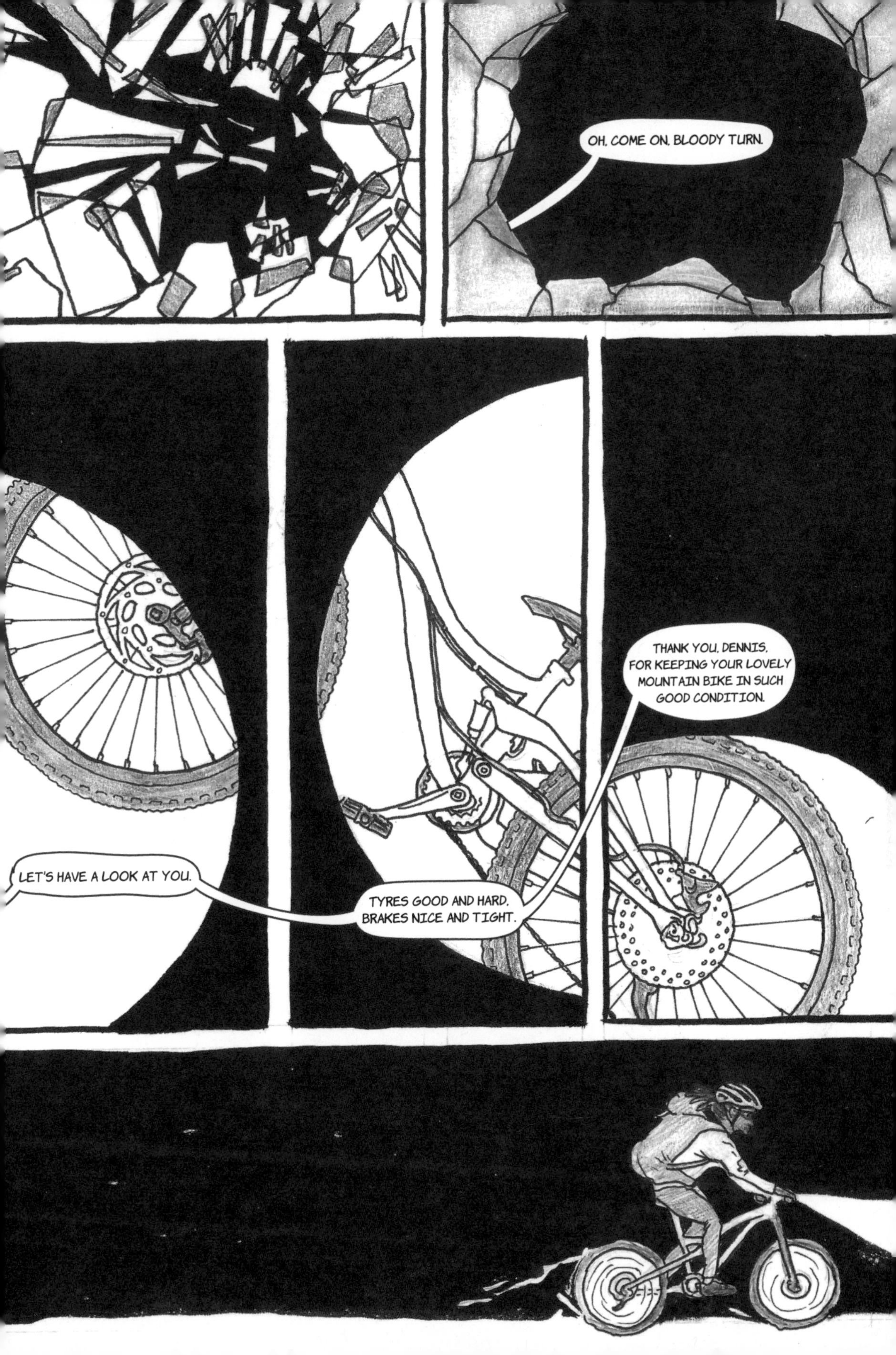
OH, COME ON, BLOODY TURN.
LET'S HAVE A LOOK AT YOU.
TYRES GOOD AND HARD, BRAKES NICE AND TIGHT.
THANK YOU, DENNIS, FOR KEEPING YOUR LOVELY MOUNTAIN BIKE IN SUCH GOOD CONDITION.

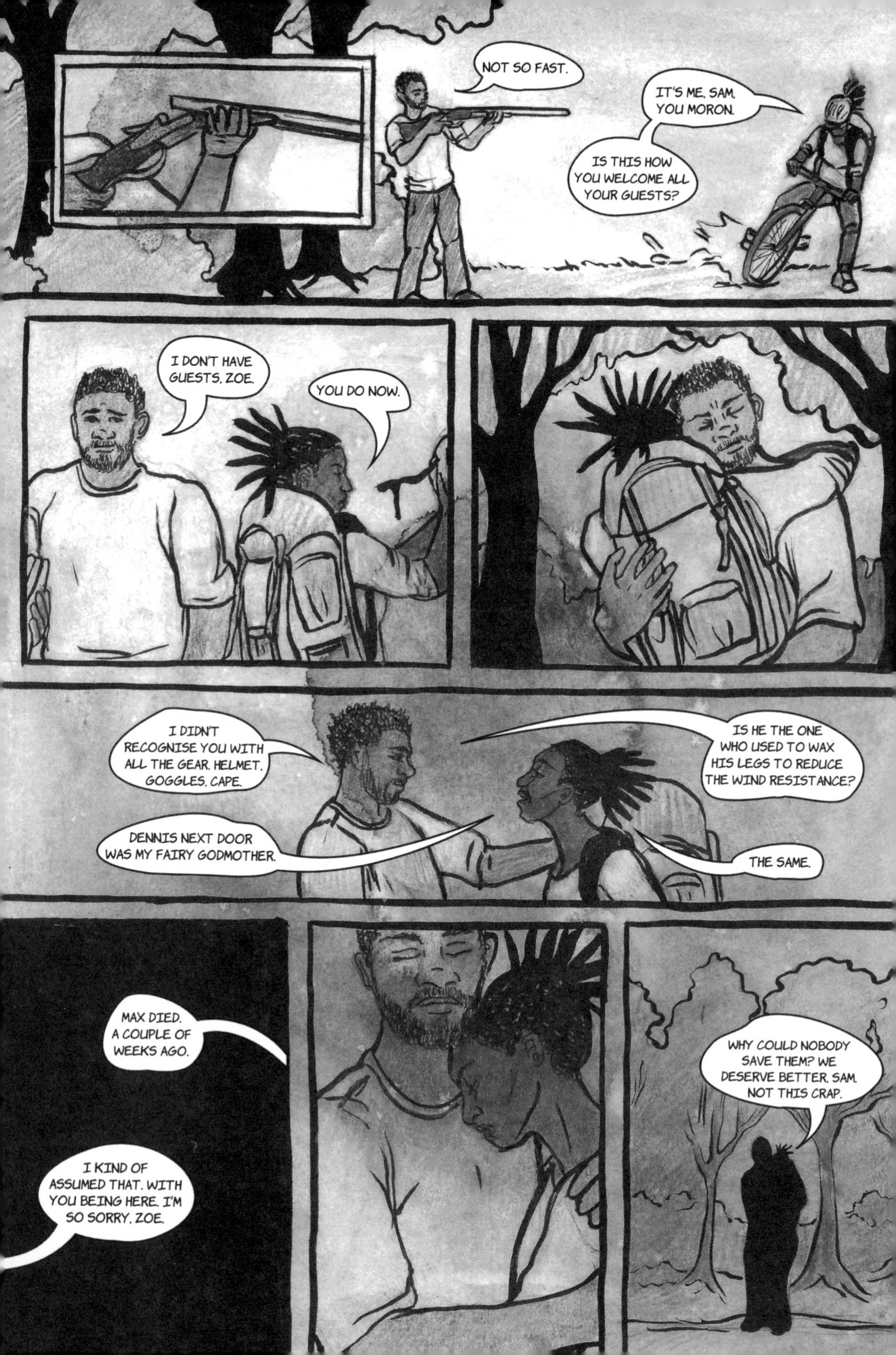
NOT SO FAST.
IT'S ME, SAM. YOU MORON.
IS THIS HOW YOU WELCOME ALL YOUR GUESTS?
I DON'T HAVE GUESTS, ZOE.
YOU DO NOW.
I DIDN'T RECOGNISE YOU WITH ALL THE GEAR. HELMET. GOGGLES. CAPE.
IS HE THE ONE WHO USED TO WAX HIS LEGS TO REDUCE THE WIND RESISTANCE?
DENNIS NEXT DOOR WAS MY FAIRY GODMOTHER.
THE SAME.
MAX DIED. A COUPLE OF WEEKS AGO.
I KIND OF ASSUMED THAT. WITH YOU BEING HERE. I'M SO SORRY, ZOE.
WHY COULD NOBODY SAVE THEM? WE DESERVE BETTER, SAM. NOT THIS CRAP.

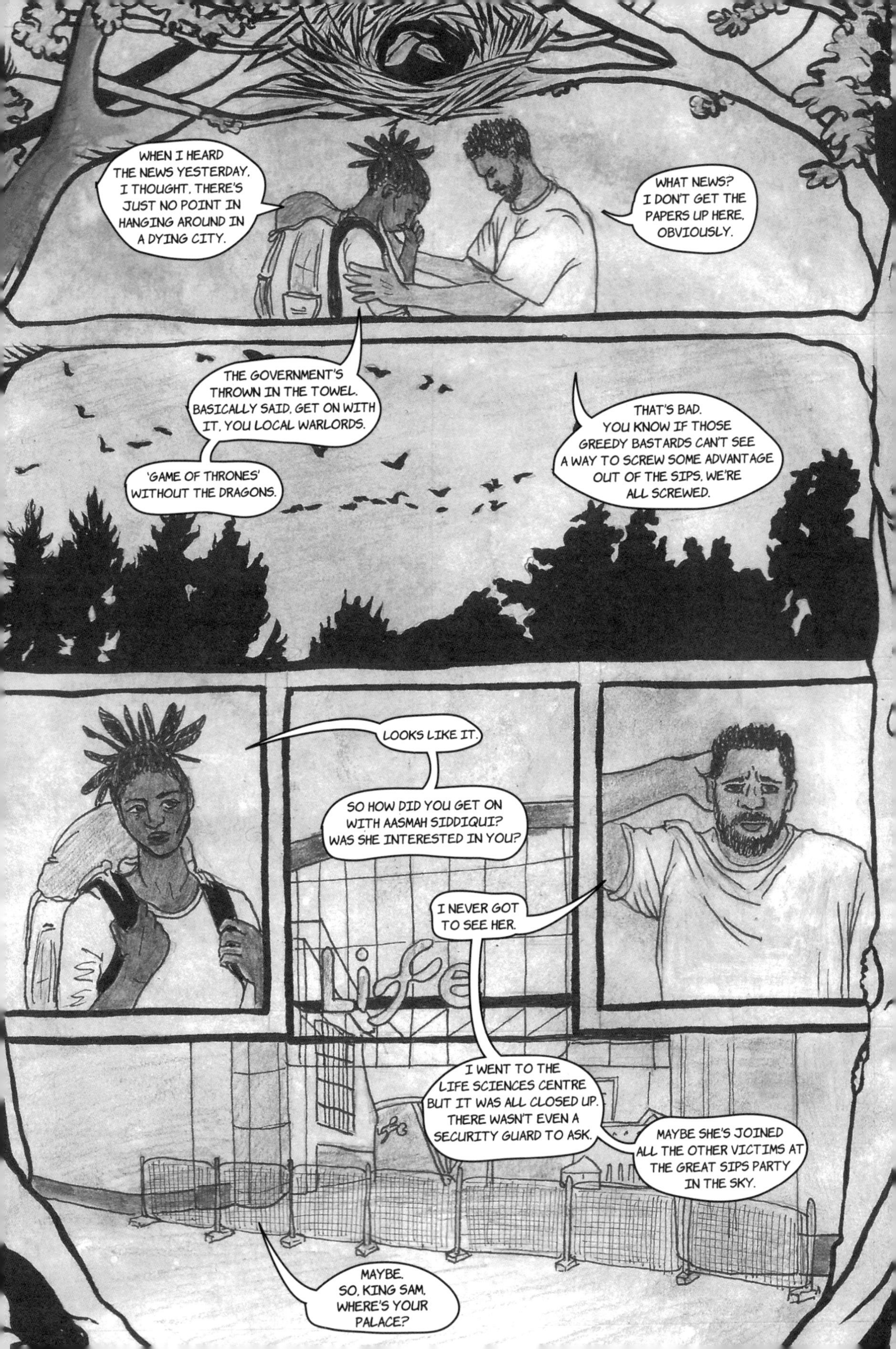

WHEN I HEARD THE NEWS YESTERDAY, I THOUGHT, THERE'S JUST NO POINT IN HANGING AROUND IN A DYING CITY.
WHAT NEWS? I DON'T GET THE PAPERS UP HERE, OBVIOUSLY.
THE GOVERNMENT'S THROWN IN THE TOWEL. BASICALLY SAID, GET ON WITH IT, YOU LOCAL WARLORDS.
'GAME OF THRONES' WITHOUT THE DRAGONS.
THAT'S BAD. YOU KNOW IF THOSE GREEDY BASTARDS CAN'T SEE A WAY TO SCREW SOME ADVANTAGE OUT OF THE SIPS, WE'RE ALL SCREWED.
LOOKS LIKE IT.
SO HOW DID YOU GET ON WITH AASMAH SIDDIQUI? WAS SHE INTERESTED IN YOU?
I NEVER GOT TO SEE HER.
Life
I WENT TO THE LIFE SCIENCES CENTRE BUT IT WAS ALL CLOSED UP. THERE WASN'T EVEN A SECURITY GUARD TO ASK.
MAYBE SHE'S JOINED ALL THE OTHER VICTIMS AT THE GREAT SIPS PARTY IN THE SKY.
MAYBE. SO, KING SAM, WHERE'S YOUR PALACE?

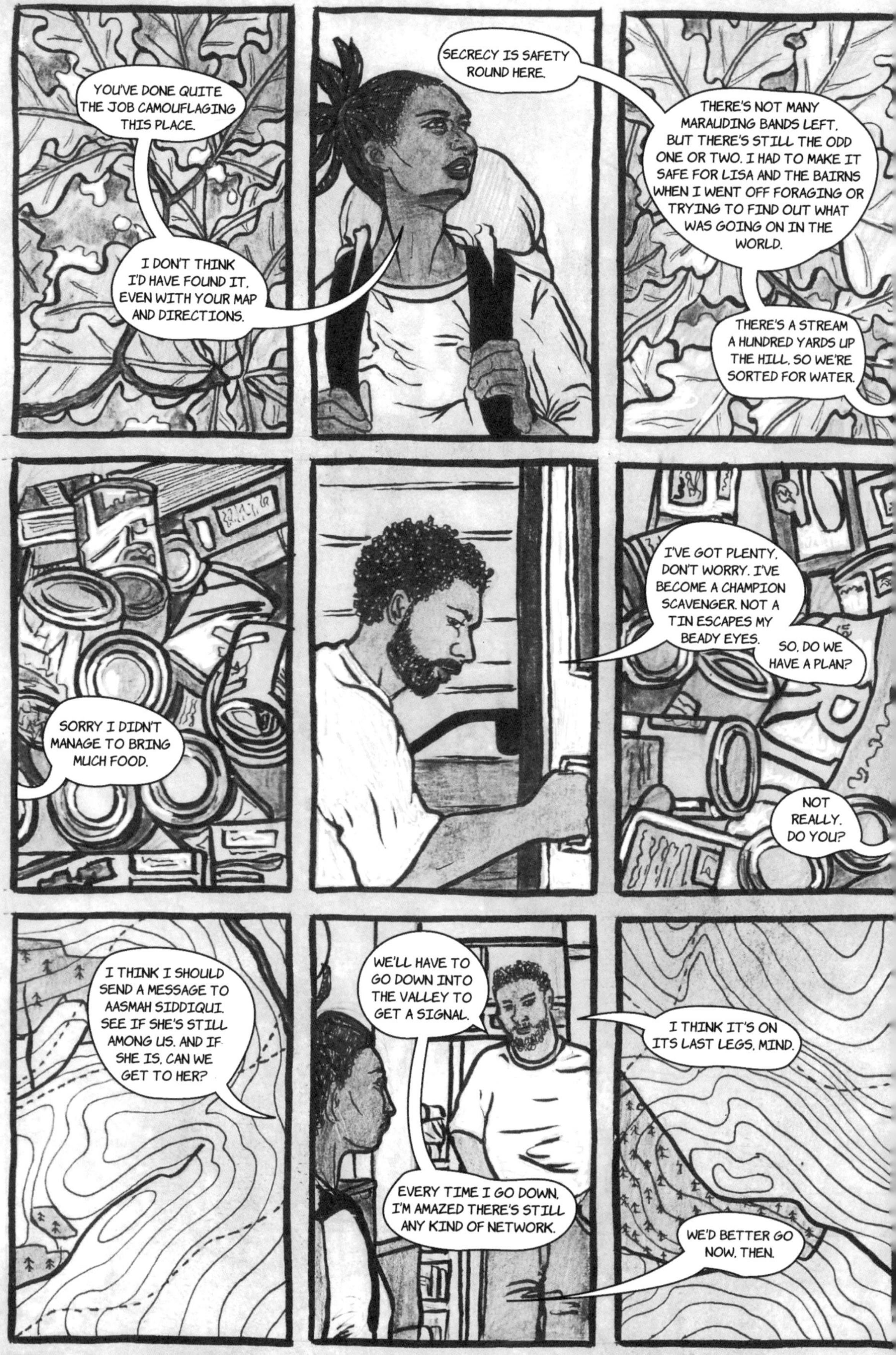
YOU'VE DONE QUITE THE JOB CAMOUFLAGING THIS PLACE.
I DON'T THINK I'D HAVE FOUND IT, EVEN WITH YOUR MAP AND DIRECTIONS.
SECRECY IS SAFETY ROUND HERE.
THERE'S NOT MANY MARAUDING BANDS LEFT, BUT THERE'S STILL THE ODD ONE OR TWO. I HAD TO MAKE IT SAFE FOR LISA AND THE BAIRNS WHEN I WENT OFF FORAGING OR TRYING TO FIND OUT WHAT WAS GOING ON IN THE WORLD.
THERE'S A STREAM A HUNDRED YARDS UP THE HILL, SO WE'RE SORTED FOR WATER.
SORRY I DIDN'T MANAGE TO BRING MUCH FOOD.
I'VE GOT PLENTY, DON'T WORRY. I'VE BECOME A CHAMPION SCAVENGER. NOT A TIN ESCAPES MY BEADY EYES.
SO, DO WE HAVE A PLAN?
NOT REALLY. DO YOU?
I THINK I SHOULD SEND A MESSAGE TO AASMAH SIDDIQUI. SEE IF SHE'S STILL AMONG US. AND IF SHE IS, CAN WE GET TO HER?
WE'LL HAVE TO GO DOWN INTO THE VALLEY TO GET A SIGNAL.
EVERY TIME I GO DOWN, I'M AMAZED THERE'S STILL ANY KIND OF NETWORK.
I THINK IT'S ON ITS LAST LEGS, MIND.
WE'D BETTER GO NOW, THEN.

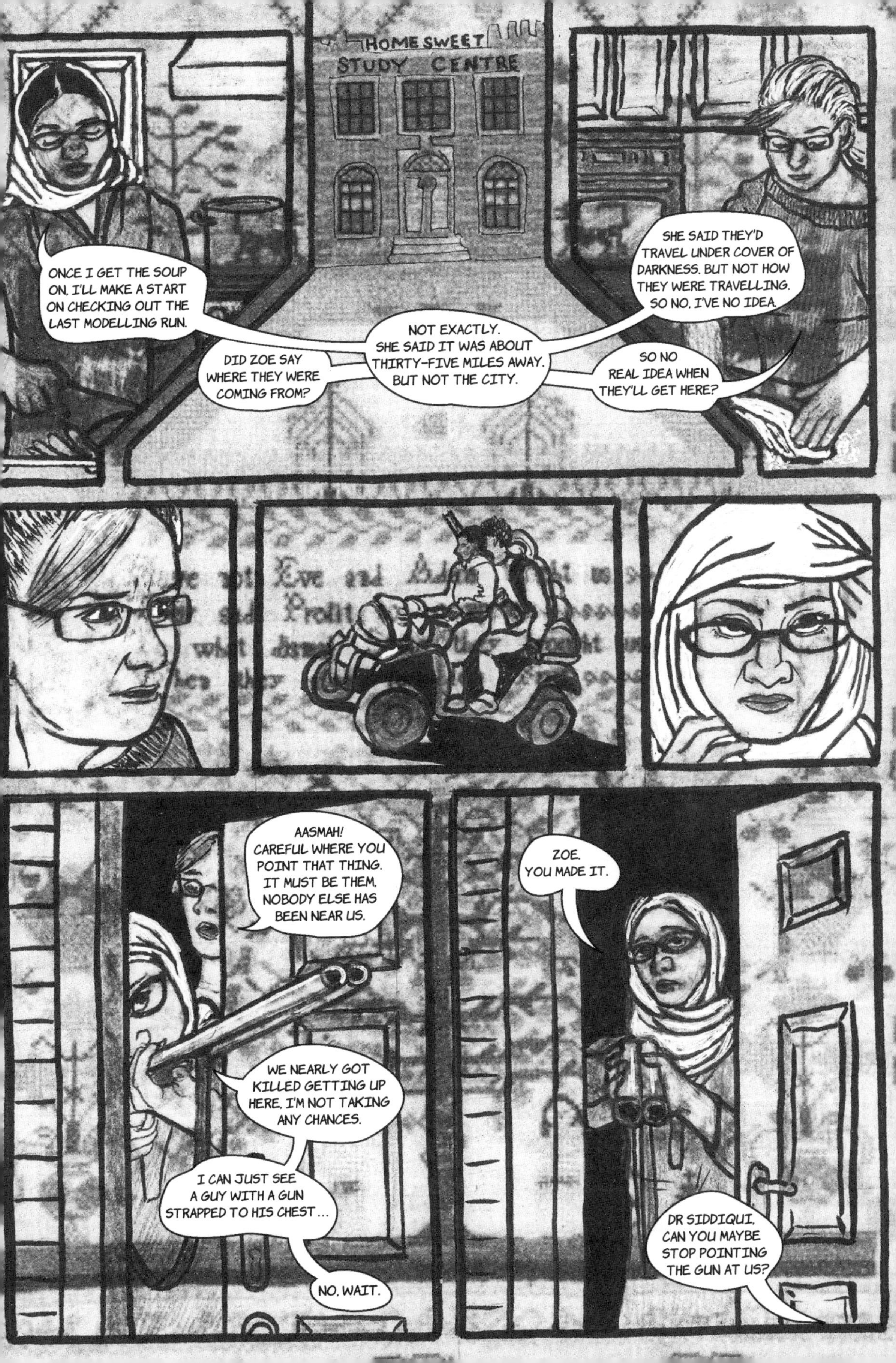
HOME SWEET
STUDY CENTRE
DID ZOE SAY WHERE THEY WERE COMING FROM?
NOT EXACTLY. SHE SAID IT WAS ABOUT THIRTY-FIVE MILES AWAY. BUT NOT THE CITY.
SO NO REAL IDEA WHEN THEY'LL GET HERE?
SHE SAID THEY'D TRAVEL UNDER COVER OF DARKNESS. BUT NOT HOW THEY WERE TRAVELLING. SO NO, I'VE NO IDEA.
ONCE I GET THE SOUP ON, I'LL MAKE A START ON CHECKING OUT THE LAST MODELLING RUN.
AASMAH! CAREFUL WHERE YOU POINT THAT THING. IT MUST BE THEM. NOBODY ELSE HAS BEEN NEAR US.
WE NEARLY GOT KILLED GETTING UP HERE. I'M NOT TAKING ANY CHANCES.
I CAN JUST SEE A GUY WITH A GUN STRAPPED TO HIS CHEST …
NO, WAIT.
ZOE. YOU MADE IT.
DR SIDDIQUI, CAN YOU MAYBE STOP POINTING THE GUN AT US?

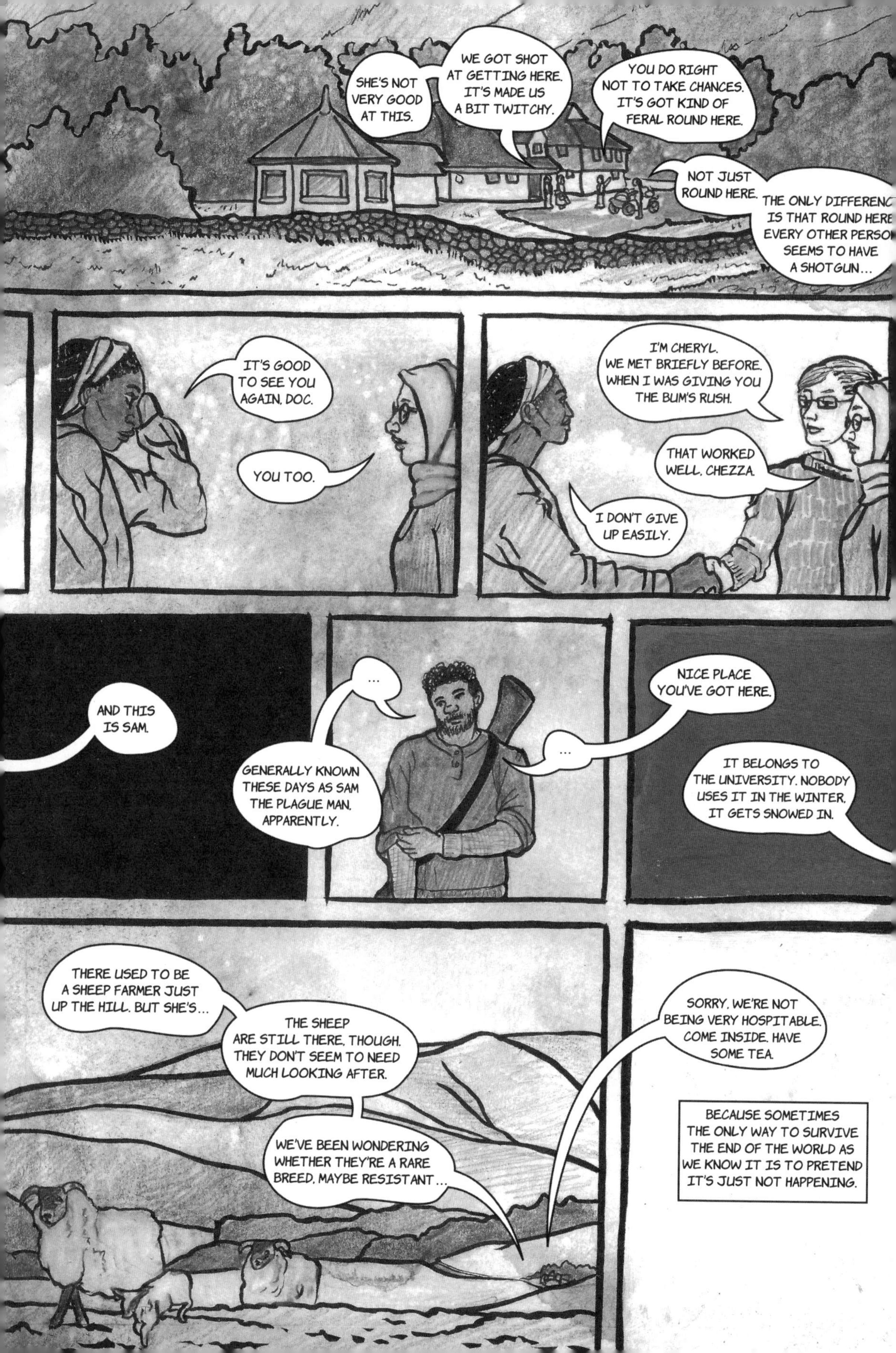
SHE'S NOT VERY GOOD AT THIS.
WE GOT SHOT AT GETTING HERE. IT'S MADE US A BIT TWITCHY.
YOU DO RIGHT NOT TO TAKE CHANCES. IT'S GOT KIND OF FERAL ROUND HERE.
NOT JUST ROUND HERE.
THE ONLY DIFFERENC IS THAT ROUND HERE EVERY OTHER PERSO SEEMS TO HAVE A SHOTGUN…
IT'S GOOD TO SEE YOU AGAIN, DOC.
YOU TOO.
I'M CHERYL. WE MET BRIEFLY BEFORE. WHEN I WAS GIVING YOU THE BUM'S RUSH.
THAT WORKED WELL, CHEZZA.
I DON'T GIVE UP EASILY.
AND THIS IS SAM.
…
GENERALLY KNOWN THESE DAYS AS SAM THE PLAGUE MAN, APPARENTLY.
NICE PLACE YOU'VE GOT HERE.
…
IT BELONGS TO THE UNIVERSITY. NOBODY USES IT IN THE WINTER, IT GETS SNOWED IN.
THERE USED TO BE A SHEEP FARMER JUST UP THE HILL. BUT SHE'S…
THE SHEEP ARE STILL THERE, THOUGH. THEY DON'T SEEM TO NEED MUCH LOOKING AFTER.
WE'VE BEEN WONDERING WHETHER THEY'RE A RARE BREED, MAYBE RESISTANT…
SORRY, WE'RE NOT BEING VERY HOSPITABLE. COME INSIDE. HAVE SOME TEA.
BECAUSE SOMETIMES THE ONLY WAY TO SURVIVE THE END OF THE WORLD AS WE KNOW IT IS TO PRETEND IT'S JUST NOT HAPPENING.

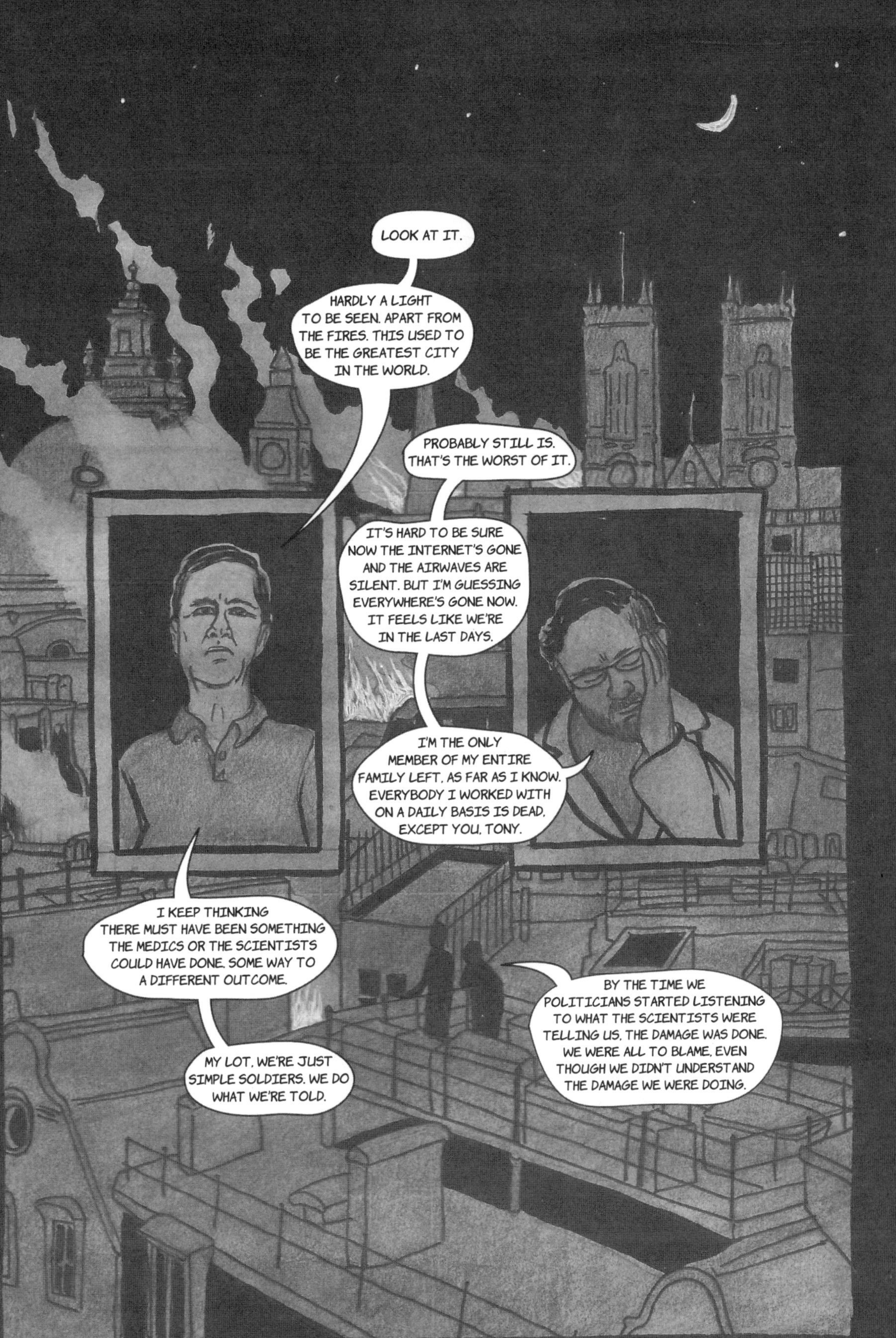
LOOK AT IT.
HARDLY A LIGHT TO BE SEEN. APART FROM THE FIRES. THIS USED TO BE THE GREATEST CITY IN THE WORLD.
PROBABLY STILL IS. THAT'S THE WORST OF IT.
IT'S HARD TO BE SURE NOW THE INTERNET'S GONE AND THE AIRWAVES ARE SILENT. BUT I'M GUESSING EVERYWHERE'S GONE NOW. IT FEELS LIKE WE'RE IN THE LAST DAYS.
I'M THE ONLY MEMBER OF MY ENTIRE FAMILY LEFT, AS FAR AS I KNOW. EVERYBODY I WORKED WITH ON A DAILY BASIS IS DEAD, EXCEPT YOU, TONY.
I KEEP THINKING THERE MUST HAVE BEEN SOMETHING THE MEDICS OR THE SCIENTISTS COULD HAVE DONE. SOME WAY TO A DIFFERENT OUTCOME.
MY LOT, WE'RE JUST SIMPLE SOLDIERS. WE DO WHAT WE'RE TOLD.
BY THE TIME WE POLITICIANS STARTED LISTENING TO WHAT THE SCIENTISTS WERE TELLING US, THE DAMAGE WAS DONE. WE WERE ALL TO BLAME, EVEN THOUGH WE DIDN'T UNDERSTAND THE DAMAGE WE WERE DOING.

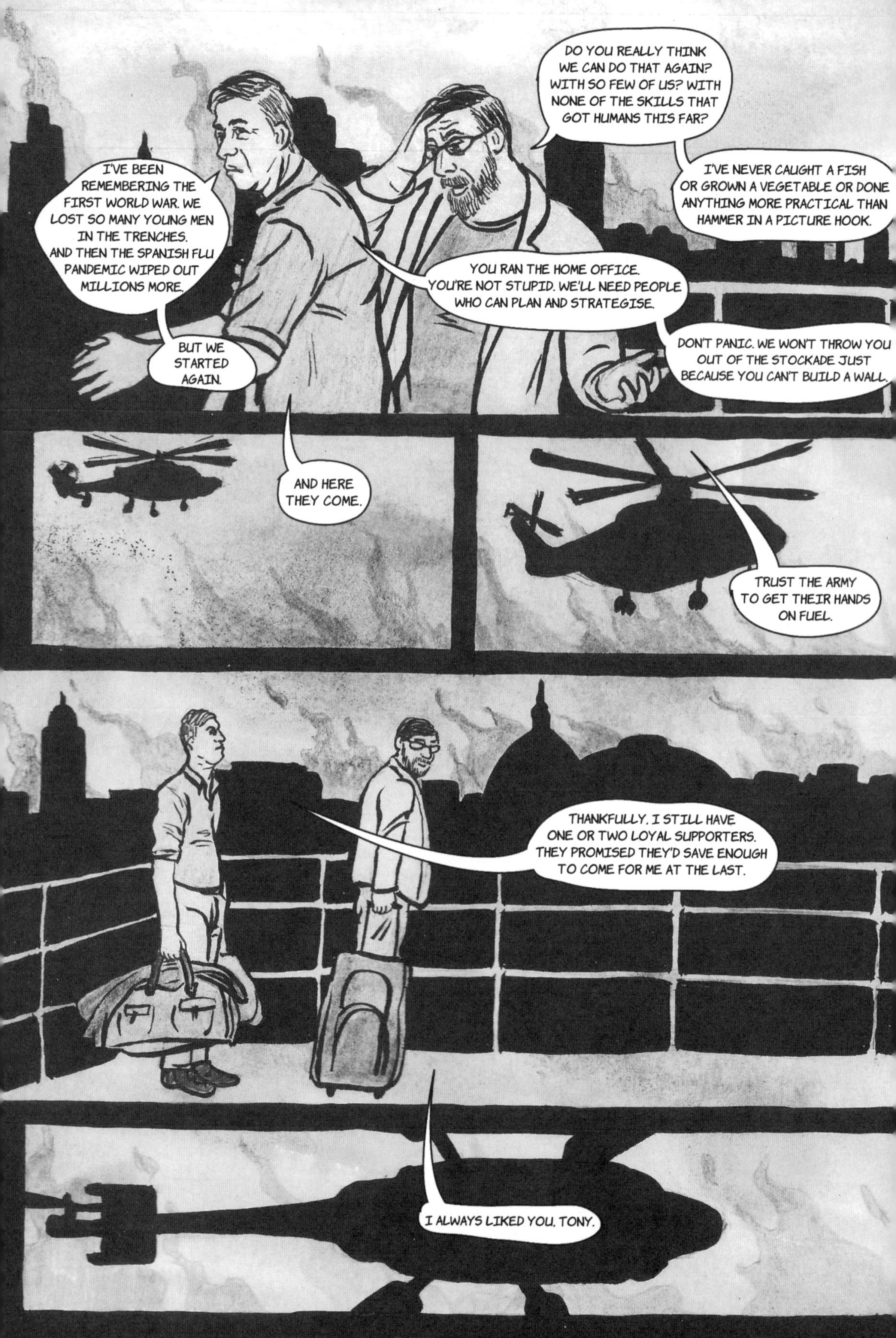

I'VE BEEN REMEMBERING THE FIRST WORLD WAR. WE LOST SO MANY YOUNG MEN IN THE TRENCHES. AND THEN THE SPANISH FLU PANDEMIC WIPED OUT MILLIONS MORE.
DO YOU REALLY THINK WE CAN DO THAT AGAIN? WITH SO FEW OF US? WITH NONE OF THE SKILLS THAT GOT HUMANS THIS FAR?
I'VE NEVER CAUGHT A FISH OR GROWN A VEGETABLE OR DONE ANYTHING MORE PRACTICAL THAN HAMMER IN A PICTURE HOOK.
YOU RAN THE HOME OFFICE. YOU'RE NOT STUPID. WE'LL NEED PEOPLE WHO CAN PLAN AND STRATEGISE.
DON'T PANIC. WE WON'T THROW YOU OUT OF THE STOCKADE JUST BECAUSE YOU CAN'T BUILD A WALL.
BUT WE STARTED AGAIN.
AND HERE THEY COME.
TRUST THE ARMY TO GET THEIR HANDS ON FUEL.
THANKFULLY, I STILL HAVE ONE OR TWO LOYAL SUPPORTERS. THEY PROMISED THEY'D SAVE ENOUGH TO COME FOR ME AT THE LAST.
I ALWAYS LIKED YOU, TONY.

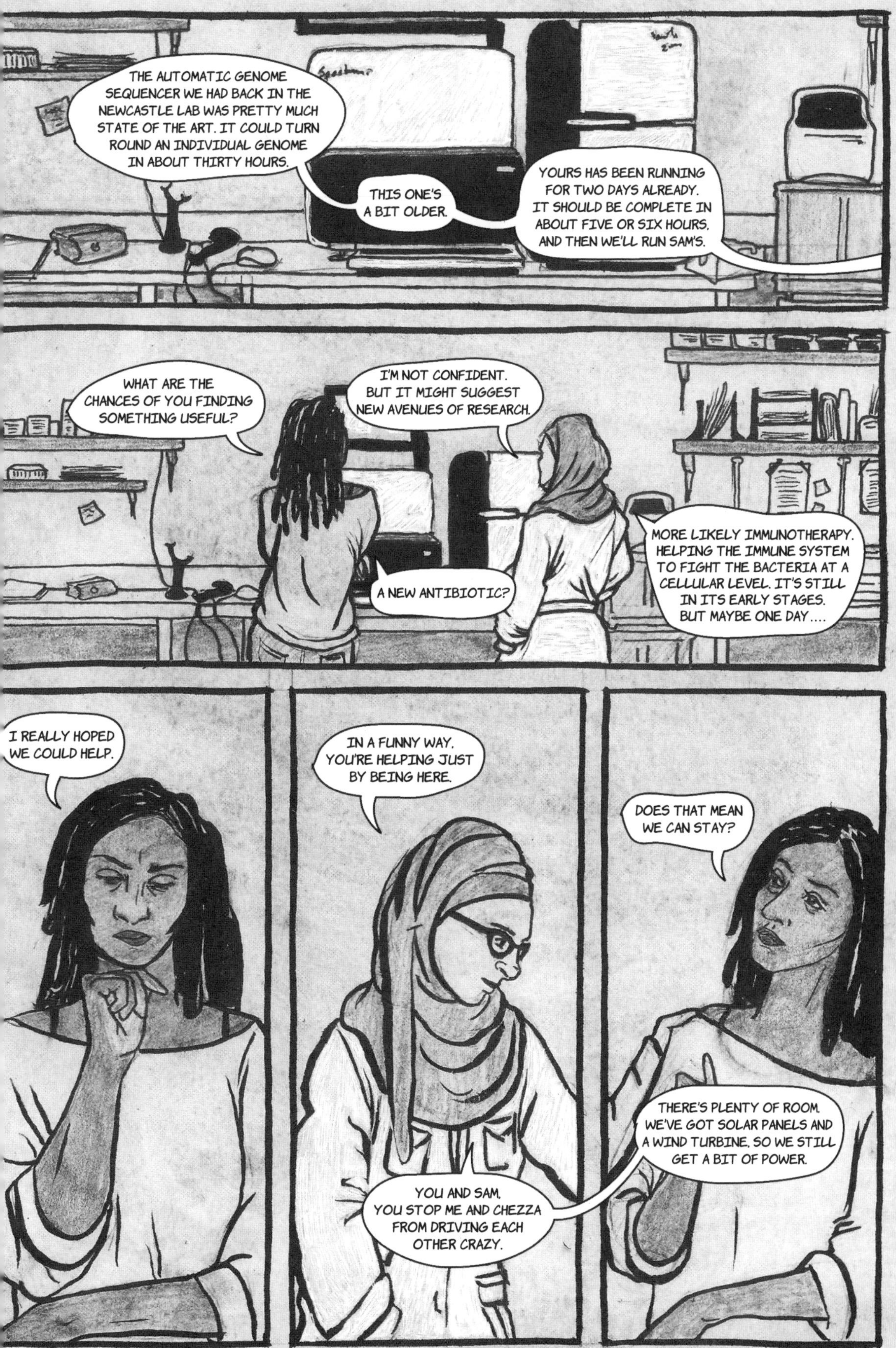
THE AUTOMATIC GENOME SEQUENCER WE HAD BACK IN THE NEWCASTLE LAB WAS PRETTY MUCH STATE OF THE ART. IT COULD TURN ROUND AN INDIVIDUAL GENOME IN ABOUT THIRTY HOURS.
THIS ONE'S A BIT OLDER.
YOURS HAS BEEN RUNNING FOR TWO DAYS ALREADY. IT SHOULD BE COMPLETE IN ABOUT FIVE OR SIX HOURS, AND THEN WE'LL RUN SAM'S.
WHAT ARE THE CHANCES OF YOU FINDING SOMETHING USEFUL?
I'M NOT CONFIDENT. BUT IT MIGHT SUGGEST NEW AVENUES OF RESEARCH.
A NEW ANTIBIOTIC?
MORE LIKELY IMMUNOTHERAPY. HELPING THE IMMUNE SYSTEM TO FIGHT THE BACTERIA AT A CELLULAR LEVEL. IT'S STILL IN ITS EARLY STAGES. BUT MAYBE ONE DAY....
I REALLY HOPED WE COULD HELP.
IN A FUNNY WAY, YOU'RE HELPING JUST BY BEING HERE.
YOU AND SAM, YOU STOP ME AND CHEZZA FROM DRIVING EACH OTHER CRAZY.
DOES THAT MEAN WE CAN STAY?
THERE'S PLENTY OF ROOM. WE'VE GOT SOLAR PANELS AND A WIND TURBINE, SO WE STILL GET A BIT OF POWER.

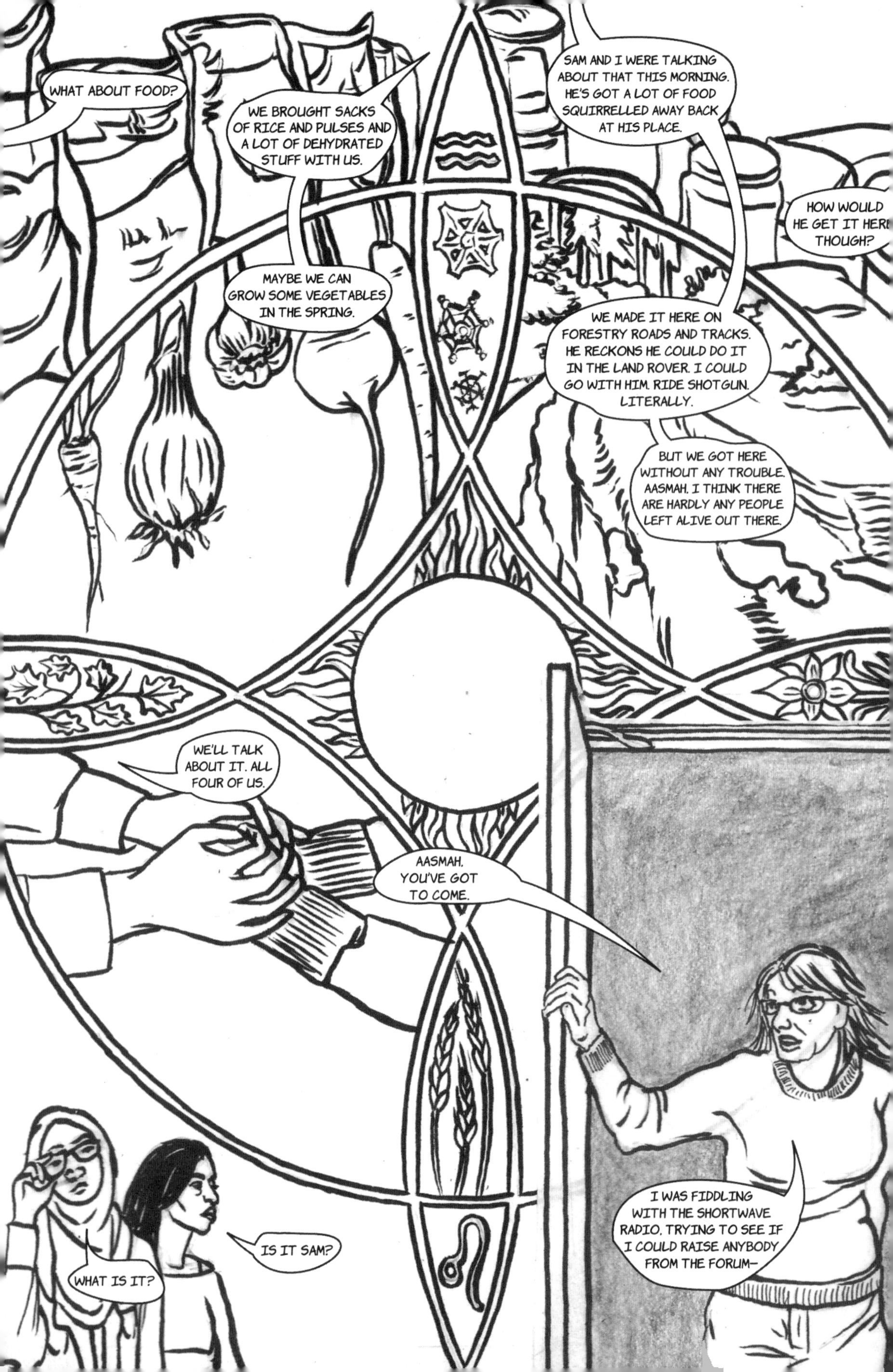
WHAT ABOUT FOOD?
WE BROUGHT SACKS OF RICE AND PULSES AND A LOT OF DEHYDRATED STUFF WITH US.
MAYBE WE CAN GROW SOME VEGETABLES IN THE SPRING.
SAM AND I WERE TALKING ABOUT THAT THIS MORNING. HE'S GOT A LOT OF FOOD SQUIRRELLED AWAY BACK AT HIS PLACE.
HOW WOULD HE GET IT HERE THOUGH?
WE MADE IT HERE ON FORESTRY ROADS AND TRACKS. HE RECKONS HE COULD DO IT IN THE LAND ROVER. I COULD GO WITH HIM. RIDE SHOTGUN. LITERALLY.
BUT WE GOT HERE WITHOUT ANY TROUBLE, AASMAH. I THINK THERE ARE HARDLY ANY PEOPLE LEFT ALIVE OUT THERE.
WE'LL TALK ABOUT IT. ALL FOUR OF US.
AASMAH, YOU'VE GOT TO COME.
WHAT IS IT?
IS IT SAM?
I WAS FIDDLING WITH THE SHORTWAVE RADIO, TRYING TO SEE IF I COULD RAISE ANYBODY FROM THE FORUM–

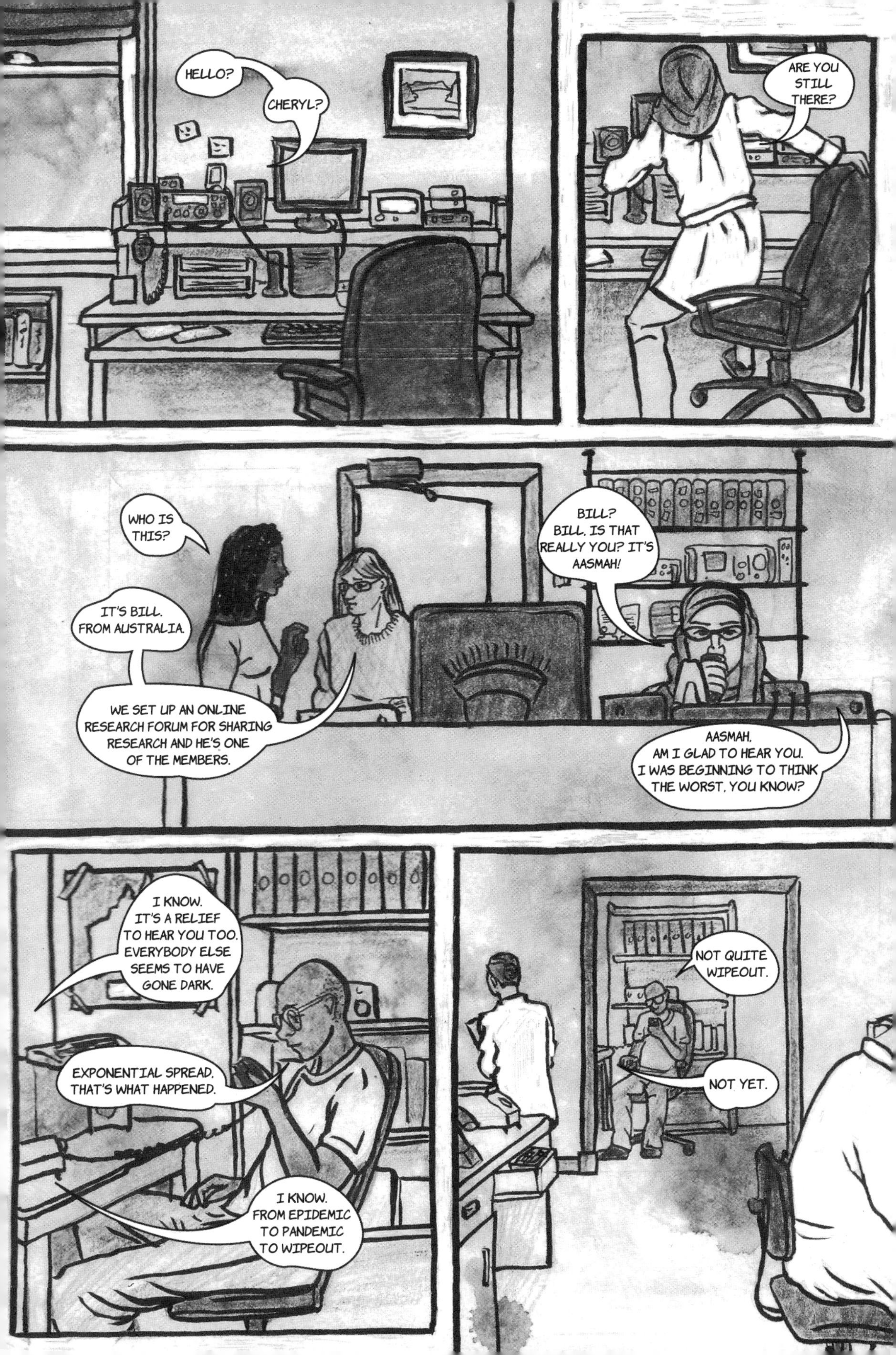
HELLO?
CHERYL?
ARE YOU STILL THERE?
WHO IS THIS?
IT'S BILL. FROM AUSTRALIA.
WE SET UP AN ONLINE RESEARCH FORUM FOR SHARING RESEARCH AND HE'S ONE OF THE MEMBERS.
BILL? BILL, IS THAT REALLY YOU? IT'S AASMAH!
AASMAH, AM I GLAD TO HEAR YOU. I WAS BEGINNING TO THINK THE WORST, YOU KNOW?
I KNOW. IT'S A RELIEF TO HEAR YOU TOO. EVERYBODY ELSE SEEMS TO HAVE GONE DARK.
EXPONENTIAL SPREAD, THAT'S WHAT HAPPENED.
I KNOW. FROM EPIDEMIC TO PANDEMIC TO WIPEOUT.
NOT QUITE WIPEOUT.
NOT YET.

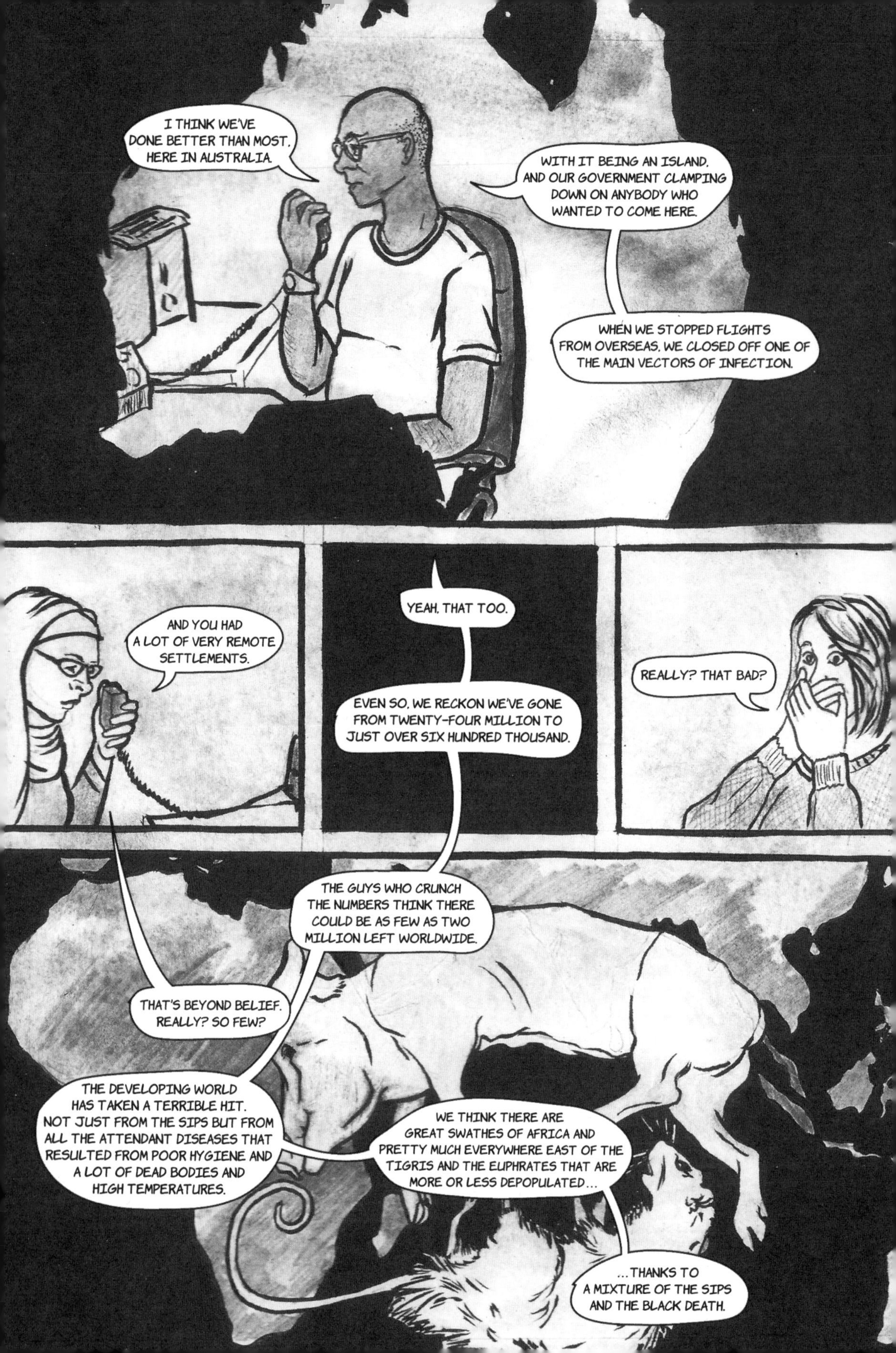
I THINK WE'VE DONE BETTER THAN MOST, HERE IN AUSTRALIA.
WITH IT BEING AN ISLAND, AND OUR GOVERNMENT CLAMPING DOWN ON ANYBODY WHO WANTED TO COME HERE.
WHEN WE STOPPED FLIGHTS FROM OVERSEAS, WE CLOSED OFF ONE OF THE MAIN VECTORS OF INFECTION.
AND YOU HAD A LOT OF VERY REMOTE SETTLEMENTS.
YEAH, THAT TOO.
EVEN SO, WE RECKON WE'VE GONE FROM TWENTY-FOUR MILLION TO JUST OVER SIX HUNDRED THOUSAND.
REALLY? THAT BAD?
THE GUYS WHO CRUNCH THE NUMBERS THINK THERE COULD BE AS FEW AS TWO MILLION LEFT WORLDWIDE.
THAT'S BEYOND BELIEF. REALLY? SO FEW?
THE DEVELOPING WORLD HAS TAKEN A TERRIBLE HIT. NOT JUST FROM THE SIPS BUT FROM ALL THE ATTENDANT DISEASES THAT RESULTED FROM POOR HYGIENE AND A LOT OF DEAD BODIES AND HIGH TEMPERATURES.
WE THINK THERE ARE GREAT SWATHES OF AFRICA AND PRETTY MUCH EVERYWHERE EAST OF THE TIGRIS AND THE EUPHRATES THAT ARE MORE OR LESS DEPOPULATED…
…THANKS TO A MIXTURE OF THE SIPS AND THE BLACK DEATH.

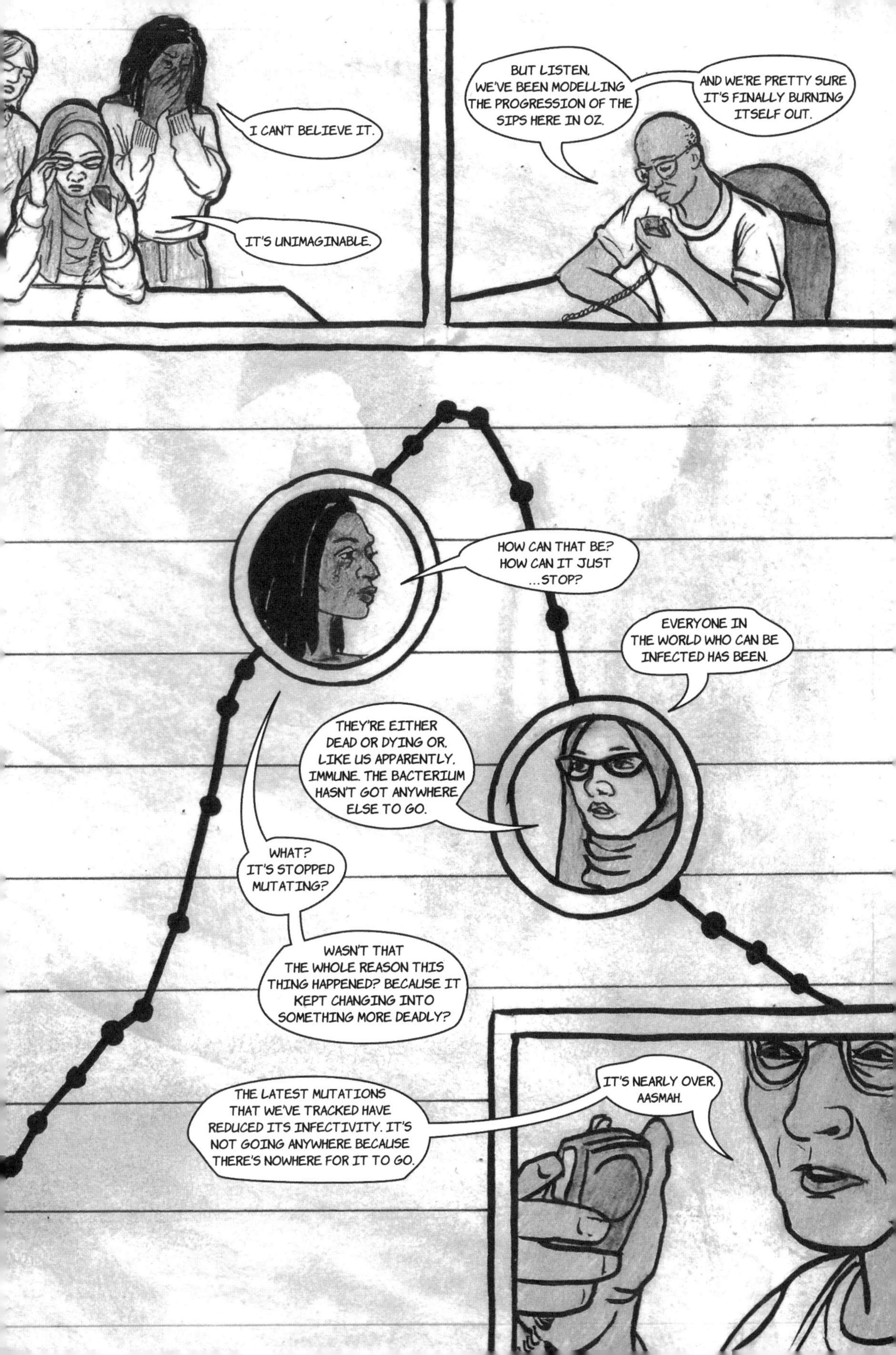
I CAN'T BELIEVE IT.
IT'S UNIMAGINABLE.
BUT LISTEN, WE'VE BEEN MODELLING THE PROGRESSION OF THE SIPS HERE IN OZ.
AND WE'RE PRETTY SURE IT'S FINALLY BURNING ITSELF OUT.
HOW CAN THAT BE? HOW CAN IT JUST ...STOP?
EVERYONE IN THE WORLD WHO CAN BE INFECTED HAS BEEN.
THEY'RE EITHER DEAD OR DYING OR, LIKE US APPARENTLY, IMMUNE. THE BACTERIUM HASN'T GOT ANYWHERE ELSE TO GO.
WHAT? IT'S STOPPED MUTATING?
WASN'T THAT THE WHOLE REASON THIS THING HAPPENED? BECAUSE IT KEPT CHANGING INTO SOMETHING MORE DEADLY?
THE LATEST MUTATIONS THAT WE'VE TRACKED HAVE REDUCED ITS INFECTIVITY. IT'S NOT GOING ANYWHERE BECAUSE THERE'S NOWHERE FOR IT TO GO.
IT'S NEARLY OVER, AASMAH.

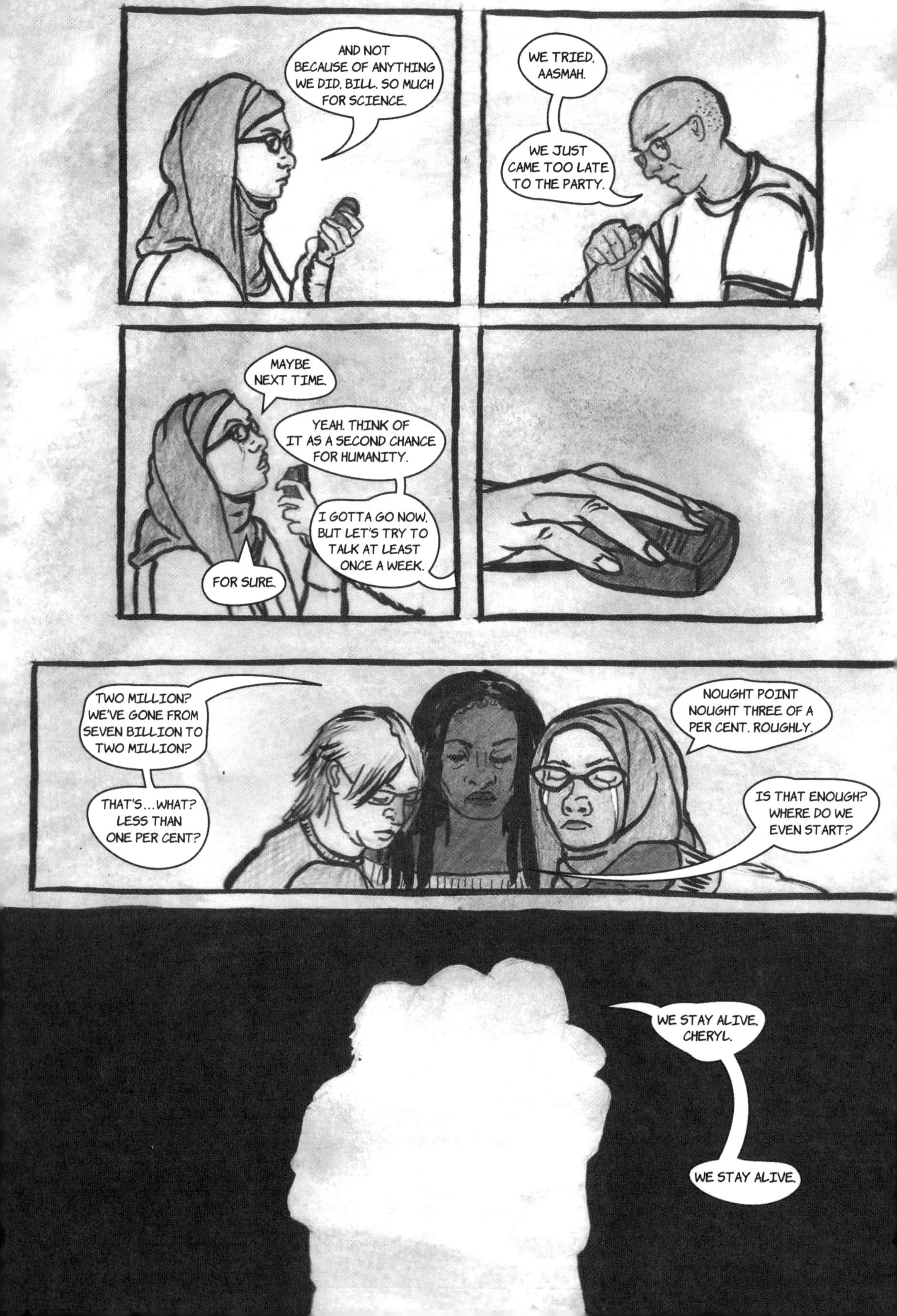
AND NOT BECAUSE OF ANYTHING WE DID, BILL. SO MUCH FOR SCIENCE.
WE TRIED, AASMAH.
WE JUST CAME TOO LATE TO THE PARTY.
MAYBE NEXT TIME.
YEAH. THINK OF IT AS A SECOND CHANCE FOR HUMANITY.
FOR SURE.
I GOTTA GO NOW, BUT LET'S TRY TO TALK AT LEAST ONCE A WEEK.
TWO MILLION? WE'VE GONE FROM SEVEN BILLION TO TWO MILLION?
THAT'S…WHAT? LESS THAN ONE PER CENT?
NOUGHT POINT NOUGHT THREE OF A PER CENT. ROUGHLY.
IS THAT ENOUGH? WHERE DO WE EVEN START?
WE STAY ALIVE, CHERYL.
WE STAY ALIVE.

 OT MUCH OF A MANIFESTO, IT'S TRUE.

BUT AT LEAST IT WAS A PLACE TO START. SO WE DID WHAT WE HAD TO DO TO STAY ALIVE.

CHERYL BECAME A DAB HAND WITH THE CHAINSAW, BUILDING A WOODPILE TO SEE US THROUGH THE REST OF THE WINTER. AASMAH FEEDS US AND TALKS TO BILL ON THE SHORTWAVE AND SPENDS LONG HOURS IN THE LAB WITH CHERYL TRYING TO FIND ANSWERS TO A QUESTION THAT DOESN'T REALLY MATTER MUCH ANY MORE.

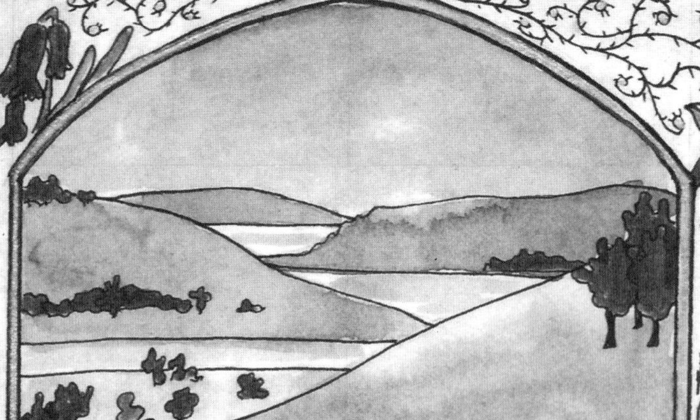

SAM AND I GO SCAVENGING.

THERE'S PLENTY OF FUEL OUT THERE FOR THE LAND ROVER AND THE QUAD BIKE.

WE TALK ABOUT LISA AND JAMIE AND OUR KIDS.

STORIES THAT KEEP THEM ALIVE. STORIES THAT HELP US BEAR THE GRIEF.

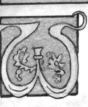

E BRING BACK FOOD AND BOOKS AND BOARD GAMES. AND SOMETIMES PEOPLE.

WE FOUND TWO FILTHY, STARVING KIDS IN A FARMHOUSE NEAR KIELDER AND WE BROUGHT THEM BACK WITH US.

THEY'VE STARTED TALKING AGAIN IN THE PAST FEW DAYS. THEY STILL WAKE UP WITH NIGHTMARES THOUGH. I TRY TO MOTHER THEM. BUT SOMETIMES IT'S JUST TOO BLOODY PAINFUL.

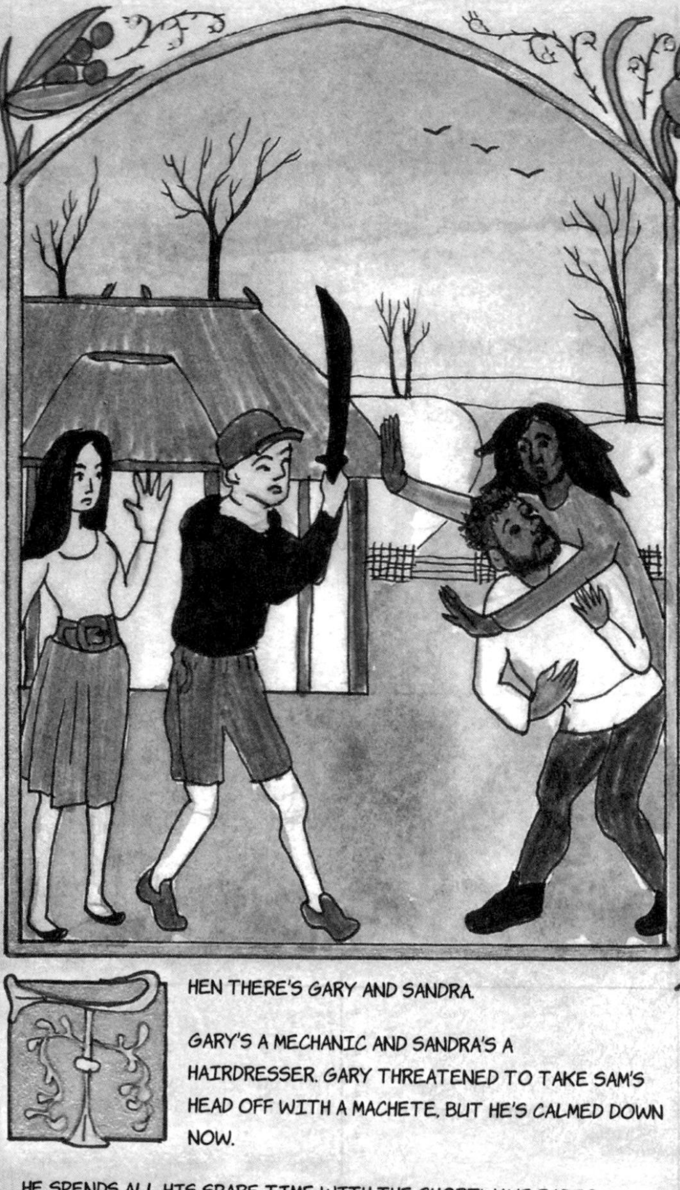

THEN THERE'S GARY AND SANDRA.

GARY'S A MECHANIC AND SANDRA'S A HAIRDRESSER. GARY THREATENED TO TAKE SAM'S HEAD OFF WITH A MACHETE, BUT HE'S CALMED DOWN NOW.

HE SPENDS ALL HIS SPARE TIME WITH THE SHORTWAVE RADIO, TRYING TO FIND SOMEBODY APART FROM BILL TO TALK TO. WE ALL TRY NOT TO DWELL ON EVERYTHING WE'VE LOST.

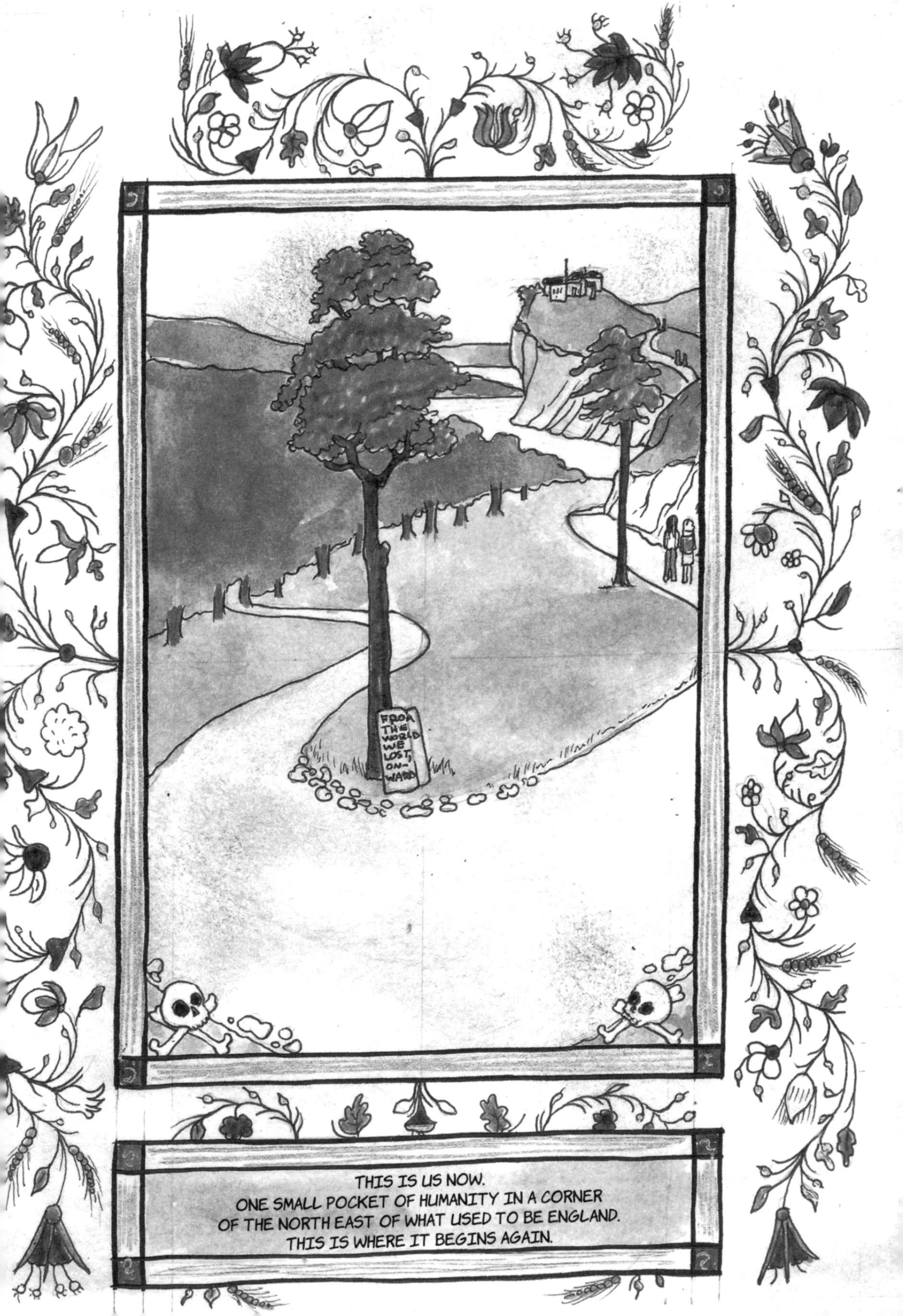
FROM THE WORLD WE LOST, ON-WARD
THIS IS US NOW.
ONE SMALL POCKET OF HUMANITY IN A CORNER
OF THE NORTH EAST OF WHAT USED TO BE ENGLAND.
THIS IS WHERE IT BEGINS AGAIN.

VAL MCDERMID, THE 'QUEEN OF CRIME', HAS PUBLISHED
THIRTY-FOUR CRIME NOVELS, WHICH HAVE SOLD OVER
SEVENTEEN MILLION COPIES WORLDWIDE, BEEN
TRANSLATED INTO FORTY LANGUAGES AND WON MULTIPLE
AWARDS. HER SERIES FEATURING CRIMINAL PROFILER
TONY HILL WAS THE BASIS FOR THE TV SERIES
THE WIRE IN THE BLOOD FOR ITV.

KATHRYN BRIGGS IS AN AWARD-WINNING GRAPHIC
NOVELIST, ILLUSTRATOR AND ARTS EDUCATOR. AFTER
STUDYING HER MASTER'S AT DUNCAN OF JORDANSTONE
IN DUNDEE, SHE BECAME AN ACTIVE MEMBER OF
SCOTLAND'S VIBRANT INDIE COMICS SCENE. SHE MOVED
BACK TO HER HOME STATE OF PENNSYLVANIA IN 2018.

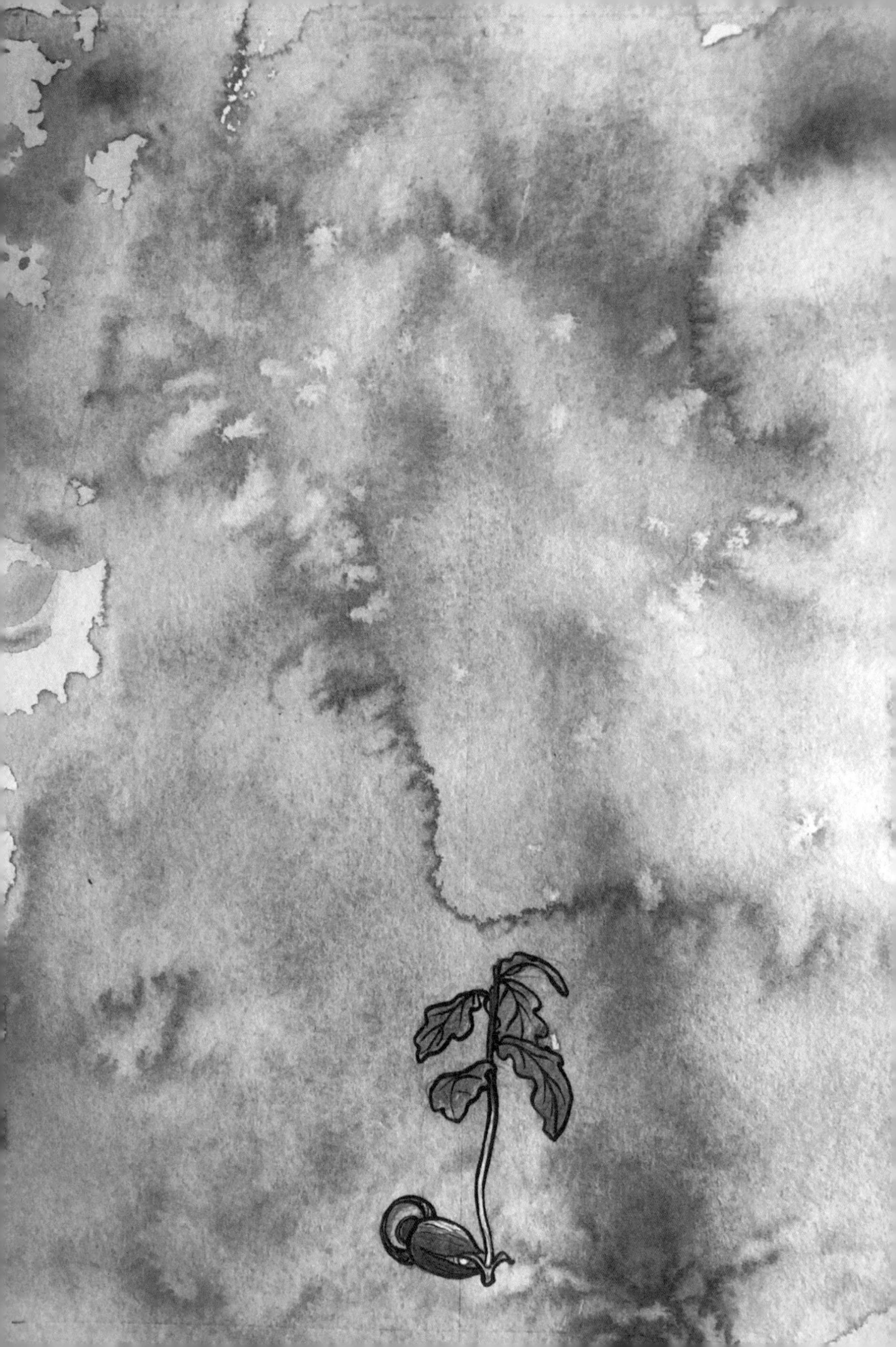

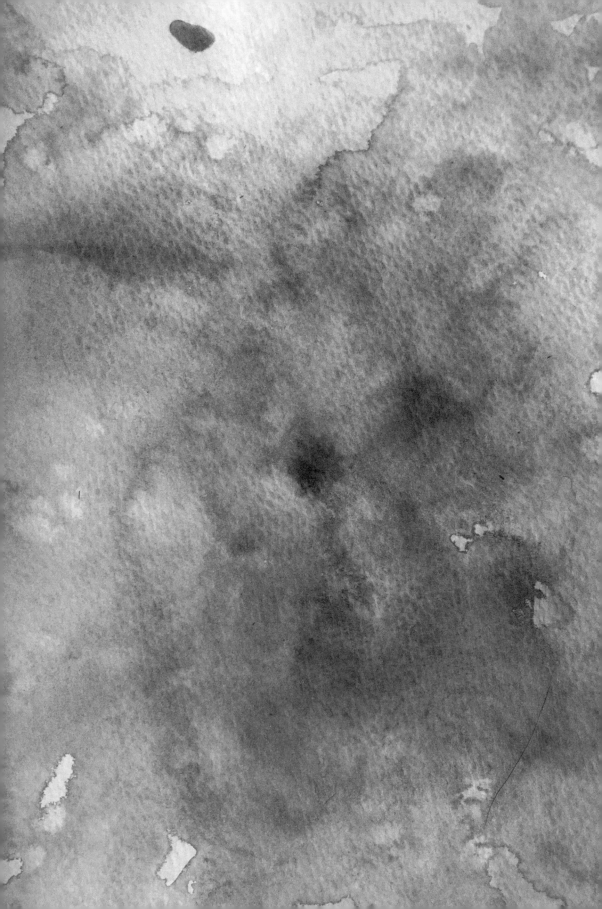